STUDIES IN HISTORY, ECONOMICS
AND PUBLIC LAW

Edited by the
FACULTY OF POLITICAL SCIENCE OF
COLUMBIA UNIVERSITY

NUMBER 429

THE UNITED STATES AND

THE DISRUPTION OF

THE SPANISH EMPIRE

1810–1822

BY

CHARLES CARROLL GRIFFIN

THE UNITED STATES AND

THE DISRUPTION OF

THE SPANISH EMPIRE

1810 - 1822

A study of the relations of the United States with Spain
and with the rebel Spanish Colonies

BY

CHARLES CARROLL GRIFFIN

1968

OCTAGON BOOKS, INC.

New York

Reprinted 1968

by special arrangement with Columbia University Press

OCTAGON BOOKS, INC.
175 FIFTH AVENUE
NEW YORK, N. Y. 10010

Library of Congress Catalog Card Number: 67-18765

Printed in U.S.A. by
NOBLE OFFSET PRINTERS, INC.
NEW YORK 3, N. Y.

TO

EVARTS BOUTELL GREENE

PREFACE TO THE OCTAGON EDITION

SINCE the publication of this book in 1937 a number of important works have appeared which should be read by any one interested in the relations of the United States and Spain in the era of Spanish American independence. In 1939 Philip C. Brooks published *Diplomacy and the Borderlands: The Adams-Onis Treaty of 1819*. It provides a fuller account of the treaty as a territorial settlement than that which is given here. It also makes some judgements which are in conflict with interpretations contained in the present volume. It is not possible to discuss these differences here. However, the author does not believe that he has reason to change any of his views in the light of Dr. Brooks' book. He refers the reader to the two accounts of the treaty and suggests that he make up his own mind on the basis of the evidence submitted in each work.

On a broader topic Arthur P. Whitaker later published a widely acclaimed book: *The United States and the Independence of Latin America* (Baltimore, 1941). It is only here and there in connection with questions of emphasis in interpretation that the author can take issue with this excellent and comprehensive study. Whitaker's useful bibliographical essay lists all significant material on the subject up to the date of publication. Since that time additional contributions to our knowledge of the subject have appeared. Among these the primacy must be given to Samuel F. Bemis' *Latin American Policy of the United States* (New York, 1943) and his *John Quincy Adams and the Foundations of American Foreign Policy* (New York, 1949). These works incorporate the research of the dean of American diplomatic historians as well as the work of several of his students. Important among these are Benjamin Keen's *David Curtis DeForest and the Revolution of Buenos Aires* (New Haven, 1947) and Laura Bornholdt's *Baltimore and Early Panamericanism: a Study in the Background of the Monroe Doctrine* (Northampton, Mass., 1949). Mention should also be made of

3

Harold Bierck's *Vida publica de Pedro Gual* (Caracas, 1947). The present author has himself made a small additional contribution to this subject in his essay "Privateering from Baltimore in the Era of Spanish American Independence," *Maryland Historical Magazine,* May, 1940.

Sir Charles Webster's important investigations on the subject of British policy were taken into account in the original edition of this book, but the summary which he published as an introduction to his two volumes of the pertinent documents: *Britain and the Independence of Latin America, 1812-1830* (London, 1938) unfortunately appeared too late for consideration. The conclusions of this work, however, as well as those of William S. Robertson, *France and Latin American Independence* (Baltimore, 1939) are essentially at harmony with the views expressed in the present work.

Finally, the author would like to say that the chief value of this work—if it has any—lies in the study which it makes of Spanish policy toward the United States. He does not believe that any one else has as yet made an equally thorough study of that policy during the critical years from 1815 to 1822. If this contention is correct, it may justify the reprinting of this book in its original form in spite of the fact that much new information relevant to it has became available since it was written. For critical comment on the historical works referred to see R. A. Humphreys, *Latin American History, a Guide to the Literature in English* (London and New York, 1958) and the annual volumes of the *Handbook of Latin American Studies* (1935 —).

CHARLES C. GRIFFIN

VASSAR COLLEGE,
POUGHKEEPSIE, NEW YORK

PREFACE

THIS volume is an outgrowth of the author's study of the Adams-Onís treaty of 1819. While engaged in research on the causes of the two-year delay in the ratification of that agreement it became evident to him that the subject could only be intelligibly handled in connection with the more general story of the relations of the United States with Spain and with the revolutionary governments of Spanish America.

The year 1815 might perhaps have been chosen for the beginning of the study, for it was after the return of peace in Europe, and between the United States and Great Britain that the two threads of this story—the treaty negotiations with Spain, and the question of recognition of the rebel governments —became closely interwoven. As the reader will notice, the greater part of this study deals with the period from 1815 to 1822, ending with the ratification of the Spanish treaty followed a year later by recognition of Spanish American independence. In order to clarify the issues involved and to trace developments which later assumed importance, some attention has been given to the period 1810 to 1815.

No attempt has been made to chronicle in detail the border strife which was a continuing factor in the relations of the United States with Spain, and to a lesser extent with the Spanish American rebels. The author has leaned heavily in dealing with these events on the work of others who have made detailed studies of frontier incidents and has devoted less space to them than he originally planned. He believes this exclusion to be justifiable, for the principal aim of this volume is to study policies and attitudes in the United States, Spain, and Spanish America. Border rivalry, therefore, is considered not for its own sake but only for its effect, like that of other factors, on the development of policy.

Another clarification must be made with regard to the treatment of the negotiations between John Quincy Adams and Luis de Onís which led to the treaty of 1819. The author has made a study of the sources covering this subject, but as a monograph by Dr. Philip C. Brooks is about to appear on the treaty as a territorial agreement, he has thought it best to cover boundary negotiations only in relation to the wider conflict between the two states.

Though fully conscious of the difficulty of giving unity to a story which can by no means be said to fall entirely within the chronological limits of this work, and which is complicated by diverse and sometimes apparently unrelated factors, it is the author's hope that he has been able to contribute to a better understanding of this phase of American foreign relations, both by study of hitherto unused material for part of his work, and by bringing together aspects which have been considered separately.

The author is indebted, in the first place, to the late Professor William R. Shepherd of Columbia University under whose guidance he began his study of history. To the Library of Congress, and in particular to Dr. J. F. Jameson, Chief of the Division of Manuscripts, the author owes the opportunity to carry on research in Spanish archives while engaged in work for the *European Mission* of the Library. Columbia University, by awarding a University fellowship for the year 1933-34, made possible further study.

Professor Samuel F. Bemis kindly allowed the author access to his then unpublished *Guide to the Diplomatic History of the United States*. Professors John A. Krout and Frank Tannenbaum have read the manuscript and given the author the benefit of their criticism. Lack of space prevents adequate acknowledgment of the author's indebtedness to many other scholars and library and archive officials, among them: Dr. Martin, Miss G. G. Griffin and other members of the staff of the Library of Congress, Mrs. Summers and other members of the staff of the archive of the Department of State, Dr. Roscoe R. Hill, now of the National Archives, Dr. Philip C. Brooks of the same institution, Sr. Miguel Gómez Campillo of the *Archivo Histórico Nacional,* Madrid, Sr. Angel de la Plaza of the *Archivo de Simancas,* Dr. Victor Paltsits of the New York Public Library, Miss Fanny Borden and other members of the staff of the Vassar College Library.

CHARLES CARROLL GRIFFIN

POUGHKEEPSIE, N. Y.
APRIL, 1937.

KEY TO ABBREVIATIONS USED IN FOOTNOTES ASIDE FROM THOSE IN GENERAL USE

AAE.   Archives du Ministère des Affaires Étrangères, Paris.
AGS.   Archivo General de Simancas, Simancas, Spain.
AHA.   American Historical Association.
AHN.   Archivo Histórico Nacional, Madrid.
AHR.   American Historical Review.
AME.   Archivo del Ministerio de Estado, Madrid.
ASP. FR. American State Papers, Foreign Relations.
C. P.   Correspondance Politique.
Cor. Pol. Correspondencia Política.
DS.   Department of State, Washington, D. C.
Est.   Estado.
FO.   Foreign Office.
HAHR.   Hispanic American Historical Review.
LC.   Library of Congress, Washington, D. C.
Leg.   Legajo.
MHS.   Massachusetts Historical Society.
MVHR.   Mississippi Valley Historical Review.
MP.   Monroe Papers.
NYP.   Division of Manuscripts, New York Public Library.
PRO.   Public Record Office, London.

CONTENTS

PAGE

CHAPTER I

REPUBLIC AND EMPIRE, TO 1815

The Panorama of 1810 15
Antecedents of Rivalry 16
American Aggression in Florida 28
Spanish Diplomacy, 1812–1815 34

CHAPTER II

THE UNITED STATES AND THE REVOLUTION IN SPANISH AMERICA, TO 1815

Contacts and Attitudes, North and South 42
United States Reaction to News of the Revolt 46
Rebel Agents in the United States 50
Attitude of the Revolutionists Toward the United States 55

CHAPTER III

NEGOTIATIONS, THE UNITED STATES AND SPAIN, TO MAY, 1818

Resumption of Diplomatic Relations 69
The Policy of Cevallos 73
Pizarro at the Helm 80
Onís and Adams Cross Swords 82
The Evolution of Pizarro's Policy 83

CHAPTER IV

THE NEUTRALITY QUESTION

Conflicting Points of View 97
Rebel Privateers 99
Filibustering from the United States 106
Spanish Protests and American Defense 115
Neutrality Enforcement, Legislation and Opinion 117

CHAPTER V

THE UNITED STATES AND THE REBELS, 1815–1818

" Patriot " Propaganda in the United States 121
The Movement for Official Recognition 130
The Policy of Monroe and Adams 137
Rebel Agents in the United States 145
The Attitude of the " Patriot " Governments 149
American Public Opinion 157

PAGE

CHAPTER VI

THE FLORIDA CRISIS AND THE ADAMS-ONIS TREATY, 1818-1819

The Development of the Crisis 161
High Tension at Washington 164
The Crisis in Spain 167
Ministerial Change, the Policy of Irujo 172
Jackson Attacked and Defended 177
Final Treaty Negotiations 180

CHAPTER VII

SPAIN WITHHOLDS RATIFICATION

The Land Grant Complication 191
Forsyth's Diplomacy, the Fall of Irujo 197
Spain Refuses to Ratify 205
Monroe and Adams Postpone the Issue 209
A New Crisis Approaches 212

CHAPTER VIII

RATIFICATION OF THE ADAMS-ONIS TREATY

European Beginnings of the Vives Mission 221
The United States Congress and Spanish Affairs 224
Factors Influencing American Opinion and Policy 227
Cabinet Deliberations and Negotiations with Vives 231
The Spanish Constitutional Government and the Treaty 235

CHAPTER IX

RECOGNITION OF SPANISH AMERICAN INDEPENDENCE

The Policy of the United States, 1819-1821 244
American Opinion, Congress and the Public 249
The Diplomacy of Manuel Tórres 252
American Agents in Spanish America, and the Attitude of the
   "Patriot" Governments to the United States 254
Spanish America in the United States Congress, 1821 265
The United States Takes the Final Step 267

CHAPTER X

LOOKING BACKWARD

Recapitulation 277
Concluding Remarks 285

PAGE

BIBLIOGRAPHY

Manuscript Sources 289
Contemporary Newspapers and Periodicals 292
Diaries, Memoirs and Printed Correspondence 293
Documentary Collections, Printed 295
Miscellaneous Primary Sources 296
Secondary Authorities 297
Articles in Periodicals 301

INDEX 303

CHAPTER I

REPUBLIC AND EMPIRE, TO 1815

IN the summer of 1810 American newspapers published, among the accounts of European battles and political maneuvers which filled their columns of foreign correspondence, reports of certain disturbances in the Spanish colonies. Had the editors been able to foretell the farreaching consequences of the movement whose first stirrings they now witnessed, they might have given these items a more prominent place. The first incident reported was the overthrow of the government at Caracas, on the southern coast of the Caribbean, and the assumption of power by a popular *Junta*.[1] Before many weeks passed news arrived of a similar uprising at Buenos Aires,[2] and the movement spread rapidly until by the end of the year most of Spain's vast American empire was in turmoil.

Among these reports one was particularly interesting to American citizens. It related to an insurrection in the Spanish province of West Florida on the southern border of the United States.[3] This revolt, though to the uninitiated it might seem part of the movement under way elsewhere in Spanish America, was produced by a different combination of forces.

Though foreign influence, British, French and American, had stimulated a desire for political and economic change,[4] the revolution in the Spanish colonies was a native movement, and

1 *New York Spectator*, June 2, 1810; *Philadelphia Aurora*, June 7, 1810.

2 *Philadelphia Aurora*, Aug. 28, 1810.

3 Rumors of this movement reached Philadelphia in August. (Onís to Bardaxí, Aug. 18, 1810, AHN., Est. Leg. 5636.) See also comments in the *Philadelphia Aurora*, Sept. 10, 1810. The actual declaration of independence at Baton Rouge came at the end of September.

4 W. S. Robertson, *Rise of the Spanish-American Republics* (New York and London, 1918), pp. 15-19; Jules Mancini, *Bolívar et l'emancipation des colonies espagnoles* (Paris, 1912), pp. 70-78, 89-99.

not subservient to any foreign power.[5] The region bordering the United States was an exception to this rule for there the territorial ambitions of the United States and the hopes of foreign adventurers were to be the dominant factors. In Florida, and to a certain extent in Texas, successive revolutionary movements must be considered as episodes in the expansive movement of the United States which led to the acquisition of Florida, to the extension of the boundary of the United States to the Pacific, and which paved the way for the absorption of Texas in the following generation. In this border area, therefore, the United States was directly responsible for the end of Spanish rule. In the rest of Spanish America, also, its activities and that of its citizens, both in the political and economic sphere, in many ways affected the final result. It is the purpose of this volume to survey the relations of the United States to the Spanish Empire in the critical years from 1810 to 1822; to trace the part played by the United States in the break up of that empire, both on the border and in other regions, and to show the interrelation of these two aspects.

The antecedents of rivalry between the United States and Spain go back to the sixteenth century, for the national prejudices of Elizabethan England were inherited by British colonists. These were intensified by territorial conflicts which became acute with the extension of English control to the Carolinas and later to Georgia.[6] Colonial troops took part in border forays against Spanish posts in Florida,[7] and in the attack on Cartagena by Admiral Vernon during the war of the

5 This is shown by the firm repulse of the British attack in the River Plate immediately before the outbreak of the revolution; by the failure of Miranda's expedition to Venezuela in 1806 in association with foreign adventurers; and by the resistance to Napoleon's emissaries to the colonies after 1808.

6 H. E. Bolton, " The Debatable Land " in *Arredondo's Historical Proof of Spain's Title to Georgia*, ed. by H. E. Bolton (Berkeley, 1925), pp. 28-110.

7 *Ibid.*

Austrian Succession.[8] At sea Yankee privateers attacked Spanish commerce.[9]

During the American Revolution the Colonists had been suitors for Spanish favor and had been given financial aid by the government of Charles III, but Spain feared and distrusted the new republic and recognized its independence only after the close of the war. During the peace negotiations at Paris Spain attempted to confine the United States to the Atlantic coast,[10] and in subsequent negotiations at Washington continued its efforts to check American expansion in the Mississippi valley. Through Spanish officials in Louisiana, intrigues were conducted with discontented Westerners with the aim of detaching Kentucky and the rest of the West from the Union.[11] The admission of Kentucky as a state in 1790 checked this agitation, but its embers still smoldered. General James Wilkinson, for one, maintained his treasonable relations with the Spanish government.[12]

Thomas Pinckney, who was sent to Spain by Washington, secured a settlement of the Florida boundary at the thirty-first parallel, and the free navigation of the Mississippi for Americans, including a right of free deposit at New Orleans, marking the end of this chapter in Spanish-American rivalry.[13] The

8 Ellis Ames, "Expedition against Cartagena" in *M. H. S. Proceedings*, First Series, XVIII, 364-379.

9 *Privateering and Piracy in the Colonial Period*, ed. by J. F. Jameson (New York, 1923), pp. 378 ff.

10 S. F. Bemis, *The Foundations of American Diplomacy: The Revolution* (New York, 1935). A more detailed account from the Spanish point of view is J. F. Yela Utrillo, *España ante la independencia de los Estados Unidos* (Lerida, 1925).

11 A. P. Whitaker, *The Spanish-American Frontier, 1783-1795* (Boston and New York, 1927), Chaps. V-VIII.

12 *Ibid.*, *cf.* W. R. Shepherd, "Wilkinson and the Beginnings of the Spanish Conspiracy" in AHR., IX (1904), 490-506.

13 S. F. Bemis, *Pinckney's Treaty* (Baltimore, 1926), covers these negotiations exhaustively. Whitaker, *op. cit.*, p. 197 ff. gives the story from the point of view of the frontier.

treaty of San Lorenzo, however, did not end friction. Spain retained military posts at Natchez and elsewhere north of the boundary until 1798. With their evacuation a lull might have been expected. Exports from the American West via the Mississippi increased rapidly, but rumors of a cession of Louisiana to France gave the " men of the Western Waters " a sense of the precarious state of their economic future.[14]

Negotiations for the return of Louisiana to France had commenced in 1795 during the Franco-Spanish peace negotiations of that year. Spain was not eager to keep so troublesome a colony, inhabited almost entirely by aliens and difficult to govern according to the established Spanish colonial system. No agreement was reached, however, until 1800, when the ' Preliminary Articles of San Ildefonso ' sanctioned the retrocession in exchange for dynastic advantages for the house of Bourbon in Italy.[15] No official notice of this transaction was given the United States,[16] and the wars in Europe prevented the French Republic from actually occupying its newly acquired American territory.[17]

Jefferson, disquieted by rumors of French designs on the Mississippi Valley, continued the earlier efforts of Federalist diplomacy to purchase New Orleans and Florida,[18] but his

14 A. P. Whitaker, *The Mississippi Question, 1795-1803* (New York and London, 1934), pp. 51-154.

15 A. P. Whitaker, " The Retrocession of Louisiana in Spanish Policy " in AHR., XXXIX (1934), 454ff. *Cf.* E. W. Lyon, *Louisiana in French Diplomacy, 1759-1804* (Norman, Okla., 1934), chaps. iv-v, especially pp. 101-109. For the convention see Alejandro Cantillo, ed., *Tratados de paz y comercio* ... (Madrid, 1843), p. 692.

16 Cantillo, *op. cit.*, p. 697, gives the text of the treaty of Aranjuez signed a few months later, which put the preliminary treaty into force.

17 Whitaker, *The Mississippi Question*, pp. 176 ff.

18 H. B. Fuller, *The Purchase of Florida* (Cleveland, 1906), p. 99 ff. is the only detailed account of these negotiations, prior to 1800. But see H. Adams, *History of the United States* (New York, 1889-1891), I, 401-402 and 413-414 for a more balanced story.

agents were unsuccessful both at Madrid and at Paris.[19] In the meantime an act of the Spanish intendant of Louisiana precipitated a crisis. This was the suspension of the right of deposit at New Orleans provided for in the treaty of 1795, which caused consternation in the western country and created a grave problem for Jefferson.[20] The Federalist opposition tried to embarrass the President by forcing him to risk his hold on the sympathy of the West by submitting to the Spanish action, or to engage in a Spanish war which might prove equally disastrous to his administration.[21] It was to evade this issue that Jefferson sent Monroe on his famous mission to Paris, which ended so unexpectedly with the purchase of Louisiana.

The Spanish government, alarmed by the violence of American feeling, ordered the reopening of the right of deposit,[22] and the acquisition of Louisiana by the United States soon after put an end to the troublesome Mississippi question which had been the central point in Spanish-American disputes since the American Revolution. Again, as in 1795, it appeared that a period of peace might ensue, but as in the earlier case other questions still remained unsettled and Jefferson was soon to make use of them in order to force greater concessions.

The United States had claims against Spain, which originated from the inroads made by France and Spain on American shipping from 1797 to 1801.[23] The captures for which the United States held Spain responsible were of two classes: those effected by Spanish vessels, and those made by French privateers in Spanish waters or condemned by French consuls in

19 H. Adams, *History of the United States, loc. cit.* Spain refused to cede territory but advised the United States of the Louisiana cession.

20 Whitaker, *The Mississippi Question,* pp. 189, 191-196.

21 *Ibid.,* pp. 203-205.

22 *Ibid.,* pp. 230-232.

23 J. B. Moore, *History and Digest of the International Arbitrations to which the United States has been a Party* (Washington, 1898), p. 4487 ff.

Spanish ports.[24] The first group of claims was amply justified by an article in the 1795 treaty which established the principle of " free ships, free goods " between the contracting powers.[25] Spain made no serious effort to avoid responsibility for them, but it denied stubbornly any liability for damages done by the French privateers which were more important.[26] A complete settlement of the controversy proved impossible. Charles Pinckney did, however, conclude a convention with Don Pedro Cevallos, the Spanish foreign minister, providing for the liquidation of the claims of the first category.[27] Ratification by the United States was delayed more than a year by factional Federalist opposition; [28] and when finally it was consented to, Spain demurred in its turn. American reservation of the additional claims and resentment at the Mobile Act of 1804, which legislated for territory Spain considered its property, were the reasons given.[29]

The United States also claimed that the entire produce of the western country for a year had been lost in consequence of the suspension of the right of deposit and asked for exaggerated amounts in compensation,[30] though the available statistics of American exports show that much freight continued to pass through New Orleans throughout the period of suspension.[31]

24 *American State Papers, Class I, Foreign Relations* (Washington, 1832-1859), cited hereafter as ASP. FR., II, 636, Monroe and Pinckney to Cevallos, Jan. 28, 1805, summarizes the American contention.

25 *Treaties and Other International Acts of the United States of America,* ed. by D. H. Miller (Washington, 1931-), II, 329.

26 ASP. FR., II, 445-458, 481.

27 D. H. Miller, *Treaties,* II, 492-497, Convention for Indemnification, Aug. 11, 1802.

28 H. Adams, *Hist. of the U. S.,* II, 249 ff.

29 ASP. FR., II, 541, Cevallos to Monroe and Pinckney, Feb. 10, 1805.

30 ASP. FR., II, 636, Monroe and Pinckney to Cevallos, Jan. 28, 1805.

31 Whitaker, *The Mississippi Question,* pp. 228-229; and note on page 319. The author shows that the decline in exports was due to renewed peace in Europe rather than to the Spanish government's action.

These pecuniary items were made subsidiary to the American claim to West Florida and Texas as part of the Louisiana purchase. This was made possible by the vague language of the treaty of San Ildefonso of 1800 retroceding Louisiana to France " with the same extent that it now has in the hands of Spain, and that it had when France possessed it, and such as it should be after the treaties subsequently entered into between Spain and other states ".[32]   The Louisiana Purchase treaty of 1803 referred to the region defined in the 1800 treaty and fixed no specific boundaries.[33] West Florida as far east as the Perdido River had once been part of French Louisiana, but this territory had been ceded to England in 1763,[34] acquired by Spain from the latter by conquest during the war of the American Revolution and definitely ceded to Spain with the rest of Florida in the Treaty of Paris of 1783.[35] As it had never been ceded to Spain by France it could hardly have been retroceded to the latter.

When it became apparent in 1804, however, that the language of the purchase treaty made such an interpretation possible, Jefferson, prompted thereto by Livingston, adopted the claim to this region,[36] and it was tenaciously maintained by the American government until the treaty of 1819 with Spain finally put an end to the controversy. The claim had only a quibbling justification. Spain had not retroceded West Florida to France in 1800. It definitely refused to do so, though

32 Cantillo, *Tratados*, p. 692, Artículos preliminares de San Ildefonso, Octubre, 1800, Art. 3, the translation is that given in the Louisiana Purchase Treaty.

33 Miller, *Treaties*, II, p. 499.

34 Cantillo, *Tratados*, p. 492, Tratado definitivo de paz entre España y Francia por una parte y la Gran Bretaña por otra, Paris, 10 Feb., 1763, Art. 20.

35 *Ibid.*, p. 587, Tratado definitivo de paz entre las coronas de España é Inglaterra, Versailles, 3 Sept., 1783, Art. 5.

36 Adams, *History of the U. S.*, II, 302.

France brought pressure to bear on the Spanish court.[37] France, though it might have encroached on this region if its plans for a new American empire had not been cut short, definitely went on record, after the cession to the United States, with regard to the eastern boundary of Louisiana, stating that the line should run from the Mississippi via the river Iberville and lakes Maurepas and Pontchartrain to the Gulf of Mexico, thus officially contradicting the American claim.[38] Jefferson, as it has been said, insisted on receiving from Spain a territory which that power claimed it had never sold and which France denied having bought.

The American claim to Texas was more reasonable. It was supported by the statement of the French commissioner at New Orleans and by the traditional claims of France to which the United States had now fallen heir. The exact boundary between French Louisiana and Spanish territory had never been formally established. If occupation is made the criterion, Spain's claim was infinitely superior to that of France. Numerous Spanish forts and missions in central and western Texas bore witness to Spanish activity. The eastern part of the province was more debateable ground. The United States, however, constantly refused a settlement on the basis of the *uti possidetis* of 1763 as the Spaniards were amply provided with documentary evidence and maps to support their contentions, whereas the Americans had little proof of this nature. They preferred, therefore, to stand on the territorial pretensions of Louis XIV and the grants made during his reign.[39]

37 E. W. Lyon, *op. cit.*, pp. 90-98, 106-107, 191; Adams, *op. cit.*, I, 402.

38 For the statements of the French government and its officials see Talleyrand to Gravina, 12 Fructidor, XII; *idem* to *idem*, July 27, 1804; Talleyrand to Santibañez, 5 Germinal, XIII, AHN., Est. Leg. 6797. See also *Louisiana under the Rule of Spain, France, and the United States*, ed. by J. A. Robertson (Cleveland, 1911, 2 vols.), II, 171-173, Laussat to Salcedo and Casa Calvo, Jan. 18, 1804.

39 For the Spanish arguments see the summary in Onís to Adams, Mar. 23, 1818, AHN., Est. Leg. 6797; for the American contentions, Adams to Onís, Mar. 12, 1818, ASP. FR., IV.

Jefferson first sought to gain his purpose through the good offices of Napoleon.[40] This proving impossible, Monroe proceeded to Madrid to try his hand at direct negotiations. The Spanish court had been forced to withdraw its most justifiable protest against the sale of Louisiana to the United States, but in return it now received assurances of French support against Monroe's pretensions. Accordingly it had nothing to fear from a discussion of them.[41] Though relations between Pinckney, the American envoy, and the Spanish court had been strained, Cevallos raised no obstacle when he and Monroe showed a wish to negotiate.[42]

All the issues were canvassed by the Americans in their lengthy correspondence with Cevallos. They had hoped to make Spain accept their claims to West Florida and Texas, and had been authorized to agree to a neutral desert zone between the Sabine and Colorado rivers in Texas if Spain would accept the latter as the international boundary. They were also permitted to offer two million dollars for Spanish territory east of the Mississippi.[43] The offer of cash was never made, but Monroe and his associate did agree to give up all other claims and to establish the neutral zone if Spain would cede the Floridas and ratify the 1802 Convention.[44] Cevallos, secure behind French backing, refused the final offer and the negotiation ended as a complete failure.[45]

In the United States the failure at Madrid and the bellicose tone of the President's message [46] led to talk of war, but Jeffer-

40 II. Adams, *Hist. of the U. S.*, II, 305 ff.

41 I. J. Cox, *West Florida Controversy, 1798-1813, a Study in American Diplomacy* (Baltimore, 1918), p. 109 f.

42 ASP. FR., II, 636, Cevallos to Monroe and Pinckney, Jan. 31, 1805.

43 Fuller, *The Purchase of Florida*, p. 148 citing DS. Instructions, vol. vi, Madison to Monroe and Pinckney, July 8, 1804.

44 ASP. FR., II, 665, Monroe and Pinckney to Cevallos, May 12, 1805.

45 ASP. FR., II, 666, Cevallos to Monroe and Pinckney, May 15, 1805.

46 J. D. Richardson, *Messages and Papers of the Presidents, 1789-1908* (Bureau of National Literature and Art, 1909, no place of publication given), I, 388, Jefferson to Congress, Dec. 6, 1805.

son had decided on another method. Hearing that his wishes might succeed if money were judiciously employed at Paris,[47] he decided, after consulting his cabinet, to try once more to secure Florida by negotiation.[48] He sent a secret message to Congress contradicting the tenor of his public one and asked for an appropriation to purchase Florida. This double policy created a breach between the administration and John Randolph who had for some time been dissatisfied. A number of Republicans followed Randolph's lead, but party discipline finally prevailed and the " Two Million Act " was duly passed.[49] The debate had caused delay, and not until March, 1806, could the necessary instructions be sent to Armstrong at Paris. By the time he was authorized to act the French government no longer showed any disposition to fall in with the scheme.[50]

During the next few years the possibility of such an arrangement was often dangled before the United States and as often withdrawn; the policy of France fluctuating as European politics made the good will of the United States more or less important. After 1808 and the beginning of the war in Spain, the United States was no longer tempted, for a title to Florida given by Joseph Bonaparte could hardly be adequate as long as the mastery of Europe was still doubtful.[51]

During these episodes of Jeffersonian diplomacy the situation on the Spanish-American frontier had been becoming

47 H. Adams, *Hist. of the U. S.*, III, 105.

48 *Writings of Thomas Jefferson*, Paul L. Ford, ed. (New York and London, 1904-1905), I, 308-309. Memo. of cabinet meeting Nov. 12 and 19, 1805.

49 H. Adams, *Hist. of the U. S.*, III, chap. vi, pp. 126-46.

50 *Ibid.*, III, 386 ff.

51 J. S. Reeves, *The Napoleonic Exiles in America; a Study in American Diplomatic History, 1815-1819* (Baltimore, 1905), cited hereafter as Reeves, *Napoleonic Exiles*, p. 114 ff., relates the attempts of France and Bonapartist Spain to sell Florida to the U. S. See Russell to Madison, Jan. 2, 1811; Barlow to Madison, Dec. 30, 1811, p. 121; Madison to Barlow, Feb. 29, 1811, p. 134.

steadily worse. In western Louisiana the anomalous situation created by the presence of both Spanish and American troops in the disputed area was settled by an agreement between General Wilkinson and the Spanish military commander in Texas, which maintained the existing lines of military occupation and provided for a neutral strip between the Sabine river and the Arroyo Hondo.[52] This agreement, though not authorized by either government, was so convenient to both that it was continued while a definitive solution remained pending.

East of New Orleans conflict could not be so easily postponed. Spanish officials, lingering in New Orleans, were selling West Florida lands against the will of the American authorities, nor did the expulsion of Morales, the principal offender, and others relieve the situation.[53] Additional trouble arose over the right of navigation of the Mobile. Free use of the river was important to the Americans because the stream was the easiest means of access to the Mississippi Territory from New Orleans and the Gulf. The right was at first withheld; then, as opinions differed among the Spanish officials, it was sometimes allowed and on other occasions denied. Irritation ensued which increased the tension between Governor Folch of West Florida and W. C. C. Claiborne, governor at New Orleans.[54]

Spanish officers, increasingly short of funds, were hard pressed to maintain a semblance of order among the turbulent inhabitants of West Florida, for the most part non-Spanish in origin. Certain men, like the notorious Kemper brothers, were able to live a lawless existence on the frontier and to escape punishment by flitting to American soil when they were in danger. Before long, reports began to reach Folch of discon-

52 I. J. Cox, " The Louisiana Texas Frontier during the Burr Conspiracy," MVHR., X (1934), 284; W. F. McCaleb, *The Aaron Burr Conspiracy; a History Largely from Original and Hitherto Unused Sources* (New York, 1903), p. 148 ff.

53 Cox, *West Florida Controversy*, pp. 174, 181-183.

54 *Ibid.*, pp. 168-187.

tent and insubordination in the Baton Rouge district, which he believed to be encouraged by Governor Claiborne.[55]

In Washington the diplomats were on no better terms. The Marquis of Casa Irujo, the Spanish minister, engaged in a series of encounters with the administration which ended in a demand for his recall. Irujo had been in good favor at the beginning of Jefferson's first term. He had done his best to secure the reopening of the right of deposit at New Orleans. An estrangement began with the Mobile Act which the Marquis considered an insult to his country and over which he used violent language to Madison. Soon after, the Spaniard was accused of having attempted to bribe a journalist, and finally one of his notes criticizing the presidential message of 1805 led to a permanent breach with Madison. Irujo did not on that account leave the country, and he was to prove a thorn in the side of the administration a year later by publicly accusing it of complicity in Francisco de Miranda's filibustering expedition to Venezuela.[56] Through Valentin de Foronda, who succeeded him as chargé d'affaires, Irujo continued to launch protests and threats at the United States government. Such was the situation when Napoleon's intervention in Spain, the dethronement of the Bourbons and the national uprising which followed put an end to normal relations between the two countries. The United States refused to recognize either party in the struggle for control of the Peninsula, and was left free meanwhile to pursue its aims, unhampered by the stubborn court at Madrid or its diplomatic representatives.

This was the only course open to the administration unless it wished to invite international complications, for Great Britain backed the Spanish *Junta* which had undertaken the opposition

55 *Ibid.*, pp. 152-153, 361.

56 H. Adams, *History of the U. S.* still the best account of Irujo's activities in the U. S. Use index under the head "Yrujo." For Jefferson's early favorable attitude toward Irujo see *Writings of Thomas Jefferson* (Monticello edition, Washington, 1904), X, 244.

to French rule, while Joseph Bonaparte's government was naturally championed by his brother. The *Junta Central,* at the instance of its British allies,[57] sent a minister to the United States with the hope of securing recognition. The new appointee, Don Luis de Onís y González, was one of the abler Spanish civil servants of his day. He belonged to a noble family of Castile with a tradition of public service and entered the diplomatic service as a young man, having in 1809 reached the rank of under secretary at the foreign office.[58] He was an ardent patriot and espoused the cause of Ferdinand VII and the *Junta* without hesitation. Onís had all the pride and rigidity of the class to which he belonged, but it was tempered in his case by high intelligence and a wide store of information. A better appointment could not have been made.

When he arrived in the United States Onís found that he was not to have an easy task. Though it was once proposed that the government should admit him, news of French successes in Spain soon scotched the proposal,[59] and it was not until 1815 that his status became official. The commissions of Spanish consuls issued before 1809, however, were regarded as valid and through them, Onís was able to put his claims and protests before the State Department, but as political questions were considered outside the consular province the American government was able to avoid discussion of them.[60]

Though cut off from his regular duties, Onís did not remain inactive. He did what he could to organize shipments of neces-

57 Juan de Garáy to Ruíz de Apodaca, July 27, 1809, AHN., Est. Leg. 3446.

58 F. de Antón del Olmet, *Proceso de los orígenes de la decadencia española. El cuerpo diplomático español en le guerra de la independencia* (Madrid, no date), II, pp. 66 ff.

59 Onís to Bardaxí, No. 158, July 28, 1810, AHN., Est. Leg. 5636.

60 Monroe to Consul Chacón, Mar. 19, 1814, AHN., Est. Leg. 5557 Expediente No. 2 sums up the U. S. viewpoint. For Onís' method of acting through consuls see, Onís to the Marqués de las Hormazas, No. 117, Jan. 6, 1810, AHN , Est. Leg. 5636.

sary supplies to the Spanish patriots and to combat Bonapartist propaganda, and not many months passed before his duties became infinitely more overwhelming with the outbreak of revolt in many widely separated provinces of Spain's American possessions.

In Florida the storm broke first in the Baton Rouge region, closest to New Orleans and containing the greatest number of American settlers. In July, 1810, a revolutionary convention met, deposed the Spanish commander, and shortly afterward declared the independence of West Florida.[61] The occupation of the region by American forces soon put an end to the infant republic. The Spanish officials at Pensacola and Mobile regarded the whole proceeding as a thinly disguised intrigue of the United States to get possession of the area without an open attack on Spanish forces. There is some truth in this assertion. Governor Claiborne of Louisiana and Holmes of Mississippi Territory encouraged the revolt with the tacit consent of Madison, and American citizens joined the rebels in considerable numbers.[62] Further, it is probable that the rebels had no desire to maintain their independence and that their motives were divided between a wish to bring American occupation and hopes of securing titles to lands irregularly obtained.[63]

The action taken by the President in West Florida was tacitly agreed to by Congress, against the strong objections of Federalists like Josiah Quincy and Timothy Pickering. Under the theory that the region occupied was part of the Louisiana purchase, no action was considered necessary to regularize the occupation,[64] but in January, 1811, Congress went further and in

61 ASP. FR., III, pp. 395-6. Declaration of Sept. 26, 1810.

62 Julius W. Pratt, *The Expansionists of 1812* (New York, 1925), quoting a Nashville paper, p. 72; Cox, *West Florida Controversy*, p. 330; Madison's proclamation of occupation, Oct. 27, 1810 is in ASP. FR., III, 396-397.

63 H. Adams, *History of the United States*, V, 36; I. J. Cox, "American Intervention in West Florida," AHR., XVII (1911), 297-300.

64 *Annals of Congress*, XXII, 11 congress, 3 session, p. 514.

secret session authorized the occupation of the rest of Florida, if the local authorities would consent, or if a foreign power should attempt to take possession of it.[65] This resolution was voted in response to Governor Folch's offer to deliver his province to the American authorities if he were not reinforced before a certain date.[66] This offer, which was made before the American occupation of Baton Rouge, apparently for the purpose of forestalling an extension of that movement to the rest of the province, was soon withdrawn and Folch showed great indignation at the conduct of the United States.[67]

Commissioners were sent by Madison to treat for the delivery of the Floridas, but they failed to achieve their object. General George Mathews, the commissioner to East Florida, however, went so far as to stir up a revolt there. He offered land to those who would undertake the move against the Spanish authorities at St. Augustine and secured the menacing presence of American military and naval detachments on the border. With this encouragement a group of men attacked and captured Amelia Island on the frontier between Georgia and Florida, and were proceeding against St. Augustine when Madison and Monroe, realizing that they could not defend these too public machinations, disavowed his actions. They did not, however, immediately withdraw the troops from the sector giving the excuse that they were needed to protect the rebels who had trusted to United States.[68]

65 Pratt, *Expansionists of 1812*, p. 74.

66 Cox, *West Florida Controversy*, p. 471 f.; ASP. FR., III, 398. Folch to R. Smith, Dec. 2, 1810.

67 Cox, *op. cit.*, pp. 509 f., 525 f.

68 R. K. Wyllys, "The East Florida Revolution of 1812-1814," HAHR., IX (1929), 415-445, a detailed study of events in Florida; Pratt, *The Expansionists of 1812*, pp. 76 ff. This is an exhaustive study of the Mathews affair based on MSS sources. The author finds Monroe definitely implicated and that he halted only under fire from the Federalists and from Great Britain. *Cf.* I. J. Cox, "Border Missions of General Mathews," MVHR., XII (1925), 312 ff.; also ASP. FR., III, 571.

These events took place shortly before war broke out between the United States and Great Britain. That government protested repeatedly against the action taken against Spain in Florida.[69] At the time, this was considered proof of sinister British designs on the province, and after the declaration of war Congress was asked to authorize the occupation of Florida as a war measure without the qualifying restrictions of the previous year. The bill failed in the Senate by a narrow margin owing to the alliance of northern Republicans with the Federalist opposition.[70] A year later Congress authorized occupation of West Florida to the full extent claimed by the United States under the Louisiana treaty, but maintained its negative as to the eastern portion of the province.[71] Aside from the fact that the United States had no claim to Florida east of the Perdido River, the attitude of Congress may be explained by the nature of material interests. The direction of settlement in Georgia was principally toward the Indian country in the south and west of the state. East Florida was not an important objective for land-hungry settlers, while West Florida, together with its more desirable lands, contained streams important to the transportation system of a large area in the Southwest.

The larger plans of the administration had met with a check, but the occupation of Mobile and its vicinity was carried out according to plan. Troops under General Wilkinson took possession on April 15, 1813 without opposition, after bluffing the Spanish garrison into evacuation.[72]

The war with the Creek Indians, which broke out soon after the occupation of Mobile, temporarily prevented any further action in Florida, but after General Jackson's successful campaign against that tribe it was renewed. Jackson had long been

69 ASP. FR., III, 399, Morier to Smith, Dec. 15, 1810; *ibid.*, 542-543, Foster to Monroe, July 2, 1811 and Sept. 5, 1811.

70 H. Adams, *History of the U. S.*, VI, 243.

71 *Ibid.*, VII, 209.

72 Cox, *West Florida Controversy*, p. 619.

strongly hostile to Spain [73] and like many of his Tennessee and Mississippi neighbors considered the acquisition of Florida one of the objects of the war. Though Spain was officially neutral, it was an ally of the enemy and in 1814 breaches of Spanish neutrality took place which gave the General an excuse for a Florida campaign. Jackson made much of the refusal of Spanish officials to surrender or to punish the Creeks who had fled from his vengeance across the frontier, and a more valid excuse was furnished by the activities of Major Nichols, a British officer who landed at Pensacola with troops and supplies to organize Indian resistance to the United States.[74] Jackson's answer was to march to Pensacola and occupy it.

American troops, thus, had occupied since 1810 all the territory claimed from Spain in the Floridas, and had twice invaded other parts of the territory. It remained to be seen whether upon the conclusion of peace Spain would be able to resist further, or whether these blows had completely destroyed its hold on the province.

One could hardly say that Madison's Florida policy was over-scrupulous, but the President's naturally cautious temperament made him eager to avoid open war with Spain. Subjected as he was to pressure for aggressive action, and notwithstanding his personal interest in the acquisition of West Florida for which as Jefferson's lieutenant he had struggled for years with the chancelleries of Spain and France, he was unwilling to trust to force alone and endeavored to keep open a line of communication with Spain. He kept Onís at a distance, for his protests were vigorous and he hardly seemed a good channel for conciliatory moves,[75] but he sent an emissary to the Spanish com-

73 *Correspondence of Andrew Jackson,* John Spencer Bassett, ed. (Washington, 1926-1933), I, 153, Jackson to Claiborne, Nov. 12, 1806. " I hate the Dons."

74 Fuller, *The Purchase of Florida,* pp. 205-207.

75 Though Onís was forced to act principally through the Spanish consuls he did have occasional contact with Secretary Dallas of the Treasury; see: Onís to Bardaxí y Azara, Nos. 211 and 217, Dec. 4 and 17, 1810, AHN., Est. Leg. 5636; No. 27, Jan. 31, 1811, *id.,* Leg. 5637.

mander of the *Provincias Internas,* the northern border region
of New Spain. Dr. John H. Robinson, who was despatched on
this errand during the summer of 1812, had other interests of
his own, but his instructions were to do all he could to assure
the Spaniards that the United States was not hostile to them,
that it wished to cooperate with Spain for proper policing of
the frontier, and that its actions in West Florida had not been
taken except with the purpose of preserving order.[76] This
mission was not very successful for Salcedo, the Spanish governor at Chihuahua, was deeply and justifiably suspicious of
Robinson's aims.[77]

As the war with England wore on with scant success for the
United States and the maintenance of peace with Spain became
more important, Madison sent Anthony Morris, a Quaker
and a personal friend of the President and his family, to Spain
on a semi-official mission.[78] Morris was ordered to maintain
that the West Florida controversy should be considered settled
in favor of the United States, and to suggest a cession of the
rest of Florida in return for a cancellation of American claims
or in advance of a future boundary negotiation.[79] This agent
was not officially received when he presented himself in December, 1813 to the government of the Regency at Cadiz, for
it was felt necessary to retaliate for the treatment afforded
Onís.[80] He did have unofficial contact with the foreign office,
however, adopting a milder tone than that contemplated in his
instructions and merely suggesting that Spain acquiesce in a

76 Monroe to Robinson, July 1, 1812. DS., Mexico, Filibustering Expeditions against the Government of Spain, 1811-1816.

77 Robinson to Monroe, July 26, 1813, DS., *ibid.*

78 His commission is preserved in AHN., Expediente No. 2, Leg. 5557,
see also H. M. Wriston, *Executive Agents in American Foreign Relations*
(Baltimore and London, 1929), p. 471.

79 Monroe to A. Morris, June 9, 1813, in John Bassett Moore, *Digest of
International Law* (Washington, 1906), I, 132-133.

80 Cevallos to Onís, to Jan. 20, 1815, AME., Cor. Pol., Estados Unidos,
Leg. 237.

temporary occupation of the disputed territory, without prejudice to Spanish rights.[81] The Regency was then on the verge of dissolution, as Ferdinand VII was shortly to return to Spain. This impending change, and the preoccupation of the ministry with schemes for securing American objectives through European intervention,[82] prevented Morris' mission from leading to any concrete result.

As these moves suggest, Madison was not eager to force the issue with Spain after the outbreak of the Anglo-American war. Jackson's march against Pensacola was undertaken without specific instructions from the War Department. In October, 1814 he was ordered to " take no measures which would involve this government in a conflict with Spain ",[83] and a subsequent order expressed anxiety as to whether the order had been received in time.[84] Orders unpalatable to Jackson were strangely slow in reaching him, and these pacific letters did not arrive until after Pensacola had been taken.[85]

Popular support for the forceful measures of the administration in Florida was strong, even before the outbreak of war with England and the resulting fear of British occupation. In 1811 Claiborne was clamoring for the capture of Mobile,[86] and even suggested the annexation of Cuba.[87] A Georgia newspaper called for the occupation of all Florida, and the historian of American expansionism in this period has shown that the whole of the South and West favored strong measures against

81 Wriston, *op. cit.*, p. 471.

82 See pp. 36-37, *infra*.

83 Monroe to Jackson, October 21, 1814, MP. LC.

84 Monroe to Jackson, Dec. 7, 1814, *ibid.*

85 Bassett, *Correspondence of Andrew Jackson*, II, 110.

86 Claiborne to C. A. Rodney, Feb. 18, 1811, Rodney Papers, LC.

87 *Official Letter Books of W. C. C. Claiborne, 1801-1816*, ed. by Dunbar Rowland (Jackson, Miss., 1917), V, 290, Claiborne to P. Hamilton, July 6, 1811.

Spain.[88] From Virginia came a plea to " lay aside all fastidious delicacy and strike the blow called for by National safety ".[89] From Europe, a relative of the ex-Secretary of State Robert Smith wrote urging the United States to take Florida. " All this morality does not answer nowadays ",[90] he remarked, perhaps impressed by the apparent success of the Napoleonic technique. The opposition was limited to the East, and principally to New England, but even there irritation against Spain was not lacking, for Spanish privateers in the South Pacific operating ostensibly against the rebels of Chile captured several American ships and added to the number of unsatisfied claims against the Spanish government.[91]

The inconsistencies in Madison's character are nowhere more in evidence than in the mixture of caution and boldness with which he occupied disputed territory, encouraged revolution, and at the same time tried to maintain friendly intercourse with his victims. Was this policy to have the justification given by success, or, were the President's political opponents to prove correct in the prophecy that, " Our policy toward Spain in seizing upon West Florida; in stirring up and actually aiding the insurrection in East Florida: . . . are crimes there is a reason to suspect an atonement will be called for "?[92]

The answer to this question depended largely on the outcome of the wars in Europe and America. To the Spanish government it seemed to depend first of all on the attitude of the powers, particularly Great Britain, toward the conflict between

88 Pratt, *Expansionists of 1812*, pp. 110 ff.   The author has surveyed the press at this time in detail.

89 J. Minor to Monroe, Nov. 1, 1812, MP., Johnson Collection, LC.

90 John S. Smith to Samuel Smith, Paris, Jan. 22, 1811, Smith Papers, LC.

91 *Philadelphia Aurora*, July 23 and 24, 1812.

92 William P. Cutler and J. P. Cutler, *Life, Journals, and Correspondence of the Rev. Manasseh Cutler* (Cincinnati, 1888), II, 346, Rufus Putnam to Cutler, June 25, 1814. For a Spanish view of Federalist anti-expansionism, see Onís to Bardaxí, No. 165, Sept. 9, 1811, AHN., Est. Leg. 5637; *cf.* on the same subject Pratt, *Expansionists*, pp. 110 ff. and 120 ff.

Spain and the United States. Soon after the outbreak of the Anglo-American War the foreign office of the Cadiz Regency deliberated on the course of action to be taken. The decision was to maintain neutrality, as Spain was in no position to undertake hostilities in America, and as a peace policy might be the most effective curb to American expansionist aims. The fact that British and Spanish armies in the Peninsula were dependent on provisions exported from the United States was also a restraining factor.[93] A few months later, in December, 1812, the foreign office prepared a memorandum on the conflict with the United States which was considered in a secret session of the Cortes.[93] No action was taken by that legislature, but the Secretary of State approached Sir Henry Wellesley, the British ambassador, on his own responsibility, asking that Spanish grievances against the United States be considered by Great Britain during the eventual peace negotiations with the former power.[94] The question of policy was also raised in the Council of State, and confiscation of American property in Spain was discussed as a possible retaliation for occurrences in Florida. This measure was not approved as it was felt that Spain would lose more than the United States if war should result.[95]

When the news of Wilkinson's occupation of Mobile arrived, the Council reconsidered its previous decision in the light of this further aggression. War was declared justifiable but impolitic; direct negotiation, impracticable; and the mediation of

93 Extracto (precis) on relations with the United States, Oct. 15, 1812, AHN., Est. Leg. 5557, Expediente, No. 1. The decision for neutrality was reached Aug. 12, 1812. On the nature and volume of the provision trade between the United States and Spain, see W. F. Galpin, "American Grain Trade to the Spanish Peninsula" in AHR., XXVIII, 24 ff., see also, A. C. Clauder, *American Commerce as Affected by the Wars of the French Revolution and Napoleon, 1793-1812* (Phila., 1932), pp. 226-229.

94 Pedro Labrador to the Secretary of the Cortes, Dec. 31, 1812, AHN., Est. Leg. 5557, Expediente, No. 1; Pedro Labrador to H. Wellesley, Jan. 4, 1813, *ibid.*

95 Report of the Council of State, Jan. 31, 1813, *ibid.*

Russia was suggested as a way to put a stop to American encroachments. If this mediation could be secured, certain concessions might be made to induce the United States to cease its pressure on Florida: the free navigation of the Mobile river, and a promise not to cede Florida to Great Britain which appeared to be the chief fear of the American public.[96]

In June, 1813, the Spanish government heard of the probable peace negotiations between Great Britain and the United States at St. Petersburg and renewed its request for British aid in securing the recognition of Onís and the restoration of West Florida.[97] A few weeks later the British, who had till then remained silent to both appeals, replied that the interests of their Ally would at all times be sustained, but as they avoided specific promises [98] the Spaniards fixed their hopes on the Tsar. Instructions were sent to the Spanish minister at the Russian court to seek mediation even though the Anglo-American negotiations failed to materialize.[99] Unfortunately for Spain, its cause was neglected by the powers, then occupied with the final campaigns against the tottering French Empire.

With these unsuccessful *démarches* the efforts of the Cadiz Regency closed. Early in 1814 Napoleon freed Ferdinand VII and the exiled prince was soon making a triumphal progress toward his capital.[100]   The reactionary policy which the King immediately put into effect in domestic affairs was paralleled by great ineptitude in the handling of foreign relations. The ablest men of the constitutionalist era were dismissed, and Spain failed to take proper advantage of its position in the coalition against Napoleon. This seems to have been due partly to the

96 Minute of the session of the Council of State, August 14, 1813, AHN., Est. Leg. 5557, Expediente No. 1.

97 Secretary of State to H. Wellesley, June 15, 1813, *ibid.*

98 Castlereagh to Fernan-Nuñez, August 28, 1813, *ibid.*

99 Secretario de Estado to the Minister in Russia (draft), Sept. 6, 1813, *ibid.*

100 Hermann Baumgarten, *Geschichte Spaniens vom Ausbruch der französischen Revolution bis auf unsere Tage* (Leipzig, 1868), II, 25-27.

preoccupation of the Spanish court with matters of dignity and protocol, but even more to its failure to adopt an alignment with one of the great powers. It demanded the adroitness and mental agility of a Talleyrand to succeed in the ambitious plan of playing one power against another. For bankrupt, devastated, war-weary Spain, with its best political talent proscribed, it was an impossible attempt. In the end Spain gained nothing.[101]

Spain's efforts to secure redress from the United States during the general peace negotiations in Europe illustrate the way its other interests were handled. In June, 1814, the reconstituted monarchy took up American affairs, turning first to Great Britain, and suggesting to Sir Henry Wellesley at Madrid that the King was ready to put himself entirely in accord with England to oblige the United States to make peace, as well as to negotiate with it.[102] This virtually offered Spanish participation in the Anglo-American war, but though the offer was repeated through the ambassador in London,[103] Spain was to be disappointed. Castlereagh saw no advantage in Spanish cooperation in the war with the United States, for Spain had no troops in America available for offensive action, and only Spanish neutrality prevented a complete occupation of Florida by American forces. England also saw no advantage in the inclusion of the Spanish-American dispute with the other problems that would eventually face the Anglo-American peace

101 Jerónimo Becker, *Historia de las relaciones exteriores de España durante el siglo XIX* (Madrid, 1924), vol. i, chaps. xxi, xxiii and xxiv; see also, Wenceslao Ramírez de Villaurrutia, " España en el congreso de Viena " in *Revista de Archivos, Bibliotecas y Museos* (Madrid), vols. xv and xvi.

102 San Carlos to H. Wellesley, June 10, 1814, AHN., Est. Leg. 5557, Expediente No. 1. The Spanish text of the passage is as follows: " El Rey mi amo est á pronto á ponerse en un todo de acuerdo con S. A. R. el Pr. Reg. de la G. B. así para obligar á la Paz como para tratar de ella con los Estados Unidos."

103 Fernan-Nuñez to Castlereagh, July 6, 1814, enclosed with Fernan-Nuñez to San Carlos No. 481, 1814, AHN., Est. Leg. 5557, Expediente No. 1.

negotiations. Castlereagh therefore declared that Great Britain would continue to protect Spanish interests from the United States as it had in the past, but that the proposed joint negotiation could not be considered. The hint at warlike cooperation was completely ignored. According to the British note:

... under the existing circumstances it would be fruitless to attempt a negotiation of this character and in proportion as the blending the settlement of the differences between Great Britain and America with that of the just complaints of Spain against the latter State would tend to remove the period of our pacification, in that proportion would the real interests of Spain be in fact sacrificed.[104]

Disappointed by this reaction, Spain, though it did not entirely give up hope of British aid, turned to other schemes.

In January, 1814, the Spanish foreign office, in anticipation of the general peace negotiation in Europe, prepared a memorandum stating Spanish objectives and how they were to be obtained. These *desiderata* were: the return of Louisiana, unjustly taken from Spain by Napoleon; a large indemnity and the return of spoils taken from Spain by the French; and, in view of the dynastic interests of the king, the restoration of the Bourbon king of Naples. To secure these ends the aid of powers which were rivals of France were to be sought in the following order of desirability: Great Britain, Austria, and Russia.[105] Dissatisfaction with the Allies brought a change in policy, however. The powers would not allow Spain an equal place with the " Big Four " in the final peace negotiations at Paris, and expected Ferdinand's government to accede to the first treaty of Paris after it had been concluded as did the minor European states.[106] Spain refused to do this and saved

104 Castlereagh to Fernan-Nuñez, Aug. 4, 1814, AHN., Est. Leg. 5557, Expediente No. 1.

105 J. Becker, *Historia de las relaciones exteriores de España durante el siglo XIX*, I, 327 f.; see also, Ramírez de Villaurrutia, *op. cit.*

106 Becker, *op. cit.*, I, 339.

its dignity by signing a separate peace with France, in which, in addition to the general provisions of the treaty between France and the Allies, certain secret articles were included. In one of them France promised to aid Spain to secure redress for the Bourbons of Italy and indemnity for the non-execution of the Italian provisions of the treaty of Aranjuez of 1801 in return for which Spain had ceded Louisiana.[107] The policy of Spain was incoherent for at the same time that it concluded a treaty of commerce and alliance with Great Britain, promising not to renew the Family Compact,[108] it was secretly cooperating with France, the country against which the major claims of Spain must necessarily be directed.

The stage was now set, or so the Spanish government believed, for presenting its demands at the Congress of Vienna. Before the opening of the Congress instructions were sent to the Spanish representative to insist on the return of Louisiana to King Ferdinand.[109] Pedro Gómez Labrador, the somewhat nearsighted and obstinate envoy, who with all his faults has been unduly criticized for his failure to achieve the impossible, reported soon after the Congress assembled that he had no hope of obtaining Louisiana, for it was objected that it was not a province conquered by France, but ceded to it by treaty and later alienated by France to the United States. The Allied plenipotentiaries considered that Spain had a claim against France, but that the Congress, not having possession of Louisiana, could not return it to Spain.[110]

Pedro Cevallos, who now reappeared at the head of the Spanish foreign office in place of San Carlos, was not daunted by these reports. He outlined to Gómez Labrador an elaborate

107 Cantillo, *Tratados*, p. 741. Treaty of July 20, 1814.

108 *Ibid.*, p. 732. Treaty of July 5, 1814.

109 Instructions of August, 1814, quoted by Villaurrutia, *op. cit., Revista de Archivos, Bibliotecas y Museos*, XV, 165 ff.

110 P. Gómez Labrador to San Carlos, November 12, 1814, AHN., Est. Leg. 5557, Expediente No. 25.

scheme for securing the interest of the powers. In return for withdrawing opposition to the Austrian occupation of Etruria the good offices of Prince Metternich were to be sought to make Great Britain agree not to conclude peace with the United States without delivering Louisiana to Spain.[111] By supporting the French views on the disposition of Saxony Gómez Labrador was to secure recognition of France's obligation to restore Louisiana or to fulfill the equivalent for which it had been ceded.[112]

These schemes show the inability of the Spanish officials of this epoch to see the international relations of Europe clearly or to evaluate judiciously the importance of the various unsettled problems to each power. No one however, can accuse Cevallos of lack of persistence. To develop further the earlier plan of securing Louisiana by direct pressure on England he again approached the British cabinet. News must have reached Spain slowly in those months, for before Cevallos' orders could reach the ambassador in London the Treaty of Ghent had been concluded.[113]

The British commissioners at Ghent had hardly touched the Florida question. A casual mention of the attempt of the United States to " wrest the Floridas from a nation in amity by force of arms " was all that Great Britain cared to do for Spain.[114] Cevallos was thus forced to give up one of his plans, but another effort was made at Vienna. Gómez Labrador, under pressure from Cevallos to do something, interviewed the Duke of Wellington and suggested to that doughty warrior that though the treaty of Ghent did not provide for the return of

111 Cevallos to Gómez Labrador, Dec. 26, 1814 as quoted by Villaurrutia, *op. cit.* in *Rev. de Archivos, Bib. y Museos*, XV, 350.

112 *Ibid.*

113 Cevallos to Fernan-Nuñez, Dec. 8 and 23, 1814, AGS., Est. Leg. 8289 (2675 moderno).

114 ASP. FR., III, 713; see also, F. A. Updyke, *The Diplomacy of the War of 1812* (Baltimore, 1915), p. 274.

Louisiana, England would be justified in retaining the province in view of the dispute as to its legal ownership. He reported that the idea seemed to interest the Duke, who agreed to consult the cabinet,[115] but the matter went no further, doubtless because the news of Jackson's victory made these schemes slightly ridiculous. The ineptitude of Spain and the preoccupation of Europe with its own affairs thus checked Spanish hopes of winning its controversy with the United States by European diplomacy.

115 Cevallos to Fernan-Nuñez, April 21, 1815, AGS., Est. Leg. 8289 (2675 moderno).

CHAPTER II

THE UNITED STATES AND THE SPANISH AMERICAN REVOLUTION, TO 1815

BEFORE 1810 the contact of the United States with Spanish America was limited chiefly to the border regions: Florida, Texas, and the greater Antilles. The provinces which were to take the lead in the independence movement were but little known. Educated men, it is true, had a literary acquaintance with the Spanish colonies derived from a series of books beginning with the compilations of Hakluyt and Purchas, continuing with the seventeenth century " New Survey of the West Indies " by Thomas Gage, and increasing in volume in the eighteenth century to close with Robertson's pioneer " History of America " and the works of travel of the German scientist, von Humboldt. Meritorious as these works were, most of them were dominated by anti-Spanish feeling and did little to combat the legend of Spanish cruelty and greed as something that surpassed those qualities as they appear throughout the human race.[1]

As the era of revolution approached there are signs of an increasing interest in Spanish America among American citi-

1 Richard Hakluyt, *The Principal Navigations, Voyages, Traffiques & Discoveries of the English Nation, etc.* (London and Toronto, 1927), for a classic example of hispanophobia which runs through the whole see the account of the battle of the *Revenge*, V, pp. 1-14. For the influence of Gage's book see: Thomas Gage, *A New Survey of the West Indies* (New York, 1929), Introduction by A. P. Newton, pp. ix-xi; Lesley B. Simpson, *The Encomienda in New Spain, Forced Native Labor in the Spanish Colonies, 1492-1550* (Berkeley, 1929), Introduction, pp. 1-18, gives an able survey of the treatment of Spanish colonization by foreign writers and the influence of the ' Black Legend ' on public opinion. See also, L. Hanke, " Dos Palabras on Antonio de Ulloa and the Noticias Secretas," HAHR., XVI (1936), pp. 498-501, 509, which gives illustrations of anti-Spanish sentiment as shown by books and speeches in the United States.

zens,[2] but the lack of authoritative information about that region was still remarkable.[3] The commercial contacts of enterprising Americans with South America had been gradually increasing, since the American Revolution upset the traditional channels of Colonial trade, and they had received a great impulse during the wars in Europe, especially since 1797, when the command of the sea by Great Britain forced Spain to suspend its already weakened system of close trade monopoly.[4] Between 1797 and 1810 a more or less systematic trade had sprung up between American ports such as Baltimore and Salem and the South American cities of Montevideo, Buenos Aires, and Callao.[5] It was of trifling volume, however, com-

2 Literary interest is shown by the publication of Clavigero's, *History of Mexico*, translated by C. Cullen, Phila., 1804. Another edition of the same work appeared at Richmond, Va., 1806. A new edition of Robertson's *History* was published at Philadelphia in 1812, see, *Philadelphia Aurora*, Jan. 7, 1812.

3 In 1810 the *Baltimore Commercial Advertiser's* editor stated that he had found it impossible by referring to ten or twelve modern geographies to find anything about Caracas except the name and situation, *Gaceta de Buenos Aires* (reprint, Buenos Aires, 1910-1914), I, 369. The dearth of information during the ensuing decade is suggested by the following: C. A. Rodney to Monroe, Oct. 31, 1817, MP. LC. speaks of a current pamphlet as the only source available; *Niles' Weekly Register*, Oct. 30, 1819 makes a similar statement about another work; Manuel Tórres, *Exposition of the Commerce of Spanish America* (Philadelphia, 1816) speaks of the unacquaintance of foreigners with the geography of South America, p. 15; *Analectic Magazine*, vol. xi (1818) laments the lack of information. "The Diary of José Bernardo Gutiérrez de Lara," ed. by E. West, in AHR., vol. xxxiv, states that Americans have "never seen another man from the realm of Mexico as I am."

4 Whitaker, *Mississippi Question*, pp. 82-86; L. E. Fisher, *The Background of the Revolution for Mexican Independence* (Boston, 1934), pp. 99-120; R. Nichols, "Trade Relations and the Establishment of U. S. Consulates in Spanish America," HAHR., XIII (1933).

5 C. L. Chandler, "United States Commerce with Latin America at the Promulgation of the Monroe Doctrine," in the *Quarterly Journal of Economics*, XXXVIII, 467. C. L. Chandler, *Inter-American Acquaintances* (Sewanee, Tenn., 1917, second ed.), pp. 27, 31 and 36. See also, Rutter, *The South American Trade of Baltimore* (Baltimore, 1897), in Johns Hopkins University Studies, vol. xv, no. 9.

pared to the trade with the Spanish West Indies, and was cultivated more as an adjunct to the Far Eastern and Northwest
Coast trades.[6] Limited, as such contacts are, to small groups
of sailors and merchants in a few cities, they did not greatly
increase mutual acquaintance. The hope of further developing
profitable trade must have been a factor in the increasing interest observable in the United States.

Almost all political leaders in the United States since the
American Revolution showed interest in the political future
of Spanish America. American sentiment for the independence
of the Spanish colonies, though in many instances sincere, was
almost always coupled with American expansionist feeling.
Jefferson, as early as 1786 expressed the amazing fear that
Spain could not hold Spanish America " till our population can
be sufficiently advanced to gain it piece by piece." [7] During the
period of Citizen Genêt's intrigues anti-Spanish feeling was
strong in the West, and a plan was set on foot against Louisiana
and Mexico under the leadership of George Rogers Clark.
The French backers of the scheme spoke of liberating these
provinces, but Clark talked of " striking Spain a vital blow "
and of the ease of " conquering " all Spanish America.[8]

The interest of Alexander Hamilton, Rufus King and other
Federalists in the revolutionary schemes of Francisco de
Miranda is well known.[9] A joint Anglo-American attack on
the Spanish colonies was only averted in 1798 by the caution
and shrewdness of President John Adams.[10] In this instance,

6 For a good exposition of these conditions see Jeremy Robinson to
J. Q. Adams, Aug. 2, 1821, DS., Special Agents, vol. v.

7 *Writings of Thomas Jefferson* (Monticello, ed.), V, 260. Jefferson to
A. Stewart, Jan. 25, 1786.

8 Clark to the French Minister, Feb. 5, 1793, *Annual Report of the
American Historical Association*, 1896, I, 967 ff. See John Rydjord, *Foreign
Interest in the Independence of New Spain* (Durham, N. C., 1935), p. 118
and 110-127, an able account of this intrigue.

9 William Spence Robertson, *Life of Miranda* (Chapel Hill, N. C., 1929)
is the most authoritative account, see, I, 161-184.

10 *The Works of John Adams*, ed. by Charles Francis Adams (Boston,
1850-56), VIII, 600. Adams to Pickering, Oct. 3, 1798.

too, American ambitions and revolutionary principles went hand in hand. King wished to prevent France from dividing the Spanish colonies " into small Republics " under her influence,[11] and Hamilton, whose interest was largely one of personal and national ambition wrote that the United States " ought certainly to look to the possession of the Floridas and Louisiana," and " to squint at South America." [12]

It was in connection with the Burr Conspiracy that the " liberation " of Spanish America next came to the fore in the United States. Just what Burr himself planned may never be ascertained, but there is no doubt that most of his supporters thought of his project as one against Mexico.[13] New Orleans and the West were full of enthusiasm for an expedition against Spanish territory.[14] Here again there is a confusion as to motives. Burr spoke of " revolutionizing and taking possession of Mexico ",[15] but as a contemporary observer put it, " the enemy is easily concealed under the mask of a deliverer ".[16]

11 *Life and Correspondence of Rufus King*, C. R. King, ed. (New York, 1894-1900), II, 300-301.

12 *The Works of Alexander Hamilton*, H. C. Lodge, ed. (New York, 1885-1886), VII, 97, Hamilton to McHenry, June 27, 1799.

13 *Correspondence of Andrew Jackson*, ed. by J. S. Bassett, I, 164 footnote, 167-168.

14 For data on the Mexican Association at New Orleans, a group of several hundred men dedicated to the furtherance of Mexican independence and including many prominent figures, see, Rydjord, *Foreign Interest in the Independence of New Spain*, p. 210; see also, McCaleb, *The Aaron Burr Conspiracy* (New York, 1903), p. 29 f. The same work quotes the *Orleans Gazette*, May 5, 1807, showing the extent of revolutionary enthusiasm, p. 307. See also, *Writings of Thomas Jefferson* (Monticello ed.), XI, 185 f., Jefferson to J. Bowdoin, April 2, 1807. I. J. Cox, " Hispanic American Phases of the Burr Conspiracy," in HAHR., XII (1932), 146 ff., 155.

15 M. L. Davis, *The Memoirs of Aaron Burr* (New York, 1858), II, 376. The author asserts that Burr was deeply interested in Mexican freedom. *ibid.*, 376-382. See also, I. J. Cox, " The Louisiana Texas Frontier during the Burr Conspiracy " in MVHR., X (1923), 280 f.

16 *The American Register or General Repository of History, Politics and Science*, II, 87 as quoted in Rydjord, *op. cit.*, p. 217.

While the Burr affair was in progress Miranda came to the United States to organize an expedition to his native Venezuela. Though Burr claimed to have much interest in Spanish American independence, he would not cooperate with Miranda and spoke contemptuously of him.[17] The veteran revolutionary, however, found the atmosphere at New York favorable to his plans, and set forth from that port with a number of volunteers on what was to be a wholly unsuccessful attempt at revolution by filibuster.[18] There had been sympathy for Miranda's schemes in the cities of the Atlantic seaboard,[19] but he seems to have kept his plans rather quiet. His own men did not know in just what sort of enterprise they were engaged, and after the failure of the expedition there was a revulsion against the South American.[20] In the West, Claiborne[21] and Wilkinson[22] continued to champion the cause of Mexican liberation, and in the East even so conservative a Federalist as Charles Carroll of Carrollton talked of freeing the Spanish colonies in alliance with England, but the intrigues and agitation of the two decades preceding 1810 had been indecisive. Popular feeling on Spanish American independence was confused and fluctuated as the conflict between the United States and Spain varied in intensity.

The news of revolt in Venezuela and in Buenos Aires arrived in the United States at a time when the wars in Europe and the resulting problems for the United States largely monopolized attention. This led to much confusion, for South American occurrences were regarded as mere subordinate aspects of

17 H. Adams, *History of the U. S.*, III, 189; for more definite data *see* Rydjord, *op. cit.*, p. 213.

18 W. S. Robertson, *Life of Miranda*, I, 293-327.

19 *Ibid.*, p. 302, quoting various favorable press notices.

20 John W. Sherman, *A General Account of Miranda's Expedition Including the Trial and Execution of Ten of his Officers* (New York, 1810), p. 1.

21 *The Letter Books of W. C. C. Claiborne*, V, 22-24, 352.

22 *Richmond Enquirer*, Jan. 11, 1812, mentioning an event taking place in 1808; see also, McCaleb, *The Aaron Burr Conspiracy*, p. 367.

European schemes. It was sometimes assumed that the Caracas uprising was a Napoleonic plot, and a Federalist newspaper called on the administration to recognize the "patriot" government of Spain and its representative, Onís in order to foil the projects of Bonaparte for revolutionizing the Spanish colonies.[23] A few months later the same paper assumed that the Venezuela revolution was a mere extension of the national resistance to French domination in Spain and stressed the fact that there had been no declaration of independence.[24] The attitude of American parties toward France and England colored all the news. In commenting on the West Florida revolt the Federalists voiced fear of French influence, the Republicans, of British attack.[25]

The fluctuations of the Philadelphia *Aurora* were as noticeable as those of its opponents. At first it assumed that Napoleon directed the South American revolt, rejoiced that under French influence the colonists would not become allies of Great Britain, and hinted that Ferdinand VII might be set up in a South American kingdom subservient to France. In November, when it became apparent that such a result was unlikely and that the rebel colonists seemed to be on good terms with Great Britain the *Aurora* despondently declared:

It is probable that all the Spanish colonies will be free, under the guarantee of Great Britain and whether the British flag shall fly in their ports or not, the merchants of that nation will have all the benefit of the commerce of that fertile and extensive country.[26]

The administration was no less at sea. President Madison, in October, 1810, seemed to think that the independence of Spanish America was a *fait accompli,* and that it only remained

23 *New York Spectator*, June 6, 1810.

24 *Ibid.*, June 27, 1810.

25 *Ibid.*, September 8, 1810; *Philadelphia Aurora*, Sept. 10, 1810.

26 *Philadelphia Aurora*, Nov. 5, 1810.

to be seen whether it would be under French or British auspices.[27]

With the passage of time it was realized that the South American revolts were not directed by European governments, but opinion in the United States, though it became more consistent, still followed party lines. The Federalists, who had earlier taken up the cause of the Spanish patriots in Europe, belittled the outbreaks in South America and deplored their " excesses ".[28] The Republicans, governed partly by their sympathy for revolutionary principles, and partly by hostility to the Federalists either took up the cause of the rebels or remained indifferent.[29]

In 1811, despite the war clouds that hung over the country, interest in the Spanish American cause increased. News from that region became more plentiful, and proclamations and articles from the revolutionary gazettes were copied in the American press.[30] Public interest was strengthened by news of the abolition of the Inquisition and by the Declaration of Rights of Venezuela.[31] The partizan coloring of the news was still

27 *The Writings of James Madison*, G. Hunt, ed. (New York and London, 1900-1910), VIII, 116. Madison to Armstrong, October 29, 1810.

28 *Baltimore Federal Gazette*, June 6, July 18, 19, 1810; *New York Spectator*, Oct. 24, 1810.

29 *Niles' Weekly Register*, Baltimore, II, 71 ; *National Intelligencer*, Washington, Dec. 12, 1811; *Philadelphia Aurora*, Sept. 3, 1811. *Cf.* W. S. Robertson, " The Beginnings of Spanish-American Diplomacy" in *Essays in American History Dedicated to F. J. Turner*, p. 253. The partizan tendency of comment is borne out by the toasts given at Fourth of July banquets in 1810. The *Aurora* reported four at gatherings of Republicans. The *New York Spectator* none at those of Federalists, though at one a toast was drunk to the Spanish patriots in Europe.

30 *New York Spectator*, Aug. 29, 1811; *Niles Weekly Register*, Sept. 14, 1811 ; *Richmond Enquirer*, Feb. 8, 1812; *Louisiana Courier*, Mar. 30, 1812.

31 *Richmond Enquirer*, Jan. 30, 1812; *Niles Weekly Register*, Feb. 1, 1812; *New York Spectator*, Aug. 29, 1811. The friendly reception given to an American agent in Chile also brought gratified comment, see, *National Intelligencer*, June 25, 1812. The " Diary of Gutiérrez," AHR., XXXIV, 283 also testifies to the general enthusiasm.

evident, though there was a more generally favorable attitude. Niles, for example, deplored the failure of Caracas to declare for complete freedom of the press,[32] while a Federalist organ complimented Venezuela for so regulating the suffrage as to make it appear, " that the South Americans are not running quite so wild as might have been expected.   In going from the extreme of tyranny they do not run to the extreme of licentiousness ".[33]

The administration adopted an attitude which reflected the favorable interest that the insurgents inspired in the country, though the official stand was more cautious. At the first news of the rebellions, agents were sent to Venezuela and to Buenos Aires. One was also appointed for Vera Cruz, but conditions prevented his arrival. Their instructions emphasized the importance of developing trade relations with these countries; [34] stated the friendly interest of the United States; and also declared that the United States must remain neutral in the conflict between mother country and colonists. These agents, Joel Poinsett, Robert Lowry and William Shaler were expected to furnish the administration with information of the progress of events in the regions to which they were accredited.[35]

It is evident from the orders sent to American ministers in Europe that the friendly interest of Madison's administration

32 *Niles' Weekly Register*, Sept. 14, 1811.

33 *New York Spectator*, Aug. 29, 1811.

34 On the emphasis placed by the administration on the commercial importance of the Spanish American revolution, see, *Diplomatic Correspondence of the United States Concerning the Independence of the Latin-American Nations* (New York, 1925, 3 v.), ed. by W. R. Manning, I, 4, R. Smith to Armstrong, May 1, 1809; *cf.* the *Philadelphia Aurora*, Aug. 25, 1810 for speculation as to the consequences of a breakdown of Spanish colonial monopoly. See also, references below, note 35.

35 Manning, *op. cit.*, I, 6, Smith to Poinsett, June 28, 1810; I, 11, Monroe to Poinsett, April 30, 1811; Smith to Poinsett, August 27, 1810, DS., Despatches to Consuls, II. For the appointment of Shaler, see, DS., Special Agents, II. Shaler made a visit to Havana but could not go to Vera Cruz. For his subsequent activities, see p. 55, *infra*.

was sincere. Joel Barlow at Paris was instructed to urge the recognition of the new governments by the powers, though he was not in any way to compromise American neutrality.[36] The President's message to Congress of November, 1811, made the attitude adopted a matter of public record. In his somewhat pompous language Madison declared that, " an enlarged philanthropy and an enlightened forecast concur in imposing on the national councils an obligation to take a deep interest in their [the rebels'] destinies." [37] Following the President's lead a committee of the House of Representatives reported a resolution expressing sympathy for the rebels and the intention of recognizing them if they should become independent, but no further action was taken.[38] In 1812 Congress still further proved its good will by voting a sum of money for the relief of the sufferers in the disastrous Caracas earthquake in 1811.[39]

It was not long after the despatch of the American agents to Spanish American ports that representatives of the insurgent governments began to appear in the United States, the advance guard of a long series of agents who were to cause the American government much embarrassment. The first to arrive were those from Caracas. The Venezuelan patriots had not hesitated to seek foreign aid and had sent Juan Vicente Bolívar, a brother of the future " Liberator ", and Telésforo de Orea to the United States to secure munitions and to establish friendly relations.[40] They landed at Baltimore on June 4, 1810 [41] and

36 Manning, *Dipl. Corresp.*, I, 12, Monroe to J. Q. Adams, Nov. 23, 1811; *idem* to Barlow, Nov. 27, 1811.

37 Richardson, *Messages*, I, 494. Madison to Congress, Nov. 5, 1811.

38 *Annals of Congress*, XXIII, 12th Cong., 1st Sess., p. 427; *see also, Niles' Weekly Register*, Dec. 10, 1811.

39 Chandler, *Inter-American Acquaintances*, p. 72. The move was first suggested by Alex. Scott, later consul in Venezuela, DS., Special Agents, IV, Scott to Monroe, April 21, 1812; *Annals of Congress*, XXIV, 12th Cong., 1st Sess., 228, 1378.

40 Francisco José Urrutia, *Los Estados Unidos de América y las repúblicas hispano-americanas de 1810 á 1830* (Madrid, 1918), p. 37, Credentials of

were reported to have been well received there by the public, though their efforts to secure government aid were fruitless.[42]

Onís anxiously observed the activities of these agents, especially since he suspected the administration of secret collusion with them. He was overjoyed when he found it possible to establish relations with Bolívar whose revolutionary ardor had cooled. He proved willing to return to his Spanish allegiance, which, after all, Caracas had not yet formally denied.[43] According to Onís, Bolívar was willing to return to Caracas to work for the Spanish cause. His death shortly afterward put an end to the matter, not before some suspicion of his dealings with Spain had reached his government.[44]

At first, the fact that Venezuela had made no declaration of independence was a barrier to official contact, but in 1811, when Orea again approached the State Department to communicate the Venezuelan declaration and his new credentials from the independent Confederation of Venezuela, his request for formal recognition was still evaded by Monroe though in a conciliatory manner.[45] Shortly afterward the disintegration of

Bolívar and Orea dated April 25, 1810. A mission was also sent to London at this time.

41 *Baltimore Commercial Advertiser*, June 4, 1810, as quoted in the *Gaceta de Buenos Aires*, I (1810).

42 J. F. Blanco and R. Azpurúa, eds., *Documentos para la historia de la vida pública del Libertador de Colombia, Perú, y Bolivia* (Caracas, 1875-1877). Cited hereafter as Blanco & Azpurúa, *Documentos*, II, 412-3.

43 Onís to Bardaxí, July 15, 1810, AHN., Est. Leg. 5636; *idem* to *idem*, April 27, 1811, AHN., Est. Leg. 5637.

44 Onís to Bardaxí, Mar. 20, 1812, AHN., Est. Leg. 5638. *Cf.* W. S. Robertson, "Beginnings of Spanish American Diplomacy" in *Turner Essays in American History*, p. 249; also E. Taylor Parks, *Colombia and the United States, 1765-1934* (Durham, N. C., 1935), p. 86, quoting Gil Fortoul, *Historia constitucional de Venezuela*, I, 128.

45 *Writings of James Monroe*, ed. by S. M. Hamilton (New York, 1898-1903, 7 v.), V, 364, Monroe to J. Barlow, Nov. 27, 1811; Manning, *op. cit.*, I, 15, Monroe to Orea, Dec. 19, 1811; *ibid.*, II, 1154, Orea to Monroe, Nov. 6, 1811; C. A. Villanueva, *Napoleon y la independencia de América* (Paris, 1911), p. 282, states that Orea was also in contact with Serurier, the French

the first Venezuelan republic put an end to Orea's hopes. He is stated to have remained in the United States until 1821,[46] but his last official move was an appeal for the relaxation of the embargo of 1812 to facilitate the relief of the earthquake sufferers.[47]

Orea was associated with other revolutionary deputies. A Mexican agent made his acquaintance [48] and commissioners from Buenos Aires entrusted to him their request for assistance from the United States government.[49] He also introduced these men to Stephen Girard, who had acted as banker for the Venezuelans.[50]

The acquisition of supplies, the principal aim of the Venezuelan mission, was more successful. The deputies had imported a cargo of hides, coffee, and indigo, and from the proceeds of this shipment they were able to buy muskets. Four hundred and twenty-five were obtained in New York and shipped in April, 1811, and larger quantities followed.[51]

The commissioners from Buenos Aires who arrived in October, 1811,[52] were amiably, though not officially, received by the government, and they too were successful in buying arms, though they were not able to purchase the 20,000 muskets

minister in Washington, that the latter suggested Franco-American co-operation in favor of the rebels to Madison and that the idea was favorably received by the President (quoting Serurier to Bassano, Nov. 28, 1811).

46 Raimundo Rivas, *Relaciones internacionales entre Colombia y los Estados Unidos, 1810-1850* (Bogota, 1915), p. 9.

47 F. J. Urrutia, *op. cit.*, p. 44, Orea to Monroe, April 28, 1812.

48 " Diary of José Bernardo Gutiérrez de Lara," ed. by E. West, in AHR., XXXIV, 72.

49 Orea to Monroe, June 18, 1811, enclosing a communication from Buenos Aires, DS., Notes from Colombia, vol. i, part 1.

50 J. B. McMaster, *Life and Times of Stephen Girard* (Philadelphia, 1918), pp. 168-171.

51 D. Antokoletz, *Histoire de la diplomatie argentine* (Paris and Buenos Aires, 1914), p. 204; McMaster, *op. cit.*, p. 167.

52 Aguirre and Saavedra to Monroe, Oct. 25, 1811 (using pseudonyms, López and Cabrera), DS., Argentine Republic, Notes, vol. i.

and 1,000,000 flints that they had first hoped for.[53] They were not able to secure any formal answer to their communications to the American Secretary of State.[54]

After the patriot movement in Venezuela collapsed, various centers in New Granada still held out for independence, and a deputy from Cartagena in that country appeared at Washington in December, 1812, asking for recognition as a "public envoy".[55] This man, Manuel Palacio Fajardo, was no more successful than Orea had been, though he was privately received by Madison, who is reported to have preserved a glacial reserve on that occasion.[56]

The only other envoys who arrived in the United States before the outbreak of the War of 1812 were two men who claimed to represent the Mexican revolutionists. To these neighbors of the United States more attention was shown. José Álvarez de Toledo, a native of Cuba, had been a deputy to the Spanish Cortes. Dissatisfied with the colonial policy of the 'Liberals', he left the Peninsula with the intention of taking

53 McMaster, *op. cit.*, p. 170 f.; Antokoletz, *op. cit.*, p. 204 f.

54 Saavedra and Aguirre to Monroe, Jan. 20 and Feb. 5, 1812, DS., Argentine Republic, Notes, vol. i. The agents returned to Buenos Aires soon after this. According to McMaster, *op. cit.*, p. 163 ff. they failed to buy more arms because their credit was insufficient. Antokoletz, *op. cit.*, pp. 201-4, quoting the Argentine archives, claims that it was due to instructions from home not to assume debts. He also asserts that Monroe consented to sell surplus government stores to these men, and that it was not done for the reason given above. He cites a letter of Monroe dated Jan. 9, 1811.

55 Manning, *op. cit.*, II, 1164-5, Palacio Fajardo to Monroe, Dec. 26, 1812. It may be mentioned that even before Palacio appeared on the scene, two agents from New Granada, Omaña and La Lastra, had arrived on an arms-purchasing mission. They secured munitions but effected no contact with the State Department beyond the delivery of a letter from the Junta of Bogota. See Manning, *op. cit.*, Alamán, *Historia de México*, III, 46-8, appendix; F. J. Urrutia, *op. cit.*, pp. 46, 51-52, 56.

56 *Memorias del General O'Leary*, ed. by S. B. O'Leary (Caracas, 1879-88); cited hereafter as O'Leary, *Memorias*; IX, 403 f.; Villanueva, *op. cit.*, p. 288.

part in the independence movement. In November, 1811 [57] he communicated his presence in Philadelphia to Monroe who referred him to Alexander Dallas, secretary of the treasury, who had various interviews with the newcomer.[58] Monroe was interested in the proposed independent Cuban government and encouraged Toledo's plan to go to the West Indies. This proved impossible, however, and the Creole revolutionary turned his interest toward Mexico.[59]

Toledo at this time met José Bernardo Gutiérrez de Lara who was to make himself notorious later as a filibuster in Texas. Gutiérrez,[60] at a time when the rebel cause had fallen very low in Mexico, arrived at Natchitoches on the Louisiana-Texas frontier, and after directing a letter to Monroe from that place, set out overland for Philadelphia and Washington.[61] His published diary records interviews with many officials and men of influence in the Southwest, among them Governor Claiborne of Louisiana,[62] who wished him all success. The Mexican had an interview with Madison, who, he reported, received him with courtesy, but they could not converse for neither understood the other's language.[63] He found Monroe even more friendly; if war between the United States and Great Britain should come, the Secretary said, the United States

[57] Álvarez de Toledo to Monroe, Nov. 16, 1811, and note by Monroe on verso, DS., Mexico, Filibustering Expedition against the government of Spain, 1811-1816.

[58] Álvarez de Toledo to Monroe, Jan. 4, 1812, *loc. cit.* For the earlier history of Álvarez de Toledo see: I. Fabela, *Precursores de la diplomacia Mejicana* (Mexico City, 1926), p. 33 ff. (Archivo Histórico Diplomático Mexicano, No. 20).

[59] I. J. Cox, "Monroe and the Early Mexican Revolutionary Agents," *Annual Report*, AHA., 1911, I, 203 f.

[60] Fabela, *op. cit.*, p. 33 ff.

[61] Manning, *Dipl. Corresp.*, III, 1593; Cox, *op. cit.*, p. 201.

[62] "Diary of Gutiérrez," in AHR., XXXIV, 290. Others who encouraged him were General Overton and Governor Blount of Tennessee. *Ibid.*, pp. 65-66.

[63] *Idem*, p. 73.

would send fifty thousand men to aid Mexico.[64] In the meantime Gutiérrez was entertained and his return to Mexico facilitated, in the hope that he might assist in the formation of a regular government with which the United States could enter into relations.[65] The continued interest of the administration is shown by the contact it maintained with Gutiérrez and Toledo through William Shaler, the agent appointed to Vera Cruz, who had taken up residence in Natchitoches as a convenient post for observing Mexican developments.[66]

During the period of hostilities between the United States and Great Britain, the administration, involved in more critical tasks, paid little attention to the Spanish American revolutions. The decline of the patriot cause everywhere except in Buenos Aires and the difficulty of communicating with South America discouraged interest. The activity of agents of the rebels also slackened. During 1813 and 1814 only one man, M. García de Sena, an unofficial agent from Venezuela made contact with the Department of State.[67] The Texas area was an exception to the general trend, for Louisianians and the authorities at Washington as well, continued to observe developments there.

In the Spanish colonies—except in the areas bordering on the United States and a few seaports—the difficulty of communication, the illiteracy of the rural masses, the policy of both Church

64 "Diary of Gutiérrez," AHR., XXXIV, 73; cf. L. Alamán, Historia de México (Mexico, 1850), III, appendix, pp. 45-6.

65 Gutiérrez to Graham, Jan. 12, 1812; W. C. C. Claiborne to W. Shaler, April 7, 1812, DS., Filibustering Expeditions against the Government of Spain, 1811-1816. DS., Special Agents, vol. ii, William Shaler, contains Gutiérrez' receipt for $312 from Shaler.

66 See letters from William Shaler to Monroe, 1812-13, DS., Special Agents, II, passim. A study of these contacts has been made by Kathryn Garrett "The First Newspaper of Texas: Gaceta de Texas," Southwestern Historical Quarterly, XL (1937), 200 ff., using the above mentioned sources and many others. The paper covers a broader field than the title suggests.

67 DS., Notes from Colombia, vol. i, part 1, M. García de Sena to Monroe, Mar. 28, 1814, June 10, 1814.

and State prevented foreign influence from penetrating very deeply. Among the educated creoles in the cities, however, since the reign of the reforming monarch Charles III, ideas from abroad had begun to exert influence. The censorship exercised by the Inquisition relaxed its rigor, the restrictions on foreign trade were lightened, which made it possible for new ideas to come in together with merchandise.[68]

The attempt to weigh the relative importance of French, British and American influence prior to the outbreak of the wars of independence is rash, for many imponderables enter into account. It may be noted that British ideas worked principally for free trade; French influence to implant the political and social theories of the Revolution; while the United States furnished the only example of an actual working experiment in statecraft based on the new principle of popular sovereignty. For this reason American influence was most noticeable after the colonists were faced with specific problems of governmental organization.[69] The propaganda of certain forerunners of Hispanic American emancipation, however, shows the influence of American precedents,[70] and the names of Franklin and Washington came to be well known in liberal creole circles.[71] It must be remembered, however, that direct contacts were slight. Only a few like Miranda and Bolívar had actually visited the United States before 1810. When a Caracas

68 Bernard Moses, *The Intellectual Background of the Revolution in Spanish America, 1810-1824* (New York, 1926), chap. ii, pp. 28 ff.; J. T. Medina, *Historia del tribunal del santo oficio de la inquisición en Chile* (Santiago, Chile, 1900), II, 527, 529, 531, 542; M. L. Amunátegui, *Camilo Enriquez* (Santiago, 1911), I, 41-2, 55.

69 W. S. Robertson, *Hispanic American Relations with the United States* (New York, 1923), chap. iii.

70 J. P. Viscardo y Guzmán, "Lettre aux Espagnoles Américains" in appendix, C. A. Villanueva, *Napoleon y la independencia de América*, p. 318: Robertson, *Life of Miranda*, I, 104, 229; Sherman, *Account of Miranda's Expedition*, p. 36.

71 B. Mitre, *Historia de Belgrano y de la independencia argentina* (Buenos Aires, 1887, 3 v.), II, 30, 152.

journalist had occasion to make statements of fact about the United States in 1810 he used French sources, Dauberteuil, La Rochefoucauld-Liancourt, Mably.[72] In Mexico, however, the fact that French propaganda usually penetrated via the United States [73] led to greater knowledge of the northern republic than prevailed in other parts of Spanish America.

A point sometimes overlooked is that foreign influence often came into the colonies through the mother country, where under the Bourbons, and especially since the French Revolution, liberalism was working, as the careers of Jovellanos and other enlightened Spaniards illustrate. Many future leaders of the struggle for independence owed their ideas as much to Spanish liberalism as to direct foreign influence.[74]

After the outbreak of revolution the evidence of United States influence multiplied as contacts increased and colonial restrictions were thrown off, but generalization becomes more difficult. Buenos Aires, Chile, Venezuela, New Granada, and Mexico must be considered separately, for American influence varied greatly in these regions.[75]

72 Robertson, *Life of Miranda*, I, 34-58; Mancini, *Bolivar y la emancipación de la colonias españoles* ... (Paris, 1923), p. 158; Blanco & Azpurúa, *Documentos*, III, 96-98.

73 L. E. Fisher, *op. cit.*, 356-365; Rydjord, *op. cit.*, 128-136.

74 José de San Martín, Juan Martín de Pueyrredón, José Miguel Carrera, and many other leaders served in the Spanish army before or during the war against Napoleon.

75 Categorical assertions about the state of public opinion in Spanish America during the revolution are impossible owing to the lack of a free press (the Gazettes were almost entirely government controlled). The observations of foreigners were highly colored by prejudice. More definite statements can be made as to governmental attitudes, but care must be used to avoid taking official communications at their face value. The insurgent governments were struggling, bankrupt organizations and sought to flatter all from whom they might get aid. C. L. Chandler's otherwise valuable book, *Inter-American Acquaintances* is marred by an uncritical use of official utterances.

In Buenos Aires, though the chief foreign influence from 1810 to 1815 was British,[76] that of the United States was appreciable. The leaders of the first years of the revolution were acquainted with North American precedents. Belgrano, one of the military heroes of the Argentine revolution, was an admirer of Washington and translated the " Farewell Address." It was published with Belgrano's preface and conclusions as a sort of political gospel in 1813.[77] Mitre, Belgrano's biographer, however, maintains that his hero was at this time a believer in constitutional monarchy rather than republicanism.[78]

Mariano Moreno, perhaps the ablest, and one of the most conspicuous leaders of the year 1810 in Buenos Aires, had read Jefferson's " Notes on Virginia ".[79] He, too, admired Washington.[80] Yet the tone of the Buenos Aires gazette was still conservative in many ways under Moreno's editorship, publishing articles condemning the excesses of the French Revolution and showing distrust of North American political precedents.[81] Perhaps partly because of the efforts of American agents,[82] the political influence of the United States increased. In 1813 the representative assembly which met at Buenos Aires showed the effect of this propaganda.[83] The familiarity of some leaders with the American Declaration of Independence is

76 Manning, *Dipl. Corresp.*, II, 688-9, Sumter to Monroe, July 23, 1814, also, *ibid.*, II, 683.

77 *Ibid.*, I, 533, Worthington to Adams, Mar. 7, 1819.

78 Mitre, *Historia de Belgrano*, II, 152-3.

79 *Gaceta de Buenos Aires*, I, 695, Nov. 28, 1810.

80 W. S. Robertson, *Rise of the Spanish American Republics as Told in the Lives of their Liberators* (New York, and London, 1918), p. 157.

81 *Gaceta de Buenos Aires*, July 3, 1810.

82 Manning, *Dipl. Corresp.*, I, 325, W. G. Miller to Monroe, April 30, 1812. Poinsett while in B. A. translated the Constitution of the U. S. into Spanish. A copy reached the president of the *Junta* in 1812.

83 W. G. Miller to Monroe, July 26, 1813, DS., Consular Letters, Buenos Aires, vol. i, part 1.

proved by the language of one official proclamation which contained a leading sentence translated literally from the preamble of that famous document.[84] Patriotic songs of the era mention Washington,[85] and by 1813 translations of articles from the American press became frequent.[86] Even Dr. Francia, the gloomy dictator of Paraguay, had a picture of Franklin,[87] but his subsequent career suggests that the influence of the Philadelphian was not very deep.

Another figure of the revolution in the viceroyalty of La Plata who appears to have been influenced by ideas of federal government derived from the United States was José Gervasio Artigas, the leader of the *gauchos* in the region that is now Uruguay. A document issued in his name in 1813 seems to bear out the point. Artigas was a man of action and no scholar, though a shrewd thinker, and it is probable that the ideas were suggested by one of his secretaries, one Monterosa.[88]

The *Junta* at Buenos Aires was eager for American aid.[89] Poinsett, the American agent, had created a favorable impression,[90] and Diego de Saavedra and Juan Pedro Aguirre, the agents who returned from the United States in 1811, brought a good account of the friendliness they had encountered there,[91] but Poinsett left the city for Chile in 1811, and Buenos Aires was so dependent on British trade that the government, though

84 *Gaceta de Buenos Aires*, I, 291.

85 *Idem*, Oct. 25, 1810.

86 Chandler, *Inter-American Acquaintances*, p. 58 f.

87 Mitre, *Historia de Belgrano*, II, 30.

88 Hugo Barbagelata, *Artigas y la revolución americana* (Paris, n. d.), pp. 59, 62, suggests Artigas' own authorship (see appendix for the document in question). For a contrary view see: *Strictures on "A Voyage to South America, etc."* ... (Baltimore, 1820), p. 23.

89 Cornelio de Saavedra to the President of the U. S., June 26, 1811, DS. Argentine Republic, Notes, vol. i.

90 W. G. Miller to Monroe, Dec. 30, 1811, DS., Consular Letters, Bueno Aires, vol. i, part 1.

91 Manning, *Dipl. Corresp.*, I, 320, Miller to Monroe, July 16, 1812.

not anglophile, became subservient to Great Britain. During the War of 1812 no attempt was made to enforce the neutrality of the port and the British took American ships in territorial waters.[92] This weakens the force of letters written by the *Junta* to Madison in 1813 in which an alliance with the United States was suggested.[93] Throughout the period the chief motive behind the friendly communications of the Buenos Aires government to the United States was the pressing need of arms and munitions which could not be obtained in sufficient quantity from Europe. To Buenos Aires, threatened by Spain and Portugal, this was a cause of great alarm.[94]

In Chile a very different state of affairs existed in the early years of the revolution. American influence became strong, largely through the exertions of two men: Camilo Enriquez and Joel Poinsett. Enriquez, a liberal friar, poet, and journalist, who edited the first Chilean revolutionary periodical *La Aurora de Chile,* was an enthusiast for things North American.[95] A man of rebellious spirit, he had for years taken an interest in the literature of revolt and had suffered imprisonment by the Inquisition in consequence.[96] He took an active part in propaganda after the establishment of the revolutionary *Junta* in Santiago, and in the *Aurora* devoted much space to translations

92 Poinsett to J. Q. Adams, Nov. 4, 1818, DS., South American Commission; Poinsett to Sec. of State, June 14, 1814, DS., Special Agents, vol. iii. But note W. G. Miller in a letter to Monroe, Mar. 25, 1812, DS., Consular Letters, Buenos Aires, vol. i, part 1, says that though the executive is Anglophile the people are disillusioned about British aid.

93 N. Rodriguez Peña, *et al.* to Pres. of the U. S. A., July 21, 1813, DS., Argentine Republic, Notes, vol. i; also, J. Manuel de Luca to Vice-consul of the U. S. (Miller), Feb. 10, 1813, DS., Consular Letters, Buenos Aires, vol. i, part 1.

94 All communications from the Buenos Aires government emphasize this point, see especially p. 52, *supra* and Ignacio Álvarez to T. L. Halsey, May 10, 1815, DS., Consular Letters, Buenos Aires, vol. i, part 1.

95 M. L. Amunátegui, *Camilo Enriquez* (Santiago, 1911), pp. 60 ff.

96 Medina, *Historia ... de la inquisición en Chile,* II, 539.

of the speeches of Washington, Jefferson and Madison.[97] His own articles breathe the most visionary and pure romanticism.[98] The United States, according to Enriquez was the " sun of America " and the " beacon which we should follow ".[99] On the Fourth of July, 1811, he made a speech in honor of the " Bostoneses ". He became a fast friend of Poinsett [100] and may be called one of the earliest of Pan-Americanists in the broadest sense of the term. His political verse, more important from a didactic than from a literary point of view, was influential in building up the morale of the patriots in Chile.[101]

Poinsett was no laggard, and he encouraged the favorable sentiment he encountered. In a speech in 1811 he assured Chile of the friendship of the United States, his command of Spanish giving him a greater opportunity to influence his hosts than most American agents who succeeded him in South America.[102] On the American patriotic anniversary a year later Poinsett gave an elaborate banquet at which the decoration consisted of American and Chilean flags intertwined.[103]

97 *La Aurora de Chile, reprint* (Santiago, 1903), Nov. 12, 1812; Dec. 10, 1812.

98 *Ibid.*, Sept. 3, 1812.   99 Amunátegui, *op. cit.*, p. 26.

100 A. Palomeque, *Oríjenes de la diplomacia arjentina* (Buenos Aires, 1905), I, 174-175.

101 Palomeque, *op. cit.*, I, 176, attributes the following verse to Enriquez. It is a stanza of a longer poem.

> " Al Sud Fuerte le extiende sus Brazos
> La Patria Ilustre de Washington.
> El Nuevo Mundo todo se reune
> En Eterna Confederación."

102 On the influence of Poinsett on the Chilean revolution see in addition to references in the text, *infra* the following:

J. F. Rippy, *Joel R. Poinsett, Versatile American* (Durham, N. C., 1935), pp. 35-60, a biography, based on all material available in the United States. W. C. Collier y G. Feliú Cruz, *La primera misión de los Estados Unidos en Chile* (Santiago, 1927) is more detailed on this part of Poinsett's career and is based on Ms. sources in Chile. D. Barros Arana, " El primér consul extrangero en Chile, Mr. Joel Roberto Poinsett" in *Obras completas* (Santiago), vol. xi, pp. 41-58.

103 *Aurora de Chile*, July 9, 1812.

Poinsett's engaging personality and his enthusiasm for the cause of South American independence, to say nothing of his prestige as the only foreign agent in Chile, led to a close friendship with José Miguel Carrera, then the dominant figure in Chilean politics.[104] The American consul identified himself so closely with the Carrera faction that when it fell from power and the rival faction of the Larrains, headed by Bernardo O'Higgins, gained control, Americans were regarded with suspicion.[105]

Poinsett urged Carrera to buy supplies from American merchants and offered to act as intermediary for such purchases.[106] It may also have been through his influence that the Chilean government bought two American merchant vessels and converted them into privateers.[107] The arrival of the American frigate *Essex* at Valparaiso in 1813 helped to strengthen the existing cordiality as it challenged the command of the southern Pacific waters by Spanish cruisers operating from Callao and encouraged Chileans to hope for a prompt formal recognition of their independence by the United States.[108]

Some writers have accused Poinsett of exerting anti-clerical influence, and of being responsible for the omission of the word " Roman " from the official title of the Chilean church in the proposed constitution of 1812.[109] Carrera's anti-clericalism, however, may well have been derived from Europe where he had served in the Spanish army, but true or untrue, the accusation made the clergy anti-American.

104 Manning, *Dipl. Corresp.*, II, 896, Poinsett to Monroe, Feb. 20, 1813. *Cf.* also, secondary works noted above.

105 Manning, *Dipl. Corresp.*, II, 932, Worthington to J. Q. Adams, July 4, 1818.

106 Collier y Feliú Cruz, *La primera misión,* . . . , p. 57.

107 *Ibid.*, p. 135; S. Johnson, *Diario de un tipógrafo yanqui en Chile y Perú durante la guerra de la independencia* (Madrid, 1919), p. 123 ff.

108 David Porter, *Journal of a Cruise to the Pacific Ocean* (Philadelphia, 1815), I, 102.

109 Collier y Feliú Cruz, *op. cit.*, p. 20; Amunátegui, *Camilo Enriquez,* I, 97.

The adventurous disposition of the consul led him to quite undiplomatic extremes. He took part in a campaign against the royalists in southern Chile, and though he did not formally enlist in the patriot army, served as Carrera's aide and enjoyed the General's confidence.[110] The friendliness of the Carreras toward the United States is illustrated by the offer of Luís Carrera to serve on the *Essex* when a battle with a British vessel was impending in 1814.[111] That incident took place after Carrera had suffered military reverses and had lost his controlling position. The government in power when the *Essex* was finally destroyed forced Poinsett to leave the country.[112] The British naval officer on the Pacific station had gained great influence through his position as mediator between the royalists and the disheartened patriots, and Poinsett believed that he owed his expulsion to this officer.[113]

In Venezuela and New Granada from 1810 to 1812 the influence of the United States was greater than in any other part of Spanish America. Translations of American books and documents on political subjects were published [114] and the experience of the older republic was much deferred to.[115] The proclamation of the *Junta* of the province of Socorro in New Granada to the *Audiencia* at Bogotá in July, 1810 declared that its constituents enjoyed:

. . . that character of virtue which history points out to us as a political phenomenon of which there was no example before the revolution of North America, and which seemed to be reserved exclusively for the happy inhabitants of Philadelphia.[116]

110 Collier y Feliú Cruz, *op. cit.*, pp. 126-151; Amunátegui y McKenna, *La dictadura de O'Higgins* (Madrid, 1917), p. 74.

111 Porter, *Journal of a Cruise . . .*, I, 109.

112 Manning, *Dipl. Corresp.*, I, 335, Poinsett to Monroe, June 14, 1814.

113 *Ibid.*

114 Robertson, *Hispanic American Relations with the U. S.*, pp. 71, 75-6 (translations of the Constitution of the U. S., and of Paine's "Common sense").

115 *Archivo Santander*, ed. by E. Restrepo (Bogotá, 1913), I, 29.

116 Blanco & Aspurúa, *Documentos*, II, 519-21.

In New Granada local jealousies sharpened a dispute on the advantages of federalism *versus* centralism until a desultory civil war broke out. The interior provinces under the leadership of General Nariño adopted a centralized government and waged war against a confederation headed by Cartagena on the Caribbean coast.[117] This led to the isolation of Cundinamarca, the interior state, though one effort at communication with the United States was made in 1811.[118] Cartagena, on the other hand came to have close commercial relations with Baltimore, New Orleans, and Philadelphia until the Anglo-American war temporarily checked them.[119]

In Venezuela, after a constitutional debate of great bitterness, a federal government was established similar in some ways to that of the United States. The Venezuelan Declaration of Rights, however, was more closely modeled on French than on North American precedents.[120] In other instances American influence is evident. When the Congress of Venezuela was faced with the problems of organization and procedure the examples furnished by the American Continental Congress were cited,[121] and here also the phrases of the Declaration of

117 *The Emancipation of South America*, being a Condensed Translation by William Pilling of the History of San Martín by General Don Bartolomé Mitre (London, 1893), pp. 312-24.

118 Urrutia, *Páginas de historia diplomática*, p. 46 f. gives data regarding a mission to the United States from the *Junta* of Bogotá in 1811. The envoys, La Lastra and Omaña apparently delivered a letter to Monroe which is on file in the DS., but no other data exist there. Onís, however, reported the departure of these men for Cartagena in August 1811 with a cargo of arms, and declared that the U. S. government had refused to consider them independent because they still officially recognized the sovereignty of Ferdinand VII. Onís to Bardaxí, Aug. 13, 1811, AHN., Est. Leg. 5637, *cf.* Fabela, *Precursores,* p. 35.

119 *Richmond Enquirer*, Jan. 18, 1812 mentions a shipment of 1500 stand of arms, Onís to Cevallos, April 16, 1815, AHN., Est. Leg. 5640, reports another shipment.

120 Blanco & Aspurúa, *Documentos*, III, 122 ff.

121 *Idem*, III, 144.

Independence of 1776 found a place in the rebel proclamations.[122]

The United States was indirectly responsible for Venezuela's early declaration of independence. In the discussion which preceded that action in 1811 it was argued that it would induce the United States to recognize the new government. This belief was not unreasonable; for Robert Lowry, the American agent at La Guayra and Caracas, openly urged formal independence, and the reports of Orea from the United States also insisted on the necessity of an immediate declaration.[123]

Lowry was energetic in guarding the interests of his country and in trying to extend its influence. Though his commission was not sufficiently formal to satisfy the sense of dignity of the Caracas government, he was officially received and allowed to act as consul. The authorities sought his help in securing supplies and treated him in a manner highly flattering to his self-esteem. His reports insisted on the friendliness of the Venezuelan government, but he expressed fear that the commercial influence of Great Britain might have unfavorable consequences, and he was particularly alarmed by certain import duties which discriminated in favor of British goods.[124]

The *Sociedad Patriótica,* founded to carry on propaganda in Venezuela against a return to the old régime, favored an imitation of the example of the " United States of the North ",[125] and a speech made before the society on July 4, 1811 was a panegyric on the revolution of 1776.[126] The attitude of some leaders was not so adulatory. Miranda, the pioneer revolution-

122 *Gaceta de Buenos Aires,* I, 375, Sept. 10, 1810, quoting a Venezuelan proclamation.

123 Blanco & Aspurúa, *Documentos,* III, 126 ff.

124 Manning, *Dipl. Corresp.,* II, 1148-63, *passim.* See especially, Lowry to R. Smith, Nov. 30, 1810; to Monroe, Aug. 21, 1811; Feb. 2, 1812. Regarding British rivalry, Lowry to R. Smith, Sept. 6, 1810, DS, Consular Letters, La Guayra, vol. i.

125 Blanco & Aspurúa, *Documentos.* III, 138.

126 *Ibid.,* III, 141.

ary, who had come to Venezuela soon after the *coup d'état* of 1810, though not hostile to the United States, relied more on England and certainly did not favor the wholesale adoption of North American political forms.[127] Simón Bolívar was also an opponent of federal government and hence of a close imitation of the United States,[128] but he had not as yet reached his eventual commanding position in the country.

A heated debate on religious toleration in the columns of the Caracas gazette tended to cool enthusiasm for the United States. An article by William Burke printed in the gazette favored toleration and cited the example of the Philadelphia constitution.[129] In refuting his argument the partizans of intolerance made a general attack on the people of the United States which must have affected public opinion, considering the great influence of the clergy who took part in it. The United States was declared to be a government without God or religious law. The masses in that country were a " vast lodge of freemasons ", in which, with " a monstrosity unparalleled in history ", men occupied themselves in material traffic alone.[130]

The arrival of the American subsidy after the earthquake came too late to have much political effect.[131] The weakness of the patriot government and the energy of a royalist commander, Monteverde, completed the downfall of the first Venezuelan republic before the year 1812 was over.[132] The

127 Robertson, *Life of Miranda*, I, 57, 104.

128 *Cartas del Libertador*, Vicente Lecuna, ed. (Caracas, 1929-30), Proclamations of Nov. 27, 1812 and Dec., 15, 1812, I, 31-46.

129 Blanco & Aspurúa, *Documentos*, III, 49-51.

130 *Ibid.*, III, 97.

131 Alexander Scott, who was sent to deliver relief supplies testified to the gratitude of the people, but failed to get on with either Miranda's government or with Monteverde. He left disillusioned after a few months. Scott to Monroe, Nov. 7, 1812, DS., Special Agents, vol. iv.

132 F. Loraine Petrie, *Simón Bolívar 'El Libertador,' a Life of the Chief Leader in the Revolt against Spain in Venezuela, New Granada and Peru* (London, 1910), p. 59 ff.

new Venezuela, which was to arise from the ruins of the first experiment, was inspired, under the leadership of Bolivar, by ideas that differed widely from those of 1810-12.

In Mexico, the character of the revolutionary movement— which derived its energy largely from the support of the oppressed Indians and had a marked religious cast—helps to explain its relative isolation from foreign contacts. Unlike the movements in South America the Mexican revolt failed in the capital and had its strength in the mountains, where the patriots after a few initial successes were forced to lead a hunted existence. American influence was exercised almost entirely on the exiles who flocked to New Orleans and to the debatable land of Texas between United States and Spanish territory.

The early Mexican rebels did, however, make several fruitless attempts to establish contact with the United States government. The priest, Hidalgo, commissioned Pascasio Ortíz as agent to the United States in 1810,[133] but the envoy was captured and never left Mexico.[134] After the execution of Hidalgo, General Allende sent the *Licenciado* Ignacio Aldama as his " ambassador " to seek arms in New Orleans, but he, too, was captured and executed in Texas while on his way to his destination.[135] The need of the rebels was so desperate that at one time Morelos, who succeeded to the leadership of the cause, contemplated ceding Texas to the United States in return for assistance.[136] His efforts were continued in 1813 by General Ignacio Rayón, who sent Francisco Antonio Peredo to negotiate a treaty of alliance. Peredo made two trips to New Orleans but made no efforts to carry on any diplomatic action.[137]

133 Lucas Alamán, *Historia de Méjico . . . hasta la época presente* (Mexico City, 1850), II, 85, see also text of commission, *ibid.*, II, appendix.

134 Fabela, *Los precursores*, pp. 29-31.

135 Alamán, *op. cit.*, II, 96, 170-172; H. H. Bancroft, *History of Mexico*, IV, 271 quoting Hernández y Dávalos, *Colección de documentos . . . ,* I, 231-232.

136 Alamán, *op. cit.*, III, 341.

137 *Ibid.*, III, 506; Fabela, *op. cit.*, p. 60.

When rumors of American help reached the Mexican rebels on one occasion there were laudatory comments in their gazette,[138] but when they were disappointed, articles of a very different nature, containing bitter reproaches against the cold-blooded and ambitious aims of the United States also appeared.[139]

To sum up the somewhat complex and disparate tendencies mentioned in this chapter, the United States after initial confusion, began to show increasing interest in the Spanish American revolts. Though the government adopted a carefully neutral policy, it was a benevolent one. American influence is discernible in the constitutional experiments of the rebel governments, especially in northern South America. The insurgents all sought American aid, though unsuccessfully, but trade in munitions did spring up between 1810 and 1812 and often supplied vital wants of the revolutionaries. The War of 1812 cut communications between the United States and the rest of America and brought a decline, not only in commercial, but also in political contacts. At the same time the rebel cause lost ground everywhere except in Buenos Aires. British commerce was instrumental in checking American prestige, and turning the people of South America toward Europe.

138 Alamán, *op. cit.*, IV, appendix; *cf.* Fabela, *op. cit.*, pp. 73-75; *Mexico á traves de los siglos*, ed. by Riva Palacio (Mexico and Barcelona, no date given), III, 400, 432, quoting Hernández y Dávalos, *Documentos*, V, 570.

139 *Correo del Sur.*, April 22, 1813 (Mexican rebel gazette) as quoted in full in Alamán, *op. cit.*, III, 482.

140 See note 119 *supra*.

CHAPTER III

NEGOTIATIONS: THE UNITED STATES AND SPAIN, 1815 TO MAY, 1818

BEFORE Spain exhausted its attempts to secure an indirect settlement of its complaints against the United States through the influence of European powers, steps were taken toward a renewal of diplomatic relations between the two countries. In 1814, not long after the return of Ferdinand VII to Spain, President Madison appointed George W. Erving, a diplomat with experience in various minor diplomatic posts in Europe including service as chargé in Madrid, to be minister to Spain.[1] In September, Erving wrote to the Duke of San Carlos from Paris announcing his appointment and asking for a passport,[2] but he found that his reception was not to be a matter of course. The Spanish government, engaged in the complicated diplomacy of the European peace, was in no hurry to receive an American envoy. Spanish pride also demanded previous recognition of the long-suffering Onís before admitting Erving. This was made clear to Anthony Morris, Madison's informal agent at Madrid.[3] Erving, who received no reply to his note, returned to the United States much nettled and filled with suspicions of Morris, whom he suspected of plotting to supplant him in the Spanish mission.[4]

1 DS., Despatches from Spain, vol. xiii, Erving to the Sec. of State acknowledging appointment, Oct. 12, 1814. For data on Erving see J. L. M. Curry, " Diplomatic Services of George William Erving," in *Proceedings of the Mass. Hist. Soc.*, second series, vol. v (1890), 9 ff.

2 Erving to San Carlos, Sept. 26, 1814, AHN., Est. Leg. 5557, Expediente No. 2.

3 Cevallos to Morris, Nov. 20, 1814; Cevallos to Onís, Jan. 20, 1815, AME., Leg. 237.

4 Sarmiento to Onís, Jan. 20, 1815 which dealt with objections to Erving and favored Morris as minister, became known to Erving through T. Brent, sec. of legation at Madrid, *cf.* Brent to Erving, Feb. 27, 1815; Brent to Monroe, Feb. 29, 1816; Erving to Monroe, private, Aug. 31, 1816, all in DS., Despatches from Spain, vol. xiii.

Madison and Monroe, who now cherished hopes of an accommodation with Spain,[5] were nonplussed by the strong terms of Cevallos' communication,[6] but sure that compliance with the Spanish demands would be taken as a sign of weakness, they decided to maintain their objection to Onís. The latter's notes demanding recognition were countered by personal objections to him based on his alleged hostility to the United States.[7] It was claimed further that Onís' credentials, which had been issued by the *Junta* in 1809 and not formally renewed since the restoration of Ferdinand, were not in order.[8]

As Onís proved difficult, it was decided to communicate directly with Madrid.[9] Onís' notes were not answered, and he was kept in play through informal conferences with Secretary Dallas of the Treasury. Meanwhile, Monroe wrote Cevallos asserting his desire to reestablish diplomatic relations, but protesting against the Spanish insistence on the reception of a minister who was *persona non grata*. He offered, however, to withdraw his objection to Onís, if it were requested as a favor by Spain, in which case he assumed that Erving would also be received.[10] The conciliatory tone of Monroe's communication was partly due to a suspicion that Spain's cause was being supported by Great Britain, a fear that was heightened by current rumors of a cession of Florida to that power. John Quincy Adams, then minister at London, was ordered to find out what truth there might be in this supposition and to use all his influ-

5 Monroe to Giles, Feb. 22, 1815, MP. LC.

6 Madison to Monroe, April 18, 1815, MP. LC.

7 Onís to Cevallos, No. 33, April, 1815. AHN., Est. Leg. 5640. Letters from Onís to the Capt. Gen. of Caracas in 1810 reflecting on the United States had been intercepted and were later published in the U. S.

8 Monroe to Onís, May 5, 1815, AHN., Est. Leg. 5557, Expediente No. 2.

9 Madison to Monroe, no date, MP. LC., the context fixes the date as April-June, 1815.

10 Monroe to Cevallos, July 17, 1815, AHN., Est. Leg. 5557, Expediente No. 2.

ence to prevent British interference.[11] In the mean time, a letter having arrived from Cevallos which proved satisfactory to American punctilio, Onís was at last formally recognized as minister of his Catholic Majesty.[12]

As soon as his official position was settled Onís renewed his protests of previous years, summing them up in a note to Monroe of December 30, 1815. He stated Spanish grievances to be: the occupation of West Florida, the failure of the administration to prevent the organization of filibustering expeditions against Texas by Álvarez de Toledo and others, and lastly, the facilities granted to rebel privateers in American ports.[13] Monroe vigorously rebutted the Spanish contentions and attempted to turn the discussion toward a general settlement of reciprocal claims by means of a new treaty.[14] Though the Spaniard insisted that Spain was eager to reach an accommodation and hinted at a possible exchange of Florida for territory west of the Mississippi, Monroe soon discovered that Onís had no authority to conduct such a negotiation and that he preferred to refer such matters to Madrid.[15]

Six months earlier Monroe had preferred the Madrid channel of communication,[16] but his correspondence with Cevallos had led him to hope that Onís had been given wide powers. Disappointed in that expectation, he was willing to charge Erving with the business. He was eager to obtain a new treaty for which he felt the time was ripe, as the situation in Spain and in Spanish America made resistance to American claims dangerous.[17] Erving was ordered to proceed immediately to

11 Monroe to J. Q. Adams, Dec. 10, 1815; Feb. 2, 1816, DS., Instructions to Ministers, vol. viii.

12 Monroe to Onís, Dec. 8, 1815, enclosed with Onís to Cevallos, No. 121, 1815, AHN., Est. Leg. 5640.

13 Onís to Monroe, Dec. 30, 1815, AHN., Est. Leg. 5641.

14 Monroe to Onís, Jan. 19, 1816, *ibid.*

15 Onís to Cevallos, Feb. 8, 1816, AHN., Est. Leg. 5660.

16 Madison to Monroe, June 26, 1815, MP. LC.

17 Bagot to Castlereagh, May 3, 1816, PRO. FO-5, vol. 114.

Madrid [18] and was soon given powers to negotiate a settlement of claims and boundaries.[19]

It was an exceedingly worried Spanish minister who reported from Philadelphia the results of his first official contacts with the American government. He had himself advised a cession of Florida to England less than a year earlier,[20] but when he saw the consternation caused by the rumor that this had taken place [21] and that it might lead to further occupation of territory by the Americans, he took care to deny the reports categorically.[22] Convinced that the United States contemplated some aggressive move against Spain, he urged on his government the necessity of defensive preparations and of enlisting the aid of the powers.[23]   At the same time he begged for more explicit instructions, for those he had were out of date and quite inadequate to deal with current problems.[24]

The lack of proper *liaison* between Onís and his superiors, that is suggested by his correspondence at this time, was to cause difficulty throughout the next three years. It was due not so much to personal shortcomings of the staff of the Spanish foreign office, though that was a factor, but more definitely to the general disorganization of the Spanish government at the top. The absolutist reaction in Spain was by no means carried out with the systematic efficiency and paternalism that would have pleased a Metternich. It was, rather than a settled policy, a government by caprice, devoid of system and subject to changes dictated by sudden fancies and suspicions of the

18 Sec. of State to Erving, Mar. 11, 1816, DS., Instructions to Ministers, vol. viii.

19 Monroe to Erving, May 30, 1816, *ibid.*

20 Onís to Cevallos, July 15, 1815, AHN., Est. Leg. 5640.

21 Baker to Castlereagh, Mar. 12, 1815, PRO. FO-5, vol. 106, mentions the persistence of this rumor, *cf.* p. 70, *supra.*

22 Onís to Cevallos, Jan. 1, 1816, AHN., Est. Leg. 5641.

23 Onís to Cevallos, May 30, 1816, *ibid.*

24 Onís to Cevallos, Apr. 3, 1816, AHN., Est. Leg. 5660.

monarch.[25] The ordinary machinery of government was sub-ordinated to a sort of "kitchen cabinet" called the *camarilla* composed of a heterogeneous group of men: valets, buffoons, grandees of Spain, priests, and obscure adventurers, united only by their intimacy with the King and their desire to control pat-ronage and all the other sources of wealth at the court.[26] The demoralizing influence of an inner circle of this description can easily be imagined. Ministers, who for the most part were not in the confidence of their master, were only able to handle the routine work of their offices and, if they attempted to do more, ran the risk of sudden dismissal.[27] The Duke of San Carlos, a companion of Ferdinand's youth and a sharer of his exile in France, who became the first foreign minister after the res-toration, was soon retired to honorable exile as ambassador to Great Britain.[28] The turnover of ministers was phenomenal, especially in the treasury which faced staggering deficits.[29]

San Carlos' successor was no newcomer to Spanish politics. Don Pedros Cevallos, a stubborn, narrow-minded and conceited bureaucrat, had begun his career during the previous reign through the favor of Godoy, Charles IV's all-powerful favorite. As foreign minister from 1801 to 1808 he had been a subser-vient henchman of his patron, but in that year he transferred his allegiance to Prince Ferdinand, and gained his esteem by championing his cause when the Bourbons were summoned by

25 Baumgarten, *Geschichte Spaniens...*, II, 51, 133; *The Diary and Cor-respondence of Henry Wellesley, First Lord Cowley, 1790-1846*, ed. by F. A. Wellesley (London, 1930), p. 85; *cf.* Montmorency-Laval to the Duke of Richelieu, June 29, 1818, AAE. C.P. Espagne, vol. 701. These contemporary opinions are supported by the memoirs of Pizarro, Heredia, Mesonero Romanos, Alcalá Galiano and others. See, chaps. vi and vii, *infra.*

26 Rafael Altamira, "Spain, 1815 to 1845" in the *Cambridge Modern History*, vol. x, is the best brief survey; *cf.* Baumgarten, *Geschichte Spaniens...*, II, 61-2, 72-3; *Memoirs of Don Juan Van Halen*, 2nd ed. (London, 1830), I, 114 ff.

27 Baumgarten, *op. cit.*, II, 135-6, for an example; *cf.* pp. 171-73, 201-202, *infra.*

28 Antón del Olmet, *Cuerpo diplomático español...*, II, 34 ff.

29 Baumgarten, *op. cit.*, II, 174-5.

Bonaparte to Bayonne. During the Constitutional period he played a minor role in the diplomatic service, but again rose to prominence with the downfall of the liberals in 1814. Cevallos' previous experience and especially his negotiations with Monroe and Pinckney in 1805, gave him an excuse to pretend that he was an expert in American affairs. He was doubtless aware of details, but with the broader aspects of the situation in America he was even less acquainted than with those of Europe beyond the Pyrenees.[30]

In 1816 the Russian ambassador to Spain, Dimitri Pavlovitch Tatistcheff, had already acquired the ascendancy at Madrid which led one historian to declare he was the virtual dictator of Spanish foreign policy for six years.[31] Ferdinand VII, like most of the minor crowned heads of Europe at that time, greatly admired Tsar Alexander. He had unsuccessfully sought a match with a Russian Grand Duchess[32] and Tatistcheff[33] took advantage of the King's sentiments to build

30 Antón Del Olmet, *Cuerpo diplomático español*, II, 34-44, gives details of Cevallos' career. Cevallos was a native of Santander, born 1759, and died 1838. He entered public service in 1791. Erving disliked him and thought him stupid. Erving to Monroe, Sept. 22, 1816, MP. LC.; *cf. idem* to *idem*, Aug. 31, 1816, DS., Despatches from Spain, vol. xiii. Pizarro who succeeded Cevallos accuses him of laziness and overfondness for office, *Memorias del Exmo. Señor Don José García de León y Pizarro, escritas por si mismo* (Madrid, 1894-1897), II, pp. 1-9.

31 Ramírez de Villaurrutia, " España en el congreso de Viena " in *Rev. de Bibl. Archivos y Museos*, vol. xv, p. 165 ff. makes the statement referred to in the text; *cf.* C. K. Webster, *The Foreign Policy of Castlereagh, 1815-1822* (London, 1925), using index under Tatistcheff. The French ambassador's despatches are also illuminating. In 1817 he wrote that the influence of Tatistcheff was such that "elle se sentirait de force á écrire directement au Roi pour l'engager á prendre un part contraire á l'avis de son cabinet et en être écouté et á porter un coup mortel au ministre so créature." Montmorency-Laval to Richelieu, No. 111, Nov. 18, 1817, AAE., C. P. Espagne, vol. 701; see also, Nos. 110 and 123, *ibid.*

32 Becker, *Relaciones exteriores de España...*, I, 357 ff.

33 Ramírez de Villaurrutia, *Fernan-Nuñez el embajador* (Madrid, 1931), p. 148.

up his own position. He held forth prospects of military and diplomatic aid from Russia,[34] and with this bait managed to play a powerful part in Ferdinand's councils. Aside from personal ambition the Russian was moved by jealousy of Great Britain, and with his colleague at Paris, General Pozzo di Borgo, was working for a Russo-Bourbon understanding to include France, Spain, and Naples which would enhance Russian prestige and enable it to counteract the apparent domination of the Allied councils by Great Britain and Austria.[35]

Pozzo do Borgo and Tatistcheff found Cevallos an obstacle to their plans, and undermined his position,[36] while his opposition to the King's projected Portuguese marriage created other enemies.[37] Unknown to Cevallos, Ferdinand was corresponding with the Tsar.[38] He signed the treaty of the Holy Alliance without the previous knowledge of his own foreign office [39] and entrusted the negotiations of his marriage to individuals not under the control of the ministry.[40]

Cevallos' instructions to Onís during the year 1815 had been pugnacious. They required the minister not only to protest against Jackson's invasion of 1814 and to demand the restoration of those parts of West Florida occupied by the United States since 1810,[41] but also to ask for the return of Louisiana.[42] Onís on his own responsibility avoided the latter requirement, too well aware of the ill effect it would have on American

34 Laval to Richelieu, Nov. 10, 1817, AAE. C. P. Espagne, vol. 701.

35 C. K. Webster, *Foreign Policy of Castlereagh, 1815-22*, pp. 92, 411.

36 Pizarro, *Memorias*, II, 11 ff.; Baumgarten, *op. cit.*, II, 158.

37 Becker, *op. cit.*, I, 485.

38 *Ibid.*, I, 418, Alexander to Ferdinand, Mar. 31, 1816.

39 Ramírez de Villaurrutia, in *Rev. de Archivos, Bibl. y Museos*, vol. xv, p. 165 ff.

40 Becker, *op. cit.*, I, 419.

41 Cevallos to Oníis, June 27, 1815, AME., Cor. Pol. E. U. Leg. 237.

42 Cevallos to Onís, Mar. 11, 1815; *ibid.* for Onís' reasons for not demanding La. *see*, Onís to Cevallos, No. 4, Jan., 1816, AHN., Est. Leg. 5641.

opinion and of the hopelessness of regaining a region in which a new state had already been admitted to the Union. His instructions, however, led him to believe that his government was in a position to back up such large demands, either by force or through foreign influence, and his tone to Monroe was abrupt, as we have seen. Onís' reports soon showed Cevallos how tense the situation was in the United States and when Lord Castlereagh commented disparagingly on the style of Onís' communications [43] he began to realize that Spain must change its tune. He wrote to the Spanish envoy that the use of force against the United States was out of the question, noting pessimistically on the back of one of Onís' reports that it was impossible for a government with a deficit of five hundred million *reales* to think of sending an army to Texas or Florida.[44] Though he realized that he must speak more softly, Cevallos did not moderate his aims and reiterated in 1816 the necessity of maintaining the Spanish claim to Louisiana.[45]

Unwilling to make any concessions to American ambition and uncertain how to oppose it, Cevallos again turned to Great Britain and France.[46] He was not in a position to demand aid, for delay over negotiations for the abolition of the slave trade, had greatly irritated the British cabinet,[47] while the conduct of Spanish domestic affairs had created hostility in British liberal circles and had produced attacks in the London press.[48] Neither

43 Fernan-Nuñez to Cevallos, No. 935, May 17, 1816, AGS., Est. Leg. 8289 (2675 moderno).

44 Cevallos to Onís, Dec. 10, 1815, AHN., Est. Leg. 5640 (draft), see also note on the back of Onís to Cevallos of Jan. 15, 1816 and No. 4 (date?) 1816, AHN., Est. Leg. 5641.

45 *Ibid.*

46 Cevallos to Fernan-Nuñez, April 10, 1816, AGS., Est. Leg. 8289 (2675 moderno) ; Cevallos to Conde de Peraleda, April 10, 1816, AHN., Est. Leg. 5660.

47 Becker, *Relaciones exteriores de España* ..., I, 423-431.

48 Baumgarten, *Geschichte Spaniens* ..., II, 145-6.

were relations with France very cordial.[49] The Richelieu ministry refused to declare the sale of Louisiana to the United States null and void, or even to define the boundaries of the province.[50]

The attempt to interest Britain was more successful. Lord Castlereagh refused to take any formal action on the ground that it would only embitter the dispute, but he made a verbal statement to the Spanish Ambassador that was to have great influence on Spanish policy for years to come. It described an interview with John Quincy Adams, in which he had warned the United States not to attempt an expansionist policy. As reported to Cevallos, Castlereagh's words taken out of their context in the original conversation with Adams have a more menacing ring than they seem to have in Adams' report.[51] According to the Duke of Fernan-Nuñez, Lord Castlereagh told him that he had warned Adams that though Great Britain maintained a scrupulous neutrality in the disputes of the United States and Spain, the future conduct of the British government would depend on that of the United States, and that if the Americans should attempt, taking advantage of Spanish weakness, to advance their frontiers on the bordering provinces of Florida and Texas the British government:

even if Spain should desire, either as an indemnity or sale to cede any territory in those dominions, would not admit it, nor could it consent that the United States should extend its boundaries, as in such case the British cabinet would completely change its policy, and would adopt the course it considered most convenient to its own interests and that of its ally, Spain.[52]

49 Becker, *op. cit.*, I, 351 ff., 431 ff.

50 Peraleda to Cevallos, April 27, 1816, AHN., Est. Leg. 6797.

51 Adams, *Memoirs*, III, 289-92, Jan. 25, 1816.

52 The quotation given is a somewhat free translation of a confused original which is given below: "Aunque la España quisiera ó por indemnización ó venta cederles cualquier territorio en aquellos dominios no lo admitirían. Tampoco consentían en que los E. U. se extendiesen de sus

This statement of policy gave great satisfaction to Cevallos, though he would have preferred a still stronger statement in writing. It was communicated to Onís to give him the encouragement he sadly needed, for he had been ordered to temporize, as the decision whether or not to negotiate a treaty with the United States was to be postponed until Erving arrived in Madrid and his attitude could be sounded.[53]

That diplomat had reached his post early in the summer and as soon as he received authorization to begin negotiations he opened his offensive. In addition to the old claims for spoliations, the suspension of the right of deposit, West Florida, and Texas the American note included a new list based on alleged Spanish breaches of neutrality during the War of 1812. These dealt with aid supposedly furnished to the British and Indians in Florida against the United States, and the destruction of the American frigate *Essex* by the British in Chilean territorial waters.[54] Erving had been authorized to agree to a western boundary of Louisiana at the Sabine River as the last resort, if Spain would cede Florida and include enough public lands to settle the pecuniary claims. He was expected not to surrender so much western territory, if it could be helped, and to settle, if possible, on the terms offered by Monroe in 1805.[55]

Erving was given little chance to make use of his instructions for the negotiation at Madrid was cut short. Cevallos was not enthusiastic at the prospect of dealing with Erving's formidable note, nor did he feel that his opponent's personality augured an easy diplomatic victory for Spain. He therefore decided to

limites, pues en este caso mudaría totalmente de sistema este gabinete y tomaría el curso que creíese conveniente repuesto á los intereses de su aliada la España y á los suyos propios." Fernan-Nuñez to Cevallos, May 17, 1816, AGS., Est. Leg. 8289 (2675 moderno).

53 Cevallos to Onís, June 10, 1816, AME., Cor. Pol. E. U. Leg. 222. *Idem* to *idem* (draft), May 7, 1817, AHN., Est. Leg. 5660.

54 Erving to Cevallos, Aug. 26, 1816, AHN., Est. Leg. 5660.

55 Monroe to Erving, May 30, 1816, DS., Instructions to Ministers, vol. viii, see p. 23, *supra*.

evade the issue by what he believed an ingenious scheme to gain time, but which was to prejudice the Spanish cause when its real import became apparent. A memorandum, unsigned, but written in Cevallos' characteristic cramped, almost illegible handwriting sets forth the scheme in his mind.

The state of our affairs in Mexico, the desire Onís says the United States have to declare war on us, and our general situation seem to indicate that in the negotiation about to begin we should bring to our aid the influence of another foreign power such as Russia, *and prolong the discussion since it is not likely that we shall benefit in the end.* Therefore it would be advisable to seek the mediation and influence suggested, and charge Onís with the business *that he may have a pretext to ask for orders and instructions and so gain time if the matter is not going to our liking.* To minister Erving it might be stated that Onís is being ordered to enter into negotiation and that instructions are being sent to Onís, giving Erving some plausible excuse.[56]

The plan thus outlined was carried out in part, and the plausible excuse was found in a phrase of Monroe's note to Onís of June 10 announcing that Erving had been given authority to conclude a treaty. Monroe had mentioned that the United States would have preferred to treat in Washington, but that to save time the other channel was agreed to.[57] Cevallos pretended to understand this as a request for a re-transfer of the business to the United States and declared to Erving that this suited his plans.[58]

Erving had not yet seen the note from Monroe to Onís, but he protested, expressing surprise that his chief should have wished to return the negotiations to Washington in view of

56 Holograph memorandum by Cevallos, AHN., Est. Leg. 5564, Expediente No. 5. Italics are the author's.

57 Monroe to Onís, June 10, 1816; Onís to Monroe, July 3, 1816, AHN., Est. Leg. 5641.

58 Erving to Cevallos, Sept. 19, 1816 in reply to Cevallos to Erving of Sept. 15 (not found), AHN., Est. Leg. 5660.

his recent instructions to proceed at Madrid. Cevallos pleaded that other pressing business prevented him from giving the American problem his personal attention, and in the end Erving was forced to acquiesce. In vain he talked of the warlike temper of the American people and the danger of the delay that might occur in Washington if Onís should not have ample powers to settle.[59]

Plenary power to conclude a treaty was sent to Onís. He was solemnly ordered to negotiate a treaty, but told that no instructions were being sent him, as he already knew the Spanish position in the pending disputes.[60] These orders disheartened Onís. Without concessions to tempt the Americans he was helpless; he could only argue and temporize. Cevallos' plan was not carried out in full due to a flurry at Madrid which threw the foreign office temporarily into confusion. Six weeks after Erving's attempt to negotiate, the opposition succeeded in ousting Cevallos and in replacing him with José García de Léon y Pizaro.[61]   The Russian faction was at the bottom of the intrigue which led to the minister's downfall. The occasion was furnished by the king's contentment with the Portuguese marriage which Cevallos had used all his influence to prevent.[62]

His successor, Pizarro, had served Spanish diplomacy since 1793, his chief claim to renown having been his mission to Prussia in 1813, at which time he had represented Spain at the Allied headquarters and had met the major personages of European politics. For a brief term he had also served as

59 Erving to Cevallos, Sept. 19, 1816, AHN., Est. Leg. 5660; Erving to Monroe, Sept. 22, 1816, AHN., Est. Leg. 5643 (copy of intercepted letter), cf. ASP. FR., vol. iv, p. 434; Erving to Monroe, Sept. 11, 1816, DS., Despatches, Spain, vol. xiii.

60 Cevallos to Onís, Sept. 10, Sept. 15, 1816, AME., Cor. Pol., E. U., Leg. 222.

61 According to usual Spanish practice his appellation should be García or García de Leön. Actually he was universally called Pizarro. I have followed the contemporary practice.

62 Baumgarten, Geschichte Spaniens..., II, 163.

foreign minister under the Regency and had been distinguished by his anti-British attitude.[63] This recommended him to Tatistcheff, and a personal dispute with Cevallos made Pizarro not unwilling to intrigue against his chief. He was used by Ferdinand and the *camarilla* to draft some of the notes of the monarch's secret negotiations with the Tsar and his subservience in that affair furthered his claims to office.[64]

Though the manner in which he came into office was not far from shady, the ministry of which Pizarro formed a part was in many ways a promising one. Tatistcheff, following the tendency of his master at that time, was a champion of liberalism in Spanish domestic policy. He secured the appointment of Martín de Garáy, an able politician of the constitutional period, as Minister of Finance, and steps were soon being taken, which, if they could have been carried to completion, might have improved the desperate finances of the monarchy.[65] In foreign affairs Pizarro showed much assiduity and increasing independence. He considered himself to have a flair for diplomacy and was never happier than when immersed in the details of notes and counter notes or in the preparation of memoranda. His failing was in timidity rather than in lack of perception of the best interests of the country. In fairness, however, it must be said that the power of the *camarilla* tied the minister's hands in many cases.[66]

63 Pizarro began his career as secretary at the embassy in Vienna in 1793. After 1799 he served as *precis* writer at the ministry of state. In 1812 he was for a short time minister. In 1813 he went on a mission to Sicily and then to Prussia. He was in Paris in 1814 at the conclusion of peace. The above data are taken from his personal dossier, AHN., Est. Leg. 3420.

64 Pizarro, *Memorias*, II, 11 ff. gives circumstances of his appointment to the ministry in 1816.

65 Baumgarten, *Geschichte Spaniens* ..., II, 177-80 ff.

66 Erving had a high opinion of Pizarro, see, DS., Despatches Spain, vol. xiii, Erving to Monroe, Dec. 15, 1816; *cf.* Pizarro, *Memorias, passim.* On Pizarro's talents Francisco Martínez de la Rosa, *Bosquejo histórico de la política de España desde los tiempos de los Reyes Católicos hasta nuestros días* (Madrid, 1857), II, 76.

It was some months before Pizarro awoke to the urgent necessity of deciding what to do about the Washington negotiation. In the interval matters stagnated, much as if Cevallos' plan of deliberate procrastination had been adhered to. Onís, when he received his plenary powers at the beginning of January, 1817, faced one of the most difficult situations that can confront a diplomat: that of negotiating a treaty with an aggressive and hostile government without authority to make any concessions. He might well have recalled the complaints of the Israelites to their Egyptian taskmasters. The failure of the foreign office to inform him of the passages between Cevallos and Erving during the previous summer led Onís to make ludicrous missteps. He actually complained to Monroe of the new shift of negotiations to Washington, believing that it had been an American move.[67]

Monroe, having heard from Erving that Onís had received instructions, submitted the proposals of the United States. These were: the cession of Florida, the execution of the claims convention of 1802, and a western boundary for Louisiana at the Colorado river in Texas. If these terms were accepted other claims against Spain would be dropped.[68] Onís refused to answer these propositions, sparred, temporized, and was at last forced to admit that he did not know whether a cession of territory would be considered by the Spanish court or not. To calm Monroe's manifest irritation he suggested that his instructions must have been intercepted by one of the insurgent privateers or otherwise delayed in transmission. On the territorial question he argued that Florida was worth more than Louisiana, but that if the United States should propose to exchange these provinces he would be glad to forward such an offer to Madrid.[69] Negotiations were again blocked, for Monroe refused

67 Onís to Cevallos, No. 7, Jan. 10, 1817, reporting his conference with Monroe, AHN., Est. Leg. 5660.

68 Onís to Cevallos, No. 9, Jan. 12, 1817, reporting conference with Monroe of preceding day, ibid.

69 Ibid.

to continue discussion of boundaries, Onís rejected a suggestion that a separate treaty might settle the other claims.[70]

Onís did his best to justify the uncompromising attitude he was forced to maintain. Taking the offensive, he complained of the freedom with which rebel privateers operated from ports in the United States. At the same time he did his best by flattering Monroe, who was soon to assume the presidency, to quiet the animosity of the American government. Onís was terribly anxious and wrote his government that it would not be possible to draw out discussion much longer.[71] He feared the effect of the coming publication of his correspondence with Monroe on Congress and the public and on March 3 reported that a crisis had arrived and that hostile action by the United States could hardly be delayed more than six months.[72] He asked repeatedly for more ample instructions; worked out a draft of a treaty he considered feasible and suggested British mediation. April came and went and still he received no word from Madrid except routine communications and the general advice to hang on and to do what he could to prevent a break.[73]

Meanwhile Pizarro had at last taken notice of the state of affairs at Washington. He ordered a report to be prepared on the background of the American dispute and began himself to work on a plan of action.[74] Onís had recommended shifting

70 Monroe to Onís, Jan. 14, 1817, AHN., Est. Leg. 5642.

71 Onís to Pizarro, No. 28, Feb. 22, 1817, AHN., Est. Leg. 5660.

72 Onís to Pizarro, No. 32, Mar. 3, 1817, AHN., Est. Leg. 5642.

73 Draft treaty, AHN., Est. Leg. 5660. One suggestion was the sale of Florida to the United States for four million dollars. See, Pizarro to Onís, Mar. 19, 1817, AHN., Est. Leg. 5660 for an example of the tone adopted by Madrid.

74 Memorandum of the sub-secretary (primer oficial), April 1, 1817. This man was Narciso de Heredia. He was in charge of relations with the United States under Cevallos, Pizarro and his successor and provided a certain continuity despite ministerial change. A man of ability, he later rose to the ministry. The exact influence he had it is difficult to measure. The writer feels that he usually provided the ideas but had little to do at this time with final decisions. Cf. *Escritos del Conde de Ofalia, publicados por*

negotiations to Europe where they would be removed from the influence of the American populace. Pizarro would have liked to handle the business himself,[75] but he realized that another shift would be dangerous as it would be taken by the Americans as a new scheme for delay; he therefore sought another solution.[76]

Pizarro's position at the court was far from strong. For the time being he had the support of Tatistcheff and the *camarilla*,[77] but Ferdinand kept his new foreign minister at a distance, apparently because he could not quite forgive his activities under the constitutional government of Spain.[78] In order to protect himself as far as he could from hidden attack, Pizarro brought all questions of importance before the Council of State, an advisory body which had fallen into disuse during the last few years since the return of the king. Ferdinand almost invariably attended the meetings of this organization and minutes of its deliberations were regularly kept. By keeping important decisions in the open it was possible partially to disarm attack.[79]

Pizarro read a memorandum before the Council on June 10, 1817 summing up the antecedents of the current dispute with the United States. In it he presented a number of alternative proposals ranging from a declaration of war against the United States or a cession of Florida to Great Britain, to a more peaceful solution in which, with the mediation of a European power, Spain would acquiesce in United States possession of Louisiana if the latter would agree to the boundaries as Spain understood them. Another idea was an exchange of Florida for

su nieto el Marqués de Heredia, senador por derecho propio (Bilbao, 1894), pp. 42-44.

75 Erving to the Sec. of State, private, April 6, 1817, DS., Despatches, Spain, vol. xiv.

76 See note by Pizarro on back of Onís to Pizarro, May 1, 1817, AHN., Est. Leg. 5660.

77 Laval to Richelieu, No. 8, Jan. 22, 1818, AAE., G. P. Espagne, vol. 701.

78 *Ibid.*, see also, Wellesley, *Diary* . . . , p. 85.

79 Pizarro, *Memorias* . . . , II, 112.

Louisiana, as Onís had hinted recently in Washington. Pizarro thought that this would not be acceptable to the United States, but that the offer might give Spain time to secure mediation. He even hoped that it might divide opinion in the United States and that schemes of dismemberment of the Union, like those used before Spain lost Louisiana, might again prove useful. The observation showed that Pizarro was not yet well acquainted with the situation in America and that his information was derived chiefly from reading rehashes of old correspondence. A number of alternative territorial exchanges with the United States were also put forward, but the Council came to no decision except to advise that the attitude of the powers should again be sounded.[80]

A period of great activity followed at the Spanish foreign office. Pizarro had already attempted to secure British backing, but he had received no answer.[81] Inquiries were now urgently renewed in such a tone as to suggest that England, no less than Spain itself, was interested in preventing the expansion of the United States, a view no doubt encouraged by Castlereagh's statement to Fernan-Nuñez a year earlier.[82] At the same time similar demands were made to the French government.[83]

Pizarro found it hard to get replies to these demands and decided to carry on conversations with Erving in order to stave off American hostility and gain time for the completion of the steps being taken at London and Paris. He was not very successful, for when he suggested to Erving that without interrupting the Washington negotiations it might be well to carry on parallel discussion at Madrid, the latter was able to score

80 *Ibid.*, III, 225 ff. Pizarro to the King, June 4, 1817. Minute of the Council of State, June 11, 1817, AHN., Est. Leg. 5661.

81 Pizarro to H. Wellesley, April 6, 1817, and Pizarro to Campuzano (chargé d'affaires in London), June 22, 1817, Campuzano to Castlereagh, July 12, 1817, AGS., Est. Leg. 8289 (2675 moderno).

82 See p. 77, *supra.*

83 Fernan-Nuñez to Richelieu, Aug. 12, 1817, AHN., Est. Leg. 6797. Fernan-Nuñez to Pizarro, No. 300, Aug. 16, 1817, AHN., Est. Leg. 5660.

decidedly on his opponent and to show by apt citations from the Spanish notes of the past year that they contained prevarications and contradictions.[84] He declined to be drawn into any negotiation and offered only to accept or reject such terms as Pizarro might wish to offer.[85] The Spaniard, who had acquired a healthy respect for Erving's acuteness,[86] could delay no longer and submitted a project of a treaty for his consideration.

This document did not even approach the minimum demands of the United States. It is important, however, as the first formal offer made by Spain to cede the Floridas. The draft submitted by Pizarro maintained the Spanish point of view on the spoliations question, excluding those which had been left unsettled in 1802; the cession of Florida was to be offset by the surrender of Louisiana to Spain; and the whole made conditional on the consent of Great Britain to the proposed exchanges of territory. The Spanish proposal also included an article obliging the United States to prevent its citizens from aiding the American rebels of Spain in any way whatsoever, thus adding to the long existent issues in dispute a new complication based on two diametrically opposed views of neutral obligations.[87] Erving wasted no time in discussion and rejected these terms without hesitation.[88]

It was now dangerous to wait longer before sending instructions to Onís. On August 27 accordingly they were drafted by Pizarro and his assistant, Heredia, and approved by the Council of State.[89] As approved they did not transcend the

84 Erving to Pizarro, July 19, 1817, AHN., Est. Leg. 5660.

85 *Idem* to *idem*, July 29, 1817, *ibid.*, also Erving to Adams, Aug. 27, 1817, DS., Despatches, Spain, XIV.

86 Pizarro, *Memorias*, II, p. 11.

87 Erving to Adams, Aug. 27, 1817, DS., Despatches, Spain, vol. xiv; Pizarro to Erving, Aug. 17, 1817, AHN., Est. Leg. 6797.

88 Erving to Pizarro, Aug. 19 and 23, 1817, referred to in Pizarro's acknowledgment of Aug. 31, 1817, AHN., Est. Leg. 5660.

89 Memo. of instructions for Onís, Aug. 27, 1817, AHN., Est. Leg. 5660; Pizarro to Onís, Aug. 31, 1817, AHN., Est. Leg. 5660.

terms already rejected by Erving. The minister favored giving Onís more latitude, but feared to give way too rapidly lest he destroy his own position at the Spanish court, for the King and the Council of State were not convinced of the need for sacrifice.[90] The instructions despatched on August 31 ordered Onís to engage first in general discussion, then to offer Pizarro's draft treaty recently submitted to Erving. If that failed, he was to suggest the arbitration of two or more powers, and lastly the mediation of one power, presumably England. One loophole was left for the Spanish negotiator, for in the last resort and as if on his own responsibility *sub spe rati,* he was given permission to make certain other proposals taken from those suggested to the King in Pizarro's memorandum of the previous June, for an arrangement of the Louisiana boundary question. On this point, therefore, Onís had some leeway, but not on any of the other questions in dispute.[91]

Soon after these instructions were despatched replies to Pizarro's requests for diplomatic support were received from the French and British governments. The British answer com-

90 Erving to J. Q. Adams, Aug. 27, 1817, DS., Despatches, Spain, vol. xiv; Pizarro to Onís, Feb. 20, 1818, AHN., Est. Leg. 5643. *Idem* to *idem,* April 6, 1818, AME., Cor. Pol. E. U. Leg. 224.

91 Pizarro, holograph memo. of instructions for Onís. The original instructions could not be found by the writer in the Spanish archives. There is ample evidence, however, that they were sent. The concessions in territory mentioned above were not part of the instructions but were authorized by reference to a copy of Pizarro's memo. attached. They were:

(1) To cede West Florida west of the Perdido, and to fix the western boundary of Louisiana at a line running from the Gulf between the Calcaseu and Mermentas rivers, passing between Los Adaes and Natchitoches, then north to the Osage and thence to the Missouri, unless it could be diverted eastward to the Mississippi.

(2) To cede all of Florida, and to fix the western boundary of Louisiana at a line following the La Fourche mouth of the Mississippi, up that river to the Missouri and along the latter to its source.

(3) To cede both the Floridas, and to fix the western boundary at a line following the Mississippi to the Arkansas River, up that river to its source, and thence northwest indefinitely. AHN., Est. Leg., 5660; *cf.* Pizarro, *Memorias,* III, 225 ff.

municated by Sir Henry Wellesley at Madrid was not very satisfactory to Spain, though no less so than reports from London had warned. Great Britain declined to exert pressure on the United States, but agreed to act as mediator if both parties so requested.[92]

The Duc de Richelieu, the French prime minister, though willing to cooperate with Spain to restrict privateering activities of the rebels from bases in the United States,[93] and to counteract the plots of Bonapartist exiles in America against Spanish possessions, was unwilling to back the Spanish court on the two points on which it particularly desired French aid: the boundaries of Louisiana and the spoliations committed by the French in Spanish waters. Richelieu gave Fernan-Nuñez, now Spanish ambassador in Paris, some verbal encouragement, which the latter reported as a promise to relieve Spain from the American demands regarding these claims,[94] but he refused to commit himself in writing. Richelieu pointed to the position of France, occupied by foreign troops, which made it impossible for him to take the tone that he might otherwise wish to adopt toward foreign countries.[95] The final French reply, only given after much insistence by Pizarro proved disappointing. It evaded the claims question, raising doubts as to the responsibility of France for the seizures, and on the boundaries of Louisiana merely stated vaguely that instructions had been sent to Hyde de Neuville, the French minister in the United States, to assist the Spanish cause. This proved of scant value, for Hyde de Neuville avoided making any statement on the matter because, as he told Onis, if he supported the Spanish contention in West Florida, as was just, he would also have to support the

92 Pizarro to H. Wellesley, Sept. 28, 1817 in which he acknowledges Wellesley's note of Sept. 23, AHN., Est. Leg. 5643; cf. Castlereagh to Bagot, Nov. 19, 1817, PRO. FO-5, vol. 120.

93 Fernan-Nuñez to Pizarro, No. 215, July 24, 1817, AHN., Est. Leg. 5660.

94 Fernan-Nuñez to Pizarro, No. 272, Aug. 9, 1817, ibid.

95 Fernan-Nuñez to Pizarro, Aug. 23 and 26, 1817, ibid.

American claim to the west of Louisiana, for France maintained that Louisiana extended to the Rio Grande.[96]

To study these replies from London and Paris a session of the Council of State was held. Erving had impressed on Pizarro that recognition of the rebel governments or even war might result if the instructions for Onís were not more ample than the terms he had rejected during the preceding summer. In the autumn, therefore, the principal aim of Spain in the negotiation at Washington was to prevent either of these eventualities.[97] To avoid them Onís was to be instructed to make the offer of exchange of Florida for Louisiana without the previous reservations which made British consent a requisite. He might also agree to ratify the 1802 convention, reserving the right of Spain to maintain claims arising since that date. He might also hint at possible commercial privileges in the Spanish colonies after they had been reduced to obedience.[98]

Onís received the instructions authorized in August in the following November and immediately proceeded from Philadelphia, his usual residence, to Washington to renew negotiations, this time with John Quincy Adams, who was to prove a more difficult adversary than the good tempered Monroe.[99] The Spaniard found Adams in a bad humor over what he called the absurd terms offered to Erving a few months earlier. He was no less annoyed that Onís' new proposals were essentially the same,[100] for Erving had led him to expect that Spain would

96 Richelieu to Fernan-Nuñez, Sept. 12, 1817, AHN., Est. Leg. 6797; cf. Richelieu to Hyde de Neuville, Sept. 1, 1818, AAE., C. P. États Unis, vol. 76; see also, Onís to Pizarro, July 12, 1818, AHN., Est. Leg. 5644.

97 Pizarro, Memorandum to the King, Oct. 2, 1817, AHN., Est. Leg. 5661.

98 Pizarro to Onís, Nov. 3, 1817, AME., Cor. Pol. Estados Unidos, Leg. 224.

99 Onís to Pizarro, Nos. 196 and 198, Nov. 17 and 29, 1817, AHN., Est. Leg. 5642.

100 The Memoirs of John Quincy Adams, ed. by C. F. Adams (Philadelphia, 1874-1877) (cited hereafter as Adams, Memoirs), IV, 26.

now make further offers.[101] Onís declared that he was ready
to receive proposals, and in various conversations and notes in
December, 1817, and January, 1818, upheld the Spanish claim
to Texas and West Florida most ably and in great detail. But
he refused to make new proposals and insisted on his protests
against the aggressive conduct of the United States.[102] Adams
wished to avoid discussion of the Spanish complaints and to
make a general transaction in which the individual specific
claims of both parties should be lumped and cancelled.[103]

At this juncture Onís received the supplementary instructions sent from Madrid in October. They afforded him scant
satisfaction, and he advised his superior at once that the terms
he was at liberty to offer would not be acceptable to the United
States. His despatches of early 1818 were full of dire prognos-
tications of an attack on Florida. He offered his resignation if
leave could not be granted him, giving as justification his thirty-
eight years of public service, the bad climate of the United
States and the impossibility of negotiating under the instructions given him.[104] He also complained that the British and
French ministers had not been as positive in support of his
efforts as he had been led to expect.[105]

Having failed to elicit any offer from Onís, Adams summed
up the American demands in a note of January 16, 1818. The
offer was identical to that made a year earlier by Monroe and
was as unsatisfactory to Onís as the Spanish proposals had
been to Adams.[106]

101 Erving to J. Q. Adams, Aug. 27, 1817 and Sept. 10, 1817, DS.,
Despatches, Spain, vol. xiv.

102 This correspondence is printed in ASP. FR., vol. iv; see also, Adams,
Memoirs, IV, 37, and the following despatches from Onís to Pizarro: No.
202, Dec. 10, 1817, Leg. 5660; No. 209, Dec. 18, 1817, Leg. 5642; No. 1,
Jan. 5, 1818; No. 5, Jan. 11, 1818, both in Leg. 5643; No. 2, Jan. 1, 1818,
Leg. 5644, all in AHN., Estado.

103 Adams, *Memoirs*, IV, 35.

104 Onís to Pizarro, No. 2, Jan. 1, 1818, AHN., Est. Leg. 5644.

105 *Idem* to *idem*, No. 209, Dec. 18, 1817, AHN., Est. Leg. 5642.

106 ASP. FR., IV. Adams to Onís, Jan. 16, 1818, for the previous offer
by Monroe, see, p. 82, *supra*.

At the end of January a diversion was caused by the British offer of mediation made in accordance with the previous understanding with Spain. The move was made by Sir Charles Bagot at Washington in a tentative manner and was phrased in terms quite friendly to the United States, but it was decided at a cabinet meeting held for the purpose to decline the offer.[107] Adams, the cabinet member least hostile to this proposal, so worded the refusal as to leave Bagot with a pleasant impression.[108] After this, though Onís made desperate efforts to keep a correspondence going, and offered to ratify the 1802 convention and to accept a western boundary at the westernmost mouth of the Mississippi, the negotiations languished.[109] Adams refused to give way an inch on the territorial question and Onís was forced to admit for a second time that he could negotiate no longer and must again write for instructions.[110]

In view of the impasse it was the view of some observers that the United States would occupy Florida, but that war was not an immediate probability.[111] As a matter of fact no such aggressive decision was reached by the administration, but the failure of Adams and Onís to reach common ground for discussion led to greater insistence on the American claims. Erving was informed that negotiations had lapsed in Washington and that the President would not object to their being shifted to Madrid, but he was told that the previous American offer to accept the line of the Colorado River in Texas should be withdrawn if not accepted shortly.[112]

Pizarro realized in April from the tone of Onís' reports that everything possible must be done to encourage him. Though

107 Adams, *Memoirs*, IV, 51.

108 Bagot to Castlereagh, Feb. 8, 1818, PRO, FO-5, vol. 130.

109 Onís to Adams, Feb. 10, 1818, AHN., Est. Leg. 5643.

110 *Idem* to *idem*, Mar. 23, 1818, AHN., Est. Leg. 6797.

111 Bagot to Castlereagh, Jan. 6, 1818, PRO, FO-5, vol. 130; *idem* to *idem*, May 6, 1818, PRO, FO-5, vol. 132.

112 Adams to Erving April 20, 1818, DS., Instructions to Ministers, vol. viii.

he did not feel that he could authorize any further concessions of importance, he praised Onís' conduct of affairs and urged him to maintain his serenity in the existing difficult situation.[113] Already in the previous autumn Pizarro had come to feel that the negotiations with the United States, if they accomplished nothing else, must prevent the recognition of the Spanish American rebels by the government at Washington. In his memorandum of October 2, 1817, he had considered an amplification of Onís' instructions to be necessary because a halt in the discussions under way would bring with it the unwelcome recognition.[114] Subsequently he dwelt repeatedly on the same point. The way to prevent recognition, according to Pizarro, was to " stop their mouths with the negotiation ".[115] Onís was further ordered to inform Adams that the mediation of the powers in the Spanish American revolution was well advanced. The departure of an American commission for South America caused perturbation at Madrid as it was considered the prelude to more formal action. If that should come Onís was instructed to leave the country, but not to close the legation.[116]

The relative importance of the issues involved in the dispute between Spain and the United States had undergone a considerable change since the resumption of diplomatic relations in 1815. The relations of the United States to the insurgents in America, which had been considered a minor matter by Cevallos in 1816,[117] had grown in importance in the eyes of the Spanish foreign office, chiefly due to alarming reports from Onís. Four articles of a draft treaty prepared by Onís for his superiors dealt with restrictions on privateering.[118] The passage of a Neutrality

113 Pizarro to Onís, April 6, 1818, AME., Cor. Pol. E. U., Leg. 224.
114 Pizarro to the King, October 2, 1817, AHN., Est. Leg. 5661.
115 Pizarro to Onís, Feb. 20, 1818, AHN., Est. Leg. 5643.
116 Pizarro to Onís, Feb. 25, 1818, AME., Cor. Pol. E. U., Leg. 224.
117 Erving to Monroe, Sept. 22, 1816, DS., Despatches, Spain, vol. xiii.
118 Draft, in AHN., Est. Leg. 5660.

Act in 1817 lulled Spanish fears for a while,[119] but as it became
evident that the act was not completely effective Spanish appre-
hension reappeared. Pizarro instructed Onís to keep careful
records of damages suffered by Spain from privateers armed
in the United States,[120] and similar instructions were sent to
all the colonial authorities throughout Spanish America. At the
same time efforts were made to interest France and Great
Britain in the suppression of this privateering. This was
partially successful, at least the French government gave instructions to Hyde de Neuville to cooperate with Onís for this
object.[121] It was through these incidents that Spain came to
realize that its quarrel with the United States was not a local
issue but an aspect of the colonial revolt, a realization which
deepened as the movement for recognition of the rebels gathered momentum in the United States. Erving was not mistaken
in his opinion that the sending of an American mission to
South America would make Pizarro more conciliatory,[122] and
his conviction was strengthened in February, 1818, when he
learned of the failure of attempts at mediation by the powers
in the Spanish American revolution.[123] Pizarro's attitude was
so amicable in conversation that the American minister was
convinced that the end of the negotiations was in sight.

At this time Pizarro considered the objectives in the negotiation to be as follows in the order of their importance; first,
to prevent recognition of the rebels by the United States; to
secure strict observation of neutrality by the United States; to
secure a boundary which should adequately protect New Spain
and New Mexico; and last, to settle the mutual pecuniary claims
of the two governments. The center of gravity of the nego-

119 Erving to the Sec. of State, April 6, 1817, DS., Despatches, Spain,
vol. xiv.

120 Pizarro to Onís, July 3, 1817, AME., Cor. Pol., E. U., Leg. 223.

121 Richelieu to Fernan-Nuñez, Aug. 6, 1817, AHN., Est. Leg. 5660.

122 Erving to J. Q. Adams, Jan. 10, 1818, DS., Despatches, Spain, vol. xv.

123 *Idem* to *idem*, Feb. 10, 1818, *ibid.*

tiation as far as Spain was concerned had thus been displaced. Pizarro hoped in April, 1818, that it might be possible to insert a clause in the eventual treaty binding the United States not to recognize the insurgent governments. This was not too much to ask, he suggested to Onís, in view of the offer made by Charles Pinckney in 1803 to guarantee Spanish possessions beyond the Mississippi in partial recompense for the cession of New Orleans and West Florida.[124]

To secure these ends Onís was authorized to reduce his claims at the western boundary. In April he was told that *in case of extreme danger of war or of recognition of the rebels* he might agree to the line of the Sabine River.[125] In June the whole Spanish claim to Texas was practically abandoned, under similar restrictions, when a boundary at the Colorado was authorized.[126] The restrictions placed on these new concessions, Pizarro made clear, were due to the reluctance of the Council of State to give ground, and it was evident to Onís that his new orders could only be used safely as long as Pizarro held to his precarious position at the head of the ministry.

Though now committed to a policy of some concessions to the United States, Spain continued to press its cause on the French and British governments. It was advanced that Great Britain had guaranteed the American possessions of Spain in the treaty of Utrecht (1713) and in that of Versailles (1783).[127] Lord Castlereagh, though he made a show of friendship for Spain declared that the former treaty was no

124 See chapter i, *supra*. The offer was made by Pinckney in accordance with instructions from Madison, July 26, May 11, 1802; *cf.* Fuller, *The Purchase of Florida*, pp. 104-108. For Pizarro's views stated above see Pizarro to Onís, April 25, 1818, AHN., Est. Leg. 5643.

125 Pizarro to Onís, April 25, 1818, AHN., Est. Leg. 5643.

126 Pizarro to Onís, June 15, 1818, AME., Cor. Pol. E. U., Leg. 224, Leg. 5643 contains parts ciphered in original.

127 San Carlos to Pizarro, No. 80, Mar. 4, 1818, AGS., Est., Leg. 8294 (2676 moderno) ; *idem* to *idem*, Mar. 27, 1818, AGS., Est., Leg. 8288 (2675 moderno).

longer in force and that the United Kingdom would not fight the United States for the sake of Spain. He advised a peaceful settlement of the dispute as soon as possible.[128]

In the hope of bribing France to do what argument alone had failed to induce, Pizarro hinted at a cession of the Spanish half of the island of Santo Domingo.[129] Richelieu showed interest and an interview was arranged between Fernan-Nuñez and the Count de Molé, the French minister of war. The Frenchman seemed to think that a statement favorable to Spain could be made on the Louisiana boundary question, but he shied from any commitment on the spoliation claims. Molé, though interested in Santo Domingo, felt that it would not be an immediate asset on account of the long continued civil war on the island and suggested that Puerto Rico would be more acceptable to France. He offered tentatively for that island the loan of ships, arms, and even some French troops.[130] Pizarro, when this was reported, felt that he could not carry these conversations further for the King and the Council of State would not back him in making such a sacrifice. Accordingly there was no more talk of a territorial cession to France.[131]

French jealousy of British trade expansion in Spanish America led the Richelieu ministry to court the United States, Britain's chief maritime rival. Though much was said about the friendship of Louis XVIII for Spain, French policy was not pro-Spanish, though attempts were made to give Spain that impression.[132] The French project of creating Bourbon prin-

---

128 Castlereagh to San Carlos, April 28, 1818, AHN., Est., Leg. 5643.

129 Pizarro to Fernan-Nuñez, Feb. 11, 1818, AHN., Est., Leg. 5643.

130 Fernan-Nuñez to Pizarro, No. 847, Mar. 16, 1818, AHN., Est., Leg. 5643.

131 Note in Pizarro's hand on back of despatch cited in note 130.

132 Laval read Pizarro extracts from his instructions to give that impression, copy of extract Richelieu to Prince de Laval, Feb. 21, 1818, AHN., 5643. For actual French attitude see Richelieu to Laval, Aug. 24, 1818, AAE., C. P. Espagne, vol. 702; Richelieu to Hyde de Neuville, Sept. 1, 1818, AAE., C. P. États Unis, vol. 76.

cipalities, independent of Spain, in South America as a barrier to republicanism and to British influence also proved an obstacle to close Franco-Spanish cooperation.[133]

The negotiations undertaken with so much confidence by Monroe in 1816 had thus been unconscionably delayed. Spain turned from one pretext to another and only in the spring of 1818 did the changes in Onís' instructions make progress possible. During this period, however, the nature of the controversy changed. The status of the rebellious colonists of Spain which had seemed earlier a separate question now complicated the efforts of diplomats in Madrid and Washington. In 1815 the rebel cause had seemed doomed to an early collapse, but it had taken on new life, and great victories had been won by the patriots in Chile. In Venezuela Bolívar returned with fresh energy to the struggle, and on the sea rebel privateers swept Spanish merchantmen from the Atlantic. Toward this resurgent movement the United States seemed to be leaning. Could Madison, Monroe and Adams maintain a neutral position between the rival contestants in Spanish America?

133 Carlos A. Villanueva, *Bolívar y el General San Martín, la monarquía en América* (Paris, 1913), pp. 79 f. and 139 f.; *Writings of Albert Gallatin,* ed. by Henry Adams (Philadelphia, 1879), II, Gallatin to Adams, Aug. 10, 1818; Laval to Richelieu, Aug. 21, 1818, Oct. 5, 1818, both in AAE., C. P. Espagne, vol. 702.

CHAPTER IV

THE NEUTRALITY QUESTION

IN 1816 a question came to the front which had previously played only a minor part in the disputes between Spain and the United States: the controversy over the rights and duties of the United States as a neutral in the Spanish American Revolution. The United States had early taken an important part in the formulation of doctrine and practice on the subject of neutrality. The course chosen by President Washington during the Anglo-French wars after 1793 had created a body of precedent, though the American view was not then, nor has it ever been, universally accepted. The legislation of 1794 had laid the foundation for American practice on neutrality enforcement.[1] It prohibited Americans from engaging in, or preparing for, hostilities against any power, with which the United States was at peace, from within the territory of the Union.[2] Severe sanctions were provided and the law had, on the whole, been effective.

It was the maritime aspect of the question which assumed the greatest prominence in the period of the Spanish American revolts. During this conflict a new aspect of the problem appeared, for the struggle was not between two previously organized and independent states, but between one such power and rebellious provinces within its territory. Madison's administration decided to apply the existing law to this case, thus virtually recognizing the belligerency of the rebels. This was not done by proclamation, but by executive orders directing

1 C. G. Fenwick, *The Neutrality Laws of the United States* (Washington, 1913), p. 15 ff.; *cf.* also C. S. Hyneman, *The First American Neutrality, a Study of American Understanding of Neutral Obligations during the Years 1792 to 1815* (Urbana, Ills., 1934), pp. 74-98, 155-165.

2 John Bassett Moore, *Digest of International Law* (Washington, 1906), VII, 1010, gives text of these laws.

that the shelter of American ports be extended to all ships whatsoever their flag or nationality.[3]

Spain claimed that the rebel ships should be considered pirates, just as many Americans during the Civil War felt that Confederate cruisers should be treated. The United States not only refused to accept this view, but declared its right to carry on commerce with both belligerents, free from seizure except for contraband of war or in case of attempted forcing of a legally constituted and effective blockade. Spain denied the right of any foreign ships to trade with her empire, including the portions in revolt, except in accordance with prevalent Spanish commercial decrees.[4]

The revolution had given further impetus to the break-down of the Spanish trade monopoly, already greatly weakened during the preceding century. Spain was still able, however, to harass the trade which had sprung up between its oversea dominions and foreign nations. Great Britain, as Spain's ally, was given temporary permission to trade with Spanish America but no such authorization was given American ships. It was not long, therefore, before disputes arose over blockades, seizures of ships, and imprisonment of crews. Before 1815 Spain's naval power in the Caribbean and in the South Pacific was greater than that of the insurgents. Spanish privateers and cruisers captured a number of American merchantmen and whalers accused of smuggling or illegal trade.[5] During the war of 1812 American commerce was swept from the seas, but after the peace similar trouble arose. General Morillo, the Spanish military commander in northern South America, proclaimed the coast of Venezuela and New Granada in blockade,

3 Moore, *Digest of International Law*, I, 170, instructions to collectors of customs, July 3, 1815.

4 Onís to Monroe, Dec. 30, 1815, AHN., Est., Leg. 5641; Monroe to Onís, Jan. 19, 1816, *ibid.*

5 R. Lowry to Monroe, Nov. 1, 1811, DS., Consular Letters, La Guayra, vol. i, also David Porter, *Journal of a Cruise* ..., I, 103-107, *Philadelphia Aurora*, July 23-24, 1812.

and, when he captured the rebel stronghold of Cartagena, confiscated all neutral vessels he found there and imprisoned the crews. This elicited a strong protest from the United States.[6] Madison sent Christopher Hughes as special commissioner to Cartagena on the frigate *Macedonian* to negotiate for the return of the vessels and the release of the seaman.[7] The envoy was successful in the latter, but failed in the former part of his objective. Indeed, had it not happened that British subjects were among those imprisoned it seems doubtful whether the crews would have been released.[8]

A recurrence of earlier conditions on the Pacific coast of South America was one reason for the despatch of Captain Biddle with the U. S. S. *Ontario* to that area in 1817 to protect the extensive whaling fleet in those waters,[9] which was being molested by Spanish privateers operating from Peru. The Viceroy at Lima declared, in reply to Biddle's protests, that some of these vessels had introduced arms to ports held by the rebels and should therefore be treated as belligerents. The American officer was able, however, to induce the Viceroy to relax his practice with regard to neutral shipping.[10]

More important to Spain than these conflicts and more productive of controversy in the United States was the treatment afforded the armed vessels of the insurgents in American ports. The rebels had few ships of war until after the close of the wars in Europe and America, for until that time all the available shipping that was not engrossed by Great Britain and her

6 Erving to Cevallos, Oct. 25, 1816, DS., Despatches, Spain, vol. xiii; Manning, *op. cit.*, I, 26, Monroe to Onís, Mar. 20, 1816.

7 Monroe to C. Hughes, Mar. 25, 1816, DS., Instructions to Ministers, vol. viii; Hughes to Monroe, Mar. 21, 1816, MP. LC.

8 C. Hughes to Monroe, July 6, 1816, DS., Special Agents, vol. iv.

9 J. Robinson to J. Q. Adams, Aug. 12, 1818 and Dec. 6, 1818, DS., Special Agents, vol. v, states that 60 to 70 whalers were in the Pacific and 40 merchantmen engaged in the trade with the Northwest coast and other points of call.

10 Joaquin de Pezuela to Biddle, April 18, 1818, DS., Special Agents, vol. v.

allies was in the service of the United States or blockaded in
its ports. Even during this period, however, there was a small
beginning of naval activity under patriot flags in the Gulf of
Mexico under the auspices of Cartagena and of Mexican
rebels.[11] These activities were at first insignificant. The peace of
1815, however, brought with it a decline in business for American shipowners and unemployment for seamen as the carrying
trade to Europe faded away. This released a number of ships
and men just at the time when there was an opportunity to
take service with the Spanish American rebels who lacked capital and trained seamen, but were eager to attack Spanish commerce by the only means in their power—privateering.[12]

Venezuela began its naval activities after the fall of Cartagena, licensing privateers and organizing a squadron of government vessels under the command of Admiral Brion.[13] The
Buenos Aires privateers also began their activities at this time.
In 1815 a single vessel was fitted out and brought two prizes
to the home port.[14] In the following year the practice gained
greater impetus. Thomas Taylor, an American in rebel service,
came to Baltimore with a supply of letters of marque in blank
which he found it easy to dispose of.[15] At that time there were
many notices in the American papers offering ships for sale

11 Álvarez de Toledo was responsible for the beginning of privateering
under the flag of the Mexican Congress. Morelos at the former's suggestion
furnished a prize code, letters of marque, and some funds to begin the enterprise, I. Fabela, *Precursores de la diplomacia Mejicana*, p. 43.

12 For the decline of American shipping and the carrying trade see
Timothy Pitkin, *A Statistical View of the Commerce of the United States*,
etc. (New York, 1817), p. 296; *cf*. E. R. Johnson and others, *History of the
Domestic and Foreign Commerce of the United States* (Washington, 1915),
II, 33.

13 B. Irvine to J. Q. Adams, July 20, 1818, DS., Special Agents, vol. viii.
Brion had a flagship and ten other vessels which engaged in privateering,
as well as smaller craft.

14 T. S. Currier, *Los corsarios del Rio de la Plata* (Buenos Aires, 1929),
p. 23.

15 British consul at Baltimore to Bagot, July 6, 1816, PRO, FO-5, vol. 115.

and many owners were glad to engage in a business which promised large gains with ships that might otherwise lie idle.[16] Sailors accustomed to a generation of service on men-of-war and privateers were no less willing to adventure their services.

Two of the first rebel privateers equipped in Baltimore were the *Romp* and the *Orb,* swift schooners of about one hundred and seventy tons, low, sharp, and with rakish masts. They carried ten guns and a large pivot gun amidships. Average crews for such vessels numbered about one hundred men.[17] Similar ships had proved remarkably efficient as American privateers in the recent war and had shown their ability to outsail and outmanouver any vessel afloat. To avoid difficulty with the United States authorities, the *Romp* and the *Orb* cleared as American merchantmen with crews of normal size and took on the rest of their complement after leaving port. The two vessels had a successful cruise and it was reported that the share of a foremast hand amounted to about fifteen hundred dollars.[18]

New Orleans was another center for privateering activity. Ships fitted out there were usually operated under the colors of Cartagena, and later of Venezuela or Mexico. A British naval officer on duty in the Caribbean in 1816 stated that there were then no less than fourteen such ships fitting out in New Orleans.[19] A year later Louis Aury established a privateering base at Matagorda, Texas, where at one time as many as thirteen vessels were anchored. This leader abandoned Texas for a Florida base soon after, but privateers under Lafitte, the

16 Currier, *op. cit.,* p. 20.

17 British consul at Baltimore to Bagot, July 6, 1816, PRO, FO-5, vol. 115; Currier, *op. cit.,* p. 22.

18 *Ibid.*

19 Admiral J. E. Douglas to Bagot, Nov. 21, 1816, PRO, FO-5, vol. 121; for further evidence of illegal augmentation of armament in the United States see, *Prize Cases Decided in the United States Supreme Court, 1789-1918* (Oxford, 1923, 3 v.), ed. by J. B. Scott, II, 1096-7, 1168-9, 1200; DS., Consular Letters, Galveston, I, Beverly Chew to W. H. Crawford, Aug. 30, 1817. Chew encloses a list of 11 privateers in New Orleans at this time.

ex-pirate from Barataria, continued to frequent the Texas coast and by the end of 1817 had practically swept Spanish shipping from the Gulf.[20]

The reports of the profits to be gained in these ventures led to many desertions from the American merchant marine. At Buenos Aires vessels were sometimes stranded for lack of men, and it has been estimated that as many as 3500 American seamen were engaged aboard these privateers between 1816 and 1821.[21] As early as March, 1817 a number of specific instances of fat profits were reported. The *Romp*, it was claimed, took prizes to the value of $290,000.[22] In January, 1817 a New Orleans vessel had deposited $105,000 in the Bank of Louisiana after deducting the shares of the captain and crew amounting to nearly $200,000.[23] The cases just mentioned were reported by Spanish consuls to Onís and may perhaps be regarded with suspicion, but a British consul at Norfolk declared at about the same time that a single vessel had taken prizes worth $200,000 and that $50,000 of it had to his knowledge been deposited in a Baltimore bank.[24]

Some of the tricks used by the privateers to avoid molestation by the United States government have been mentioned. In those days it was customary for merchant ships bound on distant voyages to carry some armament, and if false clearance papers were secured as to destination, and if precautions were taken to avoid showing an excessive crew it was fairly easy to

20 H. H. Bancroft, *History of the North Mexican States and Texas*, II, 38, 42, quoting *Gaceta de Mexico*, VIII (1817), 787-789; Lafitte to Graham, Aug. 28, 1818; DS., Consular Letters, Galveston.

21 Currier, *op. cit.*, p. 32. On desertion at Buenos Aires, see also, T. L. Halsey to G. Tagle, July 31, 1815, DS., Consular Letters, Buenos Aires, vol. i, part 1 and Halsey to Monroe, Mar. 14, 1816, *ibid*.

22 Manning, *Dipl. Corresp.*, III, 1923, Onís to Adams, Mar. 26, 1817.

23 *Ibid.*, III, 1910, Onís to Monroe, Jan. 2, 1817; also *idem* to *idem*, Jan. 16, 1817, *ibid.*, III, 1914.

24 P. Savage to St. John Baker, Mar. 19, 1917, PRO, FO-5, vol. 122.

avoid trouble, especially in ports where public opinion was strongly favorable to the Spanish American cause.[25]

These ships usually cruised in the West Indies, but they also frequented the trans-Atlantic routes and even hovered off the coast of Spain.[26] Prize goods if valuable and easily handled, were occasionally shipped to the United States.[27] More often they were shipped to certain West Indian islands where marks were changed and papers falsified to make it possible to send the merchandise to almost any port. St. Thomas and St. Bartholemew were much used for this purpose.[28] The Buenos Aires privateers sent a certain number of their prizes, though a small percentage of the whole, to the home port. Fifty such prizes were conducted there during the period of privateering activity from 1815 to 1821.[29] The ports controlled by the insurgents in the Caribbean and the Gulf of Mexico were more common resorts. Margarita Island, off the coast of Venezuela, Galveston and Boquilla de Piedras in Texas, and for a while Fernandina, on Amelia Island off the Florida coast near the mouth of the St. Mary's, were rendezvous for the privateers.

At first only Spanish commerce suffered, but in 1818 the privateers began to resort to forcible provisioning from neutral vessels and before long the dearth of Spanish shipping and the desperate character of many privateer captains led to attacks on ships of almost any flag. In 1819, complaints of depredations on British and American commerce became common.[30]

25 For an example of this procedure see J. B. Scott, *Prize Cases Decided in the United States Supreme Court*, vol. ii, p. 1285, Case of the *Fanny*.

26 *Niles Weekly Register*, April 5, 1817 reported one in the North Sea; *idem*, Mar. 20, 1819, reports privateers active off the coast of Spain; *cf. Moniteur*, Paris, Jan. 18, 1819; *Documentos del archivo de San Martín* (Buenos Aires, 1910-1911), VIII, 209.

27 Currier, *op. cit.*, p. 30; *cf. Columbian Museum and Savannah Gazette*, Mar. 16, 1818.

28 Adams, *Memoirs*, V, 15; Currier, *op. cit.*, p. 28.

29 Currier, *op. cit.*, p. 23.

30 *Columbian Museum and Savannah Gazette*, Jan. 21, 1819; *idem*, Feb. 8, 1819; *cf. New York Evening Post*, Jan.-Mar., 1819, *passim*.

Other abuses became frequent. Occasionally the crews mutinied and continued their activity without even a show of legality, sometimes abandoning their ships and escaping ashore with their booty.[31] Letters of marque also came to be issued by governments with only a shadowy existence, and by some without seaports.[32] Privateering was at its best a shady business near the line of piracy, but carried on by foreigners in the name of governments as yet unacknowledged by the established nations, it differed from piracy only because of the legal fiction preserved by the letters of marque.

American capital and American seamen carried on much of this business. The Spanish Americans had neither men nor ships to carry it on themselves. Even the regular government ships of Buenos Aires and Chile were largely manned by foreigners.[33] Onís' notes to the State Department often give names of merchants who were concerned in privateering [34] and British reports speak of the American ownership of the Baltimore privateers as a matter of common knowledge.[35] Even officials of the Federal government: the postmaster at Baltimore and the collectors of the ports of Baltimore and Savannah were accused of being financially interested in the business.[36] Halsey, an American consular agent at Buenos Aires made a large fortune in privateering,[37] and some of the first prizes sent to Buenos Aires were consigned to an American ex-agent at that port, W. G. Miller.[38] Many other Americans were publicly

31 For one example see J. Lewis to J. Q. Adams, Port au Prince, Aug. 7, 1818, DS., Special Agents, vol. iv; also J. B. Scott, *op. cit.*, p. 1165, case of the *Bello Coruñes*, p. 1270, case of the *Nereyda*.

32 As in the case of Artigas and of the Mexican Congress after 1815.

33 *Strictures on 'A Voyage to South America, etc.'* (Baltimore, 1820), p. 59.

34 Manning, *Dipl. Corresp.*, III, 1910 (Mr. Dupuy of New Orleans), III, 1971 (Darcy and Didier, Baltimore).

35 British Consul at Baltimore to St. John Baker, July 6, 1816, PRO, FO-5, vol. 115.

36 Adams, *Memoirs*, IV, 186, V, 151; Currier, *op. cit.*, p. 52.

37 *Dictionary of American Biography*, T. L. Halsey.

38 He was not then active as viceconsul. Currier, *op. cit.*, p. 20.

reported to be owners of privateers.[39] The most conclusive evidence is that of the courts, whose records give ample proof of American participation.[40] As for the captains of these vessels their nationality was certainly not Spanish-American, if their names can be taken as a guide.[41]

So dangerous had the high seas become for Spanish merchantmen that the ship owners of Málaga petitioned the crown for the right to make simulated sales to foreigners in order to ship goods more safely to the colonies.[42] The boldness of vessels which cruised for weeks at a time near Cadiz, intercepting incoming and outgoing ships, and of others which took prizes within sight of the Morro at Havana is astounding.[43]

39 *Baltimore Federal Gazette*, Jan. 7, 1819; *New York Evening Post*, Feb. 26, 1817; *Columbian Museum and Savannah Gazette*, Mar. 16, 1818.

40 For examples of American ownership see J. B. Scott, *op. cit.*, II, p. 1154 (*Bello Coruñes*); p. 1285 (*La Republicana*).

41 Captains Fisk, Brown, Huffington, Stafford, Jenkins, Boyle and Davey are mentioned by Correa da Serra, the Portuguese minister in Washington, to Bagot, PRO, FO-5, vol. 121. Onís adds others to the list, Captains Chaytor, Hodgeson, Smith, Taylor, Barnes, Chase, Mason, Moore, Jewett, Onís to Pizarro, April 20, 1818, AHN., Est. Leg. 5644.

42 Imaz to Irujo, April 8, 1819, Archivo de Indias, Papeles de Estado, América en General, Leg. 86, Expediente 12 (LC. Photocopies).

43 *Documentos del archivo de San Martín*, VIII, 209, M. de Irigoyen to San Martín, regarding ships off Cadiz, especially the *Independencia del Sud*. For a capture off Havana, see *Columbian Museum and Savannah Gazette,* May 15, 1818.

The following figures give some idea of the magnitude of the privateering industry:

LIST OF PRIVATEERS ARMED IN THE UNITED STATES

Port	Sources of Information				
	1	2	3	4	5
New Orleans	—	4	7	7	—
Barataria	—	1	1	1	—
Philadelphia	—	2	2	2	—
Charleston	—	2	2	2	—
Baltimore	12	12	12	12	33
New York	—	2	2	4	—
Totals	12	23	26	28	33

1. Partial statement for Baltimore only, 1816. Correa da Serra to Bagot,

The widespread system of privateering discussed in the fore-going pages was the chief occasion for Onís' protests against alleged violations of neutrality, but the same principles were involved in filibustering expeditions against Spanish territory which used the United States as a base. The first of these ex-peditions was organized by Francisco de Miranda against Venezuela and sailed from New York on the *Leander* in 1806. Partly as a result of the protests of the Spanish minister, Irujo, the backers of this attempt were arrested and prosecuted. They escaped conviction and this added strength to the Spanish con-tention that Madison and Jefferson were in collusion with the Venezuelean adventurer.[44] The episode made a deep impression on the Spanish government and was one cause of the increasing hostility of Spain thereafter.[45]

The next similar case occurred in 1812 when a group of Americans and Mexicans, headed by the revolutionary leader Gutiérrez de Lara in company with an ex-officer of the U. S. Army, Augustus Magee, set out from Louisiana and for a short time gained control of most of Texas including San Antonio

PRO, FO-5, vol. 121 (1816).

2. Onís to Pizarro, April 20, 1818, AHN., Est., Leg. 5644.
3. Correa da Serra to Bagot, PRO, FO-5, vol. 141 (1818).
4. Onís to Adams, Nov. 16, 1818, ASP. FR., IV, 534-5.
5. *National Intelligencer*, Washington, D. C., June 16, 1819 (gives figures to September, 1818).

ACTIVITIES OF BUENOS AIRES PRIVATEERS

Year	No. of Ships Active	Prizes sent to B.A.
1815	1	2
1816	4	14
1817	14	21
1818	23	11
1819	14	6
1820	10	—
1821	2	—

Currier, *op. cit.*, p. 23.

44 W. S. Robertson, *Life of Miranda*, I, 293 ff. surveys the expedition. For repercussions in the United States *cf.* Henry Adams, *History of the U. S.*, III, 191 ff.

45 There is a large *dossier* on Miranda's expedition in AHN., Est., Leg. 5544.

and declared the independence of the province from Spain.[46] The ubiquitous Álvarez de Toledo next appeared on the scene, and carried on a campaign of propaganda and intrigue against Gutiérrez.[47] Magee died, and in the summer of 1813 Toledo managed to oust Gutiérrez and assume leadership. After some desultory skirmishing he was forced out by a Spanish force and retreated to New Orleans, his following completely broken up.[48]

The government at Washington had made no effort to interfere with the expedition. It had aided Gutiérrez to return from Washington to Texas,[49] and it was well informed of the filibuster's plans.[50] Recruiting was carried on openly in Louisiana, and proclamations were issued by the rebels there.[51]

Toledo continued to plot another incursion, together with Juan Pablo Anaya, an agent of the Mexican revolutionary leaders whose aid and countenance he desired for his project. Before long, however, various factions developed among the plotters. Toledo distrusted General Humbert, Picornell, Juan Cortes, and others whom he suspected of French affiliations and refused to cooperate with them.[52] He was also at odds with Dr. J. H. Robinson, Monroe's onetime agent, who was now actively

46 Lucas Alamán, *Historia de Méjico*, III, 481 ff.; I. Fabela, *Precursores de la diplomacia Mejicana*, pp. 38-9.

47 *El Mexicano*, vol. i, no. 2, June 19, 1813, Natchitoches; *Gaceta de Texas*, Nacogdoches, May 25, 1813.

48 I. J. Cox, "Monroe and Early Mexican Revolutionary Agents" in *Annual Report*, AHA., 1911, vol. i, p. 203 ff.; Fabela, *op. cit.*, pp. 38-9; Bancroft, *Texas*, II, 19-26.

49 See chapter i, *supra*.

50 William Shaler to J. Monroe, Oct. 1, 1812, DS., Special Agents, vol. ii. Shaler had played an active part in the movement which ousted Gutiérrez and placed Toledo in control, *cf.* Garrett, *op. cit.* in *S. W. Hist. Quar.*, XL (1937).

51 *Alexandria* (La.) *Herald*, Aug. 31, 1812.

52 Toledo to Shaler, Nov. 28, 1813; Toledo to Picornell, Jan. 15, 1814, DS., Mexico, Filibustering Expeditions against the Government of Spain, 1811-1816.

associated with revolutionary aims in northern Mexico.[3] Robinson had taken it upon himself to recruit volunteers from Pittsburgh to New Orleans and to purchase arms for another Texas expedition,[54] but Toledo believed that his purpose was pecuniary gain through land grants to be obtained in Texas.[55] Much wrangling took place at Natchitoches where the adventurers made their rendezvous. Robinson was checkmated by Toledo, who in turn had to give up his plans after a short-lived effort to lead the Mexican members of the filibustering group into the disputed province. The Louisiana authorities could not permanently ignore this open violation of American neutrality. Warrants were issued for the arrest of Robinson and of Toledo which, though evaded for a time, contributed to the failure of the expedition planned.[56]

These activities and rumors of continued plotting in Louisiana so alarmed Onís in 1815 that he made them the principal subject of his first note to Monroe after his formal reception as minister of Spain.[57] In September, 1815, President Madison had issued a proclamation of neutrality disavowing and outlawing the filibusters.[58] Toledo and others were indicted for infraction of the neutrality laws, but as insufficient evidence was presented they were shortly discharged.[59] These episodes show the extreme reluctance of the United States to interfere. The protests of injured innocence addressed by Monroe to

53 Cox, "Monroe and Early Mexican Revolutonary Agents," in *Annual Report*, AHA., 1911, vol. i.

54 Robinson to Toledo, Jan. 4, 1814, DS., Mexico, Filibustering Expeditions, etc., see also a proclamation issued by Robinson for recruits, Pittsburg, Nov. 19, 1813, *ibid.*

55 Toledo to Shaler, Jan. 10 and 16, 1814, *ibid.*

56 Toledo to Shaler, Sabine River, May 30, 1814, *ibid.*

57 Onís to Monroe, Dec. 30, 1815, AHN., Est., Leg. 5641.

58 ASP. FR., IV, 1, Proclamation of Sept. 1, 1815.

59 Manning, *Dipl. Corresp.*, I, 32 ff. John Dick to Sec. of State, New Orleans, March 1, 1816 (also printed in ASP. FR., IV, 431). American citizens were among those indicted, Bancroft, *Texas*, II, 34.

Onís [60] do not at all harmonize with the complete and timely information of the movements of the filibusters which the Secretary of State possessed.

The next filibustering attempt was that of Javier Mina, a Spaniard who belonged to the proscribed "Liberal" party. This young exile, after a brief sojourn in England, came to the United States resolved to aid the revolutionary cause in Mexico. He arrived at Norfolk in the summer of 1816, moved thence to Baltimore, which he made his headquarters, and visited New York, Philadelphia, and Washington.[61] He remained most of the summer in Baltimore where he underwent a series of vicissitudes. Onís attempted to check his plans,[62] and Toledo, who had become a turncoat and now acted as *agent provocateur* for the Spanish government,[63] almost broke up the expedition by reporting the collapse of the revolution in Mexico.[64] Mina was popular in Baltimore, making many friends, among them General Scott,[65] but he found it difficult to raise money, and until he obtained funds from a Mr. Dennis A. Smith was almost destitute.[66] In September, however, he was finally able to sail. The expedition first touched at Port au Prince. There Mina met Bolívar who attempted to turn him toward Venezuela, but the Spaniard preferred to act independently and to lead his small band of American and French volun-

60 Manning, *Dipl. Corresp.*, I, 19 f., Monroe to Onís, Jan. 19, 1916, denies all knowledge of Toledo's moves.

61 Negrete, *México en el siglo XIX*, IX, 12 ff.; W. D. Robinson, *Memoirs of the Mexican Revolution, Including a Narrative of the Expedition of General Xavier Mina* (Philadelphia, 1820), p. 54 ff.

62 Bagot to Castlereagh, Aug. 12, 1816, PRO, FO-5, vol. 115.

63 P. Gual to Wm. Thornton, Nov. 19, 1816, Thornton Papers, LC.

64 I. Fabela, *Precursores de la diplomacia Mejicana*, p. 68.

65 Gen. Scott to Thornton, Jan. 6, 1817, Thornton Papers, LC. F. Larrazabal, *Vida del Libertador, Simón Bolívar*, II, 47, quoting the *Maryland Journal* and the *Baltimore Advertiser*.

66 Negrete, *México en el siglo XIX*, IX, 52, 65 ff.

teers against Mexico.[67] From Hayti he proceeded to the Texas coast and joined Louis Aury. There Mina left his forces and sailed for New Orleans for further aid. He secured it only with difficulty, for though various men were willing to back a privateering venture or a filibuster against Pensacola, few cared to risk funds on a direct attack on Mexico.[68] In March, 1817, Mina left his base at Galveston and invaded Mexico. After a few initial successes his small force was dispersed, and after a further period of guerilla tactics the leader was captured and shot.[69]

The aid received by Mina in the United States was small. At Port au Prince he had fifty men only,[70] though he may have gathered additional recruits from New Orleans, but money had been given him and armed men had been enlisted on American soil. The affair was a definite breach of the neutrality laws.

The year after Mina's departure from Baltimore considerable stir was made by an adventurous Scot, Gregor McGregor. This man had served with the patriots in Venezuela and for a while had been in the good graces of Bolívar. A quarrel with some of his fellow officers, however, had led him to resign from that service, but he did not give up his desire to distinguish himself at the expense of Spain.[71] Early in 1817 he appeared in the United States talking much of his great deeds, past and future, and making a good deal of capital from his connections with Bolívar about whom there was much public interest. His plans were at first indefinite.

67 F. Larrazabal, *Vida de Simon Bolívar*, I, 442.

68 W. D. Robinson, *Memoirs of the Mexican Revolution*, p. 127 ff.

69 Negrete, *op. cit.*, IX, 27 gives Mina's proclamation. For Mina in New Orleans see report of the British consul in that port to Consul General St. John Baker, March 4, 1817, PRO, FO-5, vol. 122. His campaign in Mexico is covered in M. Torrente, *Historia de la independencia de Méjico* (Madrid, 1918), pp. 205-221.

70 O'Leary, *Memorias*, XI, 347, Mina to Montilla, Sept. 17, 1816.

71 A. Hasbrouck, *Foreign Legionaries* ... gives a caustic, but well documented account of McGregor's career.

In April, 1817, he called on Sir Charles Bagot, the British minister, and talked of the commercial importance to Britain of Spanish American independence and of the danger that the United States might damage British prestige by openly aiding the rebels. Would it not be possible for England to aid an expedition in an undercover manner? McGregor said that he had a commission from the Venezuelan patriots and was prepared to lead an adventure. He spoke of offers from Bonapartist exiles to take part in an invasion of Mexico, and suggested the advisability of hindering an American occupation of Florida by secretly countenancing a venture against the province in the name of the patriots.[72] Bagot distrusted McGregor, but felt that it would be well to watch one whose schemes might lead to serious consequences.[73]

Not long after this the Scotchman approached Richard Rush, then in charge of the Department of State pending the arrival from England of John Quincy Adams, the newly appointed secretary. Rush listened to McGregor and does not seem to have erred on the side of discretion. His strong sympathies for the patriots apparently affected his judgment. The scheme related to him was for the United States to purchase Florida after the filibusters had taken it from Spain. Officially Rush refused to have anything to do with the idea but he seems to have allowed McGregor to feel that he would not personally be sorry to see such an outcome.[74]

Failing to secure aid either from Great Britain or the United States, McGregor organized an expedition in alliance with certain Spanish Americans then resident in the country: Vicente Pazos, Pedro Gual and others.[75] These projects finally simmered

72 Bagot to Castlereagh, April 25, 1817, PRO, FO-5, vol. 122.

73 *Ibid.*

74 Adams, *Memoirs*, IV, 53; *cf.* Thornton Papers, L. C., vol. v, Thornton to Adams, Feb. 9, 1818, probably the source of Adams' information.

75 Pedro Gual to Thornton, N. Y., July 7, 1817, Thornton Papers, LC., vol. v.

down to an attack on Amelia Island, the scene of Mathews'
activities during the War of 1812. Strategically located for
smuggling on the border of the United States, it naturally
attracted the attention of the filibusters. In June, 1817,
McGregor was in Charleston where he was feted and dined in
grand style. Here he secured a brig which he despatched ostensibly to New Orleans, but actually to his Florida rendezvous.[76]
He then proceeded to Savannah, and here as at Charleston
openly enlisted volunteers for his expedition, though the destination of the adventure was kept under cover. In Savannah
McGregor tried to raise money by subscription to be repaid
from the proceeds of lands which he expected to conquer, and
it was reported that a number of Georgians were led to invest
in the scheme.[77]

McGregor had little trouble in taking the Spanish post at
Amelia which was poorly defended, but he could not control his
own followers who soon became openly insubordinate. After
a short time he withdrew from the enterprise and his place
was taken by Louis Aury who had sailed from the Texas
coast when he heard of McGregor's coup at Amelia. Under the
latter's rule the island became a hotbed of smuggling and a
thriving base for the rebel privateers.[78] The whole episode was
a flagrant breach of neutrality and was to lead to much controversy and finally to intervention by the United States
government.

Another affair, not so widely publicized at the time and still
somewhat obscure, was regarded with great anxiety by the
governments of Spain and France: the scheme of a group of
Bonapartist French exiles in the United States, most of whom

---

76 Benjamin Moodie to Consul General St. John Baker, June 21, 1817,
PRO, FO-5, vol. 122.

77 James Wallace, viceconsul at Savannah, to Consul General St. John
Baker, June 12, 1817, PRO, FO-5, vol. 122.

78 Monroe's Messages to Congress, Dec. 2, 1817, and Jan. 13, 1818,
Richardson, *op. cit.*, vol. ii, pp. 14 and 23, also published with accompanying
documents in ASP. FR., IV.

were adventurous, poverty-stricken, and discontented. Rumors of their plans began to circulate in 1816. In the following year the French Minister discovered documents purporting to deal with the aims of a Napoleonic Association. Among papers dealing with plans for recruiting volunteers, notes on Indian languages of the trans-Mississippi area, etc., was an appeal to Joseph Bonaparte, now living in retirement near Philadelphia, to support an attempt to establish a Bonapartist empire in Mexico. The documents were signed by Lakanal, an ex-member of the French National Convention, and, as a regicide, anathema to the representative of Louis XVIII.[79]

Hyde de Neuville showed these documents to his colleagues Onís and Bagot as well as to Adams. Like Onís the Frenchman regarded them as proof of a dangerous conspiracy, but Adams was inclined to regard them merely as productions of the fevered brains of a few impractical enthusiasts.[80] Through American citizens who were intimate with the circle of exiled Frenchmen Adams and Monroe were able to obtain further information on the alleged plot. Lakanal and his association remained obscure, but General Charles Lallemand and other Napoleonic officers were found to be planning an expedition into Spanish territory. This project was related to another and less militant enterprise of the Bonapartists. Some of them organized as the " Tombigbee Association or the Society for the Cultivation of the Vine and the Olive," proposed to establish a settlement on the river of that name in Alabama in order to provide homes for French exiles and to promote the development of the area. From Congress the society received a conditional grant of land on generous terms and at the time reports of the Lakanal conspiracy were in the air the French began to

79 J. S. Reeves, *Napoleonic Exiles in America* (Baltimore, 1905), in *Johns Hopkins University Studies*, vol. xxiii, p. 44 ff. gives a detailed account of this affair based on MSS in the Department of State and on the J. Q. Adams papers.

80 *Ibid.*, p. 69 ff. See also, J. Q. Adams to Monroe, Oct. 8, 1817, MP. LC.

arrive at the Tombigbee. The enterprise came to nothing due to poor management, faulty land surveys, and the unwillingness of many of the colonists to undergo the trials of American frontier life.[81]

Some of the men involved in this scheme tried to pass on their land claims to speculators in return for cash and joined another project, this time for a settlement on the Trinity River in Texas. Rather romantically, this post was called *Le Champ d'Asile*. The leader of this group, General Charles Lallemand, led a force to the Trinity early in 1818 via New Orleans and Galveston.[82] Before his departure there had been much talk that taken together with the earlier Lakanal affair kept the administration on the alert, to say nothing of the anxiety of the foreign diplomats. One account had it that the Bonapartists had their eyes on a part of South America, others that they were preparing for action in Mexico in alliance with revolutionaries in that country. Americans were involved in these schemes. A Charleston merchant promised Lallemand to contribute money and two ships. Other merchants at New York and Philadelphia were ready to join in the venture, including a Mr. Courcier of the latter city and a Mr. Adams of Boston.[83]

In the end this scheme also proved a fiasco. With the aid of the pirate Lafitte the French reached the Trinity, built a fort, and inaugurated a short-lived military colony, but many fell ill and on the approach of a small detachment of Spanish troops the heroes who had talked of conquering Mexico and even of freeing the ex-Emperor from St. Helena beat an inglorious

81 J. S. Reeves, *op. cit.*, pp. 34-38; for the land grant, see, *Niles' Weekly Register*, XIV, 393.

82 *Ibid.*, p. 91. Reeves credits the larger figure of 400 men. Nicholas Biddle to Monroe, Feb. 25, 1818, MP. LC., declares that only 150 men were involved. He may have had knowledge of only one detachment, *cf. Niles' Weekly Register*, XIV, 394.

83 William Lee to Monroe, Sept. 27, 1817, MP. LC.; Nicholas Biddle to Monroe, Feb. 25, 1818, MP. LC.; Bagot to Castlereagh, May 6, 1818, No. 38, PRO, FO-5, vol. 132; Reeves, *op. cit.*, p. 80 ff.

retreat to New Orleans.[84] Though the expedition was unsuccessful, American citizens had aided the filibusters and had proved the willingness of American as well as European adventurers to profit if they could at Spanish expense.

The reaction of the Spanish government to these manifold activities may be related briefly. Ever since the outbreak of the revolutions highly colored reports had been reaching Madrid of the aid furnished to the rebels in the United States. At first it was the shipment of munitions by American merchants that aroused the ire of Onís, though at the same time American flour and other produce were helping to maintain the Spanish and British armies in the Peninsula.[85] In 1812 and 1813 Onís also made much of the activities of Álvarez de Toledo and other adventurers in Louisiana and Texas, hinting that these men were in closer contact with the administration than he was able to prove.[86] These reports, together with the encroachments of the United States in the Floridas, led to the diplomatic efforts of the Spanish constitutional government that were described in a previous chapter.[87]

After he was officially received Onís increased the frequency and bitterness of his protests. He declared that the stores, munitions and men sent from the United States to Cartagena in 1815 were important factors in the strong resistance of that city to the attacks of the royalist general, Morillo.[88] His protests dealing with Toledo's second attempt to invade Texas

84 In addition to sources cited above, note 83, see the *Columbian Museum and Savannah Gazette*, Dec. 18, 1818.

85 Onís to Bardaxí, Sept. 9, 1810, AHN., Est. Leg. 5637; *id.* to *id.*, July 22, 1811, Aug. 13, 1811, AHN., Est. Leg. 5638. On the grain trade with Spain see W. F Galpin "American Grain Trade to the Spanish Peninsula, 1810-1814" in AHR., vol. xxviii.

86 Onís to Bardaxí, Jan. 20, 1812, Mar. 4, 1812, AHN., Est. Leg. 5638. Onís to Pezuela, Jan. 9, 1813, AHN., Est. Leg. 5639.

87 See especially Minutes of the Council of State, August, 1813, AHN., Est. Leg. 5557, Expediente No. 1.

88 Onís to Cevallos, Mar. 31, 1815, April 16, 1815, April 17, 1815, AHN., Est. Leg. 5640.

have already been mentioned. As the privateering business at Baltimore and New Orleans grew in 1816 and 1817 his notes on that subject must have taken up a large part of his time. They contained detailed reports collected by Spanish consuls of alleged breaches of neutrality in American ports, principally Baltimore and New Orleans,[89] and insisted that federal officials were negligent in enforcing the provisions of the 1795 treaty dealing with the conduct of privateering.[90]

Monroe and his successors in the State Department indignantly denied the truth of Onís' wholesale accusations and claimed that in the rare instances where unneutral conduct had occurred the authorities had taken adequate measures to punish it. Evidence was forwarded to Onís to prove that the district attorneys in New Orleans and Baltimore had prosecuted many cases and the Spaniard was accused of believing every rumor he heard.[91] There was some truth in this accusation, but it was also true that many of Onís' complaints were well founded. The officers charged with enforcement of the law of neutrality could act only on the presentation of legal evidence sufficient to make conviction a possibility. With the memory of the Prohibition experiment still fresh, it is not hard today to realize the difficulty that faced officials. Jury convictions, in view of the state of public opinion in the ports where suits had to be tried, could be secured only when the evidence was water-tight. In some cases, too, United States attorneys and marshalls were negligent, affected by the public toleration of the acts that it was their duty to suppress.[92]

89 Manning, *Diplomatic Correspondence*, III, 1910 ff.

90 Articles 14 of the treaty of San Lorenzo, 1795, provided that any citizen of either contracting power taking out letters of marque against the other should be treated as a pirate. See text in Miller, *Treaties*, II, 328.

91 Manning, *Diplomatic Correspondence*, I, 35. Monroe to Onís, June 10, 1816.

92 B. Chew to Crawford, Oct. 17, 1817, DS., Consular Letters, Galveston, I; Bagot to Castlereagh, June 3, 1817, PRO, FO-5, vol. 122; Manning, *Diplomatic Correspondence*, III, 1953 ff.

The administration at length came to realize that a change in the legislation dealing with neutrality enforcement was desirable, and Madison in one of his final messages recommended a new law to correct the defects in the existing statutes.[93] John Forsyth of Georgia introduced the bill in the House as an administration measure. It reinforced the previous law by prohibiting the sale of armed vessels to foreigners to use in a way that would be illegal for a citizen. In suspicious cases bond could be required before vessels were allowed to depart.[94]

John Randolph with his usual bitter wit called this proposal a bill to make peace between the town of Baltimore and his Catholic Majesty.[95] The debate wandered far afield and afforded an occasion for members of Congress to express their sentiments in favor of the Spanish American insurgents. Henry Clay, seconded by Sharp of Kentucky and Root of New York, attacked the bill as unfair to the rebels, while Randolph, and Smith of Maryland, supported it.[96] The administration forces won after a sharp fight. In the House the vote stood 94 yeas to 60 nays. Of the latter, thirty-two votes were cast by members from constituencies south and west of Pennsylvania, while only three New Englanders voted against the bill.[97] The vote was illustrative of the sectional and occupational interests of the members rather than of their political labels. Jefferson, in commenting on the vote in the Senate declared that it was contrary to the wishes of the people.[98]

Expressions of opinion in the press tend to support his estimate, though the feeling of the country was by no means unanimous. The most forceful presentation of the opposition view

93 Richardson, op. cit., I, 582, Madison to Congress, Dec. 26, 1816.

94 Abridgement of the Debates of Congress, ed. by T. H. Benton (N. Y., 1857-1861), V, 695, 701; Annals of Congress, XXX, 14 Cong., 2 session 715 ff.; Fenwick, C. G., Neutrality Laws of the United States, p. 32 ff.

95 Annals of Congress, XXX, 14 Cong., 2 Session, 732.

96 Ibid., XXX, 715.

97 J. B. McMaster, History of the People of the U. S., IV, 376.

98 Ford, Jefferson, X, 90, Jefferson to Gallatin, June 16, 1817.

outside the halls of Congress was that of William Cobbett. The veteran " Peter Porcupine " regarded the situation from a position astride the Atlantic in a letter " On the measures of the United States and on the conduct of the Borough-mongers with regard to Spanish America ". He considered the new act unfair, for the rebels without organized shipyards or merchant marine were at a disadvantage in resources. He felt also that the act tended to interfere with the legitimate right of neutrals to trade in contraband of war, subject to confiscation by belligerents. Was it neutral, he asked, to refuse to arm an unarmed man fighting with an armed one? Further, the act might be construed to give Spain the right to arm ships in the United States because the rebels were not " states or princes " with which the United States was at peace.[99]

The American editor of Cobbett's letter adopted a similar stand from somewhat different motives. In his preface he declared that the United States had allowed its fear of foreign intervention to lead it too far, and that in endeavoring to be more just than the law of nations " we are unjust to ourselves and to the patriots of Spanish America ". He also feared that Great Britain might take advantage of the act to supplant the United States in the estimation of the insurgents.[100]

Erving, at Madrid, objected to the new legislation because he believed that it tended to dissipate Spanish apprehensions and to stiffen the opposition of the court to any concessions in the current treaty negotiations.[101]

The *Baltimore Patriot* was one of the most outspoken opponents of the neutrality law. It held that it would hamper legitimate trade, and that it showed disgraceful compliance with the wishes of Spain, for which nation the editor exhibited a deep

99 William Cobbett, *Our Neutral Conduct Reviewed, Letter III to Major Cartwright from Cobbett's Political Register* (New York, 1818). The letter purports to have been written from N. Hempstead, L. I. in December, 1817.

100 *Ibid.*, preface.

101 Erving to the Secretary of State, April 6, 1817, DS., Despatches, Spain, vol. xiv.

contempt.[102] Niles was voicing a widely held opinion when some time earlier he stated that though the government could not rightly interfere in the Spanish American struggle, citizens had a right to do so. He pointed out that British subjects were doing more than Americans to help the rebels in spite of the fact that Great Britain was Spain's ally.[103]

The difficulty encountered in enforcing the new law is the most convincing proof of its unpopularity. This varied according to local prejudices and interests. Onís stated that the law was stringently enforced only in Massachusetts, Rhode Island and Pennsylvania.[104] Even at Philadelphia, however, the arrest of certain British officers who had volunteered for service with Bolívar caused great public commotion which only subsided when the grand jury refused to commit them.[105]

The administration was not without its supporters, however, even in Baltimore and New Orleans which were the strongholds of opposition. The *Baltimore Federal Republican* attacked the privateers [106] and the *New Orleans Gazette* declared that " anxious as we are for the success of the patriots, we are not less anxious that they should be taught to respect the laws and dignity of the United States ".[107] The *New York Evening Post* wished the patriots well, but insisted that they should be taught to respect the rights of their " natural ally ".[108] Especially interesting, coming from a state bordering Spanish territory and

102 *Columbian Museum and Savannah Gazette*, Feb. 5, 1817, quoting the *Baltimore Patriot*, Jan. 27, 1817; the *New York National Advocate*, Dec. 3, 1817 also declared the law unfair.

103 *Niles' Weekly Register*, IX, 33 (1815).

104 Note by Onís on the back of Pizarro to Onís, July 3, 1817, AME., Estados Unidos, Cor. Pol., Leg. 223.

105 Bagot to Castlereagh, Nov. 7, 1817, No. 69, PRO, FO-5, vol. 123; *id.* to *id.*, Jan. 6, 1818, *ibid.*, vol. 130.

106 Currier, *op. cit.*, p. 47, quoting issue of Oct. 29, 1816.

107 Quoted by the *New York Evening Post*, Jan. 2, 1817.

108 *Ibid.*, Jan. 30, 1817; *New York National Advocate*, Nov. 26, Dec. 2, 1817 was critical of the privateers under Aury.

strongly prejudiced against Spain, is the comment of the *Columbian Museum and Savannah Gazette* which protested editorially against " the species of piracy which at this moment disgraces the character of the American sailor . . . under the pretense of aiding the cause of the Spanish patriots. . . ." [109]

The current of opinion upholding strict neutrality legislation grew stronger in 1817 as the actions of privateer captains became progressively more lawless. During 1818, amendments to the 1817 act in the direction of still further severity aroused less opposition than the legislation of the previous year. The advocates of Spanish American independence had by that time found a more direct opportunity to bring forward their views in the movement for immediate recognition of the rebel governments which began to assume importance in 1817 and gathered impetus during the following year.

[109] *Columbian Museum and Savannah Gazette*, April 20, 1817.

CHAPTER V
THE UNITED STATES AND THE REBELS,
1815 TO 1818

IN the United States the year 1817 marked an appreciable increase of interest in the struggle for Spanish American independence. This interest had been growing ever since 1815 from its low ebb during the war with Great Britain. Rebel successes during these years tended to animate their partisans in the northern republic. In the far south General San Martín's brilliant campaign, beginning with his march across the Andes and ending with the battle of Maipú, again won Chile for the patriots. In the northern sphere Bolívar, after repeated failure, had given up direct attack on the Venezuelan coast and had shifted his base to the Orinoco valley. On the *llanos* that bordered this river and its tributary the Apure he could maintain himself indefinitely and was in a strong position to threaten the Spanish garrisons in the north. Under General Paez the patriots were developing that body of hardy light cavalry which was to be the essential factor in future successes. At Angostura, Bolívar's capital, the forms of civil government were inaugurated, a fact not without significance in its effect on foreign opinion.

One sign of increasing interest, and a factor in producing it, was the appearance of pamphlets and books and an increasing volume of newsprint dealing with Spanish American affairs. A book which received wide notice was the *Outline of the Revolution in Spanish America* published anonymously by Manuel Palacio Fajardo. The author, whose position as agent for Cartagena had been ended by the fall of that city to Morillo, employed his leisure to good purpose in preparing this volume. It was a fairly detailed account of the revolutions from the patriot point of view, and it was especially valuable as propaganda because the writer knew how to please and flatter his audience in the United States.[1] The book received favorable notice from several reviews and was often praised as the only convenient and accessible source of information on a subject made difficult for the average newspaper reader by conflicting reports.[2]

Another work enjoyed great popularity and sold so cheaply that the British minister suspected that it was subsidized by the administration.[3] It was a pamphlet called: " A letter to James Monroe . . . upon the present State of South America ". Its author, H. M. Brackenridge, espoused the patriot cause with ardor.[4] The principal thesis of the work was its advocacy of official recognition of the rebel governments, or at least that of Buenos Aires, which had maintained a *de facto* independence since 1810. Brackenridge characterized the policy of the administration as overscrupulous: the conduct of Spain, he declared, would have led any other nation to occupy Florida and Texas; the United States, no longer a " patchwork republic ", had nothing to fear; it should be the first to win the honor of recognizing the new states, thereby spreading republicanism and American commercial interests, both of which were threatened by reactionary Europe and the commercial ambitions of Great Britain.[5] The spirit which animated the Monroe Doctrine appears in a passage where he speaks of the United States as the natural leader of the Americas, and of the common continental interests which bound the people of the New World in opposition to the Old.[6] He did not favor the idea of an

1 *Anonymous* (M. Palacio Fajardo) *Outline of the Revolution in Spanish America, or an Account of the Origin, Progress, and Actual State of the War Carried on between Spain and Spanish America*, by a South American (New York, 1817).

2 *Analectic Magazine*, XI (1818) ; *American Monthly Magazine*, III (1818), 54 f. See also Rodney to Monroe, Oct. 31, 1817, MP. LC.

3 Bagot to Castlereagh, Dec. 2, 1817, PRO, FO-5, vol. 123.

4 H. M. Brackenridge, " Letter to James Monroe, etc." in the *Pamphleteer* (London, 1818). Reprinted from the American edition of 1817.

5 H. M. Brackenridge, *op. cit.*, p. 50.

6 *Ibid.*, p. 44.

international congress, nor any formal alliances, but hoped that some less rigid form of cooperation would be possible.

The bitter denunciation of Spanish rule which prefaced the pamphlet was an appeal to popular prejudice, though in all probability it was regarded as sober historical truth at the time in the United States.[7] The wide circulation and the importance attached to this pamphlet are attested in the preface to the London edition of 1818, and the mere fact of its republication in England reinforces the editor's remarks.

Another slender volume of a similar nature was the work of a political exile from the United Provinces of South America, as the region headed by Buenos Aires was then denominated. Vicente Pazos, the author, was a native of Upper Peru (present-day Bolivia). He had taken a considerable part in the revolution of his native province and in Buenos Aires, had edited in that city a newspaper of pronounced republican views, and finally had been forced to leave the country by the government of Pueyrredon which was conservative and monarchical in tendency and intolerant of criticism.[8] This pamphlet, like that of Palacio Fajardo devoted much space to diatribes against the obscurantist and cruel conduct of Spanish officials in America.

A work which seems to have been less widely read at the time of its publication, but which has especial interest today because it antedates the others mentioned in this chapter, was *A Cursory View of Spanish America* by William Davis

---

7 Brackenridge, *op. cit.*, pp. 2-6.

8 Vicente Pazos, *Letters to Henry Clay on the Revolution in South America* (New York, 1819). For data on the career of this interesting character see Bartolomé Mitre, *Historia de Belgrano y de la independencia argentina* (Buenos Aires, 1887), III, 48; II, 436. Pazos, who according to Mitre had Aymara indian blood in his veins, was intensely anti-Spanish. He had travelled widely in Europe and America, was a linguist, skilful writer, but eccentric and flighty. His rashness will appear in the foregoing pages.

9 William D. Robinson, *A Cursory View of Spanish America*, reprinted from the 1815 edition by the *Magazine of History*, vol. xxxvi. W. D. Robinson should not be confused with Dr. John Robinson who was sent by

Robinson.[9] The author, who wrote during the stress of wartime feeling against Great Britain, was a bitter anglophobe and warned his fellow countrymen of the danger of encroaching British influence in the New World. Anti-Spanish as well, he described Spanish atrocities, dungeons, mutilations and executions in a blood-curdling manner. The creoles were declared to have great natural endowments including acuteness, high spirit, and enthusiasm for liberty.[10] On the attitude of the American West, Robinson stated:

> To assist in the emancipation of Mexico from the dominion of Spain has long been a popular feeling among all classes of society in the States before mentioned. So strong indeed has been that feeling occasionally, that our government could scarcely prevent its embroiling us with Spain.[11]

The pamphleteers who have been mentioned were by no means the only propagandists working in favor of the rebels in the United States. William Duane, editor of the *Philadelphia Aurora,* worked steadily towards popularizing the Spanish American cause. Duane was an intimate of Manuel Tórres, an agent from Colombia, who furnished him with material and was probably partly responsible for the editor's views on these subjects.[12]

Baptis Irvine, a Scotch journalist who for a time edited the *New York Columbian* and later transferred his activities to the *Washington City Gazette,* was another enthusiast for the

---

Monroe on a mission into northern Mexico. W. D. Robinson was a business man who carried on a trade in munitions, etc. with some of the Mexican rebels. He was captured by the royalists, sent to Spain and imprisoned. Paroled with the understanding that he would appear for trial, Robinson jumped his bail and escaped to Gibraltar.

10 W. D. Robinson, *op. cit.,* p. 276.

11 *Ibid.,* p. 280.

12 R. Rivas, *Relaciones internacionales entre Colombia y los Estados Unidos, 1810-1850* (Bogota, 1915), p. 20. See also letters of Duane to Jefferson and to Tórres in *Massachusetts Historical Society, Proceedings,* 2nd series, XX, 375, 380.

patriot cause. Irvine became greatly attached to José Miguel Carrera during the visit of that Chilean leader to the United States. Consequently in addition to his general enthusiasm for South American liberty he took sides in the factional dispute in Chile and Buenos Aires, favoring Carrera and his allies and attacking O'Higgins, Pueyrredon and others hostile to the Carreras.[13]

Thomas Ritchie, the editor of the *Richmond Enquirer,* was one of the earlier champions of South American independence. His paper was influential not only in Virginia but throughout the South and West, standing for old-time Jeffersonian principles. Ritchie was credited with much influence with Monroe, which added weight to his editorials.[14] In 1817 Ritchie favored recognition of the insurgents but he lost his enthusiasm after that year, perhaps because his attention was diverted subsequently to the attack on Jackson.[15] It was in the *Enquirer* that a series of letters signed " Lautaro " appeared in 1817 in favor of recognition of the rebels. They were reprinted by other journals, among them the semi-official *National Intelligencer* of Washington, and much curiosity was aroused as to their authorship. By some they were ascribed to Skinner, the postmaster at Baltimore and an intimate of the patriots in that city.[16] Others believed them to be the work of a number of men.

Hezekiah Niles, the editor of the *Weekly Register,* devoted more space to reports from Spanish America than most of his colleagues. He reprinted rebel proclamations and decrees on

13 Adams, *Memoirs,* V, 57, and under Irvine in Index. *Niles' Weekly Register,* Nov. 24, 1821; Collier and Feliú Cruz, *op. cit.,* p. 236 ff.; *Strictures on "A Voyage to South America"* (Anonymous), p. 158.

14 For early favorable comment on Spanish American cause see *Richmond Enquirer,* Jan. 7, 1812 and frequently thereafter. *Cf.* C. H. Ambler, *Thomas Ritchie* (Richmond, 1913), p. 71.

15 *Ibid.,* pp. 72, 83.

16 Adams, *Memoirs,* IV, 318; V, 158-9, George Hay to Monroe, Oct. 26, 1817, MP. LC. Collier and Feliú Cruz, *op. cit.,* p. 233. B. Vicuña McKenna, *El ostracismo de los Carreras* (Santiago, 1857), p. 81 ff.

numerous occasions. Though less critical of the administration's policy than some of the enthusiasts, he was none the less sincerely interested in the success of the revolutionary cause.[17]

Baltimore, which was the center of the privateering business, was also the rendezvous for most of the Spanish American agents and exiles in the United States.[18] Associated with these men were numerous Americans: Brackenridge and Irvine, journalists; Skinner and McCulloch, federal officials; William Pinkney, the famous lawyer; and Theodoric Bland, judge of the United States district court.[19] Skinner was especially active in pressing the rebel cause, carrying on a correspondence with Monroe urging the administration to look with a more indulgent eye on the revolutionists.[20]

The American who maintained the closest and most friendly contact with the rebels in the United States was Dr. William Thornton, head of the Patent Office at Washington. He was an uncritical disciple of Paine and Rousseau and had espoused the Spanish American revolutionary cause at the beginning of the movement.[21] The doctor's interest was due to a mixture of motives, however. His republican and democratic sympathies led him to draft model constitutions, banking codes, and other such documents which he submitted to the governments of Venezuela and of Colombia;[22] his humanitarianism led him to attempt to convert the patriots to moderate treatment of prisoners of war;[23] on the other hand as an associate of Fulton and

17 *Niles' Weekly Register*, 1811-22, *passim*. For specific examples see Sept. 14, 1811, Dec. 7, 1811, Feb. 1, 1812, Mar. 28, 1812, Sept. 11, 1813, July 20, 1816.

18 Anonymous, *Strictures on "A voyage to South America, etc.,"* p. 158.

19 Collier and Feliú Cruz, *op. cit.*, p. 236, Adams, *Memoirs*, V, 56, 154.

20 Skinner to Monroe, Jan. 13, 1817, MP. LC., Johnson Collection.

21 See *Dictionary of American Biography*, "William Thornton".

22 Thornton to Gual, Aug. 13, 1816, Thornton Papers, LC., vol. iv. *Idem* to *idem*, April 23, 1817, *ibid.*, vol. v; Thornton to Toledo, July 24, 1816, *ibid.*, vol. iv.

23 Thornton to Gual, July 25, 1816, *ibid.*, vol. iv.

other early steamboat constructors he had an ambition to exploit the possibilities of South American rivers for the new means of transportation. From his patriot associates he acquired a rather vague concession to operate steamboats on the Magdalena and tried unsuccessfully to get a similar patent for the River Plate.[24]

Thornton's closest friend among the rebel agents was Pedro Gual, a native of New Granada. Until 1816 he had represented the government of Cartagena and later assumed a sort of general agency for all patriot interests in the United States, which never became official.[25] Through Gual, Thornton made contacts with Manuel Tórres, later agent of Colombia, and with J. G. Roscio, J. R. Revenga, and other associates of Bolívar.[26] These men, owing to the precarious status of their cause and the lack of any organized civil government in their country until 1819, had no official contacts with the government of the United States, but they carried on important activities, among them the encouragement of privateering, spreading verbal and written propaganda and securing supplies of munitions and food. Thornton also corresponded with Álvarez de Toledo, General Mina, Lino de Clemente and others.[27] Thornton was of great assistance to these men, introducing them to influential Americans and translating and composing articles for publication in the press.[28]

Among the Spanish Americans resident in Baltimore were Vicente Pazos, Manuel Dorrego, José Agrelo and Manuel Moreno, the latter a brother of the great leader of the 1810 revolution at Buenos Aires, Mariano Moreno. These men had

24 Certificate issued by Gual, Dec. 26, 1816; *ibid.*, vol. iv.

25 I. Fabela, *Precursores de la diplomacia Mejicana*, p. 67. Thornton Papers, L.C., Gual to Thornton, Oct. 7, 1815, vol. iv.

26 Thornton to Gual, April 23, 1817; J. R. Revenga to Thornton, June 20, 1817, Thornton Papers, LC., vol. v.

27 *Ibid.*, vol. iv, Thornton to Toledo, July 24, 1816.

28 *Ibid.*, vol. v, Gual to Thornton, Sept. 3, 1818, Pazos to Thornton, April 3, 1818, Gual to Thornton, July 23, 1817.

been exiled by Pueyrredon, the " Supreme Director " at Buenos Aires, for their opposition to his policy.[29] Naturally this group was critical of the existing regime in Buenos Aires, though still fervently in favor of independence. Directly and indirectly, through American friends such as Skinner and Irvine, these men were responsible for revealing the factional disputes in the United Provinces; and their activities, though not calculated to produce that end, disillusioned many as to the political capacity of the South Americans.[30]

The most conspicuous and one of the most popular Spanish Americans to visit the United States during these years was José Miguel Carrera, the arbiter of Chilean affairs during Poinsett's stay in that country. A deep antagonism separated Carrera from the rival faction headed by O'Higgins. When San Martín, with the cooperation of O'Higgins, reconquered Chile for the patriots, Carrera took no part in the campaign. Before it began he had made up his mind to achieve Chilean freedom in another way. To further his plans he came to the United States where Poinsett and Commodore Porter had led him to think he might secure aid.[31]

Armed with introductions from these American friends, Carrera was well received when he arrived in the United States in 1816. The list of the friends he made is an imposing one; he established contact with Joseph Bonaparte and some of his satellites among the Napoleonic exiles, with De Witt Clinton, Aaron Burr, Thurlow Weed, and John Jacob Astor.[32] He even

29 For Pazos see p. 123, *supra*; B. Mitre, *Historia de Belgrano*, III, 48; *Documentos del archivo de Pueyrredon* (Museo Mitre) (Buenos Aires, 1912), III, 273-8; José T. Guido, *Biografía de Manuel Dorrego*, p. 15.

30 *Documentos del archivo de San Martín* (Buenos Aires, 1910-1911), IV, 533, Pueyrredon to San Martín, Nov. 24, 1817; Vicente Pazos, *Letters to Henry Clay, etc.*, p. viii; Anonymous, *Strictures on "A Voyage to South America,"* pp. 28, 39.

31 Amunátegui y McKenna, *La dictadura de O'Higgins* (Madrid, 1917), p. 147 ff.

32 Collier and Feliú Cruz, *op. cit.*, pp. 217 ff., 223 ff.; Vicuña McKenna, *op. cit.*, p. 74.

had an interview with Madison who seems to have treated him with cordiality.[33] For a time Carrera was depressed by the failure of his efforts to secure financial aid. Volunteers were to be had for the asking, but what he needed was money to buy ships and munitions.[34]

Finally, with the assistance of the indefatigable Skinner, who made Carrera a personal loan of $4,000, and introduced him to the Baltimore firm of Darcy and Didier, the South American was able to fit out a small squadron with which he planned to begin the reconquest of his country from the Spaniards. He sailed from Baltimore in the autumn of 1816 with four ships, taking with him a small band of volunteers and a considerable amount of munitions and armament.[35] His plans met with an abrupt check when his expedition arrived at Buenos Aires. Pueyrredon detained Carrera's ships and took over the supplies for his own use.[36]

Though Carrera's plans thus ended in failure, his stay in the United States was important in its effect on public opinion. As in the case of the Buenos Aires exiles, his friends adopted a hostile attitude toward the dominant faction in Chile and tended to create a state of confusion in the public that was to militate against the success of the campaign for immediate recognition of the insurgent governments.[37]

33 Porter to Monroe, Jan. 3, 1819, M.P. I.C., cf. Collier and Feliú Cruz, op. cit., p. 202.

34 Vicuña McKenna, op. cit., p. 44. Carrera has been accused of having amassed a fortune in Chile which he took with him to the United States, but according to most of those who have studied the matter he was penniless on landing; cf. Amunátegui y McKenna, op. cit., p. 147 ff.

35 Collier and Feliú Cruz, op. cit., p. 233 ff.; Amunátegui y McKenna, op. cit., p. 147 ff. Authors vary as to the character and amount of Skinner's loan. About 60 volunteers accompanied Carrera, Collier and Feliú Cruz, op. cit., p. 245.

36 Manning, Diplomatic Correspondence, I, 349, Halsey to Monroe, March 3, 1817; Carrera to H. Didier, Dec. 12, 1817, MP. LC.

37 For an example of this effect see an article attacking Pueyrredon in the Baltimore Patriot, May 29, 1817, quoted by Pelliza, Dorrego, p. 460; New York National Advocate, July 25, 1817.

Against this considerable group of propagandists Onís, aided only by his legation staff and a few outsiders like the turncoat Alvarez de Toledo, was able to do comparatively little. His influence principally affected wealthy and socially prominent groups in Philadelphia, his residence. Something was accomplished in other ports by the Spanish consuls of whom Morphy (Murphy?) at New Orleans and Bernabeu at Baltimore were the most active. Onís with the aid of his secretary, José de Heredia, wrote a series of pamphlets under the pseudonym " Verus " in which he defended the Spanish contentions in the current diplomatic dispute with the United States and tried to overcome American prejudice against his country.[38] He asked for funds to support a writer of newspaper articles and to buy newspaper space, but he was unsuccessful, for the depleted Spanish treasury kept minister, staff, and consular officers continually in arrears of salary.[39]

The cumulative result of all these controversial writings and verbal or personal propaganda efforts must not be underestimated in seeking an explanation for the public stir in the United States during 1817 and 1818 on the question of recognition of the rebels. The change in public opinion was marked. Niles, who had complained in 1815 of the lukewarmness of the public, was able to say a year later that the people of the United States

38 On Spanish propaganda efforts see Onís to Bardaxí, Jan. 10, 1812, AHN., Est. Leg. 5638 re a pamphlet written against the Mexican filibusters in Texas. The *Aurora* of Philadelphia, Jan. 8, 1812 contains reference to a monthly publication edited by Cabral Noronha, a writer in Onís' pay. For Onís' attempts to get funds for propaganda see Onís to Cevallos, Feb. 3, 1816, AHN., Est. Leg. 5641, *id.* to *id.*, Oct. 8, 1816, *ibid.*, Onís to Pizarro, Feb. 21, 1817, AHN., Est. Leg. 5642. On Onís' attempts to influence public opinion on privateering see his letter to Pizarro, Nov. 23, 1818, AHN., Est. 5643. Onís' pamphlets signed Verus are to be found filed with his despatches for 1817 and 1818, AHN., Est. Leg. 5643, 5643, 5660. One is also published in Spanish in the appendix of his *Memoria* . . . (Madrid, 1820), Onís failed to secure propaganda funds but Spain was less chary in dealing with British opinion. See instructions from San Fernando to San Carlos, Oct. 30, 1819, AGS., Est. Leg. 8294 (2676 Moderno).

39 Onís to Cevallos, Feb. 3, 1816, AHN., Est. Leg. 5641.

generally were "heartily devoted to the success of the patriots."[40] The following lucubration of a writer in the *American Monthly Magazine* may be taken as an illustration of a widespread attitude. In a review of Palacio Fajardo's *Outline* the author states:

The subject of our discussions is . . . the approaching liberation of millions, starting from the long and heavy sleep of a slavery that threatened to be immortal; the speedy expulsion of every hostile foreign foot from the great western world; the establishment throughout its regions of a pure and rational liberty; the progress of civilization, arts, commerce, refinement; the desert itself bursting forth into bloom and verdure . . . the new and glorious lights in which the character and capabilities of man will shine out in the consequence of this momentous revolution; . . . are all combined in one grand tableau.[41]

The pages of the daily press, the reviews, and the *Annals of Congress* contain numerous similar expressions of faith in a new era of progress, freedom and liberty following the liberation of Spanish America from Bourbon rule.[42]

Much of this enthusiasm was superficial. The insurgent agents in the United States occasionally bewailed the public indifference as loudly as Onís proclaimed the strength of its sympathy for the rebels.[43] One commented that despite general pop-

40 *Niles' Weekly Register*, Nov. 4, 1815 and July 20, 1816.

41 *American Monthly Magazine*, 1818, vol. iii, 254 ff.

42 For categorical statements on the strength of opinion in favor of the insurgents during the period 1816 to 1819, see: Bagot to Castlereagh, July 4, 1816, PRO, FO-5, vol. 114; Onís to Cevallos, Jan. 15, 1816, AHN., Est. Leg. 5641; Onís to Pizarro, No. 5, Jan., 1818, AHN., Est. Leg. 5643; J. S. Skinner to Monroe, Jan. 13, 1817, MP. LC (Johnson Collection); Ford, *Jefferson*, X, 90, Jefferson to Gallatin, June 16, 1817; C. Hughes to Monroe, Mar. 14, 1816, DS., Special Agents, vol. iv; Brackenridge, *op. cit.*, p. 58; *Blackwood's Magazine*, Oct., 1817; *Analectic Magazine*, vol. xi, 21 (1818); M. Pelliza, *Dorrego*, p. 432 appendix, Dorrego to Gonzalez Balcarce, May 19, 1817; Hyde de Neuville, *Mémoires et souvenirs*, II, 203, 205.

43 Palomeque, *Orijenes de la diplomacia arjentina* (Buenos Aires, 1905), I, 47, Aguirre to J. Q. Adams; Collier and Feliú Cruz, *op. cit.*, pp. 195-6; P. Gual to William Thornton, Nov. 2, 1816, Thornton Papers, L. C.

ular support for the cause he was unable to borrow money for his personal expenses.[44] Even among sympathizers doubt was occasionally expressed as to the ability of the Spanish Americans to govern themselves,[45] and this feeling increased as news of factional disputes among the patriots reached the American press.[46] This undertone of less optimistic opinion increased in volume as the attempts of the rebel enthusiasts to entangle the United States in the Spanish American struggle gathered strength.

The expression of opinion on Spanish American affairs in Congress was at least in part a result of the propaganda which has been described above. Beginning in an insignificant way in 1816, it grew in volume and intensity until in 1818 an attempt was made to force recognition of the insurgent governments on the executive. This movement in Congress had an importance beyond its immediate sphere, for at that time the debates of Congress were reported more fully in proportion to the other types of news than at present. During the sessions a whole page or more of the small four and eight page newspapers of the day was devoted to Congressional debates. It is safe to surmise that many Americans first had the subject of Spanish American independence brought to their attention by the Congressional agitation.

Since the early sympathy for the insurgents expressed before the war of 1812 [47] there had been no discussion of Spanish

44 F. J. Urrutia, *Los Estados Unidos de America y las repúblicas hispanoamericanas de 1810 á 1830, páginas de historia diplomática* (Madrid, 1918), p. 155, Lino de Clemente to Secretary of Foreign Relations of Venezuela, Dec. 27, 1818.

45 *Columbian Museum and Savannah Gazette*, Feb. 19, 1817, *North American Review*, V, 226 ff (1817) ; *Niles' Weekly Register*, X, 199; Manning, *Diplomatic Correspondence*, I, 39, Poinsett to Monroe, May 23, 1817; Ford, *Jefferson*, X, 84.

46 Collier and Feliú Cruz, *op. cit.*, p. 195 f., see also pp. 128, *supra* and 247 ff., *infra.*

47 See pp. 46 ff., *supra.*

American independence in Congress until 1816.[48] In January of that year, during a speech on the direct tax and the state of the Union, Clay took up the subject. He did not then suggest any immediate action, but, he declared, it was impossible " not to see that in the progress of things we might be called upon to decide the question whether we would or would not lend them [the rebels] our aid." [49] Onís was much disturbed by Clay's attitude at this time [50] but the public was not yet fully aroused, and John Randolph ridiculed Clay's enthusiasm as a fever recently acquired in Europe, a bellicose spirit out of place in the United States.[51]

The fact that Clay began his public advocacy of the insurgent cause as early as 1816 seems to indicate that John Quincy Adams' interpretation of Clay's policy, as motivated by a spirit of factious opposition to the Monroe administration and to himself, in particular,[52] can hardly be maintained, for at this time Clay had not yet been disappointed by his failure to receive the office of secretary of state. This does not, of course, preclude the possibility that the motive suggested by Adams may have played a part after the spring of 1817, but it can hardly have been the principal one. Though Clay's advocacy of immediate recognition of the rebels came in 1818, it was a natural consequence of his earlier views in favor of the rebels.

48 Except for an incidental expression of interest by Clay, see *Annals of Congress,* 12 Cong., 2 Sess., HR., p. 663, Jan. 8, 1813. I am indebted to Prof. Van Deusen of the University of Rochester for this example of Clay's early interest.

49 *Works of Henry Clay, Comprising his Life, Correspondence and Speeches,* ed. by C. Colton (New York and London, 1904), VI, 96.

50 Onís to Cevallos, Jan. 28, 1816, AHN., Est. Leg. 5641.

51 *Annals of Congress,* XXIX, 14 Cong., 1 Sess., HR., 718.

52 Adams, *Memoirs,* Mar. 18, 1818, IV, 62-3.

53 It is to be noted that as late as January, 1817 Clay did not foresee the part he was to play in this controversy, for he then declared that nothing of importance would be touched upon in the current session of Congress. Clay to Thomas Bodley, Jan. 4, 1817, Clay Papers, LC.

Though Clay was the center of the Congressional agitation on this subject from 1816 to 1821, the part he played has been overestimated, perhaps because of Clay's outstanding personality and the importance of his career in American politics. The interest of the country in the cause Clay championed was clear before he took up the cudgels for it. It could not have been stimulated by one man, not even by the greatest orator of the day. The exact balance of motives which led Clay to take the lead remains hidden. It is enough to realize that he saw enthusiasm for the rebel cause growing throughout the country and that the subject was one which offered great possibilities for the use of his oratorical gift. It was in the West, furthermore, among Clay's own constituents that the greatest feeling of interest in the patriot cause was to be found.[54]

In 1817 during the discussion of the Neutrality Bill in the House many Congressmen, not all of whom were followers of Clay, expressed their desire to see the rebel cause succeed. Even those who supported the administration's neutrality measures were quick to proclaim their friendly feeling for the rebels. Indeed the debate wandered far from the question at issue, and led to opinions for or against the insurgents. Sharp of Kentucky wondered how his colleagues could be " the spectators of a struggle for liberty and independence by any portion of the human family and feel indifferent as to the result." [55] Clay and others who spoke against the bill expressed sympathy for the patriots and animosity toward Spain in which anti-Catholic feeling was mixed with objections to the Spanish system of government and the Spanish policy toward the United States.[56]

54 For Kentucky sentiment, see, *Niles' Weekly Register*, XIII, 371, XIV, 295. It was not limited to the West, however. Some years later a supporter of Clay writing from Pennsylvania stated that one of the reasons that sentiment in that region supported Clay for the presidency was his South American policy. C. Minor to Clay, Nov. 16, 1822, Clay Papers, LC. Other evidence has been given in the text, *supra*, p. 124.

55 *New York Evening Post*, Jan. 30, 1817.

56 *Annals of Congress*, XXX, 14 Cong., 2 Sess., HR., 715 f., 730, 734, 736.

On the other hand John Randolph objected to linking such unrelated matters and ridiculed the "visionary idea" that "the struggle in question was one for the right of self government." [57] Sheffey of Virginia protested against the emotional support of the insurgent cause and gloomily predicted that in South America there would be "strife and bloodshed of long duration . . . which will settle down in a despotism perhaps more dark than has heretofore prevailed there." [58]

In December, 1817, Clay and others attacked [59] the president's message in which the decision to occupy Amelia Island and Galveston was announced,[60] at the same time that Onís was protesting from entirely different motives.[61] The issue of recognition was formally broached in March, 1818. Early in that month Clay declared his intention of bringing the South American question before the House. His first attempt was to provide for recognition of status that would give the patriots all the benefits of an acknowledged independence in the courts of the United States.[62] When this proposal was tabled, he turned to the apropriation bill to which he proposed an amendment calling for eighteen thousand dollars for expenses and salary of a minister to the United Provinces of Rio de la Plata.[63] One of the Kentuckian's speeches in the course of the debate on this motion has been considered his greatest oratorical effort up to that time. Clay lost no opportunity in the course of this speech to attack Spain in the most abusive language; to criticize its colonial system and its policy toward the United States at the same time that he lauded the rebels. Nothing indicates more clearly than this the close connection between the Spanish boundary dispute and the so-called South American question.

---

57 *Ibid.*, p. 731. 58 *Ibid.*, p. 735 f.

59 *Ibid.*, XXXI, 15 Cong., 1 Sess., HR., 401-415, *passim*.

60 Richardson, *op. cit.*, II, 13-14.

61 Onís to Adams, December 6, 1817, AHN., Est. Leg. 5660.

62 J. Forsyth to N. Biddle, March 20, 1818, Biddle Papers, LC.

63 *Annals of Congress*, XXXII, 15th Cong., 1 Sess., pp. 1468-9.

In his peroration which expressed the spirit in which he wished the question to be considered Clay clearly voiced the doctrine of America for the Americans.

I have no hesitation in asserting my firm belief [he declared] that there is no question in the foreign policy of this country which has ever arisen, or which I can conceive of as ever arising, in the decision of which we have had or can have so much at stake. This interest concerns our politics, our commerce, our navigation. There can not be a doubt that Spanish America, once independent, whatever may be the form of the governments established in its several parts, these governments will be animated by an American feeling and guided by an American policy. They will obey the laws of the system of the new world, of which they will compose a part in contradistinction to that of Europe.[64]

This speech and others delivered in the course of the next few days excited deep interest. It is said that members of the House had themselves transported from sickbeds to the floor in order to vote on the resolutions.[65] All but one of the speakers declared their sympathy with the rebel cause,[66] but the resolution failed by a vote of 115 to 45. The only section of the country which gave a majority for the measure was the West.[67]

It may be significant that the supporters of the administration dwelt on the danger of European complications. Forsyth, one of Clay's opponents, declared that there was a " great gang " in the House who were ready to help Clay but " trembled

64 *Works of Henry Clay*, ed. by Colton, VI, 136.

65 F. L. Paxson, *The Independence of the South American Republics, a Study in Recognition and Foreign Policy* (Philadelphia, 1916), p. 134. If interest was extraordinary on this occasion it must have been equally so a year earlier when the vote on the Neutrality Bill totalled 154 or only 6 less than on this occasion. See p. 117, *supra*.

66 *Works of Henry Clay*, ed. by Colton, VI, 165.

67 *Abridgement of the Debates of Congress*, ed. by Benton, VI, 170. The vote of the sections was as follows: *Yeas*: New England 5, Middle Atlantic 16, South Atlantic 9, West 15; *Nays*: New England 31, Middle Atlantic 33, South Atlantic 41, West 8, Unaccounted for 2.

in their shoes at the mere mention of a war with Spain." [68]
Another reason for Clay's failure may have been his attack on
the Florida policy of the administration. Many Southerners
who were friendly to the South American cause were alienated
by Clay's lukewarmness toward the acquisition of that territory and his support of the Amelia Island adventurers. [69]

Meanwhile the policy of Monroe's government, like that of
Madison, had been to maintain an official neutrality and at the
same time to try to convince the Spanish American rebels that
the United States viewed their cause with sympathy. So close
was the continuity between the two administrations that no
distinction can be made between their policy on this phase of
foreign affairs. Of Monroe's personal feeling of cordiality
toward the insurgents there can be no doubt. In 1815 he could
already say:

They insist on the acknowledgement of their governments by
the United States, and when it is considered that the alternative
is between governments which, in the event of their independence
would be free and friendly, and the relation which, reasoning
from the past, must be expected from them, as colonies, there is
no cause to doubt in which scale our interest lies. [70]

In the spring of 1817 he spoke of the progress of the revolution in the Spanish provinces " always interesting to the United
States, and now much more so because of a well founded hope
that it will succeed ". [71]

As for the members of Monroe's cabinet, they seem to have
agreed with the President's views with the exception of Adams,
who had a line of thought of his own. When he assumed charge
of the State Department he was inclined to favor strict neutral-

68 J. Forsyth to N. Biddle, Mar. 20, 1818, Biddle Papers, LC., vol. v.

69 *Idem* to *idem*, Mar. 27, 1818, *ibid.*

70 Monroe to J. Q. Adams, Dec. 10, 1815, DS., Instructions to Ministers,
vol. viii.

71 Manning, *Diplomatic Correspondence*, I, 39, Monroe to Poinsett, April
25, 1817.

ity, not only because it was expedient in view of the danger of European intervention, but also because he believed that such a policy was in itself best suited to the interests of the country. Furthermore, he did not disregard the moral and legal aspects of the problem. " Who, in this case of a civil war; [he asked] has constituted us the judges, which of the parties has the righteous cause? " Adams' critical outlook prevented him from falling into that indiscriminate enthusiasm for the insurgents which affected so many of his contemporaries.[72]

The maintenance of this cautious policy did not lead the administration to neglect the cultivation of the good will of the rebel governments. Though formal recognition was withheld, a series of semi-official agents were sent to South America. None of the agents despatched in 1810 remained at their posts after the close of the war with Great Britain. Poinsett had been forced to leave Chile in 1814. Lowry and Scott had both left Venezuela not long after the collapse of the patriot cause there in 1812; Shaler, as we have seen, was never able to reach his destination at Vera Cruz.[73] To replace these men various appointments were made. To Buenos Aires a Providence merchant, Thomas Lloyd Halsey, was sent as consul. He was despatched in 1812, but owing to the war he did not take up his duties until 1815.[74] In 1816 Joseph Devereux, a merchant planning a trip to South America, was requested to inform the government of the conditions he encountered.[75] A few months later J. Lewis was given a consular appointment to the

72 The quotation is taken from Adams to A. H. Everett, Dec. 29, 1817, in the *American Historical Review*, XI, 113, see also Adams to Erving, June 10, 1816, in *Writings of John Quincy Adams*, ed. by W. C. Ford (New York, 1913-1917), VI, 45.

73 See chapter I, *supra*.

74 Halsey to Monroe, Oct. 21, 1812 acknowledges his appointment. His despatches from Buenos Aires begin in 1815. DS. Consular Letters, Buenos Aires, vol. i, part i.

75 Monroe to J. Devereux, Jan. 12, 1816, DS., Despatches to Consuls, vol. i.

" Spanish Main " with permission to proceed to Chile and Peru if he found business insufficient to warrant his stay in the former area. Lewis, however, never went further than the West Indies.[76] These men, who, it will be noted, were all engaged in trade, were not expected to do more than report on conditions and to look out for the interests of American merchants and seamen. Though they held commissions similar to those issued to Poinsett and Lowry in 1810, their instructions did not authorize them to deal with political or diplomatic matters.

In 1817 W. G. D. Worthington was appointed special agent for Buenos Aires, Chile, and Peru, a wider field than that given to previous agents. Essentially, however, his duties were to be similar to theirs and were limited to representation of commercial interests and making reports. He was given no authority to negotiate.[77]

Meanwhile Monroe's inclination toward the insurgents and the mounting interest in their cause in the United States led him to contemplate a more formal mission to South America. There was much difficulty in organizing the commission. Poinsett was approached in May, 1817, but he declined to serve [78] and only in July were John Graham and Caesar A. Rodney chosen for the position.[79] They were to be accompanied by J. B. Prevost who was selected to serve as resident agent in Buenos Aires, Chile, and Peru and given authority over Halsey and Worthington.[80] The sudden illness and death of Rodney's son and the absence of the President from Washington on his tour of the country forced a postponement of the Commission's

76 Monroe to J. Lewis, DS., Special Agents, vol. iv, June 12, 1816.

77 H. M. Wriston, *Executive Agents*, p. 415; Worthington to J. Q. Adams, May 27, 1817, DS., Argentine Republic, W. G. D. Worthington, Special Agent, vol. i, part 1.

78 Poinsett to Monroe, May 7, 1817, MP. LC.

79 Rodney to Rush, July 13, 1817; Graham to Rush, August 7, 1817, DS., South American Commission, 1817-1818.

80 Rush to Prevost, July 18, July 24, 1817, DS., Despatches to Consuls, vol. ii; Wriston, *op. cit.*, p. 419.

departure.[81] In September it was decided to send Prevost ahead, charging him with the additional duty of taking possession for the United States of the establishment at Astoria at the mouth of the Columbia River, which according to the treaty of Ghent was to be returned by the British. Prevost sailed for the Pacific in October with orders to touch at Chile and Peru *en route* for the Northwest Coast and to remain in South America after accomplishing his other mission.[82]

The delay in the departure of the commission gave Monroe time for further thought during which he felt some misgivings as to the advisability of sending the Commission. Since the President's decision in May, John Quincy Adams had arrived to take over the State Department. In October the President gave his new secretary an opportunity to express his views in a cabinet meeting which took up the whole complex of problems presented by Spain and Spanish America. The following questions were submitted for discussion:

Has the executive power to acknowledge the independence of the new states whose independence is not recognized by the parent country and between which parties war exists?

Is sending a minister equal to recognition?

Is it expedient for the United States to recognize Buenos Aires or other revolted province?

What ought to be the future conduct of the U. States towards Spain, considering the evasion practised by her government and amounting to a refusal to make reparation for injuries?

Is it expedient to break up the Amelia Island establishment which is of a piratical and highly mischievous nature?

81 Graham to Rush, Aug. 7, 1817, DS., South American Commission, 1817-1818. The whole story of the commission's establishment is to be found in a series of letters from Rush to Monroe during the latter's absence from the capital, June 3, 4, 5, 11, 17, July 20, Aug. 24, 1817, MP. LC.

82 Adams to Prevost, Sept. 29, 1817, DS., Instructions to Ministers, vol. viii.

Is it expedient to act as was accorded in the previous May and suspended, i. e. to send a commission to South America to report on the progress of the revolution and the probability of its success? [83]

The last two questions were decided in the affirmative as the steps taken subsequently indicate. As to the right of the executive to recognize the new states, we may be sure that Adams took an affirmative view in the light of his other statements upholding the powers of the executive and claiming for it the sole conduct of foreign affairs, except where definitely limited by the Constitution. His opinion against immediate recognition, however, was agreed to by the cabinet.[84] It also appears that a more cautious policy towards Spain was decided upon at this time. Bagot [85] noticed a few days later what he considered a surprising change in the language used by the *National Intelligencer* on Spanish affairs. It now deplored aid to the rebels by United States citizens and argued against recognition of their governments.[86]

It is probable that the attitude of the European powers had a good deal to do with the moderate attitude of the administration. Adams was convinced of the hostility of the powers and of the consequent need for caution.[87] The message to Congress which was delivered soon after the cabinet meeting achieved a compromise on Spanish affairs; it stressed the neutrality of the United States and mentioned damages suffered from both contestants; it went on to relate events at Galveston and Amelia Island and the decision of the administration to suppress these establishments; and it announced the appointment of a commis-

83 Paraphrased from Memo., Oct., 1817, MP. LC.

84 Adams, *Memoirs*, IV, 15, October 30, 1817; *cf. ibid.*, 204-206.

85 *National Intelligencer*, October 30, 1817.

86 Bagot to Castlereagh, Nov. 6, 1817, PRO, FO-5, vol. 123.

87 *Writings of John Quincy Adams*, ed. by W. C. Ford (New York, 1913-1917), Adams to Erving, June 10, 1816; see also Manning, *Diplomatic Correspondence*, I, 56-7, Adams to B. Irvine, Jan. 31, 1818.

sion to South America to seek authoritative information.[88] As Monroe put it in a letter to a friend, the idea was " to elevate South America as high as we could without a compromitment with the allied powers who may probably or rather possibly, take the part of Spain. The pulse of the allied powers will be felt while the United States remain free to act." [89]

In December, when the South American commission finally sailed on the frigate *Congress,* it included, in addition to Rodney and Graham, Judge Theodoric Bland of Baltimore.[90] H. M. Brackenridge was attached as secretary.[91] From the composition of the body it was to be expected that the patriots were to be given the benefit of any doubt, for both commissioners and secretary had gone on record before their appointment as adherents of the rebel cause. Their instructions, however, stressed the fact that they were to consider themselves primarily a fact-finding body. They were to explain and justify the neutral policy of the United States as best suited to the interests of the patriots. Finally, they were to remonstrate with the Buenos Aires government against the indiscriminate issue of privateering licenses, and to ask disavowal of the proceedings of McGregor and Aury at Amelia Island.[92] Bland, who was particularly interested in Chile,[93] secured permission to proceed to that country if he should consider it advisable.

While the recognition movement was rising to its climax in Congress, the administration was faced with the critical negotiations with Spain. The close relation between the two ques-

88 Richardson, *Messages and Papers*, II, 13-14.

89 Monroe to ———(?), Dec. 2, 1817, MP. LC.

90 Manning, *Diplomatic Correspondence*, I, 46, Adams to Erving, Nov. 11, 1817.

91 Rush to Brackenridge, July 17, 1817, DS., Despatches to Consuls, vol. ii. Brackenridge to Rush, July 29, 1817, DS., South American Commission, 1817-1818.

92 Adams to the Commissioners, Nov. 21, 1817, Manning, *Diplomatic Correspondence*, I, 47; Monroe to Rodney, Nov. 20, 1817, Rodney Papers, LC.

93 Bland to Monroe, Nov. 15, 1817, MP. LC.

tions was obvious, but Monroe and Adams refused to consider them officially in that light in communications with Spain, though they were fully aware of the interrelation.[94] They knew that Spanish successes in the colonies would increase Spanish resistance in the pending negotiation [95] and they also knew that a departure from the neutral policy they had adopted would put an end to their hopes of a boundary settlement by negotiation. In dealing with the rebels, however, the administration was more frank. Adams instructed one of his agents to Bolívar's government that one reason for the reluctance of the United States to recognize the rebels was that Spanish negotiations tied the hands of the administration.[96]

These circumstances, and the cooling effect of Clay's criticism, reduced Monroe's ardor for the insurgents.[97] More important to the Secretary of State were reports from Europe of an intervention by the Allied powers in South American affairs. In February, 1818, Adams showed great cordiality towards Bagot, and mentioned his wish to act in concert with Great Britain in Spanish America, a procedure which would help the administration to withstand the pressure at home for immediate recognition of the rebels.[98]

The proposed mediation of the powers between Spain and the rebellious colonists was largely a product of the jealousy of the continental powers who felt that Great Britain alone was gaining benefit from the existing state of affairs. Early in 1817 the French minister in Washington had discussed with Richard

94 Adams to Erving, April 20, 1818, DS., Instructions to Ministers, vol. viii. At this time and others when relations with Spain were least hopeful Adams talked more freely than usual of probable recognition of the rebels.

95 Mannng, *Diplomatic Correspondence*, I, 29, Monroe to Gallatin, April 15, 1816.

96 Adams to B. Irvine, Jan. 31, 1818, *ibid.*, I, 567.

97 Adams, *Memoirs*, IV, 71.

98 *Correspondence, Despatches and Other Papers of Viscount Castlereagh*, ed. by C. Vane (London, 1850-1853), XI, 404 Bagot to Castlereagh, Feb. 8, 1818. It was at this time also that Adams was so careful to refuse the British offer of mediation between the United States and Spain with so much moderation and in such a friendly manner. See chap. iii, *supra.*

Rush the possibility of a mediation between Spain and the rebels to be undertaken by the United States and France, excluding Great Britain.[99] Later in the year, chiefly through the initiative of General Pozzo di Borgo, the Tsar's representative in Paris, Alexander began to take an interest in general European mediation between Spain and the Colonies.[100] A memorandum was issued at St. Petersburg in November, 1817 in which a plan of action was suggested.[101] This was by no means a scheme for blind support of the Spanish claims. Portugal and Spain, then embroiled over the possession of Montevideo in South America and Olivenza in the Peninsula, were first to be brought to an agreement with the aid of the allied council of ambassadors at Paris. Subsequently, liberal terms, allowing a measure of local autonomy and freedom of trade with foreign nations, were to be offered to the rebellious colonists of Spain with the prestige of all the powers behind the scheme. If this were not enough to bring the rebels back to their old allegiance, a boycott was suggested.

This attempt at compromise was a failure, for only Britain had any substantial trade with the revolted regions, and she would pay the penalty in the event of such a boycott. The British cabinet held that force should under no circumstances be used against the rebels, and that the Allies should not guaranty the success of the proposed move as Spain insisted.[102] Castlereagh was able to secure the support of Hardenburg and of Metternich on this point[103] and mediation consequently made no progress.

99 Rush to Monroe, April 24, 1817, MP. LC.

100 Dexter Perkins, "Russia and the Spanish Colonies" in AHR., XXVIII, 658. It was Pozzo who secured from the Spanish government a hint that mediation would be welcome. See Fernan-Nuñez to Pozzo quoted by Perkins, *op. cit.*, p. 660.

101 Russian Memorandum, Nov. 17, 1817, MP. NYP. also printed in Manning, *Diplomatic Correspondence*, III, 1853.

102 D. Perkins, *op. cit.* in AHR., XXVIII, 661.

103 *Correspondence . . . of Viscount Castlereagh*, XI, 385-7. Hardenburg to Alopeus, Nov. 22, 1817. Perkins, *op. cit.*, p. 664 f.; W. P. Cresson, *The Holy Alliance* (New York, 1922), p. 65.

Monroe, though he saw the Russian memorandum of November, was not well informed of the subsequent course of this affair.[104] The Spanish court attempted to spread the impression that it was progressing satisfactorily,[105] and the British government, through Bagot, gave Adams to understand that something was being done.[106] There was good reason, therefore, in the light of information at hand, for the United States to proceed cautiously with regard to the patriots of South America. The President was at first favorably disposed toward the idea of American participation in joint intervention, but he soon rejected the idea because, as he put it, the powers favored a compromise whereas the United States favored total independence of the colonies.[107]

If, from the point of view of Spain and the European powers, the United States seemed hand in glove with the Spanish American rebels, the agents of the new governments in the United States received quite a different impression. The envoys from Buenos Aires, especially, found their activities circumscribed. In 1816, after some years without any representatives in the United States, that government gave a commission to Martin Thompson, a naturalized citizen, as consul-general in the United States.[108] He proved an unsuitable choice, exceeding his instructions, talking too freely, and running into difficulties

104 He had reports from Gallatin at Paris and Erving at Madrid but it was not sufficiently definite information to use as a basis for policy. *Writings of Albert Gallatin*, ed. by Henry Adams (Phila., 1879), II, 63, Crawford to Gallatin, May 1, 1818; Gallatin to Monroe, July 18, 1817, MP. LC.; Manning, *Diplomatic Correspondence*, III, 1957, Erving to Adams, Jan. 10, 1818. As late as the following May Adams complained that he was not properly informed, *ibid.*, I, 66 ff., Adams to Rush, May 20, 1818.

105 Pizarro to Fernan-Nuñez and San Carlos, Feb. 16, 1818, AHN., Est. Leg. 5643 (draft unsigned).

106 Adams, *Memoirs*, IV, 49, Jan. 27, 1818; see also, Adams to Gallatin, May 19, and to Rush, May 20, 1818, DS., Instructions to Ministers, vol. viii.

107 Adams, *Memoirs*, IV, 72, Mar. 30, 1818.

108 Ignacio Álvarez to the President of the U. S., Jan. 16, 1816, DS., Argentine Republic, Notes, vol. i.

in consequence from Spanish agents who made his life miserable. He was soon after removed from office on account of his indiscretion.[109] A special agent was next despatched to the United States to secure a fleet of armed ships for the governments of Chile and Buenos Aires.[110] It was hoped that this envoy, Manuel Hermengildo de Aguirre, would be able to secure a loan in the United States to cover the cost of the six corvettes of from 25 to 30 guns needed to wrest the command of the South Pacific from the royalists. Aguirre also brought with him twenty-five letters of marque and seventy-five licenses for prize captains with which to bolster the Baltimore privateering business.[111] Though his errand was primarily commercial, he was invested somewhat vaguely by his commission with " diplomatic character ".

Aguirre ran into difficulty soon after his arrival. Funds promised by the Chilean government failed to arrive; he found the credit of the patriot governments at a low ebb and he was soon at his wits' end.[112] Nor were his troubles purely financial. He found that the new neutrality legislation had plenty of teeth and would probably prevent the fulfilment of his mission. An interview with Rush during the latter's incumbency at the State Department somewhat reassured the South American. He seems to have gathered more from Rush's personally friendly attitude than was justified,[113] at least Rush subse-

109 J. M. de Pueyrredon to President of the U. S., Jan. 10, 1817, *ibid.*

110 Commission of Aguirre, April 28, 1817, *ibid.*

111 Matias de Irigoyen to San Martín, April 30, 1817 in *Archivo de San Martín*, VIII, 184. Before sending Aguirre to the U. S. an unsuccessful attempt had been made to secure the ships through óne George Green in Buenos Aires, *ibid.*

112 *Documentos del archivo de San Martín*, VIII, 188, Aguirre to the Supreme Director of Chile, July 30, 1817.

113 *Ibid.*, VIII, 206, Aguirre to the Supreme Director of Rio de la Plata, *ibid.*, IV, 533-5, Pueyrredon to San Martín, Nov. 24, 1817, Palomeque, *Oríjenes de la diplomacia arjentina*, I, 214, Memo. of a conversation between Aguirre and Rush, Nov. 22, 1817. Aguirre also declared that he was encouraged by Monroe, Palomeque, *op. cit.*, I, 42.

quently claimed that Aguirre's poor command of English must have led him into error.[114]

After unsuccessful negotiation with Messrs. Darcy and Didier of Baltimore, the firm, which had aided Carrera's venture, Aguirre finally signed a contract with New York builders for three ships at a cost of $80,000 each.[115] Two ships were built, but at this point the Buenos Ayrean was arrested and tried for violation of the Neutrality Act. He was acquitted because no proof was presented to show that his ships had been armed,[116] but the delay caused by the trial so strained Aguirre's finances that he despaired of being able to clear the vessels. He wrote to Adams complaining of the unfair working of the Neutrality Act and proposed to sell the vessels, for which he had contracted, to the United States.[117] Monroe, much worried by this episode, which he feared might unfavorably affect public opinion in Buenos Aires, prevailed on Adams to soften the language of his reply to the South American.[118]

These difficulties were increased by Aguirre's demand for formal recognition of his government. Adams evaded the main issue and based his refusal on the envoy's lack of adequate credentials. He also asked embarrassing questions as to the exact nature and territorial extent of the sovereignty claimed by the United Provinces.[119] In spite of these official rebuffs, Aguirre was lionized by Washington society and created quite

114 Rush to Monroe, Nov. 22, 1817, MP. LC., cf. Adams, *Memoirs*, IV, 21. See also Remarks of R. Rush on Aguirre's letter of Nov. 14, 1817, both in DS., Argentine Republic, Notes, vol. i.

115 Manning, *Diplomatic Correspondence*, III, 1971 ff.

116 *New York Evening Post*, July 29, 1818.

117 Aguirre to Adams, Aug. 10, 1818, DS., Argentine Republic, Notes, vol. i.

118 Monroe to Adams, August 17, 1818, August 27, 1818, MP. LC. Adams refused the offer, but Aguirre was finally able to leave with his two ships unarmed (but with cannon stowed in the hold).

119 Manning, *Diplomatic Correspondence*, I, 59, Adams to Monroe, March 25, 1818, explains Adams' stand.

a problem for Onís, who was unwilling to appear where he might meet the rebel agent. His unofficial reception would have been still warmer had it not been for the exiled group from Buenos Aires which had sown seeds of doubt as to the republicanism and love of liberty of the Pueyrredon government.

During and after this episode still other complications arose. Perhaps with a hope of securing a more sympathetic reception, Pueyrredon commissioned an American, General W. H. Winder of Baltimore, as agent of Buenos Aires in the United States.[120] This gentleman consulted Monroe as to whether he should accept the office and was dissuaded from doing so.[121] The appointment of David C. De Forest, another naturalized citizen of the United Provinces, to the less pretentious post of consul-general was almost as unsuccessful.[122] De Forest came to the United States and formally requested recognition as consul-general, but he was refused on grounds similar to those given Aguirre a few months earlier.[123]

Simultaneous with these developments was a dispute between certain other rebel agents and the United States in connection with the Amelia Island episode. As announced in Monroe's message of December, 1817, the armed forces of the United States had driven out Aury and his men from Fernandina. This action led to a protest signed by Vicente Pazos and a Venezuelan emissary, Lino de Clemente. The signers accused the administration of acting in an un-neutral and unfriendly

120 Pueyrredon to the Pres. of the Congress of the U. S., Feb. 25, 1818, DS., Argentine Republic, Notes, vol. i.

121 Winder to Monroe, July 23, 1818, MP. LC., Johnson Collection; Winder to Monroe, May 3, 1818; Monroe to Winder, May 11, 1818, ed. by M. Kenway, HAHR., XII (1932), 458-60.

122 Pueyrredon to the President of the U. S., May 5, 1818, DS., Argentine Republic, Notes, vol. i.

123 De Forest to Adams, Dec. 9, 1818, *ibid.* See also Adams' reply to De Forest, Manning, *Diplomatic Correspondence*, I, 82, Dec. 31, 1818; Adams, *Memoirs*, IV, 88-90; on De Forest's earlier career, see, Chandler, *Inter American Acquaintances*, p. 27.

way towards the rebels.[124] When McGregor set out on his Amelia adventure he had a commission signed by Pazos and Gual who presumed to act, though quite unauthorized, on behalf of the " Independent Governments of Spanish America ". Pazos, the pamphleteer exile, and Gual, whose official status had long expired, had no connection with any existing patriot regime, but Lino de Clemente, a newly arrived agent from Bolívar's government, also signed the protest.[125] Adams was deeply incensed by these self-constituted backers of McGregor and Aury and refused to receive any communication from Clemente because of his implication in this affair. The unfortunate envoy was therefore obliged to return to Venezuela embittered against the United States government.[126]

The position of American agents in South America was of course very different from that of the men just mentioned. On all occasions they were welcomed, but their tasks were perhaps as difficult and they too were often in hot water. To Venezuela, in the spring of 1818, the United States sent Baptis Irvine, the journalist whose pro-patriot activities have been noted. He was to explain the American attitude towards the Amelia affair and to prosecute the claims of American citizens against Venezuela.[127] Irvine found that Bolívar knew little and cared less what happened at Amelia Island.[128] The " Liberator " was in-

---

124 Address of Don Vicente Pazos to the President of the United States, clipping from the *Washington City Gazette*, April, 1818. This protest was given much publicity and was supported by Clay in Congress and by others like Thornton (draft of letter from Pazos to Adams in Thornton's hand is in Thornton Papers, LC.). Pazos also memorialized Congress, but the House refused by a vote of 124 to 28 to consider it (Bagot to Castlereagh, April 7, 1818, PRO, FO-5, vol. 131). *Cf.* J. Forsyth to N. Biddle, Mar. 11, 1818, Biddle Papers, LC.

125 F. J. Urrutia, *op. cit.*, p. 146 ff.; R. Rivas, *op. cit.*, p. 9.

126 Lino de Clemente to Thornton, April 1, 1819, Thornton Papers, LC. For a good treatment of this episode see J. B. Lockey, *Pan-Americanism; Its Beginnings* (New York, 1920), pp. 188 ff.

127 Adams to Irvine, Jan. 31, 1818, DS., Despatches to Consuls, vol. ii.

128 Irvine to Adams, July 20, 1818, DS., Special Agents, vol. viii.

clined to magnify the significance of the arrival of the American agent and made quite a ceremony of his official reception.[129] The discovery of Irvine's informal commission somewhat dampened his enthusiasm, and when the American claims were broached Irvine soon found that he was not to have matters all his own way. These claims were for vessels captured by the naval forces of Venezuela under the command of Admiral Brion, who had declared a blockade of the coast. Bolívar's conception of neutral rights was very different from that of the United States. Though his principal argument was the existence of a legal blockade of the Orinoco, he also held that trade in munitions with a belligerent was a " belligerent act "[130] which justified confiscation. He made use of Cobbett's pamphlet on the American Neutrality Act to support his contention that the law was unfair and justified retaliatory action by Venezuela.[131] The correspondence between Irvine and Bolívar dragged on for months, becoming more and more acrimonious. Failing to agree on the facts in the case, the contestants deflected the argument into remote channels in which the South American had much the better of the matter, in spite of Irvine's strong original case. Nevertheless, in October Bolívar's patience gave way and he protested vehemently against Irvine's tone, remarking that " it is the same thing for Venezuela to fight Spain or the whole world if all the world attacks her ".[132] This war of words does not seem to have had serious consequences, for two months later Irvine was writing placidly to praise the new civil organization of the republic and to urge closer relations with the United States, which alone shared with Venezuela a govern-

129 *Cartas del Libertador*, V. Lecuna, ed. (Caracas, 1920-30), II, 33.

130 *Boletín de la Academia Nacional de Historia*, Caracas, vol. xvi (1933), Bolívar to Irvine, Aug. 6, 1818.

131 *Ibid.*, Bolívar to Irvine, Aug. 20, 1818. The original letters and Irvine's replies are in DS., Special Agents, vol. viii, see especially, July 29, Aug. 6, and Aug. 20.

132 *Boletín de la Academia Nacional de Historia*, Caracas, vol. xvi (1933), Bolívar to Irvine, Oct. 7, 1818, p. 212 ff.

ment based on right and not on feudal tradition or military violence. In lectures on the wickedness of the Holy Alliance Irvine brought his mission to an end, having failed to get any satisfaction for the spoliations of Brion.[133]

There was no anti-American sentiment in Venezuela at this time, but the almost excessive deference of the first republic of 1810-1812 had passed with the downfall of that government and its federal republican ideals. British influence was growing, encouraged by the stream of volunteers from Britain to Bolívar's army and the extension of credit to the patriots by British men of business.[134] The American Neutrality Act had created an undertone of resentment, but on the surface friendship for the United States was still the keynote.[135]

In Buenos Aires the attitude of the government towards the United States underwent wide fluctuation. After the close of the Anglo-American war the Buenos Aires government turned toward the United States with high expectations, which increased after the formal declaration of independence of the United Provinces at the Congress of Tucumán in 1816.[126] The efforts of consul Halsey contributed toward this result. He was on good terms with the government and carried on propaganda in favor of a constitution similar to that of the United States.[137] The atmosphere of good will was only partially damp-

133 *Memorias del General O'Leary*, publicadas por su hijo, Simón B. O'Leary (Caracas, 1879-1888), VIII, 344-5; B. Irvine to Bolívar, Dec. 10, 1818.

134 S. Forsyth to B. Irvine, Oct. 26, 1818; B. Irvine to Adams, Aug. 11, 1818, Oct. 21, 1819, DS., Special Agents, vol. viii.

135 Irvine to Adams, July 20, July 30, Aug. 11, 1818, also *Correo del Orinoco*, Oct. 10, 1818.

136 C. L. Chandler, *Inter-American Acquaintances* (Sewanee, Tenn., 1917), p. 63 quoting *Gaceta de Buenos Aires,* May 25, 1816. The declaration itself mentioned the example of the United States, see Palomeque, *op. cit.,* I, 28 and I, 197; *Documentos del archivo du Pueyrredon*, III, 264; *cf.* Robertson, in HAHR., I (1918), 245, which points out that the Congress favored a mission to the U. S. to seek munitions and formal recognition.

137 Halsey to Ignacio Álvarez, May 16, 1815, DS., Consular Letters, Buenos Aires, vol. i, part 1.

ened by Halsey's complaints against high duties on American goods and indirect encouragement of desertion from the American merchant marine.[138]

Juan Martín de Pueyrredon, the Supreme Director invested with executive power by the Congress of Tucumán, seemed at first to share the amicable sentiments of Álvarez, the previous ruler. At least he turned to the United States for aid, sending Aguirre to Washington, and negotiating for a $2,000,000 private loan with Devereux. Halsey implicated himself in this affair by witnessing the preliminary contract and incurred the wrath of his superiors in Washington by so doing.[139] Worthington was ordered to repudiate any connection between the United States government and such financial transactions, and though he found some disappointment when he made the announcement, he was able to report that sympathy for the United States was still strong in Buenos Aires.[140] This embarrassing incident was not entirely the fault of the American agents. Unsalaried merchants given commissions as consular agents were obviously not expected to give up private business. They were not always careful to distinguish between their private and public characters, and South American governments interpreted the acts of such agents in the way that would most deeply commit their home governments. The difficulty could have been avoided if the State Department had not employed men involved in business.[141]

As the year 1817 wore on, the high hopes of the Buenos Ayreans that their declaration of independence would bring

138 Halsey to Gregorio Tagle, July 31, 1815, Halsey to Monroe, Mar. 14, 1816, Halsey to Secretary of State, Mar. 3, 1817, *ibid.*

139 Pueyrredon to the President of the U. S., Jan. 31, 1817, DS., Argentine Republic, Notes, vol. i; Rush to Halsey, April 21, 1817, DS., Despatches to Consuls, vol. ii.

140 Worthington to Adams, Oct. 1, 1817, DS., Argentine Republic, W. G. D. Worthington, Special Agent, vol. i, part 1.

141 For Halsey's defense see Halsey to Rush, Nov. 21, 1817, DS., Consular Letters, Buenos Aires, vol. i, part 1.

recognition of their government by the United States gave way to disappointment and irritation,[142] which was aggravated by the news of the mishaps which had befallen Buenos Aires agents in the United States. An Argentine envoy recently returned from Europe declared that the North Americans, like the powers of Europe on the continent, were motivated by jealousy of Great Britain and that little or no aid was to be expected from them.[143] The writings of Pazos, Agrelo and others attacking the " Supreme Director " in the American press also annoyed Pueyrredon, and pamphlets were published in Buenos Aires to refute an article in a Baltimore paper.[144]

A minor crisis came in January, 1818. Halsey, whose popularity with the Buenos Aires authorities had waned considerably in the course of the previous year, was suddenly ordered to leave the country immediately, accused of conspiring with the Baltimore exiles to introduce anti-government propaganda into the city. The order was suspended through the conciliatory efforts of Worthington, but Pueyrredon had other grievances against Halsey. The consul had visited the headquarters of Artigas, Pueyrredon's enemy in control of the region now called Uruguay, and he was accused of furnishing him with munitions and of accepting privateering licenses issued by the " gaucho " chieftain.[145] Halsey's official career came to an end

142 Worthington to Adams, Oct. 4, 1817, Jan. 1, 1818, DS., W. G. D. Worthington, Special Agent, Argentine Republic, vol. i, part 1. See also Pueyrredon to the President of the United States, Jan. 14, 1818, DS., Argentine Republic, Notes, vol. i, see also copy of a letter from Buenos Aires enclosed with Biddle to Monroe, Jan. 11, 1818, MP. LC.

143 B. Mitre, *Historia de Belgrano*, II, 747 (appendix).

144 *Al Avisador Patriota y Mercantil de Baltimore, un ciudadano de Buenos Aires* (Buenos Aires, 1817) a series of three pamphlets dated September, 1817; *El Censor* (Buenos Aires), June 6, 1818; *Documentos del archivo de Pueyrredon*, IV, 147, letter to the editor of the *New York Columbian* (Irvine's paper).

145 Halsey to Adams, Jan. 10, 1818, Halsey to G. Tagle, Jan. 7, 1818, Tagle to Halsey, Jan. 8, 1818, DS., Consular Letters, Buenos Aires, vol. i, part 2.

soon after, his recall crossing Pueyrredon's request for his dismissal.[146]

Worthington proved himself an energetic supporter of American interests and a fervent apostle of American " Kultur ". He was also an adept at making himself agreeable, but he had traits which usually prove fatal in a diplomat: bad judgment together with a tendency to disregard his instructions. He took it upon himself to negotiate a commercial convention with Pueyrredon which included provisions for the mutual acceptance of consular officials, apparently not realizing that this was equivalent to recognition of independence. This treaty was immediately disavowed by Adams and added to the tension subsisting on other counts.[147]

The arrival of the U. S. Frigate *Congress* in February, 1818 with the much heralded commissioners, Rodney, Graham, and Bland reawakened the hopes of Pueyrredon, but he was disappointed to find that they were not invested with formal diplomatic character. This fact, the modest bearing of the commissioners who avoided ceremony and concentrated their efforts on fact-finding, and their short stay in Buenos Aires detracted from the importance of the commission in the eyes of the local authorities.[148]

In Chile the reaction against the United States since the exile of the Carreras was especially marked. Worthington and Prevost, who both arrived in that country in 1818, were well received, but reported that European influence was predomin-

146 Adams to Halsey, Jan. 22, 1818, DS., Despatches to Consuls, vol. ii, Halsey to Adams, August 21, 1818, Consular Letters, Buenos Aires, vol. i, part 2. Manning, *Diplomatic Correspondence*, I, 374 f. Pueyrredon to Monroe, Jan. 31, 1818.

147 Worthington to Adams, Jan. 1, 1818, DS., Argentine Republic, W. G. D. Worthington, Special Agent, vol. i, part 1; Adams, *Memoirs*, IV, 70, 158-159.

148 The Commissioners to Adams, May 28, 1818, DS., South American Commission, 1817-1818. The commission arrived at Buenos Aires, Feb. 28 and left April 24, 1818. For reports on their stay in the city, see Manning, *Diplomatic Correspondence*, I, 382 ff., 527.

ant.[149] Arrivals of American ships at Valparaiso became rare, while trade with Great Britain grew with rapidity.[150] Owing to Prevost's absence at the Columbia River, Worthington was the sole American agent in Chile throughout most of 1818. He kept himself busy here, as he had east of the *cordillera:* attempting to arrange a commercial convention, appointing vice consuls, offering a draft of a model constitution,[151] and attempting to protect American sailors from impressment and their masters from desertions.[152]

Worthington closed one of his reports with the following explanation of the Chilean attitude toward the United States:

It is difficult to make others believe if [the policy of the United States] is of so pure and lofty a character. You can not make these people believe, that altho' you may act with the most perfect neutrality towards them and Spain, such acting is not a lukewarm and inimical proceeding towards them.[153]

In Chile, as at Buenos Aires, a less democratic and more authoritarian type of leadership had come to the fore with the rise of men like San Martín, Pueyrredon and O'Higgins. Even without the incidents mentioned in this chapter it is likely that the constitutional monarchies of Europe would have displaced the United States in the sympathies of southern South Americans.

Owing to the uncertain and generally unfavorable fortune of the Mexican Revolution after 1814, the contacts of its lead-

149 Manning, *Diplomatic Correspondence*, II, 932, Worthington to Adams, July 4, 1818.

150 Manning, *Diplomatic Correspondence*, II, 941, Worthington to Adams, Oct. 22, 1818.

151 Worthington to José Irrisarri, Mar. 2, June 20, 1818, DS., Argentine Republic, W. G. D. Worthington, Special Agent, vol. i, part 1; Worthington to M. Zanartú, Mar. 2, 1818, *ibid.*; Worthington to O'Higgins, May 5, 1818, *ibid.*

152 Worthington to the Supreme Director, Santiago, April 21, 1818, *ibid.*

153 Manning, *Diplomatic Correspondence*, II, 941, Worthington to Adams, Oct. 22, 1818.

ers with the United States government were negligible. This
did not mean, however, that continued efforts were not made to
secure aid from the north. As early as the summer of 1814 the
Mexican Congress whose hopes were aroused by the arrival on
the Gulf coast of one General Humbert, a Frenchman who
was falsely reputed a United States agent, sent Juan Pablo
Anaya to New Orleans, hoping that a loan might be floated in
the United States. Anaya met Álvarez de Toledo and collaborated with him in his Texas schemes, but he accomplished
little, partly because his efforts were discovered and hampered
by the Spanish consul. The Congress had intended sending
Anaya a diplomatic commission and instructions, but this purpose was frustrated by the jealousy of a leader who failed to
forward these documents.[154]

In 1815, Toledo, who saw his earlier plans frustrated, led
the Mexican leaders, among them Morelos, to believe that aid
for Mexico could then be easily secured in the United States.
In response to these suggestions José Manuel de Herrera was
appointed minister to the United States, leaving Mexico in
August, 1815 for Louisiana. A letter forwarded to the State
Department from New Orleans was the sole official act of his
diplomacy, but he was active in securing supplies and in aiding
the cohorts of Aury in Texas. Herrera returned to Mexico in
1816 with large plans for the future. In the meantime, Morelos
had been captured and executed, and Teran, who continued the
struggle, distrusted Herrera and refused to give him further
countenance. His suspicion seems to have been justified, for
Herrera soon made his peace with the royalist authorities and
only reappears in Mexican history in 1821, when he served the
government of Iturbide.[155]

154 H. H. Bancroft, *History of Mexico*, IV, 605-606; Riva Palacio, *op. cit.,*
III, 433; Fabela, *op. cit.*, pp. 72-73; quoting Hernández y Dávalos, *Colección
de documentos*, VI, 43; Alamán, *op. cit.*, IV, appendix.

155 Bancroft, *op. cit.*, IV, 606; Fabela, *op. cit.*, p. 42 f.; Riva Palacio,
op. cit., III, 524.

This was to be the last effort at Mexican-American cooperation during the struggle for independence. It will be noted that
though the agents who reached New Orleans were encouraged
by the atmosphere they encountered there, they were not
strongly supported by their leaders in Mexico. This was partly
due, of course, to inability to act on account of military reverses,
but it also suggests that these leaders were not deeply impressed
with the friendliness of the United States, nor convinced of the
value to their cause of filibustering in Texas and Aury's privateers as were their agents.

In the United States, though public opinion was almost universally friendly to the patriots during these years, there was a
division of opinion as to the policy to be adopted toward their
governments. A few newspapers took up Clay's advocacy of
recognition,[156] reinforcing the pioneers in the movement such
as the *Aurora* and the *Richmond Enquirer*. Following Brackenridge's lead, a writer in Dennie's Philadelphia magazine, the
Portfolio argued that the government should establish official
relations with the *de facto* governments of Chile and Buenos
Aires.[157] In the *American Monthly Magazine* a journalist's
enthusiasm even led him to formulate a scheme for a new Holy
Alliance between North and South America for the protection
of the principle of free government.[158]

On the other hand, the conservative papers of the large seaports of the Atlantic coast favored caution and supported the
policy of the administration. In the *National Intelligencer* a
" North American " rebutted the " Letters of Lautaro " which
had been appearing in the *Richmond Enquirer*, remarking that
enthusiasm for South America was well suited for demagogs,
but that it " behooves the patriotic citizen of these states . . .
to enquire in the first place how their interests will be affected

156 *Louisiana Courier*, April 6, 1818, this paper also quotes similar statements by the *New York Columbian* and the *Kentucky Gazette*.

157 *Portfolio*, iv series, vol. v (1818), 98 ff.

158 *American Monthly Magazine*, III, (1818), 268.

by any steps taken. . . ." He supported Monroe's policy, which he declared to be based on tradition, the obligations of international law, and to be further justified by quarrels among the rebels and the monarchical tendencies apparent at Buenos Aires.[159]

The *Columbian Centinel* of Boston favored neutrality and supposed that " an alliance with the revolutionaries against Spain " did not " enter the views of any but those who are born away by the most unregulated passion for military renown ".[160] In New York the staid *Evening Post* also supported the administration.[161] The correspondent of the *Charleston Courier* in Washington attacked Clay's resolutions with vigor,[162] and even in Savannah, next to Spanish Florida, the leading commercial paper, the *Columbian Museum and Savannah Gazette,* favored neutrality, though its sympathies were with the revolutionaries. " The Spanish Americans," it declared, " are unfit in a very extensive degree for the enjoyment of liberty and the United States should not interfere to substitute one tyranny for another." [163]

Though at Baltimore the mercantile community was divided,[164] the business men of the Atlantic seaboard were generally lukewarm toward the patriots. As an influential Philadelphian put it: " we are not all patriot mad; nor disposed to risk the character and peace of our country for a set of military factions in South America. . . ." [165] The fact that trade with Spain and the loyal Spanish provinces was far greater than that as yet established with the independent areas of Spanish

159 Paxson, *op. cit.*, p. 128.

160 *Columbian Centinel*, Nov. 19, 1817.

161 *New York Evening Post*, Jan. 29, 31, Mar. 13, 1817.

162 *Columbian Museum and Savannah Gazette*, quoting the *Charleston Courier*, April 11, 1818.

163 *Ibid.*, June 19, 1817.

164 Skinner to Monroe, Jan. 13, 1817, MP. LC.

165 B. A. Konkle, *Joseph Hopkinson*, pp. 207-8; *Life and Correspondence of Rufus King*, ed. by C. R. King (New York, 1894-1900), VI, 113.

America [166] may well have played a part in determining the attitude of the mercantile class. Nicolas Biddle, who may be considered a representative man of wealth, wrote Monroe in December, 1817, to urge neutrality as " due to our own security ".[167]

Madison's view of the state of public opinion in February, 1818 was the following:

The real sense of the nation with regard to the revolutionary struggle in S. America can not, I should suppose be mistaken. Good wishes for its success and every *lawful* manifestation of them, will be approved by all, whatever may be the consequences. The nation will equally disapprove any measures unnecessarily involving it in the danger of a war which might even do less good to the Spanish patriots than harm to the U. States; or any under-hand measures bringing a just stain on the national character.[168]

There was not, of course, any one opinion to which the public at large subscribed. The foregoing pages have attempted to show the varying shades of friendship or emnity for the rebels which prevailed. Nevertheless Madison's statement was a canny estimate of the middle ground which might be expected to gain the support of the greatest number of citizens.

The caution observed by the United States in its dealings with the Spanish American governments was the result of a series of factors in which the following were predominant: the

166 *Spanish America and the United States, or Views on the Actual Commerce of the United States with the Spanish Colonies* ... By a Merchant of Philadelphia (Philadelphia, 1818). The author pointed to the 80,000 to 100,000 bbls. of flour annually exported to Cuba and the 45,759 hhds. of molasses imported thence in 1817. *Annals of Congress*, XXX, 14 Cong., 2 Sess., HR., 738. Smith of Maryland in the debate on the Neutrality Bill (1817) emphasized the value of the trade with Spain, Cuba, etc.

167 N. Biddle to Monroe, Dec. 11, 1817, MP. LC.; a few months later Biddle wrote Monroe that whatever moral and political motive there might be for American coöperation with the rebels, the hope of commercial advantage was illusory, Biddle to Monroe, Mar. 15, 1818, MP. LC.

168 Madison to Monroe, Feb. 18, 1818, MP. LC.

attraction exercised by democratic and revolutionary principles, hostility to Spain, the private interests of privateering merchants and seamen. These were checked and held in balance by the timidity and conservatism of other merchants and their interest in peace with Spain, fear of European intervention in the affairs of the Spanish colonies, distrust of the political stability of the new governments,[169] and last but not least, the pending negotiations with Spain. In connection with the last mentioned factor events of so stirring a character were to occur as to supplant the question of recognition for more than a year in the public interest.

169 In this connection it is to be noted that the administration was in possession of much more information on Spanish American political conditions from its agents on the ground than was communicated to the public, and much of it was of an unfavorable character. Even agents sympathetic to the rebels made severe criticism. For examples see Poinsett to Rush, May 23, 1817, DS., South American Commission; Poinsett, undated report on the state of parties and the character of the revolution DS., Special Agents, vol. iii; B. Irvine to Adams, July 30, 1818, DS., Special Agents, vol. viii; Halsey to Monroe, Feb. 11, 1815, DS., Consular Letters, Buenos Aires, vol. i, part 1; Worthington's report on Chile, 1818, DS., Argentine Republic, W. G. D. Worthington, Special Agent, vol. i, part 1.

CHAPTER VI

THE FLORIDA CRISIS AND THE ADAMS-ONIS TREATY

WHILE the American public turned with increasing interest toward the nascent republics of Spanish America, anti-Spanish feeling in the United States grew more intense, still further stimulated by the apparent stagnation of treaty negotiations. It would be wearisome to note many examples of the violent language in which American impatience and prejudice expressed itself. Even a diplomat in the American service spoke of the pleasure which he anticipated in seeing " the ruin of royalty and priestcraft " in Spain.[1] One newspaper referred to Ferdinand VII as the " sot of Madrid ",[2] others raked up old stories of the early days of the Spanish Inquisition and delighted in presenting statistics of its victims of three hundred years before.[3] The imprisonment of Americans at Cartagena after the capture of that fortress by General Morillo, and stories of the barbarous treatment they endured, also aroused indignation.[4] The barbarities committed by both sides in the wars, especially in Venezuela and New Granada, were frightful enough, but reports emanating from rebel headquarters were frequently published relating Spanish atrocities while savagery on the part of the patriots usually went unchronicled.[5]

In 1816 the U. S. S. *Firebrand* was fired on by a Spanish cruiser in the Gulf of Mexico. Apparently the Spanish com-

1 Erving to Monroe, Jan. 13, 1816, MP. LC.

2 *Columbian Museum and Savannah Gazette*, April 16, 1818.

3 *Niles' Weekly Register*, IX, 307.

4 Manning, *Diplomatic Correspondence*, II, 1169, Lowry to Monroe, Jan. 22, 1816; Onís to Pizarro, April 1, 1817, AHN., Est. Leg. 5660; *Niles' Weekly Register*, IX, 429.

5 *Niles' Weekly Register*, IX, 364 relates a story about a Spanish surgeon supposed to have confessed poisoning prisoners; see also *Columbian Museum and Savannah Gazette*, April 25, 1817 for other atrocity stories.

mander was not aware of the *Firebrand*'s character and believed it was assisting rebel privateers recently sighted in the vicinity. Feeling ran high in New Orleans and public resolutions were adopted calling for action by the government.[6]

By 1817, when the hostility of the Seminole Indians began to assume a more menacing character, the desire of the South for a speedy settlement with Spain became more urgent. A Georgia paper declared that if Spain was unable or unwilling to compel the Indians within its jurisdiction to be at peace, the United States should do so.[7] In January, 1818, rumors that the Spanish negotiations had been broken off and Florida ceded to Great Britain spread alarm on the border.[8] This fear of British intrigue, justifiable in view of events during the war of 1812, kept rumors flying and even influenced members of the cabinet.[9] Hostility to Spain, however, was partly the result of sympathy for the insurgents and did not proceed alone from the difficulties in process of negotiation.

The President, however, did not lack support for his peaceful policy. One of his correspondents suggested that the United States would find it easier to negotiate a boundary settlement with Ferdinand VII than with a " high spirited Mexican Republic ".[10] Another declared that " whatever may be said *de jure* the result *de facto* will be the same " for the " possession of its [Florida's] soil by individuals is taking place; which is very like a state possession of it "—a little patience and the problem would solve itself.[11] The remnants of the Federalist party led by Rufus King, senator from New York, firmly

6 Bagot to Castlereagh, Nov. 9, 1816, PRO, FO-5, vol. 115; *Columbian Museum and Savannah Gazette*, Feb. 12, 1817, reprint from the *Louisiana Gazette*; for the strength of anti-Spanish sentiment in New Orleans see *Louisiana Gazette and Commercial Advertiser,* April 28, 1818 (insults to Onís).

7 *Columbian Museum and Savannah Gazette*, June 17, 1817.

8 *Ibid.*, April 27, 1818.

9 William Wirt to Monroe, Feb. 28, 1818, MP. LC.

10 G. W. Logan to Monroe, June 5, 1818, MP. LC.

11 Benjamin Vaughan to Monroe, Nov. 21, 1817, MP. NYP.

opposed action which might lead to war,[12] but Monroe's own party contained a number of hotheads not averse to risking war by aggressive action in Florida. Early in 1818 the public seems to have been more bellicose than the administration, especially in the West and South.[13]

On the frontier between Georgia and Florida the situation had been difficult ever since the recent war. A fort built by British agents during the war and since manned by hostile Indians and negro runaways caused much anxiety until its destruction in 1816.[14] In 1817 conditions grew worse and alarm spread along the border.[15] General Gaines, commander of the United States troops in the district, finding the Seminoles resolute in their emnity, sent a force against them which burned Fowltown, an Indian village. In reprisal the savages attacked small parties of whites in the neighborhood and border homesteads were destroyed amid the horrible scenes that attended Indian warfare.[16] The federal government ordered General Jackson to take command and to bring the " war " to an end, giving him the authority it had previously given Gaines to follow the Indians if need be into Spanish territory.[17] The story of that hot-headed warrior's subsequent activities in Florida and of the celebrated misunderstanding which led Jackson to believe that he was acting in accordance with instructions is well known and need not be repeated here.[17]

12 *Life and Correspondence of Rufus King*, VI, 112 ff.

13 *Louisiana Courier*, April 20, 1818; *Columbian Museum and Savannah Gazette*, April 2, 1818, quotes the *Charleston Courier's* Washington correspondent as saying that " the people here are all elated at the prospect of war with Spain "; see also Onis to Pizarro, No. 23, 1818 and No. 202, 1817, AHN., Est. Leg. 5643; in 1817 rumors of violent feeling in Georgia were current, see, *New York National Advocate*, Nov. 17, 1817, quoting, *Washington City Gazette*.

14 S. B. Fuller, *The Purchase of Florida*, 228-231; ASP. FR., IV, 555-60.

15 Message of Acting Governor Rabun of Georgia, in the *Columbian Museum and Savannah Gazette*, Nov. 12, 1817.

16 *Ibid.*, Dec. 13, 1817.

17 The best account of these events is in J. S. Bassett, *Life of Andrew*

Onís, who had warned his government since the beginning of the year that hostile action in Florida was to be expected, protested in strong terms, first, on hearing of Jackson's occupation of the Spanish post of St. Marks and again when he heard of the capture of Pensacola.[18] Though he was indignant at the affront to Spanish authority in Florida, he did not adopt a bellicose attitude. He had just received Pizarro's instructions of the previous April, and in conversations with Adams and with Hyde de Neuville he appeared to be distressed that Jackson's incursion should have prevented negotiation at a time when he was otherwise in a position to conclude a treaty.[19] The wily Spaniard seemed to realize that the embarrassment of the administration, which was as yet undecided what course of action to pursue with regard to Jackson, gave him a momentary advantage and his despatches of this time breathe optimism.[20] Onís was well informed of the dissensions in the cabinet, and was encouraged by the weak attitude of Crawford on the western boundary question.[21]

Onís did not cut off all communications with Adams after making his protests and continued informal discussions of the western boundary question, on which the negotiation principally hinged.[22] He proposed a line following the Calcasieu River from the Gulf, thence northward from a point between Los Adaes and Natchitoches to the Missouri, the best offer he had yet made. Adams insisted on the claim to Texas and derided the Spanish claim to the Pacific coast as far north as 56 degrees of

Jackson, I, 233 ff., together with the same author's edition of the *Correspondence of Andrew Jackson*, II, 548 ff.; Fuller, *op. cit.*, gives a detailed narrative that does not do justice to Jackson.

18 Onís to Adams, June 17, and July 8, 1818, AHN., Est. Leg. 5643.

19 Adams, *Memoirs*, IV, 104, July 7-8, 1818; Hyde de Neuville to Richelieu, No. 114, July 9, 1818, AAE. CP., États Unis, vol. 75.

20 Onís to Pizarro, July 18, 1818, AHN., Est. Leg. 5643.

21 See copy of Hyde de Neuville to Richelieu, July 9, AHN., Est. Leg. 5660.

22 Adams, *Memoirs*, IV, 106, July 11, 1818.

latitude.[23] On the surface the deadlock was unchanged, but Pizarro's new instructions gave Onís further latitude in the last resort and the United States was very shortly to reduce its pretensions to western territory, because it wished to effect a general settlement which would make discussion of Jackson's acts in Florida unnecessary.

The deliberations of the American cabinet over Jackson's conduct were stormy. Adams upheld Jackson, while the rest, at first, felt that he could not be entirely justified. It was finally decided to restore the captured posts to Spain but at the same time to defend the General and to blame Spain for its failure to control the Indians.[24] The decision was largely dictated by the exigencies of domestic politics, but it was also affected by the status of negotiations with Spain. Monroe and his cabinet had heard from various sources—Onís himself, Hyde de Neuville, the French minister who was partly in the Spaniard's confidence and private individuals in Philadelphia—that Spain was close to an acceptance of the American terms.[25] A complete rebuff of the Spanish protest would almost unavoidably lead to a break; to disavow and punish Jackson would perhaps strengthen Spanish obstinacy; a middle course might save the day. As Monroe wrote during this eventful summer, the course adopted would make Spain realize the necessity of a prompt cession for her own safety. " If we escape war, which we cannot fail to do, the better will be the effect." If the government turned on its commander, hope of a cession would be at an end.[26]

23 Onís to Pizarro, July 18, 1818, AHN., Est. Leg. 5643; Adams, *Memoirs*, IV, 106, July 11, 1818.

24 *Ibid.*, IV, 112, July 19, 1818; Adams to Onís, July 23, 1818, AHN., Est. Leg. 5644.

25 Thomas Cooper to Monroe, July 27, 1818, MP. NYP.; N. Biddle to Monroe, July 28, 1818, MP. LC.; Erving to Adams, Jan. 10, Mar. 16, and April 26, 1818, DS., Despatches from Spain, vol. xv.

26 Monroe to Calhoun, Aug. 31, 1818, MP. NYP.

The volatile Hyde de Neuville now showed great activity. Authorized by his general instructions to contribute as best he could to a peaceful settlement between Spain and the United States, the Frenchman was glad to comply when he was requested by Monroe and Adams to act as intermediary. The offer he took with him when he called on Onís at the latter's country home at Bristol was a great concession by the administration. Adams, without committing himself to a verbal statement, had marked a proposed boundary on the map. It followed the Trinity River to its source, thence westward to the Rio Grande, up the latter to its source, on to the summit of the chain of mountains beyond, there to end or continue westward to the Pacific.[27] Even before this offer was made, which, it will be noted, surrendered a large part of Texas, Hyde de Neuville, acting on hints from Onís, had proposed that a compromise might be made at the Sabine River.[28] The intermediary was impressed by the small distance which separated the parties in this dispute over Texas lands and was inclined to censure Onís for his obstinacy.[29] Onís was suspicious and did not take him fully into his confidence. He succeeded in drawing from Hyde de Neuville the tentative offer suggested by Adams with regard to the boundary, but though his despatches show elation at the ground gained he did not allow his fellow diplomat to notice his feeling and told him that he had decided to make no further move until he heard from Madrid.[30] It appears that it was due to these indirect contacts that Onís and Adams failed to see that no matter how near agreement they might be on the Texas border, they were completely at odds on the northwest extension of the line.

Onís felt that the offer to restore St. Marks and Pensacola was a triumph for his diplomacy and that Spanish dignity had

27 Adams, *Memoirs*, IV, 110, July 16, 1818.

28 Onís to Pizarro, No. 134, July 18, 1818, AHN., Est. Leg. 5643.

29 Hyde de Neuville to Richelieu, No. 118, July 20, 1818, AAE., C. P. États Unis, vol. 75.

30 Onís to Pizarro, No. 138, Aug. 4, 1818, AHN., Est. Leg. 5643.

been adequately salved. Nevertheless, he acted with hesitancy, taking no further action until October, although he received Pizarro's instructions of June 15, which gave him additional bargaining power, before the end of August. When he did renew negotiations he was to find Adams and Monroe more stubborn, for the domestic and foreign dangers that had seemed so imminent in July then appeared less threatening.[31]

In discussing Spanish policy it must be realized that the views of the government at Madrid and the acts of its minister at Washington cannot be treated as identical. There was a lapse of approximately three months, except when special messengers were used, between the date instructions were despatched and their arrival. In such an interval of time much could, and often did, occur and consequently there was a lack of coordination between Onís and his superiors, which became increasingly dangerous in 1818 as the negotiations reached a crisis. News of the seizure of St. Marks did not arrive at Madrid until July, and official news of Jackson's acts at Pensacola until August.[32]

In the meantime Pizarro had been attempting to relieve the pressure on Onís by opening a discussion with Erving. Though Onís and Adams had made no progress in the spring of 1818, relations between the negotiators at Madrid had improved notably. The Spanish minister reassured Erving when the latter sought information about the large land grants in Florida, recently reported to have been made to certain members of Ferdinand's intimate circle, which Erving rightly feared might prejudice the negotiations in progress.[33] The French Ambassador at Madrid commented on the Spanish complaisance

31 Onís to Pizarro, No. 144, Aug. 31, 1818, ibid.; Onís to Pizarro, No. 145, Sept. 1, 1818, AHN., Est. Leg. 5644.

32 Jackson occupied St. Mark's in April and Pensacola in May. Gaceta de Madrid, July 25, 1818 gives the news of the execution of Arbuthnot and Ambrister and of Jackson's departure toward Pensacola.

33 Erving to Pizarro, July 18, 1818, private, Pizarro to Erving, July 19, 1818, DS., Despatches Spain, vol. xvi.

toward Erving in contrast to the abrupt tone used to the Portuguese, then at loggerheads with Spain over the question of Montevideo.[34] Still further to clear the atmosphere Pizarro offered immediate ratification of the 1802 claims convention.[35] He also began conversations with Erving on the boundary question, declaring that the American claim to the line of the Colorado River was out of the question but hinting at a possible compromise. He caused Erving much embarrassment by suggesting that Spain would now gladly accept the offer of a territorial guaranty of its possessions west of the Mississippi River, which had been made by Charles Pinckney in 1803.[36] Erving was not aware that such an offer had been made and was much put out by Pizarro's move. In order to turn the Spaniard to another subject, he countered with a suggestion for a neutral zone on the frontier which he declared would be a better solution than a guaranty.[37] This was a scheme which the Adams, Jefferson and Madison administrations had all contemplated, but which was now less popular in Washington. Erving was eager to secure the credit for making a settlement with Spain and allowed himself to become involved in further discussion.

Impressed by Pizarro's apparent eagerness to reach an agreement, Erving reported that it would be easy to adjust a treaty on the basis of the minimum requirements mentioned in his instructions of 1816, that is, fixing the boundary at the Sabine; but that agreement on the Colorado line now required by Adams was prevented by the resistance of the court, though if it depended on Pizarro alone he believed that it might be secured. He ascribed Spanish obstinacy to the feeling of security induced by the failure of Clay's resolutions in the House, and the failure

34 Laval to Richelieu, June 7, 1818, AAE., C. P. Espagne, vol. 701.

35 Pizarro to Erving, July 9, 1818, Erving to Adams, July 13, 1818, DS., Despatches, Spain, vol. xvi.

36 Erving to Adams, July 13, 1818, DS., Despatches, Spain, vol. xvi.

37 Erving to Pizarro, July 9, 1818, Pizarro to Erving, July 9, July 19, 1818, AHN., Est. Leg. 5643.

of the administration to follow up by aggressive steps its firm stand in the negotiations.[38]

Unfortunately for Erving, his secretary, Thomas L. L. Brent, was corresponding with Monroe, commenting unfavorably on his chief and suggesting that orders be sent him to desist from further interference in the treaty negotiations, which he described as mere attempts of Pizarro to cause delay in Washington.[39] It is surprising that these negotiations were continued by Pizarro for weeks after Jackson's exploits in Florida were known to him. The news of the " Pensacola outrage ", as the Spaniards called it, finally called forth a strong protest from Pizarro,[40] but conferences with Erving continued even after that, and the American minister was still treated with favor at the court.[41]

By the latter part of August, Pizarro's wish to reach an agreement could no longer take precedence of the need to satisfy the outraged dignity of the Spanish king and court, and the problem so rudely brought to a crisis by Jackson was studied in cabinet meetings and finally ventilated in the Council of State. Pizarro's exposition to the Council blamed it for its excessive confidence in the efficacy of mediation or intervention by European powers. These illusions, according to the minister, by preventing the authorization of terms satisfactory to the United States, had led directly to the present crisis. He expressed indignation at Jackson's attack, but warned against declaring war in view of Spain's other difficulties with the Colonies and with Portugal. If dignity demanded a strong move, perhaps a suspension of diplomatic relations might be

38 Erving to Adams, July 22, 1818, DS., Despatches, Spain, vol. xvi.

39 T. L. L. Brent to Monroe, July 24, 1818, MP. NYP.

40 Pizarro to Erving, Aug. 11, 1818, AME., Estados Unidos, Cor. Pol. Leg. 224; Erving to Adams, Aug. 17, 1818, DS., Despatches, Spain, vol. xvi.

41 Laval to Richelieu, Aug. 13, 21 and 31, 1818, AAE., C. P. Espagne, vol. 702.

tried, but that would be dangerous and he advised that Onís be authorized to make the best bargain he could.[42]

The Council was the scene of a vigorous attack on Pizarro led by Guillermo Hualde, Lozano de Tórres and the Duke of Infantado, but the majority, including the prince, Don Carlos, and Pizarro's ministerial colleagues, supported him, and it was decided to choose the more cautious path. After a stormy two day session the Council approved giving Onís ample power to settle, but emphasized the necessity of settling *all* disputes between the two countries. It was distinctly stated that reparation for Jackson's conduct must be obtained; that a guaranty of Spanish sovereignty over territory not ceded should be required; and that assurances should be given by the United States that it would not aid the Spanish American rebels.[43] In the meantime the negotiation was formally suspended; a still stronger protest was delivered to Erving and communicated to the European powers.[44]

At the end of August Pizarro's latest reports from Onís were dated not later than the end of June, though he had received notice of developments in Washington to the middle of July through the French ambassador, who passed on information derived from Hyde de Neuville. Hoping within a few days to be better informed, Pizarro delayed sending the instructions agreed upon. Onís for the time being was ordered to adjust his demands for satisfaction to the manner in which the American government reacted to his offers in informal negotiations which he was to continue, notwithstanding the formal suspension announced from Madrid.[45]

42 Minutes of the Council of State, Aug. 26 and 27, 1818, AHN., Est. Leg. 5661.

43 Pizarro, *Memorias,* III, 309-11.

44 Pizarro to Erving, Aug. 29, 1818, Erving to J. Q. Adams, Aug. 27, 1818, DS., Despatches, Spain, vol. xvi; Pizarro, Circular to Ministers and Ambassadors of the King, Aug. 29, 1818, AME., Estados Unidos, Cor. Pol., Leg. 224.

45 Pizarro to Onís, Aug. 30, 1818, AME., Estados Unidos, Cor. Pol. Leg. 224.

Before Pizarro had time for further action another of the periodic political upheavals at the Spanish court had removed him from office and sent him in disgrace to a provincial city. The reason for the ministerial upset is well established. Ever since the appointment of Pizarro, his colleague, Martín de Garáy, at the head of the treasury had been subjected to severe attack by those representing the privileged vested interests. The failure of Garáy's plans to bring the expected improvement in the finances, which was due largely to the sabotage of hostile interests, led to a decline in that minister's reputation.[46] As soon as his backers, Tatistcheff and the *camarilla,* wavered, Garáy was in danger and Pizarro as his friend and associate shared his predicament. The latter further endangered his position by assuming an independent manner towards his former patrons.[47]

The fall of the ministry was also related to the diplomacy of the day, particularly to the schemes of Pozzo di Borgo and Tatistcheff. These were in turn related to the plans for bringing about mediation between Spain and the Colonies. Though the British negative had scotched the project in 1817, it was renewed in another form in the following year. The Allied Sovereigns were to meet at Aix-la-Chapelle to consider the evacuation of France by the Allied armies and the financial arrangements upon which that was to be conditional. Pozzo began to press for the inclusion of Spain in the conference; partly in order to renew the mediation plan, and partly to gain an ally for Russia which had of late often been overruled in the Allied councils by Austria, Prussia and Great Britain. This initiative was checked by Castlereagh, whose policy it was to prevent the enlargement of the limited functions of the Alliance, and who foresaw difficulties if the minor powers were admitted.

46 Baumgarten, *Geschichte Spaniens*, II, 176 f., 181-2, 184 ff.; Laval to Richelieu, Sept. 17, 1818, AAE., C. P. Espagne, vol. 702.

47 Ramírez de Villaurrutia, *op. cit.,* in *Revista de Archivos, Bibliotecas y Museos*, XVI, 182; Laval to Richelieu, May 4, 1818, AAE., C. P. Espagne, vol. 701; *id.* to *id.*, August 21, Sept. 17, 1818, *ibid.*, vol. 702; Pizarro, *Memorias,* II, 95-6.

He gained his point by a personal appeal to the Tsar that put an end to Pozzo's grand plan.[48]

Though Spanish hopes for an invitation to Aix were disappointed, the powers seemed to be somewhat better disposed for consideration of the status of the Spanish Colonies. Pizarro made a conciliatory gesture in June, 1818, which led Castlereagh to hope that something might be done.[49] The matter was actually broached at the conference at Aix, but the project failed again due to the opposition of Great Britain to any use of force. The French and Russian governments were only able to secure the consent of the conference to a proposal that the Duke of Wellington be appointed representative of the Alliance to offer good offices to Spain and the Colonies, but Wellington refused to act except on the basis set forth by Castlereagh.[50] Spain had met with a double check through British influence; Pizarro by adopting a more friendly attitude toward that power in the latter part of his term of office had therefore opened himself to attack.[51]

The circumstances of the cabinet crisis were remarkably melodramatic. On September 14, 1818, the unsuspecting ministers attended a *corrida* in the bull ring, then, after working in their offices in the basement of the palace overlooking the Manzanares, they had retired to their homes, unsuspicious of the blow that awaited them. After midnight the King announced his decision. The gates of the palace were shut in order to prevent any disturbance, and at one o'clock in the morning

---

48 Webster, *The Foreign Policy of Castlereagh, 1815-1822*, p. 126 ff., 418 ff.; D. Perkins, "Russia and the Spanish Colonies" in AHR., XXVIII, 666.

49 Castlereagh to Bagot, Aug. 8, 1818, PRO, FO-5, vol. 129; Webster, *op. cit.*, p. 417; Adams, *Memoirs*, IV, 136-8.

50 W. P. Cresson, *The Holy Alliance* (New York, 1922), pp. 75 ff., gives the most detailed account of this aspect of the conference's work. *Cf.* Webster, *op. cit.*, p. 126 f.

51 In the spring of 1818 the ministry lost Tatistcheff's support. Laval to Richelieu, May 4, June 7, 1818, AAE., C. P. Espagne, vol. 701.

Garáy, Pizarro, and Vasquez Figueroa, minister of marine, were informed in curt notes from General Eguia, minister of war, that they and their families must be out of the capital before six a. m. Escorts and passports were ready and before the city waked the three ministers had silently disappeared.[52]

Pizarro's place was taken by Carlos Martínez de Irujo, a diplomat with a long and eventful career. He had entered government employ as a page to Charles III's great minister, the Count of Floridablanca, who gave the young man a chance to rise, sending him first as attaché to The Hague and later in a similar capacity to London. Irujo was active and vivacious, had keen intelligence and great ambition together with a flair for self-advancement. He managed to ingratiate himself with Manuel Godoy when that favorite ruled at the Spanish court and made rapid progress in his profession, receiving in 1796 an appointment as minister to the United States. Irujo's checkered career in that country is well known. His hot temper and taste for intrigue made his stay far from tranquil. Twice he got into serious quarrels with the administration, once during John Adams' and again during Jefferson's presidency. In Philadelphia Irujo married the daughter of Governor M'Kean of Pennsylvania and was enough of a Yankee to make money by speculation. After leaving the United States he served as minister to the Portuguese court at Rio de Janeiro and later played a part in Spanish politics under the Cadiz Regency. Since the restoration of Ferdinand he had been living in Cadiz occupied with private interests.[53]

52 Laval to Richelieu, Sept. 17, 1818, AAE., C. P. Espagne, vol. 702; *Diary and Correspondence of Henry Wellesley, First Lord Cowley, 1790-1846*, ed. by F. A. Wellesley (London, 1930), p. 87.

53 Personal dossier on Irujo, AHN., Est. Leg. 3420; *cf.* F. Antón del Olmet, *op. cit.*, III, p. 333 ff.; for Irujo's career in the United States see Henry Adams, *History of the United States* using index under " Yrujo." For the impressions of the French ambassador see Laval to Richelieu, Sept. 28, 1818, AAE., C. P. Espagne, vol. 702.

Irujo was called to Madrid with the intention of sending him to Aix-la-Chapelle,[54] and it has been thought that his choice was due to his pronounced anglophobia,[55] a not unreasonable supposition in view of the great influence of Tatistcheff at this time. The new minister was well informed on trans-Atlantic affairs. Even before his appointment he had maintained a correspondence with Onís which is evidence of his interest.[56] Erving distrusted Irujo and it was believed in the United States that he was strongly anti-American, an opinion based on his record as minister in Washington.[57] It does not appear, however, that this was the case. His conduct of the negotiations does not bear it out. He was a belligerently patriotic, almost jingoistic Spaniard, but it may well be doubted whether he was moved by any special antipathy to the United States.

It fell to Irujo to execute what his predecessor had begun and to send instructions to Onís in accordance with the recent decision of the Council of State. Pizarro left a draft of such instructions which Irujo modified before despatching. Pizarro's draft deviated but slightly from the policy laid down by the Council. He told Onís that a momentary evacuation of the posts taken by Jackson would be considered sufficient reparation on that score, but he wished Onís to vary his demands according to the attitude of the United States on other points. On boundaries Onís was given the full authority that the Council had recommended, but Pizarro was not then aware of the American claims west of Texas, for the negotiation up to this time had dealt only with the eastern part of the Louisiana boundary near the Gulf coast. No explicit orders, therefore, were sent to Onís regarding the line west of the Great Plains. Pizarro weakened the Council's requirement of a territorial

54 J. Becker, *op. cit.*, I, 497; Martínez de la Rosa, *Bosquejo histórico de la política de España* (Madrid, 1857), II, 288-9.

55 C. A. Villanueva, *Bolívar y el General San Martín*, p. 124.

56 Onís to Irujo, Nov. 30, 1818, AHN., Est. Leg. 2770.

57 Hyde de Neuville to Dessolle, Aug. 7, 1819, AAE., C. P. États Unis, vol. 76; Erving to Adams, Sept. 20, 1818, DS., Despatches, Spain, vol. xvi.

guaranty. If Texas could be retained, he felt that the guaranty would not be of much value and need not be considered a *sine qua non*. Although Onís was to be given power to set the boundary of Louisiana at any point between the Mississippi and Texan Colorado rivers, it is evident that Pizarro expected a line as far east as the Sabine and did not wish territorial concessions to be made " except in urgent danger of war or of recognition of the rebel governments by the United States ". On neutrality enforcement Pizarro followed the Council closely: the United States should give proof of good will and " all means consistent with the constitution and laws of the country should be used to control these evils [aid to the insurgents] reinforcing as far as possible the existing provisions of the Treaty of 1795 that deal with these matters and adding other safeguards, if possible, adequate to deal with present circumstances ".[58] Pizarro also hoped that if a bad territorial bargain had to be made the United States might be induced to pay cash, though this was not to be considered a primary object.

Irujo's modifications in these instructions were not numerous, but they were important. He told Onís not to endanger a good western boundary by insisting on articles dealing with neutrality enforcement. Irujo was also more specific about the boundary. He hoped for a line northward from the source of the Sabine direct to the Missouri and along that river to its source; thence to the Pacific if necessary in a northwesterly direction. He hoped that Onís would be able to secure a line that would leave Spain in possession of the headwaters of the Red, Arkansas and Missouri rivers as a protection to the Spanish settlements in New Mexico, but he declared that the retention of Texas was all Spain could hope for.[58]

58 The foregoing paragraphs are based on Pizarro's draft of instructions to Onís (in the handwriting of N. de Heredia, the undersecretary). It bears corrections and changes in Irujo's handwriting. It was originally dated September 13, 1818, the day before Pizarro's dismissal, and was actually sent Onís in its modified form on October 10, 1818. AHN., Est. Leg. 5643.

A few weeks after these instructions were despatched Irujo heard through the French ambassador of the American boundary claims in the Northwest. Realizing that his previous letter had not been explicit enough on this part of the line, he resubmitted the question to the Council of State. That body declared that it had already gone on record in favor of ample powers to Onís and did not consider further discussion necessary.[59] Irujo, consequently, wrote Onís that he was to consider himself " fully authorized to act, negotiate and conclude the settlement according to circumstances without the necessity of further consultation." [60]

It would appear from the foregoing that Irujo had more to do with the conclusion of the Adams-Onís Treaty than he has been given credit for in the past. Onís declared subsequently that he was given impossible instructions until Irujo came into office.[61] It is true that Pizarro wished to reach an agreement earlier in the year, but he was not decisive in his policy, hampered by the opposition at the Spanish court. Jackson's incursion did have an electric effect on the negotiations, as American writers have so often noted. It was not Florida, however, but the western boundary of Louisiana which was affected by his raids, for the cession of Florida had been discounted in the negotiation since 1817.[62]   Owing to Jackson's raid the Spanish Council of State made important concessions, but not until Irujo came to office were demands for security against recognition of the rebel states, for prevention of aid to them, and

59 Minutes of the Council of State, October 17, 1818, AHN., Est. Leg. 5661.

60 Irujo to Onís, Oct. 23, 1818, AME., Estados Unidos, Cor. Pol. Leg. 225.

61 Onís to Irujo, private, Mar. 24, 1819, AHN., Est. Leg. 3446. " I shall always repeat that all the glory is yours, for I do not know how I have had patience to bear the ridiculous instructions that were given me until you took up the reins of the ministry . . . "

62 S. F. Bemis, *A Diplomatic History of the United States* (New York, 1936), p. 189, emphasizes this point. The fundamental work on the treaty is by Philip C. Brooks, " The Adams-Onís Treaty as a Territorial Agreement ", MS., University of California Library.

for a guaranty of Spanish sovereignty beyond the new frontier abandoned. Ferdinand and the influential courtiers at Madrid, who did not follow the American negotiations in detail, never favored a treaty which did not settle all these matters and definitely secure the friendly neutrality of the United States. Irujo, better informed of what was practicable, decided to give up these unattainable ends, trusting that a treaty would relieve tension and enable Spain to carry out its plans for an attack on Buenos Aires with greater possibilities of success.[63]

In the United States the controversy raised by Jackson's action dealt primarily with the constitutional aspects of the episode, but it also called forth speculation on the international consequences. According to Onís, the public was in part hostile to Jackson and the administration when the news of the capture of Pensacola arrived.[64] Bagot thought that there was a universal desire to obtain Florida, but little disposition to accomplish it at the cost of a war.[65] The middle ground adopted by Monroe, of returning the posts but refusing to censure Jackson, met the approval of most people. The elder statesmen of the Republican party, Jefferson and Madison, gave their hearty support to the way in which the crisis was handled,[66] and even King, the Federalist leader, justified Jackson, though he hoped for a peaceful cession of Florida.[67]

The old party lines no longer held. Opposition to the administration was voiced in some Federalist papers and also in old

63 Irujo was closely associated with Tatistcheff in advocating a policy of force against the rebels and bent all his efforts to preparation for the expeditionary force against Buenos Aires. See Laval to Dessolle, Mar. 23, 1819, AAE., C. P. Espagne, vol. 703, Laval to Richelieu, Nov. 30, 1818, ibid., vol. 702; Laval to Dessolle, Jan. 28, 1819, ibid., Supplement No. 25; Baumgarten, Geschichte Spaniens, II, 208-9.

64 Onís to Pizarro, July 27, 1818, AHN., Est. Leg. 5644.

65 Bagot to Castlereagh, July 24, 1818, PRO, FO-5, vol. 132.

66 Ford, Jefferson, vol. x, Jefferson to Monroe, Jan. 18, 1819; Hunt, Madison, VIII, 420, Madison to Monroe, Feb. 13, 1819; Adams, Memoirs, IV, 227.

67 King to Monroe, July 27, 1818, MP. NYP.

line Republican organs.[68] The faint beginnings of the future Whig party might be divined in the criticism of Jackson in the Northeast, by the conservative elements in the Old South, and by the followers of Clay in East and West alike. This criticism was united only in hostility to Jackson. Clay and his partizans were hostile to Spain and not averse to war with that power, though not on the Jackson issue.[69] Other critics were in favor of a moderate policy toward Spain.[70]

During January, 1819, as the debate in Congress on the Seminole War continued, it became evident that Clay's efforts were being wasted and that the country was on the whole solidly behind the administration in its defense of Jackson.[71] As Monroe stated the issue, if Jackson had been ordered to trial " the interior of the country would have been much agitated if not convulsed by appeals to sectional interests, by imputations of subserviency to the views of Ferdinand, of hostility to the cause of the colonists, etc.," [72] Monroe also believed that disavowal of Jackson would have made Spain more stubborn.[73] While this was true of the situation during the previous summer, it did not apply to conditions during the Congressional attack on the General, for Irujo's final instructions to conclude a treaty had been despatched in October and gave Onís no excuse for delay once had had received them.

68 *New York Evening Post*, Jan. 6, 1819; *Columbian Centinel* (Boston), Mar. 2, 1819; see clipping from the *Richmond Enquirer* enclosed in PRO, FO-5, vol. 141 and Ambler, *Thomas Ritchie*, p. 70 ff.

69 Robertson to Monroe, Dec. 20, 1818, MP. LC.; Onís to Irujo, Feb. 16, 1819, AHN., Est. Leg. 5661.

70 T. Ritchie to Barbour, Jan. 4, 1819, Barbour Papers, NYP.; *New York Evening Post*, Feb. 19, 1819.

71 See S. Sharp to Monroe, Jan. 10, 1819, G. W. Hay to Monroe, Feb. 12, 1819, and other letters in MP. LC.

72 *Writings of James Monroe,* ed. by S. M. Hamilton (New York and London, 1898-1903), VI, 87, Monroe to Madison, Feb. 7, 1819.

73 *Ibid.,* Onís received his final instructions in January, 1819, while the Congressional attack on Jackson was still in progress.

In another direction the administration had taken a risk in supporting its military commander, for anger had risen high in England over the summary execution of the British subjects, Arbuthnot and Ambrister, by Jackson in the course of his Florida campaign.[74] Poletica, the newly appointed Russian envoy to Washington, was in London at the height of public indignation over this incident, but he saw that the United States was safe. The English, he wrote, " die with rage over it, but they will control their feelings until the day of reckoning." [75] Fortunately the incident was to be forgotten before such an occasion arose. The British ministry saw that it had no legal right to intervene, and was equally convinced that any disturbance of the peace at this time would be disastrous to larger British interests. Castlereagh accordingly allowed the incident to pass without official protest.[76]

In Spanish America the leaders of the patriots watched the critical situation with interest. In the summer of 1818 Bolívar heard that the United States had begun hostilities against Spain in Florida. He questioned Baptis Irvine on the matter with great curiosity.[77] News of the capture of Pensacola by Jackson caused elation at Angostura.[78] Still later, intercepted despatches from Madrid to the Spanish authorities in Venezuela which spoke of the danger of war with the United States kept the patriots hopeful that they would soon find themselves in the company of a new ally against the mother country.[79]

74 R. Rush to Monroe, Jan. 17, 1819, MP. LC. "The publick anger against us amounts almost to Rage." See also Richard Rush, *Memoranda of a Residence at the Court of London*, Second series (Phila., 1845), I, 136-140.

75 W. P. Cresson, *The Holy Alliance*, p. 87, quoting Poletica to Capo D'Istria, Aug. 1/13, 1818, from the Russian Archives.

76 Castlereagh was much disturbed by the incident at first. Castlereagh to Bagot, No. 16, Aug. 18, 1818, PRO, FO-5, vol. 129, but he decided not to act. See *id.* to *id.*, No. 1, Jan. 2, 1819, *ibid.*, vol. 141.

77 B. Irvine to Adams, July 20, 1818, DS., Special Agents, vol. viii.

78 B. Irvine to Adams, Aug. 27, 1818, *ibid.*; *Cartas del Libertador*, II, 40.

79 *Correo del Orinoco*, October 10, 1818. In Buenos Aires and Chile the press also commented with interest on the American invasion of Florida and

The hopes of the Spanish Americans and of some of their friends in the United States were to be frustrated, for while the public was intent on the Jackson affair the long and bitter negotiation between Spain and the United States was concluded, thanks to the good judgment of John Quincy Adams, and to the able diplomacy of Onís, now backed by a more realistic policy in Madrid since the ministerial change of the previous autumn. Onís in his opening move in October, 1818, showed himself remarkably stubborn, though his despatches, and even more his personal letters, show that he was heartily in favor of reaching an agreement.[80] He had no instructions at this time dated later than the middle of July and was unaware as yet of the attitude of his government toward the events of the summer, yet he might have offered better terms than those he now brought forward, and he admitted as much in his reports.[81] It seems as if the Spanish negotiator feared his own superiors more than he did his opponents. He can hardly be blamed, for he knew how easily a servant of Ferdinand VII might lose the due reward for years of faithful effort through some unlucky misstep. The Spanish system of diplomacy tended to suppress initiative in its representatives. Insistence on meticulous adherence to minute and explicit instructions might be wise in negotiation between European courts, but it was not the ideal way to handle trans-Atlantic business in days when an exchange of letters between Madrid and Washington took from four to six months.

Onís opened his campaign with a conciliatory gesture, offering to exchange ratifications of the 1802 Claims Convention,[82] but the main points in his next note proved extremely disap-

the probability of war which that indicated. See *Gaceta Ministerial de Chile*, Nov. 7, 1818; *Documentos del archivo de San Martín*, VI, 368; Tomás Guido to San Martín, Mar. 22, 1819.

80 Onís to Irujo, private, Nov. 30, 1818, AHN., Est. Leg. 2770; Onís to Irujo, Dec. 28, 1818, AHN., Est. Leg. 5643.

81 Onís to Pizarro, Nov. 2, 1818, AHN., Est. Leg. 5643.

82 Onís to Adams, October 18, 1818, AHN., Est. Leg. 5643.

pointing to Adams. The Spanish note offered a western boundary already verbally refused by Adams during the summer; insisted on additional reparation for the Jackson affair; a stricter enforcement of neutrality, to say nothing of other minor points objectionable to the United States.[83] This move was obviously what Onís confessed it to be in his despatches: an attempt to prolong negotiations, until he should have received his next mail from Madrid, and to tempt the administration and the public by hints of further concessions to avoid immediate hostilities.[84]

Monroe was less disappointed than Adams [85] and showed himself less eager for an immediate settlement with Spain than he had been during the summer. Even Crawford, who had favored concessions in western territory in July, now wanted to claim territory south of the Red River.[86] After a cabinet consultation Adams replied to the Spanish proposal with an ultimatum. In it the surrender of Texas was still offered, but a definite claim to territory westward to the Pacific was now included.[87] The note firmly refused any reparation for Jackson's deeds beyond the restoration of the forts which had already been offered. The cancellation of all land grants in Florida, made since 1802, was also demanded.[88]

The exchange of notes had widened rather than closed the breach between the negotiators. Onís spoke of the American note as arrogant, haughty and dictatorial.[89] The Spaniard also came to distrust Hyde de Neuville more and more and to

83 Onís to Adams, October 24, 1818, *ibid.*

84 Onís to Pizarro, October 31, 1818, AHN., Est. Leg. 5643.

85 Adams, *Memoirs*, IV, 144, October 26, 1818.

86 *Ibid.*, IV, 145 ff.

87 The line offered by Adams followed the Sabine from the Gulf to its source; then north to the Red River; along it to its source; to the Rio Grande; along it to its source; to the mountain chain west of the Rio Grande; along the chain to 41 degrees N. Lat. and westward to the Pacific.

88 Adams to Onís, Oct. 31, 1818, AHN., Est. Leg. 5643.

89 Onís to Pizarro, Nov. 2, 1818, *ibid.*

consider him an ally of Adams.[90] On the American side there was unconcealed disappointment at Onís' reply to the ultimatum. He agreed to the Sabine line in Texas, but refused the rest of the boundary demanded by Adams, offering in place of it a line north from the Red River at Natchitoches to the Missouri and along that stream to its source. He also insisted on the other points of his October proposal.[91] The intervention of Hyde de Neuville was fruitless, for neither Adams nor Onís were willing to budge from their positions. The Frenchman was eager to bring the contestants to an agreement, but in November, when he reported Adams' bitter comments on Spanish diplomacy, he despaired of a successful transaction and spoke with irritation of the obstinacy of Spain. In spite of his leaning toward the United States he seems to have done his best to get both sides to moderate their pretensions.[92]

The United States now increased its demands. Monroe, repenting of the offer to give up Texas, induced Adams to withdraw it unless immediately accepted and to renew the previous American claim to the region as far west as the Texan Colorado River.[93] In November, too, Adams despatched to Erving his famous defense of Jackson, one of the masterpieces of special pleading in the annals of American politics.[94] Its effect when published, on the public in England and in the United States was considerable. On Spain it had little influence for it came too late to affect the decision of the Spanish government.

During the latter part of 1818 Onís' reports on the prospect of American recognition of the rebel governments were reassuring. The President's message did not recommend any change

90 Ibid.

91 Onís to Adams, Nov. 16, 1818, AHN., Est. Leg. 5643.

92 Hyde de Neuville to Richelieu, Nov. 27, Dec. 1, 1818, AAE., C. P. États Unis, vol. 76; Adams, Memoirs, IV, 172 f. and 184.

93 Ibid., IV, 175-6.

94 Adams to Erving, Nov. 28, 1818, DS., Instructions to Ministers, vol. viii (no enclosures here), see also ASP. FR., IV.

in policy and devoted little attention to the matter;[95] Clay had for the time being neglected the South American question, intent on his attack on Jackson; the public was absorbed in that issue and less was said and thought about the Spanish American rebels.[96] Onís' opinion was confirmed by reports reaching Madrid from Paris, but Irujo was not sanguine and was eager to wind up the negotiation with the United States in order to forestall any hostile move.[97] His fears were not unjustified, for irritation at the stagnation of negotiations with Onís led Monroe to take up again the possible recognition of Buenos Aires.

During the previous summer the American ministers in Europe had been ordered to ascertain the probable reaction of England, France and Russia to a recognition of the rebels by the United States and to any war with Spain that might result from the then tense situation.[98] The reports which returned from the European capitals were not definite, but were hardly reassuring. It was not the wish of any power that the United States should take independent action.[99] In December, however, Monroe made a more definite move. Informal suggestions were made to the British and French ministers in Washington that the United States would be glad to act with those powers to recognize the Buenos Aires government.[100] This might perhaps be interpreted as an attempt to light a bonfire under the ten-

95 Richardson, *Messages and Papers*, II, 43, Monroe to Congress, Nov. 16, 1818.

96 Onís to Pizarro, Nov. 17, Nov. 23, 1818, AHN., Est. Leg. 5643; Onís to Irujo, Nov. 17, 1818, AHN., Est. Leg. 2770.

97 Fernan-Nuñez to Pizarro, Sept. 15, 1818 with Irujo's comments on verso, AHN., Est. Leg. 5643; Laval to Richelieu, Dec. 14, 1818, AAE., C. P. Espagne, vol. 702.

98 Manning, *Diplomatic Correspondence*, I, 74 f., Adams to Rush, Aug. 15, 1818, to Gallatin, Aug. 20, 1818, to Campbell, Aug. 20, 1818. See DS., Instructions to Ministers, vol. viii.

99 Webster, *op. cit.*, p. 415.

100 Adams, *Memoirs*, IV, Dec. 7 and 12, 1818, p. 186 ff.

acious Onís, but it was inspired rather by the apparent hopelessness of a settlement with Spain.[101] At Adams' order, Rush
made identical advances on this subject to Lord Castlereagh,
even mentioning the intention of his government to recognize
Buenos Aires " at no remote period ".[102] No further steps were
taken, partly because they proved unwelcome both to the French
and to the British governments, but also because new developments were in store in the Spanish negotiation. Rumors about
these *démarches* continued to circulate in European diplomatic
circles for some months and created much alarm later in
Madrid.[103]

One of the reasons for Onís' unwillingness to give ground
was the news he received in November of the change of ministry at Madrid.[104] Ignorant of the events that had produced the
upset, he was doubly cautious. On January 4, however, he received Irujo's important instruction of October 10. Rather than
elation, the Spanish envoy seems to have experienced a feeling
of regret. With these instructions, he wrote, he might have
been able to get better terms during the preceding summer.
Now, owing to the increasing weakness of the Spanish military
position in the Colonies, the pressure for recognition of the
rebels which had unexpectedly flared up again, the inaction of
the European powers—he feared that he might fail. The chief
stumbling block, in his opinion, was the lack of explicit authority to concede the American claims to an outlet on the Pacific

101 On the pessimism prevalent about the negotiation, see Hyde de
Neuville to Richelieu, Nov. 27, Dec. 1, 13, 1818, AAE., C. P. États Unis,
vol. 76; Bagot to Castlereagh, Dec. 3, 1818, PRO, FO-5, vol. 133.

102 Adams to Rush, Jan. 1, 1819, DS., Instructions to Ministers, vol. viii;
Manning, *Diplomatic Correspondence*, III, 1450, Rush to Adams, Feb. 15,
1819.

103 Spanish agents were busy picking up these rumors: from Brussels,
Álava to Irujo, Feb. 17, 1819; from St. Petersburg, Zea Bermudez to
Irujo, April 2, 1819; from Copenhagen, J. Iznardi to Irujo, June 1, 1819,
AHN., Est. Leg. 5661.

104 Onís to Irujo, Nov. 17, 1818, private, AHN., Est. Leg. 2770.

Ocean as far south as 41° N. Lat,[105] but he prepared for another attack.

Through Hyde de Neuville he informed Adams that he had received further instructions, and pleaded for a boundary from the source of the Missouri to the Pacific via the Columbia River.[106] The Frenchman found Crawford and Calhoun open to argument.[107] Both wished to secure Florida and were uninterested in far western lands. Adams pricked up his ears at the first intimation he had received that Spain would agree to a boundary reaching to the Pacific and asked that Onís submit this proposal in writing,[108] but he refused the offer when it was made, though it also included a withdrawal of further demands for redress for the Florida attack.[109] A suggestion by Adams that the proposed treaty might leave the western boundary indefinite and confine itself to the other points in dispute was likewise refused by Onís.[110]

A few days later Onís received the instructions sent from Madrid on October 23, which gave him *carte blanche*. Without delay he set on foot through Hyde de Neuville an attempt to secure a compromise on the line of the Arkansas River.[111] At the same time he renewed his efforts to swing influential members of Congress and cabinet officers to favor his proposition, a lobbying attempt which greatly annoyed Adams.[112] These proposals overcame Monroe's resistance and he instructed Adams to accept the Spanish offer of the Arkansas as far west as 101° W., if Spain would agree to make no settlements on

105 Onís to Irujo, Jan. 4, 1819, AHN., Est. Leg. 5645.

106 Onís to Irujo, Jan. 10, 1819, *ibid.*

107 Adams, *Memoirs*, IV, 214, Jan. 7, 1819; Onís to Irujo, Jan. 10, 1819, AHN., Est. Leg. 5645.

108 Adams, *Memoirs*, IV, 215, Jan. 15, 1819.

109 Onís to Adams, Jan. 16, 1819, AHN., Est. Leg. 5661; Adams refused only verbally until Jan. 29.

110 Onís to Irujo, Jan. 16, 1819, AHN., Est. Leg. 5661.

111 Onís to Irujo, Jan. 26, 1819, *ibid.*

112 Adams, *Memoirs*, IV, 214, 244.

the plains north of New Mexico.[113] This was communicated to Onís through Hyde de Neuville.

The negotiation from this point was a matter of detailed bargains and compromises, a description of which can not be given here. In general, the United States conceded territory between the Arkansas and Red rivers which Spain held to be vital for the protection of New Mexico. Spain in return surrendered land west of the Rockies, at last accepting the 42nd parallel as the boundary.[114] In this final haggling the intervention of Hyde de Neuville fully justified itself. It would perhaps have been impossible to reach an agreement without his moderating influence. Monroe, too, once the matter hinged on a few thousand square miles of territory in the far distant west, was unwilling to break off the negotiations and was a restraining influence on the indomitable Adams.[115]

Not until the last moment was success assured. On February 8 Onís wrote that he believed Adams wished to break off and to occupy all the disputed territory.[116] Soon after, however, the main territorial compromise having been accepted, negotiations entered the final stage of drafts and counter drafts of a treaty, and discussion turned to a number of troublesome minor problems: the status of land grants in Florida, the navigation of border rivers, the amendment of the commercial clauses of the treaty of 1795, etc. A slight flurry arose in the middle of February when Adams, disturbed by the opposition of some Westerners, who objected to abandonment of Texas, reopened the supposedly closed boundary question—but he did not persist.[117]

113 *Ibid.*, IV, 234-5.

114 The principal sources for the final stages of the negotiation are the following: Correspondence of Adams and Onís, printed in ASP. FR., IV; Adams' *Memoirs*; the correspondence of Onís with Irujo, chiefly in AHN., Est. Legs. 5661, 5645; P. C. Brooks, *op. cit.* (in MS.) is the best account of these negotiations.

115 Adams, *Memoirs*, IV, 244, Feb. 4, 1819; Onís to Irujo, Feb. 8, 1819, AHN., Est. Leg. 5661.

116 *Ibid.*

117 Onís to Irujo, Feb. 16, 1819, AHN., Est. Leg. 5661.

The dispute on some points lasted to the eve of signature. Adams was irritated by Onís' appeals to Monroe over the head of the Secretary of State, and finally returned Onís' draft of the treaty with modifications which, he declared, embodied the ultimate concessions, threatening to break off if the slightest further objection were raised. This put an end to the long controversy on February 20. Two days later, on Washington's birthday, the treaty was signed.[118]

The basis of agreement was the cession by Spain of its possessions east of the Mississippi and the establishment of a western boundary for Louisiana that has since become familiar on schoolroom wall maps of American territorial expansion.[119] In consideration of these territorial adjustments both nations abandoned outstanding claims, and the United States agreed to pay the claims of its own citizens against Spain up to a maximum of five million dollars. Changes were also made in the commercial relations of the two countries: the return of deserting seamen was facilitated, the principle of " free ships, free goods " which had been established by the treaty of 1795 was limited in its application to those powers who themselves recognized the principle, and Spanish shipping was given preferential treatment in Florida for a period of twelve years. Two other provisions may be noted as they were causes of later difficulty. Land grants in the ceded area were declared valid if made before January 24, 1818, and Spain agreed to deliver to the American authorities all archives and records dealing with land titles in the province.[120]

118 Onís to Irujo, Feb. 20, 1819, AHN., Est. Leg. 5661; Adams, *Memoirs*, IV, 270, Feb. 20, 1819.

119 The line ran from the Gulf up the Sabine River to 32° N. thence due N. to the Red River, up that stream to 100° W., north to the Arkansas River and along the river to its source " in Lat. 42 north," and thence by that parallel of latitude to the South Sea.

120 The text of the treaty is best consulted in D. H. Miller, *Treaties and Other International Acts of the United States of America*, III, 3 ff. which contains as well extremely valuable critical notes.

The treaty was not a total victory for either country; the United States had surrendered its claim to Texas, and Spain had been forced to cede Florida for a nominal equivalent and to recognize American rights to the Oregon country. To contemporary observers in more than one country the settlement of so long and thorny a controversy seemed to be of more value to Spain than anything that might have been retained by further obstinacy. The failure of negotiations in February, 1819, would in all probability have led to war or violence of some sort which Spain could hardly afford.[121] Still, Spain received no guaranty regarding the future conduct of the United States toward the insurgent governments in Spanish America. Verbally, Monroe and Adams had hinted that the conclusion of a treaty would lead the United States to take no action hostile to Spain,[122] but the future alone was to decide what the United States considered hostility to be.

Onís had acquitted himself with distinction in the negotiations. Throughout most of his stay in the United States he had been subjected to popular hostility and aggressive pressure from the administration, while his government gave him no power to satisfy them. In the end he made a treaty which retained for Spain large areas long claimed by the United States and secured several other concessions favorable to his country. To the United States also the treaty was valuable. In the words of a semi-official commentator in the *National Intelligencer:*

It terminates the only existing controversy with any of the European powers, it rounds off our Southern possessions and forever precludes foreign emissaries from stirring up Indians to war and negroes to rebellion, whilst it gives to the Southern country

121 Adams, *Memoirs*, IV, 374, "A treaty or rupture were the only alternatives. If a rupture had ensued England could not have been long neutral and would have drawn all Europe pro or con into the struggle." *Cf.* Adams to Campbell, June 3, 1819, DS., Instructions to Ministers, vol. viii.

122 Hyde de Neuville to Richelieu, Nov. 8, 1818, AAE., C. P. États Unis, vol. 76.

important outlets to the sea. It adjusts the vast western boundary, acknowledging the U. S. to be the sovereign under the hitherto contested Louisiana treaty over all the territory we ever seriously contended for. In a word it is a treaty than which the most sanguine have not anticipated one more favorable. It is one that fully comes up to the expectations of the great body of the American people.[128]

The opinion just quoted, though exaggerated, was widely held at this time. Hyde de Neuville testified to the generally favorable reception of the treaty,[124] and editorial comment modeled on the paragraph quoted was to be met in widely separated parts of the country.[125]

The attitude of the Senate, to which the treaty was submitted immediately after it was signed, shows that opposition was negligible for the moment. Though Clay and his friends in the House had expressed dissatisfaction with the administration's conduct of the negotiation, branding it as weak in regard to Texas and over-aggressive in defense of Jackson,[126] they were unable to command any support in the upper house. The Senate approved the treaty by a unanimous vote two days after it was signed.[127]

But the rejoicing was not unanimous throughout the country. Benton of Missouri was a fervent opponent and attacked the treaty in the St. Louis press on the ground that it should not have sanctioned the loss of Texas.[128] The *Washington City*

123 *Niles' Weekly Register*, Feb. 27, 1819, quoting the *National Intelligencer*.

124 Hyde de Neuville to Richelieu, Feb. 28, 1819, AAE., C. P. Espagne, vol. 703.

125 *Savannah Republican*, May 28, 1819; *Boston Patriot*, quoted in the above; *Columbian Museum and Savannah Gazette*, Mar. 16, echoing the *New York National Advocate*; *Kentucky Reporter*, Mar. 17, 1819 copied the editorial quoted above in the text, though it later attacked the treaty.

126 Adams, *Memoirs*, IV, 276.

127 *Ibid.*

128 T. H. Benton, *Thirty Years' View; or a History of the Working of the American Government for Thirty Years, from 1820 to 1850* (New York, 1854-1856), I, 15; Benton declared that not a newspaper in the United States

Gazette, devoted to Henry Clay, deplored the treaty and hoped that the Senate would not ratify it. It emphasized the value of Texas and minimized that of the Oregon country which, it declared, " can be of no use to us for several centuries ".[129] Not for several months, however, did Western opposition to the treaty begin to crystallize. In February, 1819, even Jackson, so closely identified with Western pioneer interests, showed no interest in Texas.[130]

supported his views on the treaty. In this he was mistaken. In the spring of 1819 the following papers attacked the treaty: *Savannah Republican,* May 26, 1819, quoting the *Boston Daily Advertiser*; *Kentucky Reporter,* Mar. 10, 1819, to say nothing of others who joined in the outcry later. Benton writing later in the light of subsequent events in Texas was apparently attempting to exalt his early interest in annexation.

129 *Washington City Gazette*, as quoted by the *New York Evening Post,* Feb. 26, 1819.

130 Adams, *Memoirs,* IV, 239. This accords with Jackson's letters later in the year, see chap. viii, *infra* and contradicts Jackson's later statements. Letters to Monroe from the West prior to July, 1819 show no opposition to the treaty, if perhaps less enthusiasm than those from other regions. For examples see T. B. Robertson to Monroe, May 25, 1819, MP. NYP.; J. C. Somerville to Monroe, June 13, 1819, MP. LC.

CHAPTER VII
SPAIN WITHHOLDS RATIFICATION

ONIS regarded the treaty as the best one possible, considering the circumstance of its negotiation, but he was not sure how his handiwork would be received at home.[1] Irujo was gratified by the news of the settlement, for he had been awaiting news from Washington with interest tinged with alarm,[2] but the decision of the court at Madrid was not to depend on Irujo alone. Opposed to the minister was a heterogeneous group of personal enemies, ultra patriots and adventurous schemers. The leader of this opposition was Juan Estéban Lozano de Tórres. This extraordinary man, though completely uneducated and of obscure parentage, had managed by flattery and a certain dexterity in intrigue, together with a complete lack of scruple, to obtain the favor of Ferdinand and was at this time minister of "Grace and Justice", a key position for the distribution of patronage, control of the police, law courts, and clergy.[3]

Lozano disliked Irujo and hoped to supplant him in the higher ranking office of secretary of state. For this purpose he was able to rally others. The treaty with the United States, as it provided for cession of Spanish territory, was displeasing to most Spanish courtiers who knew little or nothing of the true state of Spain's international relations. In 1819 few Spaniards could help realizing that Spain had become a second-rate power, but they looked on this decline as a temporary result of the abuses of the previous reign and the exhaustion of the country after the Peninsular War. They could not throw off their pride and the habits of thought inherited from more fortunate generations, nor stomach a policy of expediency. It was easy for

1 Onís to Irujo, private, Mar. 24, 1819, AHN., Est. Leg. 3446.

2 Laval to Dessolle, Mar. 23, 1819, AAE., C. P. Espagne, vol. 703.

3 For Irujo's characterization of the man see Irujo's letters to Ferdinand VII, July 7, and July 16, 1819, AHN., Est. Leg. 3412. *Cf.* Laval to Dessolle, Feb. 4, 1819, AAE., C. P. Espagne, Supplement No. 25; Erving to the Sec. of State, June 30, 1817, DS., Despatches, Spain, vol. xiv; Baumgarten, *Geschichte Spaniens*, II, chap. vii, *passim.*

Lozano to encourage this sentiment and to direct it against Irujo. Public opinion was gagged, but in the *entourage* of the monarch there were many who could influence Spanish policy. Several great nobles, among them the Duke of Infantado, President of the Council of Castile, were antagonized by the proposed cession of territory.[4]

On May 1, Irujo submitted the treaty to the Council of State, opening the session by reading an address recommending ratification. The cession of territory was regrettable, he admitted, but peace with the United States was an absolute necessity in view of the colonial situation. The opposition retorted that Spain lost much and gained little by the terms agreed on; that Onís had exceeded his instructions; that to lose Florida by invasion was better than to cede it, as Spanish *rights* would then remain intact; and finally that Great Britain would object to the proposed addition to the territory of the United States. Irujo's rebuttal, which emphasized the value of Texas, saved by the treaty, and the proved unwillingness of Great Britain to intervene, was not sufficient to carry the day. None of the councillors seemed to view the treaty with approval, though a majority felt that as a choice between two evils it might be better than war. Others, among them Don Carlos, the king's brother, were perplexed and undecided. Lozano de Tórres, the Duke of Infantado and Guillermo Hualde, a protegé of Lozano, were the most bitter opponents of ratification.[5]

Irujo was disturbed by the vigor and extent of the attack, but he remained hopeful and gave the diplomatic corps at Madrid the impression that the treaty would eventually be accepted,[6] but the opposition was now reinforced by three mem-

4 Laval to Dessolle, May 11, 1819, AAE., C. P. Espagne, vol. 703; Extract from Forsyth's private journal, June 13, 1819, record of a conversation with an unnamed Spanish official, DS., Despatches, Spain, vol. xvii.

5 Minutes of the Council of State, May 1, 1819, AHN., Est. Leg. 5661.

6 Laval to Dessolle, private, May 11, 1819, AAE., C. P. Espagne, vol. 703. The news that a Spanish decoration had been granted Hyde de Neuville for his work at Washington strengthened opinion that Spain would ratify.

bers of the royal household: the Duke of Alagon, captain of the King's guards and his boon companion, Count Puñonrostro, and Sr. de Vargas, lesser luminaries of the court. These men were beneficiaries of enormous grants of land in Florida made to them by their master during the winter of 1817-1818.[7] A persistent odor of jobbery clings to this affair. Nothing could have been more pernicious than the mixture of these private interests with the public relations of the United States and Spain. Pizarro had first offered to cede the Floridas in the summer of 1817, and the Spanish government knew that if the offer was accepted the United States expected to satisfy the claims of its citizens against Spain by the sale of public lands in the territory. In spite of this the three courtiers received title to enormous tracts, comprising the whole of the public domain in the province, several months after the offer of cession.

It appears that a scheme was on foot to take advantage of the rise in land values which would inevitably follow the establishment of American sovereignty in Florida. Though the language of the grants assumed that they were made to encourage population, trade, and military security, the fact that the grantees were impecunious courtiers throws doubt on the sincerity of the alleged motives.[8] In February, 1818, Richard S. Hackley, an American merchant who had previously served as consul in Spain, was carrying on negotiations with the Duke of Alagon, the principal grantee. The plan was to transfer a large part of the Duke's lands to Hackley, who in turn was to organize a land company for the retail sale of the acreage.[9]

7 Miller, *Treaties*, III, 41 an excellent map of the lands granted. ASP. FR., IV, 509-510 contains the texts of these grants. Alagon's was in East Florida, that of Vargas in territory around Mobile already occupied by the United States. Puñonrostro's grant bordered that of Vargas on the east.

8 Erving to Adams, May 14, 1818, DS., Despatches, Spain, vol. xv.

9 A bundle of papers dealing with these grants exists in the AHN., Est. Leg. 5585, Expediente No. 10. It also contains a pamphlet titled *Legal Opinions on the Title of Richard S. Hackley to Lands in Florida* (New York, 1841), pp. 1-9 of this work give *data* on Hackley's negotiations with Alagon.

Erving heard of the grants in February, 1818, and protested to Pizarro against such concessions while the status of Florida was the subject of negotiation.[10] This vigorous action, together with Pizarro's irritation at the addition of one more difficulty to the negotiation with the United States, checked the plans of the speculators. At Pizarro's instance the Council of the Indies forbade the sale of Florida lands to foreigners.[11] This step and Pizarro's further assurance that " there would be no difficulty about the grants " allayed Erving's suspicions.[12]

During the final stages of the Adams-Onís negotiations the status of Florida lands was further discussed. Adams stated flatly that the United States would consider void all grants subsequent to 1802.[13] When Onís made objection to so drastic a requirement, an agreement was finally reached confirming all grants prior to January 24, 1818.[14] None were to be recognized, however, unless actually proved and taken possession of, and unless all conditions attached to the grants had been fulfilled.

10 Erving to Adams, Feb. 10 and May 14, 1818, DS., Despatches, Spain, vol. xv.

11 Pizarro, *Memorias*, II, 83; Pizarro to President of the Council of the Indies, April 28, 1818, AME., Cor. Pol. Estados Unidos, Leg. 224.

12 Erving to Pizarro, July 18, 1818, private, and Pizarro to Erving, July 19, 1818, DS., Despatches, Spain, vol. xvi.

13 Adams to Onís, Oct. 31, 1818, AHN., Est. Leg. 5643; Adams, *Memoirs*, IV, 145-6.

14 In November, 1818, Onís refused to cancel the grants as far back as 1802, but proposed a compromise (Adams, *Memoirs*, IV, 170-1), suggesting on Nov. 16 (Onís to Adams, Nov. 16, 1818, AHN., Est. Leg. 5643) the date January 24, 1818, the day on which he first offered to cede the Floridas. As he explained his action to Pizarro (Onís to Pizarro, Nov. 23, 1818, AHN., Est. Leg. 5643) the grants having been made " with the sole object of peopling the said territories and not in order that they should be alienated, they have been virtually annulled by the failure of the beneficiaries to comply with these conditions."   In February, 1819, on the eve of the final settlement Adams made another effort to cancel all recent grants. He was led to agree to the date previously suggested by Onís, with the proviso that from the date of the treaty grantees must comply with the terms of their grants to validate them (Onís to Irujo, Feb. 19, 1819, AHN., Est. Leg. 5661).

This compromise was reached with the understanding that the recent large grants would be excluded by these conditions.

After the treaty was signed a rumor spread in the United States that the grants were made before the date mentioned in the treaty. Adams found to his horror that though the charters corresponding to two of the grants, of which Erving had sent copies, were subsequent to the critical date, they confirmed previous royal decrees. Greatly alarmed, he interviewed Hyde de Neuville and Onís.[15] Both assured him that they had supposed the grants in question to be annulled by the treaty, but Onís in the written statement required of him only stated this as his opinion and denied definite knowledge of the dates of the concessions. Though he denied any intention to trick Adams, he left the way open for a reversal of his attitude by his government.[16]

It appears that Onís, knowing the influence of the grantees at court, had done his best to secure the latest possible date in the treaty for the confirmation of grants. He deplored the King's bounty as an obstacle to the negotiations, but he was glad to avoid the appearance of hostility to the interests of the powerful grantees.[17] Adams was not completely satisfied with Onís' declaration and John Forsyth, the newly appointed minister to Spain, was instructed to present a declaration that according to the understanding of the negotiators the treaty annulled the Alagon, Puñonrostro and Vargas grants.[18]

15 Adams, *Memoirs*, IV, 287 ff.

16 Onís to Irujo, No. 49, March, 1818; Onís to Adams, Mar. 10,, 1819, AHN., Est. Leg. 5661; Onís to Irujo, private, Mar. 24, 1819, AHN., Est. Leg. 3446; Hyde de Neuville to Richelieu, Mar. 9, 1819, Hyde de Neuville to Adams, Mar. 17, 189, AAE., C. P. États Unis, vol. 76.

17 Onís to Irujo, Mar. 24, 1818, AHN., Est. Leg. 3446. His instruction with regard to the grants had been as follows: Pizarro to Onís, April 25, 1818, AHN., Est. Leg. 5643 had instructed a defense of all grants made. Irujo to Onís, Oct. 10, 1818, AHN., Est. Leg. 5643 authorized surrender of grants later than 1804, and a day later, Irujo to Onís, Oct. 11, 1818, AME., Cor. Pol. Estados Unidos, Leg. 224, those after 1803.

18 Adams to Forsyth, Mar. 10, 1819, DS., Instructions to Ministers, vol. viii.

Much of this stir can be traced to the activities of one Nicolás Garrido, agent for the Duke of Alagon, who, after formally taking possession of his principal's lands at St. Augustine in June, 1818, had proceeded to the United States. After the treaty was signed he openly offered lands for sale and guaranteed that his title was sound under the terms of the treaty.[19] Garrido was alarmed by the turn matters took after Adams secured Onís' declaration and is said to have written to the Duke to do all in his power to sustain the legality of his title even at the cost of war. Onís wrote privately to Irujo in March that this agent had said publicly that he would give $25,000 to be sure that his letters would arrive in Spain before Forsyth appeared with the treaty and the American declaration.[20]

Obviously the grantees had a strong interest in maintaining their titles, for at a low estimate the value of their lands approached eight million dollars.[21] When news of the treaty first reached Madrid the grantees made no attack on it, for it apparently confirmed the rights of Alagon and Puñonrostro,[22] but when the subsequent correspondence between Adams and Onís regarding the validity of the grants became known, these powerful interests joined the opposition.[23] It was apparently assumed that the United States intended to annul the grants explicitly and at all costs. It was not known that Forsyth's instructions, though they ordered him to present the American declaration on the grants, did not require Spain to take action with regard to it. Indeed, the treaty having previously been ratified by the Senate without reservations, the legal right of the United States to insist on modifications was questionable.

19 N. Biddle to Monroe, June 18, 1818, MP. LC.; Onís to Irujo, Mar. 24, 1819, No. 51, AHN., Est. Leg. 5661.

20 Onís to Irujo, private, Mar. 24, 1819, AHN., Est. Leg. 3446.

21 Ibid.

22 The Vargas grant was subsequent to Jan. 24, 1818 and invalid according to any interpretation of the treaty.

23 Extract from Forsyth's Diary, June 15, 1819, DS., Despatches, Spain, vol. xvii.

According to one view, Alagon and his associate could hope for no cash return on their lands as long as Florida remained Spanish. The law forbade the sale of lands to foreigners, the only prospective customers. A surrender to the American view of the treaty would deprive them of title, but if the United States should forcibly occupy Florida, as seemed probable if Spain refused to ratify the treaty, the American courts might sustain their rights, for military conquest does not ordinarily effect title to private property.[24]

John Forsyth, the new American minister, had arrived at Cadiz on April 16, 1819, on the U. S. sloop-of-war *Hornet*, but he did not reach Madrid until the first week in May.[25] Forsyth, born a Virginian, had moved to Georgia early in life. After graduating from Princeton he practiced law and in 1813 was elected to Congress. There he made a reputation as an orator and become the chairman of the House Committee on Foreign Relations. In 1818 he was appointed to the Senate to fill an unexpired term, but hearing of the coming vacancy at Madrid he obtained the appointment through the influence of his fellow Georgian, William H. Crawford.[26]

Forsyth impressed his contemporaries as a man of talent, especially as an orator, and all unite in praising his amiability. If any criticism was made, it was that he failed to make the most of his talents owing to a fondness for society.[27] When his appointment to Madrid was announced the foreign diplomats at Washington were unanimous in approving it, Onís even declaring that he would be the best minister the United States

24 Irujo to the King, July 16, 1819, AHN., Est. Leg. 3412. *Escritos del Conde de Ofalia publicados por su nieto el Marqués de Heredia, senador por derecho propio* (Bilbao, 1894), pp. 285-289; Adams, *Memoirs*, V, 16 f.; Forsyth to Adams, Jan. 3, 1820, DS., Despatches, Spain, vol. xviii.

25 Forsyth to Adams, April 18, 1819, DS., Despatches, Spain, vol. xvii.

26 *Dictionary of American Biography*, "John Forsyth"; Forsyth to N. Biddle, Dec. 15, 1818, Biddle Papers, LC.; Adams, *Memoirs*, IV, 307.

27 E. I. McCormac, "John Forsyth" in *American Secretaries of State and their Diplomacy*, ed. by S. F. Bemis, vol. iv.

had yet sent to Spain.[28] Adams, alone, distrusted the Southerner and deplored his appointment.[29] Though in later life Forsyth was to make a name for himself as a competent cabinet officer, his choice at this time as envoy to Spain was an unfortunate one.   An amiable and clever young man, with no diplomatic experience and fond of rhetoric, was not fitted to deal with the punctilious and dilatory Spanish court. Forsyth's usefulness was further limited by his inability to speak any language but his own. This forced him to rely almost entirely on written communications and cut him off from many sources of information.

The new minister arrived at Madrid with his temper already ruffled by a brush with the customs-house officers at Cadiz, whose interpretation of diplomatic immunity differed from his. His irritation grew as time elapsed without any progress toward ratification of the treaty. A letter to Irujo on May 18 urging promptness met an evasive reply and the American realized that he was not to have smooth sailing.[30]

Irujo would have been content if the treaty had definitely annulled the Florida grants, but the discrepancy between the letter of the treaty and the understanding of the negotiators was annoying, for it forced him to take a stand that was unpopular at the court and drew upon him the enmity of the grantees. He decided, therefore, to find out just what Forsyth's stand on the grant question was, and requested Laval, the French ambassador, to interview the American. This diplomat gladly undertook the errand, for he had instructions from his government to be of service.[31]

At first Forsyth was reluctant to discuss the matter. His primary object was to secure the ratification of the treaty as

28 Onís to Irujo, Nov. 30, 1818, private, AHN., Est. Leg. 2770; Hyde de Neuville to Richelieu, December 27, 1818, AAE., C. P. États Unis, vol. 76; Bagot to Castlereagh, Jan. 4, 1819, PRO., FO-5, vol. 141.

29 Adams, *Memoirs*, IV, 521.

30 Forsyth to Irujo, May 18, June 4, 1819, AHN., Est. Leg. 5661.

31 Laval to Dessolle, May 24, 1819, Dessolle to Laval, May 25, 1819. AAE., C. P. Espagne, Supplement No. 25.

soon as possible, for he was holding the *Hornet* at Cadiz in hope of returning it on that vessel. He feared discussion that might delay action and in his turn asked Laval to impress on the Spanish government the necessity for promptness, remarking that the ratification of the treaty did not in itself affect the rights of the grantees.[32] Irujo was much encouraged by this interview and during the last week in May induced Laval to see Forsyth again and to try to secure a promise not to insist on presenting his declaration on the land grants, or on receiving any corresponding declaration from Spain. Laval in the subsequent interview told Forsyth that the only grant which caused any difficulty was that of Alagon. He argued that, though it had been the intention of Adams and Onís to annul all these large grants, the letter of the treaty seemed to confirm one of them, and as Alagon was influential at the Spanish court it might be wise for the United States not to insist on express annullment and thereby risk the benefits which the treaty assured. He also questioned the legal efficacy of a posterior declaration to overcome or modify the provisions of a treaty. These arguments seemed to impress Forsyth. He observed that the courts might sustain Alagon's rights, but that could not affect the public rights of the United States, which in that case would have recourse to Spain to indemnify the resulting loss.[33] Here Forsyth's attitude differed from that of Adams. The latter, certainly, would not have hinted at a possible further negotiation with Spain on this issue. Forsyth's eagerness to finish his mission was leading him toward dangerous ground. He even hinted that in case the rights of Alagon were recognized by the American courts it might be possible to establish a compensation for the Duke in order to induce him to give up his claims and thus prevent further annoying negotiations.[34]

32 Laval to Dessolle, May 24, 1819, *ibid.*

33 Laval to Dessolle, June 7, 1819, AAE., C. P. Espagne, Supplement No. 25.

34 Laval to Dessolle, May 31, 1819, *ibid.* Forsyth's despatches do not confirm any such communication to Laval, though he speaks of the latter's

Forsyth, as a Georgian, was more interested in Florida than he was in the extinction of claims, most of which were held in the cities of the eastern seaboard. In this he was not far removed from Monroe who observed in March, 1819 that Florida was worth more than the United States had given for it even without an acre of public land.[35] With Adams, however, the land-grant issue had become a point of pride. He felt that the difficulty had arisen partly through his own fault and he was deeply chagrined at the way in which Onís had, he thought, deliberately tricked him. He also regarded the Florida public lands as the means for providing money with which to pay private claims against Spain for which the government had assumed responsibility in the treaty.

Forsyth's observations to Laval were his own and were not covered in any way by his instructions. Laval and Irujo, however, assumed that the compensation idea emanated from Washington and the latter saw in it an escape from his difficult position. He had already used all his energy to induce the King to accept the treaty. To the arguments already used before the Council of State he added the danger of a British occupation of Florida to forestall action by the United States; he stressed the full powers that had been granted Onís in the previous autumn; he even suggested that a special council be convoked to study the matter; and to make his earnestness absolutely clear he offered his resignation. The King remained uncertain between these arguments and those advanced by Lozano de Tórres and his friends.[36] These men played on the monarch's

efforts to get some statement from him favorable to the rights of the grantees (Forsyth to Adams, June 10, 11 and 17, 1819, DS., Despatches, Spain, vol. xvii), but Laval's reports are so circumstantial that they can not be disregarded.

35 Adams, *Memoirs*, IV, 290 attributes this opinion to Monroe. Forsyth's point of view is brought out in his letters to N. Biddle, Sept. 3, and Dec. 15, 1818 and Feb. 14, 1819, Biddle Papers, LC., vol. v.

36 These arguments were recalled to the king by Irujo in his letters to Ferdinand of July 7, July 12, 1819, AHN., Est. Leg. 3412; *cf.* Laval to Dessolle, June 10, 1819, AAE., C. P. Espagne, Supplement No. 25.

pride and fear. They told him that the treaty was a blow to his honor and the integrity of his dominions, and that it would be followed by the loss of other Spanish colonies. The *Juntas*, they said, even in the darkest days of the struggle against Napoleon, had not ceded territory—was it admissible that the King himself should now give up part of the empire he had inherited from his ancestors?[37] With more justification they pointed to matters left unsettled by the treaty. It contained no assurance that rebel privateers would not continue to operate from American ports, or that the United States would not shortly recognize the rebel governments.[38] It should be noted that it was at this time that rumors of the American consultation of Great Britain and France with a view to recognition of Buenos Aires were reaching Màdrid.[39]

Irujo's position was critical. To save himself and the treaty he attempted to detach the Florida grantees from the opposition by passing on to them the hints of compensation which Forsyth had let slip.[40] He was hardly given time for his hopes to subside after making these moves. At two a. m. on the following day, June 13, he received a royal order informing him of his dismissal and consigning him to arrest in the monastery of Valverde at Ávila.[41] Alagon and Puñonrostro had gone straight to the King from their talk with Irujo and had accused him of corrupt practice, of improper interest in Florida lands,[42] and of treasonably pro-American conduct of the nego-

37 Extracts from Forsyth's journal, June 13, 1819, DS., Despatches, Spain, vol. xvii.

38 Laval to Dessolle, May 31, 1819, AAE., C. P. Espagne, Supplement No. 25.

39 See chap. vi, *supra*, p. 184, note 103.

40 Laval to Dessolle, May 31, 1819, AAE., C. P. Espagne, Supplement No. 25.

41 Irujo to González Salmón, June 16, 1819, AHN., Est. Leg. 3412.

42 According to Erving Irujo did have a grant of from six to ten thousand acres in Florida, bought fifteen years earlier while he was in the United States, DS., Erving to Adams, Feb. 11, 1819, Despatches, Spain, vol. xvi.

tiations.[43] The irrepressible Irujo did not entirely lose heart, and from his place of confinement deluged the King with letters which help to establish the course of events leading to his disgrace. A judicial inquiry of his conduct was set on foot, but was soon abandoned owing to lack of evidence and Irujo was released after two months, though still in disgrace.[44]

The fall of Irujo left the Spanish foreign office in confusion. The venal opposition to the late minister contained no leader of experience or marked ability. Lozano de Tórres was now the most prominent man at court, but he was not designated to succeed Irujo. Manuel González Salmón, the ranking subsecretary, was given temporary charge of the ministry of state, but no one, González Salmón included, knew what Spanish policy was to be.[45]

Forsyth still hoped for ratification, which, in view of Spain's current difficulties with Portugal and the war with the Colonists, seemed to him inevitable. He pressed González Salmón for a reply to his notes but found the acting minister unwilling to commit himself.[46] The French ambassador, who deplored the change, also hoped that the treaty might yet be ratified. He knew the connection between Irujo's disgrace and his advocacy of the Washington treaty, but he was inclined to believe that the treaty had been attacked principally in order to oust Irujo. Onís, who had negotiated the treaty was apparently not in disgrace, and there were rumors that he might be called to Madrid to replace González Salmón.[47] Laval attempted to hearten Forsyth who was depressed and suspected British intrigue. With some difficulty he was persuaded to hold the *Hornet* a little longer in hope of some favorable development.[48]

43 Laval to Dessolle, July 20, 1819, AAE., C. P. Espagne, vol. 703.

44 Dossier on Irujo's imprisonment, AHN., Est. Leg. 3412.

45 Laval to Dessolle, June 17, 1819, AAE., C. P. Espagne, vol. 703.

46 Forsyth to Adams, June 17, 1819, also same date, *id.* to *id.*, private, DS., Despatches, Spain, vol. xvii.

47 Laval to Dessolle, July 5, 1819, *ibid.*

48 Laval to Dessolle, June 14, 1819, AAE., C. P. Espagne, vol. 703.

The favored position of the Russian minister at the Spanish court, Tatistcheff's ambitious schemes, and his hostility to Great Britain had led during the past few years to a rivalry between Sir Henry Wellesley and Tatistcheff which did not correspond to the real policy of either the Russian or British governments. Castlereagh had cautioned his subordinate against being led into a competition for influence at Madrid and had complained to the Tsar of Tatistcheff's behavior. Alexander had reprimanded his over-active envoy, but this does not seem to have had any immediate effect at Madrid. Tatistcheff had gone too far to retreat without completely losing his influence, and he continued his anti-British agitation, though with more caution than before. To the uninitiated at the Spanish court, therefore, Russia and Great Britain appeared to be bitter antagonists.[49]

Irujo's hostility to Great Britain and his friendly relations with Tatistcheff had been conspicuous, and his fall was a sign that Russian influence was on the wane. The Russian had over-played his hand [50] and was now being deserted by his erstwhile friends in the *camarilla*. In Madrid it was now realized that hope of Russian aid for Spain was an illusion. The recently purchased Russian fleet had proved unseaworthy,[51] and the peculations of Ugarte, a member of the *camarilla* closely associated with Tatistcheff, were shortly afterward made public.[52] There was nothing left for the arch schemer to do but to retire gracefully when he was no longer granted the private audiences with Ferdinand to which he had become accustomed. He left

49 Webster, *op. cit.*, pp. 65-67, 411-412; Prevost to Metternich, Nos. 44 and 45, October, 1818 (copies), AAE., C. P. Espagne, vol. 702; Perkins, in AHR, vol. xxviii, p. 662.

50 Laval to Dessolle, June 14, 1819, AAE., C. P. Espagne, vol. 703; on Irujo's friendship with Tatistcheff see Prevost to Metternich, Oct. 21, 1818 (copied), AAE., C. P. Espagne, vol. 702.

51 Laval to Dessolle, June 14, 1819, AAE., C. P. Espagne, vol. 703.

52 *Idem* to *idem*., April 22, 1819, *ibid*.

Spain in the autumn of 1819 on a leave of absence from which he did not return.[53]

The Anglo-Russian rivalry at the Spanish court had a deplorable effect on the ignorant schemers now in power at Madrid. They reasoned that as the pro-Russian Irujo had favored the American treaty Great Britain must object to it. As a matter of fact Russian influence at Madrid had not been strongly exerted in favor of the treaty, though the Tsar deplored violence and urged a peaceful settlement. Tatistcheff in August, 1819, when his influence was already on the wane, did recommend ratification of the American treaty in order not to delay the sailing of the expeditionary army to South America,[54] but he had never taken any great interest in the negotiations.[55] The attitude of Great Britain remained what it had been. Lord Castlereagh declared to San Carlos, the Spanish ambassador, that he did not wish any misunderstanding; that Spain must not hope for support from him.[56] The new leaders in Spain, however, seemed to rely more on gossip than they did on the evidence available in the files of the foreign office; led astray by the anti-American tone of the British press, they hoped for the aid of the British government.[57]

53 His recall was requested by San Fernando to Capo D'Istria, February, 1820, AHN., Est. Leg. 3446.

54 J. Becker, *Historia de las relaciones exteriores de España*, I, 478.

55 In 1818 Tatistcheff was accused by his French colleague of abetting Spanish stubbornness, Laval to Richelieu, Nov. 30, 1818, AAE., C. P. Espagne, vol. 702.

56 San Carlos to González Salmón, July 17, 1819, AHN., Est. Leg. 5661.

57 This lack of correct information is partially explained by the fact that the subsecretary who was in charge of the American negotiations under Pizarro and Irujo was disgraced and exiled simultaneously with his chief. *Escritos del Conde de Ofalia . . .*, pp. 43-44, introduction. *The Times* (London) published a violent diatribe against the treaty; for this and reports of other comments of the British press see, *Niles' Weekly Register*, May 1, May 29, and July 3, 1819. Spanish politicians were not alone in misinterpreting British policy. Forsyth's suspicions are disclosed in Forsyth to Monroe, Aug. 7, 1819, MP. NYP; Laval to Dessolle, July 1, 1819, AAE.,

Even before Irujo's fall Lozano de Tórres sent an emissary to Sir Henry Wellesley to secure his aid in blocking ratification of the treaty. Sir Henry refused to see this man and through his secretary declared the neutrality of Great Britain.[58]

On June 21 Forsyth's patience gave way and he addressed a note to González Salmón couched in language more suited to the floor of an American legislature than to a communication between sovereign states. It was a tirade against Spanish procrastination which, however justified it may have been in substance, was unfortunate in style and was to hinder rather than advance ratification of the treaty. Forsyth spoke of rumors that the King might " refuse that which the reputation of Spain " required, " that which Spain dare not refuse to do ". He made vague bombastic threats and went on to conclude that " there is that which a just government will more cautiously avoid than ever . . . the degradation of conscious baseness . . . No wise king will dare to do an act which would deprive him of the respect of all nations, sully the reputation of his kingdom in the eyes of the civilized world." [59] If Onís had used such language in Washington one may well imagine the resentment he would have aroused, and Spaniards were more sensitive than Americans to verbal assaults, being less accustomed to the freedom of language which accompanies party politics.

When the Council of State met again, now without Irujo, its temper had changed. Of Irujo's colleagues only one, José Imaz, minister of finance, still favored the treaty because he considered it the only safe policy. Two other councillors recommended ratification if the United States would give assurances not to recognize the rebel colonies and would guarantee the sovereignty of Spain over its colonial possessions. Most of those present opposed ratification on any terms. A member who had

C. P. Espagne, Supplement No. 25; for Adams' suspicions see, *Memoirs*. IV, 400. *Cf.* also *infra*, pp. 209 ff.

58 Laval to Dessolle, July 5, 1819, AAE., C. P. Espagne, vol. 703.

59 Forsyth to González Salmón, June 21, 1819, AHN., Est. Leg. 5661.

previously been undecided spoke of the American attitude as
" unjust, irritating, scandalous "; another remarked that it was
" necessary not to have Spanish blood to remain indifferent to
such enormous insults ". Forsyth's note seems to have been one
cause for the more hostile atmosphere, but the dismissal of
Irujo and the accusations made against him had an even more
serious influence.[60]

The views of Don Carlos, who though a reactionary was
not a member of the *camarilla,* and whose patriotism was above
suspicion, illustrate the reaction of one uninfluenced by personal
motives:

> The state of this affair is very different from that which pre-
> vailed in the last session. In it I was undecided between the inde-
> corousness of the treaty and the evil consequences of not ratifying
> it, but now I do not hesitate a moment in giving my vote that it
> should not be ratified.[61]

Irujo's sobering influence was gone; Forsyth's insulting language had been the last straw which decided Spain, already disturbed by rumors of an impending recognition of the rebels by
the United States and affected by the pecuniary interests of
the Florida grantees.

Though the minutes of the Council show an almost unanimous disapproval of the treaty, no decision was announced.
On the following day a small and less ceremonious *Junta de
Ministros* was held in the royal apartments to hear the King's
decision. It was there that the monarch communicated his resolution not to ratify the agreement with the United States,
considering it " contrary to the honor and interests of Spain "
and because it did not " conclude the differences between the
United States and Spain ".[62] The *Junta* was consulted as to the
best way to avoid ratification with safety and without loss of
credit.

60 Minutes of the Council of State, June 30, 1819, AHN., Est. Leg. 5661.

61 *Ibid.*

62 Minutes of the Junta de Ministros, July 1, 1819, AHN., Est. Leg. 5661.

Now that the ruler had spoken the ministerial chorus rose in denunciation of Onís' hard-won treaty. The most extreme accused all who had participated in the negotiation of treason; recommended measures for the defense of Florida and Cuba, and a complete break with Forsyth. A new rivalry now appeared between Lozano de Tórres and the Duke of San Fernando, a young and ambitious member of the Council of State. The latter favored moderation and suggested that a new parley should be started in order to prevent or delay a war. This view prevailed and González Salmón was ordered to prepare instructions to govern the projected undertaking.[63]

The Spanish decision on the treaty, at least in its broad outline, was apparently reached at this time. There is some evidence, however, to show that the King was still uncertain. No announcement was sent to Forsyth; Ferdinand seemed preoccupied; and some of his remarks led Laval to believe that the American treaty was still under consideration.[64] The King's retirement to his hunting lodge at Sacedon, accompanied by González Salmón, and the documents relating to the treaty suggest that the matter still hung in the balance.[65]

The delay in making an announcement lends credibility to an obscure scheme in which Álvarez de Toledo was said to be involved. The one-time rebel turned royalist had received a pardon through Onís' influence and had returned to Spain in 1817. He was taken up by the court, especially by General Eguía, the minister of war, who consulted him as an expert on American affairs.[66] In July rumors began to circulate that this man had been commissioned to undertake a secret mission relating to the United States. The idea was to secure a loan in London to pay the American claims; to deliver Florida to

63 Ibid.

64 Laval to Dessolle, Aug. 2, 1819, AAE., C. P. Espagne, vol. 704.

65 Laval to Dessolle, July 1, 1819, AAE., C. P. Espagne, vol. 703.

66 See expediente on Álvarez de Toledo, AHN., Est. Leg. 5554, Expediente No. 12; Erving to Sec. of State, April 6, 1817, DS., Despatches, Spain, vol. xiv.

Great Britain as security for the loan; and thus to shelve Onís' treaty. Toledo was intimate with Lozano. The scheme fits in with that minister's obstinate belief that Britain could be induced to prevent the cession of Florida and is in keeping with the secretive diplomatic methods of Ferdinand. Neither the Spanish foreign office nor any of the regular diplomatic agents of Spain abroad were in the secret if there was one.[67] Toledo was reported to have left Madrid, to have passed through Paris, to have returned to Madrid, to have reached London and initiated some business there. Lord Castlereagh questioned the Spanish Ambassador about these rumors and declared that he would refuse to see Toledo, for no good could come of such machinations.[68] The enterprise came to nothing, if it existed at all, and is chiefly interesting as a possible explanation for the inaction of Spain during July 1819.[69]

On August 2 another *Junta de Ministros* was held and the policy approved at the previous meeting was confirmed. It was now decided to inform Forsyth that the King could not decide on the treaty without first getting certain explanations, and that with a view to securing them a person enjoying the royal confidence had been chosen to deal with the matter.[70] A note embodying this decision was sent to Forsyth on August 10. Beside the announcement of Spanish plans it included a protest against the language he had employed in his note of June 21, but to sugar the pill it concluded with effusive declarations of good will.[71]

67 San Carlos to González Salmón, July 17, 1819, AHN., Est. Leg. 5661, denies categorically any knowledge of Toledo's reported activities, and there is no evidence in Toledo's dossier to indicate the mission.

68 *Ibid.*

69 For Toledo's reputed mission see: Laval to Dessolle, July 8 and July 20, 1819, AAE., C. P. Espagne, vol. 703; Forsyth to Monroe, Aug. 7, 1819, MP. NYP.; Forsyth to Adams, Aug. 22, 1819, DS., Despatches, Spain, vol. xvii; Gallatin to Forsyth, July 9, 1819, *Writings of Albert Gallatin,* ed. by H. Adams, II, 109.

70 Minutes of the Junta de Ministros, Aug. 2, 1819, AHN., Est. Leg. 5661.

71 González Salmón to Forsyth, Aug. 10, 1819, *ibid.*

Forsyth objected to the vagueness of this note and its failure to specify reasons for the attitude adopted,[72] but González Salmón evaded his questions and insisted on continuing discussion only in Washington.[73] Forsyth was forced to admit failure. On August 21 he announced formally that, ratification having been withheld after the six months period fixed by the treaty, the United States resumed all its claims.[74]

Private interests and personal emnities had played a large part in producing this new stalemate—hostility to Irujo, the greed of Alagon and his fellows, and the intrigues of Tatistcheff, Lozano de Tórres and others. The fall of Irujo strengthened opposition to the treaty and reports of American designs to recognize Buenos Aires together with the rash and inflammatory language used by Forsyth had also contributed to defer the issue. The underlying reason for Spanish reluctance once all these factors are discounted was the feeling that the treaty gave no security that the United States would turn from its policy of bare neutrality and open sympathy for the rebels in the Spanish colonies. Perhaps it is vain to seek too reasonable an explanation. Ferdinand may have tried to reach a decision on logical grounds, but he was primarily influenced by the attachment of the men about him to his person and to his absolutist principles. Though alone responsible for Spanish policy, the King may be regarded as acting as the electorate does in a representative democracy, that is: as a deciding force choosing between alternatives it can not control, and more influenced by sentiment than by reason.

In the United States, meanwhile, the delay at Madrid led to uneasiness. Rumors of British opposition began to occupy American newspapers. As it has been noted, the comment of the British press was hostile. It was held that the cession of

72 Forsyth to González Salmón, Aug. 12, 1819, *ibid.*

73 González Salmón to Forsyth, Aug. 19, 1819, *ibid.*

74 Forsyth to González Salmón, Aug. 21, 1819, *ibid.* Forsyth to Adams, Aug. 22, 1819, DS., Despatches, Spain, vol. xvii.

Florida to the United States endangered British possessions in the West Indies and commercial interests in the whole Caribbean area.[75] This attitude was resented in the United States and remarks such as that of the *Times* that " poor old Spain has fallen into the hands of a sharper " [76] certainly did not reduce irritation. A pamphlet issued in London which urged occupation of Cuba by Great Britain in order to offset the strategic advantage gained by the United States through possession of Florida still further increased the suspicions of the American public.[77] In Parliament questions were asked on the attitude of the government to the Adams-Onís Treaty. Why, asked the Marquis of Lansdowne in the House of Lords, had the government not prevented the cession of Florida which might be dangerous to Great Britain in case of war? Lord Bathurst, answering for the Foreign Office, declared that Britain had no excuse to intervene in a dispute between Spain and America and Lord Liverpool added that opposition to the treaty was useless unless the country was prepared to back it by force.[78]

The outcome of this discussion in Parliament might have lulled American antagonism, but it was not yet known in the United States on July 9 when a vessel arrived, thirty days out of Cadiz, with news that the Spanish treaty had not yet been ratified.[79] Accounts appeared in the *Washington City Gazette* in which fear of British interference at Madrid was played up.[80]

75 *Niles' Weekly Register*, May 1, 1819. This sentiment was not new. See *Columbian Museum and Savannah Gazette*, Feb. 10, 1818, quoting *Jamaica Colonial Journal; Louisiana Courier*, April 6, 1818 quotes a Jamaica article favoring a British occupation of Florida.

76 *Niles' Weekly Register*, July 3, 1819.

77 J. F. Rattenberry, *Remarks on the Cession of Florida to the United States of America, and on the Necessity of Acquiring the Island of Cuba by Great Britain,* in the *Pamphleteer,* London, vol. xv, 1819.

78 *Parliamentary Debates,* ed. by Hansard, vol. xl, pp. 287 ff.

79 Adams, *Memoirs,* IV, 400.

80 *Ibid.* See also, *Kentucky Reporter,* Lexington, Ky., June 16, 1819; Rumors were abroad soon that Spain had ceded Florida to Great Britain,

On July 31 the *Hornet* returned with the same discouraging news of delay. Supporters of the administration's Spanish policy maintained an attitude of outward confidence, but at heart their belief in Spanish acquiescence was sadly shaken.[81]

The arrival of Forsyth's despatches led to a cabinet meeting to decide what action should be taken in case Spain should definitely prove recalcitrant. The cabinet was unanimous that Florida should be occupied in that event, but there was a conflict of opinion on the instructions to be sent to Forsyth. Crawford took the extreme view that he should ask for his passports, but he was opposed by Calhoun and Adams.[82] The moderation of Adams and of the President did not arise from lukewarm interest in the acquisition of Florida. Not long before this time Monroe had said that if Spain hesitated to agree to the treaty he would never consent to negotiate again with that country.[83] Adams on his part had vehemently declared to Bagot that the United States considered the Floridas part of the national territory, and that in case Spain refused to ratify the treaty force would be used.[84] They still hoped, however, that Spain would give in, for though the direct news was disquieting Gallatin reported that it was believed in Paris that Spain would accept the treaty, a view also corroborated by Erving.[85] A mistaken view also prevailed that the removal of Irujo was a *favorable* sign.[86] Further, Monroe heard indirectly that De la Serna, the

that California had been ceded to Russia, that Great Britain had obtained Cuba, see *Niles' Weekly Register*, Sept. 4, Nov. 27, Dec. 4, 11, 1819. *National Intelligencer*, quoted by *Columbian Museum and Savannah Gazette*, Nov. 3, 1819.

81 *Niles' Weekly Register*, Aug. 16, 1819.

82 Adams, *Memoirs*, IV, 405.

83 Antrobus to Castlereagh, Oct. 6, 1819, PRO., FO-5, vol. 143.

84 *Idem* to *idem*, Aug. 3, 1819, *ibid*.

85 *Writings of Albert Gallatin*, ed. by H. Adams, II, 103-104, 108-109; Gallatin to Adams, Nos. 105, 111, 114, May to July, 1819.

86 Hyde de Neuville to Dessolle, Aug. 7, 1819, AAE., C. P. États Unis, vol. 76.

Spanish chargé, who had been left in charge of the legation by Onís, believed that ratification would go through.[87]

The administration decided, accordingly, to instruct Forsyth to accept the Spanish ratification, even after the six months period prescribed by that instrument had elapsed, if it were given in time to reach the United States before the meeting of Congress. Orders also went to him to insist on the acceptance of the American declaration on the invalidity of the Florida grants. It was decided not to make any threat to occupy disputed territory, but to state that the decision as to future policy would be left to Congress if ratification should be withheld. With these orders the *Hornet* again sailed for Cadiz.[88]

Monroe's optimism was not to be justified. On October 7, the brig *Joseph* arrived at New York from Bordeaux with official news of the Spanish negative decision and the proposal of a new negotiation at Washington.[89] In spite of this disappointment it was necessary before taking further action to await the result of the new offer recently despatched to Forsyth.

That minister, chagrined by the check he had suffered at the outset of his diplomatic career, was to suffer further discomfiture during the autumn, and still further increase his unpopularity at the Spanish court.[90] When the American offer of a time extension for ratification reached Madrid at the end of September, Forsyth was persuaded by Laval to present it verbally.[91] An interview was accordingly arranged with the Duke of San Fernando, who was now secretary of state, having

87 C. J. Ingersoll to Monroe, Aug. 10, 1819, MP. NYP.

88 Adams to Forsyth, Aug. 18, 1819, DS., Instructions to Ministers, vol. viii; Adams, *Memoirs*, IV, 405.

89 The news reached Washington on Oct. 10, Brent to Monroe, DS., Domestic Letters, vol. vii; *Niles' Weekly Register*, October 16, 1819.

90 Dessolle to Hyde de Neuville, Oct. 21, 1819, AAE., C. P. États Unis, vol. 76; *Correspondence ... of Lord Castlereagh*, ed. by C. Vane, XII, 170, Wellesley to Castlereagh, Jan. 6, 1820.

91 Laval to Dessolle, Oct. 13, 1819, AAE., C. P. Espagne, vol. 704.

overcome the preponderance of his rival Lozano de Tórres.[92]
Though not without ability, the new minister seems to have been
sluggish and inexperienced. Laval reported that his sovereign
cure for all troubles was inaction. To a large extent he was a
mere figurehead, for the King himself now kept a closer watch
over foreign affairs.[93]

As interpreters were necessary at this meeting, most of the
advantages of personal contact were lost. San Fernando refused
to admit any moral obligation on the part of Spain to ratify
the treaty; disregarded Forsyth's talk of hostile public feeling
in the United States; and insisted on the previously announced
plan to send a minister to Washington to discuss the treaty.[94]
An exchange of notes confirming the matters touched upon at
the interview put an end to negotiation and Forsyth was again
obliged to report failure.[95]

Though no agreement had been reached, the meetings had
gone off without any display of bad temper and the personal
objections of the Spaniards to Forsyth might have evaporated,
but a few days later a note from Forsyth on the subject of the
land grants was returned by San Fernando with a curt statement that it contained inadmissible language.[96] Forsyth's re-
monstrances [97] were disregarded, and much perturbed and uncertain of his proper course, he was about to ask for his pass-

92 Laval to Dessolle, Aug. 26, 1819; DeCabres to Dessolle, Nov. 15, 1819;
Laval to Dessolle, Oct. 31, 1819, ibid. San Fernando to De la Serna, Sept. 12,
1819, AME., Estados Unidos, Cor. Pol., Leg. 225.

93 Laval to Dessolle, Oct. 31, 1819, AAE., C. P. Espagne, vol. 704.

94 Minute of conference, San Fernando-Forsyth; Forsyth to San Fernando,
Oct. 10, AHN., Est. Leg. 5661; Laval to Dessolle, Oct. 13, 1819, AAE., C. P.
Espagne, vol. 704.

95 San Fernando to Forsyth, Oct. 8, 1819; Forsyth to San Fernando, Oct.
10, 1819, AHN., Est. Leg. 5661; Forsyth to Adams, Oct. 10, 1819, Oct. 28,
1819, DS., Despatches, Spain, vol. xvii.

96 San Fernando to Forsyth, Nov. 12, 1819, AHN., Est. Leg. 5661.

97 Forsyth to San Fernando, Nov. 20, 1819, ibid.

ports.[98] This was more than the Spaniards had counted on.
They had wished to rebuke the minister without precipitating
an open break with his government, and through Count Bulgary, the Russian chargé d'affaires, Forsyth was partially
mollified. On receiving assurances that the new envoy to Washington would set out immediately, he postponed his departure,
threatening, however, to present the obnoxious note again if
Spain did not act quickly.[99]

The public temper in the United States when the attitude of
Spain became known was unmistakably bellicose. In October
popular feeling was reported to be " more actively hostile than
that of the administration " and the same observer believed that
" a declaration of war at this time against Spain would be a
very popular measure ".[100] Even mercantile New England
which had been opposed to violent measures now joined the
rest of the country. War was the first thought in Boston when
the news of the rejection of the treaty was received, even the
merchants feeling that anything would be better than the long
continued uncertainty that played havoc with commercial intercourse with Spain and its possessions.[101]

98 According to F. W. Hackett, *The Meade Claim* (Washington, 1910),
p. 9, which is an ex parte argument to support the case of a claimant
before Congress at a later time, the Spanish government at this time was
contemplating further deals in Florida lands. He states that on Sept. 30,
1819, the Spanish government on being pressed for payment of his claim
by Meade, offered to pay in Florida lands. As they were all in the hands
of Alagon and other grantees at this time the exact move contemplated is
not clear. Forsyth to Adams, Jan. 3, 1820, DS., Despatches, Spain, vol. xviii.
Forsyth was at a loss to understand the strong stand of the Spanish court
and conjectured as to whether it was due to British interference, or to a
deliberate plan to make the United States occupy Florida in order to improve
the private interests of Alagon and his associates.

99 *Ibid.* See also San Fernando to Forsyth, Dec. 16, 1819 and Forsyth to
San Fernando, Jan. 27, 1820 in AHN., Est. Leg. 5661 and 5662 respectively.

100 Antrobus to Castlereagh, Oct. 6, 1819, PRO., FO-5, vol. 143, see also
Hyde de Neuville to Dessolle, Oct. 23, 1819, AAE., C. P. États Unis, vol. 76.

101 Eustis to Monroe, Oct. 23, 1819, MP. LC.; during the previous year a
war scare had led many American ships to leave Spain hurriedly without

A host of varied influences were now brought to bear on the President. In August a Philadelphia editor suggested that the United States occupy Cuba as well as Florida, as war was inevitable in any case.[102] Though occupation of Florida was a popular idea, not many joined this man in favoring a conquest of Cuba. One Southern paper declared that there was no widespread wish to acquire that island.[103] Another repercussion of the strained situation was the suggestion of Rodney, the ex-commissioner to South America, who asked whether the rejection of the treaty did not leave the United States free to recognize Spanish American independence.[104] In the West opinion seemed to be divided between expansionism and sympathy for revolution. Desire for Texas was expressed, as was sympathy for filibusters who were working for the independence of that region.[105]

As the time for the meeting of Congress approached, there appears to have been a slight but definite reaction from the war talk that had prevailed a few weeks earlier.[106] The administration must have noticed this trend at the same time that France and Russia exerted their influence to prevent any rash decision. Hyde de Neuville was most active in his pacific efforts. His government was especially eager to prevent war,[107] and its

their cargoes, Laval to Richelieu, Aug. 21, 1818, AAE., C. P. Espagne, vol. 702. The probability of war between Spain and the United States was being discounted by Lloyds. It was considered a ten to one chance that such a war would not break out within two months, *Niles' Weekly Register*, October 23, 1819.

102 William McCorkle to Monroe, Aug. 25, 1819, MP. NYP.

103 *Columbian Museum and Savannah Gazette*, Aug. 7, 1819.

104 Rodney to Monroe, September 30, 1819, MP. LC.

105 *Kentucky Reporter*, May 5, 1819 quotes and endorses the objections of the *St. Louis Enquirer* to the surrender of Texas. The *Savannah Republican*, July 27, 1819, quoting a Natchez paper shows sympathy for the expedition of Gen. Long to Texas.

106 Eustis to Monroe, Oct. 23, 1819, MP. LC.; Hyde de Neuville to Dessolle, Dec. 5, 1819, AAE., C. P. États Unis, vol. 76.

107 Richelieu to Hyde de Neuville, July 5 and Sept. 5, 1818, AAE., C. P. États Unis, vols. 75 and 76 respectively.

envoy was in a position to be effective, for his services as intermediary between Adams and Onís had acquainted him fully
with the situation and had won him the good will of Adams and
of Monroe. Through the summer he had tried to keep Adams
in a good humor, making excuses for the Spanish delay and
holding out prospects of a speedy settlement.[108]

When Monroe heard in October that Spain was planning to
send a new minister to the United States he induced Hyde de
Neuville, who was on the point of returning to France, to
postpone his journey.[109] The President was perhaps conscious of
the abruptness as well as of the sterling ability of his Secretary
of State, and hoped with the Frenchman's aid to smooth over
the coming encounter. Hyde de Neuville, delighted by the com-
pliment implied, agreed to remain.[110]

The Russian influence at Madrid had been much distorted
by the intrigues of Tatistcheff, but the new minister in Washington, Count Pierre de Poletica, stayed within the letter of
his instructions to deplore violence and to do what he could to
bring peaceful agreement between Washington and Madrid
without committing his government to any action.[111] Soon
after his arrival Poletica announced these views to Adams and
evinced a friendly disposition toward the United States.[112] In
December, shortly before the delivery of Monroe's message to
Congress, the Russian was asked by Adams whether his government favored ratification of the treaty by Spain. He gave an
affirmative answer, an attitude in accord with that of the

108 Hyde de Neuville to Dessolle, Aug. 7, 1819, AAE., C. P. États Unis,
vol. 76.

109 Adams to Hyde de Neuville, Oct. 23, 1819, *ibid.*

110 Hyde de Neuville to Dessolle, Nov. 16, 1819, *ibid.*

111 " Correspondence of the Russian Ministers in Washington," ed. by W.
C. Ford, in AHR., vol xviii (1913), pp. 315 ff. Nesselrode to Poletica, 9/21
November, 1819 (translation).

112 Adams, *Memoirs*, IV, 380; Cresson, *The Holy Alliance*, pp. 86-87.
points out Poletica's critical attitude toward Spain.

Russian foreign office.[113] This conciliatory influence was reinforced by reports reaching Washington from Paris describing
a similar attitude on the part of Dessolle, the French foreign
minister and of Pozzo di Borgo on behalf of the Tsar.[114]

The problem before Monroe and his cabinet in November
and December, 1819 was a delicate one. The President was hesi-
tant. He inclined, at first, to sustain his earlier opinion that
Florida should be occupied.[115] A part of his message was even
drafted with this recommendation, but in a cabinet meeting on
November 26 Monroe was still undecided. He was worried by
the growing conflict between Adams and Crawford, who took
opposite sides on this as on many other questions. Crawford
favored aggressive action while Adams, perhaps influenced by
the French and Russian ministers, argued for delay. A compromise suggested by Adams was finally adopted, and the message
in its final form recommended the passage of an act authorizing
the President to take possession of Florida when and if he
should find such a course necessary or desirable.[116]

This was clever politics. The act contemplated would show
the world that the United States was in earnest and increase
the pressure on Spain, but it also left Monroe free to use force
or not as circumstances might dictate. There were good reasons
for what amounted to an evasion of the issue. One of them
was the uncertainty as to whether an occupation of Florida
would lead to war. There was no doubt that it could be regarded
as an act of war, but Adams did not believe that Spain would
fight on this issue.[117] In forming his opinion he was influenced,

113 "Correspondence of the Russian Ministers," AHR., XVIII, 321 f.
Nesselrode to Poletica, No. 27, 1819 (translation).

114 Adams, *Memoirs*, IV, 448; *Writings of Albert Gallatin*, II, 125,
Gallatin to Adams, No. 125, October, 1819.

115 *Writings of James Monroe*, ed. by Hamilton, vol. vi, Monroe to
Madison, Nov. 24, 1819.

116 Adams, *Memoirs*, IV, 446 ff.; Richardson, *Messages and Papers*, II,
pp. 54-58, Monroe to Congress, Dec. 7, 1819.

117 Adams, *Memoirs*, V, 60.

no doubt, by Gallatin's reports.[118] Still, the ultimate result of an armed occupation was impossible to calculate with certainty and Monroe was glad to postpone action until further information from abroad and expressions of opinion from the country could reach him.

Monroe's message in so far as it related to Spanish affairs was most diversely received. It was approved by hot-heads and conservatives but for very different reasons. From Boston, Philadelphia and Virginia came letters approving the President's policy as one that would avert war, while from the West came expressions of as ardent approval which assumed that war would occur.[119] As the month of January wore on the complexity of public opinion became more and more manifest and the reaction from the war spirit of the early autumn was clearly noticeable.[120]

The rumors of war with Spain which circulated during the autumn of 1819 were not entirely unjustified. Though neither government actively desired a break, both adopted measures which might well lead to war, and neither neglected preparation for eventual hostilities. In the United States Jackson was asked to prepare a plan of campaign for an attack on the Spanish forts in Florida,[121] but even before Calhoun's request reached him the fiery General had volunteered his advice on this matter to the President.[122] He anticipated a difficult task.

118 *Writings of Albert Gallatin*, ed. by H. Adams, II, 125, Gallatin to Adams, No. 125, October, 1819.

119 Letters of a pacific turn are Spencer Roane to Monroe, Dec. 13, 1819, MP. NYP.; N. Biddle to Monroe, Dec. 9, 1819, MP. LC.; Madison to Monroe, Dec. 11, 1819, and Dearborn to Monroe, Dec. 31, 1819, MP. LC., Johnson Collection. More warlike were the following: J. Desha to Monroe, Dec. 23, 1819, A. Jackson to Monroe, Jan. 15, 1820, MP. NYP.

120 Smith Thompson to Van Buren, Jan. 9, 1820, Van Buren Papers, LC.; " Correspondence of the Russian Ministers . . ." AHR., XVIII, 322-3, Poletica to Nesselrode, Jan. 31 / Feb. 12, 1820.

121 *Correspondence of J. C. Calhoun*, ed. by J. F. Jameson in *Annual Report*, AHA., 1899, vol. ii, p. 165, Calhoun to Jackson, Dec. 10, 1819.

122 Jackson to Monroe, Dec. 10, 1819, MP. NYP.

At St. Augustine a regular siege would be necessary and Fort Barranacas at Pensacola had recently been strengthened.

In Spain, also, preparations for war were being made in the last months of 1819, precipitated by the renewal of tension between Forsyth and the Spanish foreign office. The minister of war was ordered to prepare a report on the military footing of Cuba and the Floridas and to take steps to put them in a proper state for defense.[123] The minister reported that three thousand men had recently been sent to Cuba, but Florida, he thought, could not successfully be defended against a serious attack from the United States. The large forces stationed in Mexico could not safely be diverted from that area to Florida.[124] Onís, now in Madrid, was called upon for information on the military strength of the United States. His report estimated the American regular army at ten thousand men, who could be expanded in time of war to sixty two thousand for which number trained officers were available. The militia of 700,000 men was not credited with any offensive value.[125]

These reports were not encouraging and evidently dissuaded Spain from any idea of taking the offensive. Orders were sent to the chief Spanish officials in America to act with caution in their military operations and to keep in touch with the legation in Washington.[126] On another element, however, Spain prepared for the offensive. The Secretary of the Navy was ordered to furnish two hundred privateering licenses signed in blank. In case of war one hundred of these were to be sent to England and the remainder to France for distribution by the Spanish ambassadors to prospective privateers in those countries.[127] Though its own naval resources were small, Spain evidently

123 San Fernando to Sec. of War, Dec. 14, 1819, AHN., Est. Leg. 5661.

124 Alos to San Fernando, Dec. 19, and Dec. 26, 1819, *ibid.*

125 Onís to San Fernando, Dec. 23, 1819, *ibid.*

126 Alos, Circular to Officials in America, Jan. 7, 1820, AHN., Est. Leg. 5662.

127 San Fernando to the Sec. of the Navy, Dec. 14, 1819, AHN., Est. Leg. 5661; Alos to San Fernando, Jan. 5, 1820, AHN., Est. Leg. 5662.

looked forward with gusto to giving American shipping a taste of the medicine which American-owned and American-manned privateers under Spanish American colors had been dealing out to Spanish maritime commerce.

Unimportant as these warlike measures were on both sides of the Atlantic, they indicate the atmosphere of mutual distrust and uncertainty that characterized Spanish-American relations at the end of 1819. It was not to be long, however, before events unforeseen at this juncture were to occur, making possible a solution of the crisis.

CHAPTER VIII

RATIFICATION OF THE ADAMS-ONIS TREATY

SPAIN had announced in August, 1819, that a minister would be sent to the United States to thrash out questions relating to the recently negotiated treaty, but it was not until December that the appointment of General Francisco Dionisio Vives was made public.[1] Vives had distinguished himself in the Peninsular War, but he had no diplomatic experience.[2] But Ferdinand wished to be represented in Washington by a soldier and he disregarded the pretensions of the diplomats.[3] Two men first considered both offered excuses,[4] and Vives, equally reluctant, was virtually drafted. The new minister was serving in the army destined for South America then being organized in Andalusia, and quarantine for yellow fever delayed his departure for Madrid.[5] Apparently there was little interest in hastening negotiations, or some one more available would have been sent to Washington.

The instructions Vives carried when he left Madrid had been prepared during the previous summer by González Salmón, and had not subsequently been altered, though six months had elapsed. After a preliminary summary of the dispute with the United States they stated that Onís' treaty was inadmissible because it provided for large concessions to the United States

1 San Fernando to Forsyth, Dec. 16, 1819, AHN., Est. Leg. 5661.

2 *Enciclopedia universal Espasa*, LXIX, 712, Article "Francisco Dionisio Vives."

3 González Salmón had recommended J. Campuzano, ex-chargé at London. González Salmón to Ferdinand, July 29, 1819, AHN., Est. Leg. 5661.

4 Nemesio Salcedo, a retired officer with experience in northern Mexico was chosen but declined owing to ill health. A General Bonavia who was considered also was unavailable. Laval to Dessolle, Sept. 27, 1819, AAE., C. P. Espagne, vol. 704; Forsyth to Adams, Oct. 10, 1819, DS., Despatches, Spain, vol. xvii.

5 Laval to Dessolle, Oct. 13, 1819, AAE., C. P. Espagne, vol. 704.

in return for which Spain gained insufficient compensation. The American overtures to France and Great Britain, suggesting joint recognition of the Buenos Aires government (here incorrectly stated to have been made after the treaty was signed), indicated the worthlessness of the agreement to Spain. Fortunately, the United States had itself provided an excuse for delay by requiring an unjustifiable interpretation of the article in the treaty dealing with public lands in Florida.

The principal aim in the negotiation now renewed was to prevent the United States from recognizing or giving aid to the rebel governments. This could best be accomplished through a guaranty similar to that offered by the Americans in 1803. Only after this main point had been settled were the boundary and pecuniary claims questions to be considered.

To secure British aid commercial advantages should be offered to that power. Finally, the instructions declared that if the United States could be induced to renew negotiation the mission would be considered a success even if no agreement were reached.[6]

The land grant question which had been a principal factor in the downfall of Irujo and the rejection of the treaty was mentioned only as a convenient excuse for delay, and the main objection was based on the policy of the United States toward the rebels. Irujo had planned to prevent recognition of the new governments in Spanish America by satisfying American territorial ambitions and had believed that no express stipulations would be necessary. His successors discarded this policy, strained American patience, and believed that the consequent hostility of the United States justified them. In short, Spain had returned to the policy of holding the United States in play, the futility of which Pizarro had come to realize, and which Irujo had replaced by a clear-cut plan.

6 Instructions to Vives approved by the *Junta de Ministros*, of Aug. 2, 1819, AHN., Est. Leg. 5661.

On his way to England, whence he was to sail to his destination, Vives halted in Paris, where he met Pozzo di Borgo and Baron Pasquier, the new French foreign minister. Both urged promptness and advised Spain to make sacrifices to settle with the United States. They were also effusive with assurances of good will toward Spain. Vives attacked Hyde de Neuville for backing Adams on the land-grant dispute, but Pasquier retorted that even Onís had been forced to make a similar statement, and insisted that Hyde de Neuville had instructions to make himself useful to Spain. Pozzo di Borgo told Vives that Poletica had similar orders.[7]

During his stay in Paris Vives also met Gallatin, who eagerly pressed him for news. The American was disappointed to hear that Vives did not bring the Spanish ratification with him, but he gathered that Vives had authority to give some security of settlement if the replies to his " requests for information " were satisfactory. Gallatin took this to mean that Spain would in that event agree to an American occupation of Florida. Vives later denied having made any such statement, and it is probable that Gallatin counted too heavily on some vague remark made by the Spanish diplomat. Fernan-Nuñez, Ferdinand's representative in Paris, added to the confusion by hinting that Spain might give way on the land grants, and it also appears that Pasquier misled Gallatin as to the extent of Vives powers. Gallatin reported correctly, however, that the principal points to be raised by the new minister would be the interpretation of the land grant article of the treaty and the relations of the United States with the rebellious Spanish Americans.[8]

Vives left Paris on February 14 for London where he faced the arduous task of securing British intervention. The way had been partly prepared for him by the Duke of San Carlos who

7 Fernan-Nuñez to San Fernando, Feb. 14, 1820, AHN., Est. Leg. 5662.

8 *Writings of Albert Gallatin,* ed. by H. Adams, vol. ii, 133-36, 165, Gallatin to Adams, Feb. 15, 1820, Aug. 7, 1820; *cf.* Vives to Adams, May 11, 1820, AHN., Est., Leg. 5646; and Adams to Gallatin, May 25, 1820, DS., Instructions to Ministers, vol. ix.

had attempted more than once to justify to Castlereagh the rejection of the Adams-Onís Treaty. With San Carlos to assist him Vives twice interviewed Lord Castlereagh, but though he went over all the familiar Spanish arguments and made the offers of commercial privileges that had been authorized, he received no encouragement. The Spaniards were roundly lectured by the British minister. He told them that he would like to see them keep Florida, but that he would not go to war to secure that end. He ignored hints that Florida might be ceded to Great Britain and advised Spain to settle with the United States as soon as possible.[9] This discouraging result left Vives nothing more to do in England and within a few days he sailed for New York from Liverpool.

While Spain was thus attempting to prepare the ground for a coming negotiation at Washington, the American Congress was considering the Florida question and Monroe's request for optional authority to occupy that territory. A bill embodying the President's request was introduced in the House and referred to the Committee on Foreign Relations early in the session, but no report was made by the committee until March, 1820.[10] The Missouri controversy was chiefly responsible for the postponement of this issue. This report differed considerably from Monroe's original proposal. It made the occupation of Florida mandatory rather than optional. Another feature which made it objectionable to Adams and to others in the Northeast was its apparent surrender of the American claims to the public lands in Florida and its suggestion that the country should look to the region west of the Sabine River for indemnity. Practically disregarding the treaty of 1819, it did not provide any method for satisfying the claims of individual citizens. As reported, the bill was an expression of Southern and

9 San Carlos to San Fernando, Feb. 24, 1820, AHN., Est. Leg. 5662.

10 *Annals of Congress*, XXXVI, 16th Cong. 2nd. Sess., HR, p. 1618-19, Report of the Committee, Mar. 9, 1820. As early as January, 1820 there were signs of unrest in the House on the administration's Spanish policy. *Ibid.*, XXXV, 16th Cong., 2nd Sess., HR. 948.

Western interests and it was not likely to pass the House in this form.[11]

The administration favored an occupation of Florida under the theory that the treaty of 1819 was binding on Spain and might be unilaterally enforced by the United States. The bill reported did not suit the plans of Monroe and Adams at all. Vives was expected shortly; France and Russia urged moderation; Monroe decided, therefore, to forestall a vote on the bill and sent a message to Congress on March 31 in which he advised that no action be taken until after the arrival of the Spanish envoy.[12] He had difficulty in finding a plausible justification for the change in his attitude since the beginning of the session. Not wishing to declare his real motive, a desire to retain freedom of action, he spoke of the " distressed state of Spain ", where revolts had broken out, and of the expressed wishes of France and Russia. The President's action was effective in stopping the progress of the Florida bill in the House, but it became the subject of a new attack by Henry Clay.

The Kentuckian, as usual, objected to the administration's Spanish policy. " These people will put me in the opposition ", he wrote, " whether I will or no. I wanted to go with them respecting our Spanish affairs; but how can I join in such a foolish course. Instead of resorting to the natural expedient of taking possession of our own, they ask us to take (on the ground too of right) what does not belong to us ".[13] Soon after Monroe's message reached the House, Clay introduced two resolutions which expressed his views on Spanish affairs. The first declared that the House of Representatives had jurisdiction over any alienation of territory; the second, that re-

11 Adams, *Memoirs*, IV, 495-6 and V, 19, 53 and 65.

12 Richardson, *Messages and Papers*, II, 69, Monroe to Congress, March 31 1820.

13 *Life of J. J. Crittenden and Selections from his Correspondence and Speeches* ed. by Mrs. Chapman Coleman, p. 39, Clay to Crittenden, Dec. 4, 1819.

newal of the treaty of 1819 rejected by Spain was not expedient.[14]

Clay spoke in support of these resolutions with his usual vigor, attacking the conciliatory attitude of the executive toward Spain. He declared that the treaty signed during the previous year had led to nothing but failure. As for Monroe's recent message, he criticized its apparent deference to the meddling of foreign diplomats; ridiculed the idea that the United States should be influenced by " the distressed state of Spain ", which he took as an expression of sympathy by Monroe for Ferdinand to whom Clay alluded as a " vile despot of whom I cannot speak in appropriate language without departing from the respect due to this House and to myself." [15]

Clay was no less hostile to the committee report on the Florida bill. He felt that if adopted it might bring war with Spain and he did not desire a war over Florida. That region, he believed, would inevitably fall into the hands of the United States in time; there was no immediate necessity for taking it. Texas, on the other hand, was of great and pressing importance. According to Clay it was part of the United States, and he cited in support of this view the claims sustained by the State Department in the negotiation with Spain until 1818. This being the case, the executive had no right to cede the territory without consulting Congress. As for the talk of possible disunion which might result from further territorial expansion to the southwest, he was not inclined to take it very seriously; but even if disunion should result it would be preferable to the settlement of Texas by Spaniards.[16]

14 *Abridgement of the Debates of Congress*, ed. by T. Benton, VI, 574; This feeling was not limited to Clay and his western friends. *Cf.* J. Roberts (Senator from Pa.) to N. Biddle, Dec. 24, 1819, Biddle Papers, LC., vol. vi. Roberts thought it would be better to allow the treaty to lapse than to enforce it unilaterally. *Cf. Annals of Congress*, XXXVI, 16 Cong., 1 Sess., HR, p. 1752 ff.

15 *Abridgement of the Debates of Congress*, VI, 577 ff.

16 *Ibid.*, 578-581.

Lowndes of South Carolina replied for the administration. Disregarding the first resolution as a constitutional question he did not then have time to take up, he defended the expediency of Monroe's policy. The House, he declared, was not in a position to judge such questions; no one could tell the exact relative values of Texas and Florida; furthermore, Clay's argument that Florida would eventually fall to the United States could be applied to Texas just as well.[17] In spite of Clay's eloquence the resolutions were defeated by a substantial majority.

It is evident here that opinion both in Congress and throughout the country was much divided on Spanish affairs, in contrast to the almost united support given the administration at the time the Adams-Onís treaty was signed. Before that time, the interests of Southerners and Westerners, had marched hand in hand with those of the North and East. One group favored pressure on Spain for the cession of territory, the other for the reimbursement of losses suffered at the hands of Spain during the Napoleonic wars. The attitudes of these groups differed only in that the financial and commercial interests (aside from the exceptions previously noted) opposed measures that might lead to war, for the settlement of claims could only be reached by peaceful negotiation. This is evidenced by the prevailing attitude of the North and East, except in Baltimore, to the questions of neutrality enforcement and recognition of the rebel states of Spanish America.[18]

One of Onís' reports of the year 1817 brings out the influence of pecuniary interests in the Spanish negotiation. He declared that Stephen Kingston of Philadelphia approached him on behalf of certain marine insurance companies and hinted broadly at a large bribe if he would sign a treaty which recognized the claims of these companies.[19] The concentration of

17 *Abridgement of the Debates of Congress*, VI, 581 ff.

18 See chapters iv and v, *supra*.

19 Onís to Pizarro, No. 67, April 5, 1817, AHN., Est. Leg. 5642. The sum mentioned was $100,000.

spoliation claims in the hands of insurance companies was considerable as a large proportion of American shipping in that period had been insured against capture.[20]

Mercantile interests were not all identical, however. The privateering interest, the merchants interested in the Cuban trade, the Mediterranean trade, and that with loyalist and patriot provinces in South America tended to adopt diverse opinions in the controversy on Spanish affairs.[21]

The interest of Georgia and of the lower South generally was in the establishment of order on the frontier and favored the acquisition of Florida chiefly as it would bring about Indian pacification.[22] The Georgia frontier was moving into the un-

20 In May, 1820 Congress asked for information as to claims against Spain and a report was made by Adams. The largest of the 41 claims submitted, varying in amount from $564,327 to $20, 244, were geographically distributed as follows: Philadelphia, 10, Massachusetts 5, New York 2, Va., Md., and D. C. 7, Del. 1, Baltimore (given apart) 2, Charleston 4. This shows the concentration of these interests in the North and East. Doubt is thrown on Onís' accusation of Kingston by the fact that his claim and that of the Insurance Co. of North America which he represented was only for $22,210. *Compilation of Reports of Committee on Foreign Relations, U. S. Senate, 1789-1901* (Washington, 1901), I, 32. A year later when a commission was established to pass on these claims many more were submitted. Of these, 18 totalled $1,510,430.94, and 124 others $5,919,150. 744 other claims of unknown value were before the commission. *Niles' Weekly Register*, Jan. 20, 1821.

21 Merchants trading with Cuba objected to an aggressive Spanish policy which might give Great Britain an excuse to occupy the island. Peace was worth more, in their opinion, than Florida (*Niles' Weekly Register*, XVII, Feb. 12, 1820). There was also an idea abroad, which gained strength at this time, that the Spanish American continental colonies would become commercial competitors of the United States. For an early expression of this opinion see (*Philadelphia Aurora*, Aug. 25, 1810; Manning, *op. cit.*, I, 535, Worthington to Adams, Mar. 7, 1819). Adams seems to have adopted this view, see DS., Instructions to Ministers, IX, Adams to R. C. Anderson, May 27, 1823.

22 The special interest of Georgia in the acquisition of Florida is shown by a resolution of its legislature unanimously requesting the annexation of East Florida to that state, *Niles' Weekly Register*, Dec. 29, 1821. This is suggested in a letter from Forsyth to N. Biddle, Sept. 3, 1818, *cf.* also October 13, 1818 and Dec. 15, 1818 (Biddle Papers, LC., vol. v) in which

settled Indian country within the present boundary of the state, though there was some expansion southward toward the St. Mary's River. The indirect interest of Georgia in the settlement of Florida is shown by the later history of population movements. The expansion of cotton culture into Florida was not important, as the richer and more available lands westward were more inviting to the plantation owner.[23]

Though the actual settlement of Florida was not a pressing economic urge, the speculative spirit played a part here as in all frontier areas. Tennesseans and Easterners vied with Carolinians and Georgians in taking flyers in Florida lands.[24] There was even a boom in building lots in Pensacola at this time.[25]

In Louisiana and the neighboring states and territories interest was concentrated on Texas. The support that Mexican filibustering expeditions were able to command there has already been noted.[26] With the exception of this one region,

he states the interest of Georgia in the prompt survey of the 1795 boundary line which had never been completed due to unsettled conditions. The cession of Florida would pacify the area and make the survey possible. See *supra*, pp. 164, 190. The indifference of men from the Old South such as Lowndes of South Carolina, Andrew Jackson, Forsyth and Crawford of Georgia to expansion west of the Mississippi was characteristic of the section at this period.

23 For maps and statistics showing regional distribution of cotton production and of population, see L. C. Gray and E. K. Thompson, *History of Agriculture in the Southern United States to 1860* (Washington, 1933, 2 v.), II, 684; 890-891; 895, 902. On population trends, see also C. O. Paullin, *Atlas of the Historical Geography of the United States* (Washington, 1932), plates 75 and 76.

24 *An Original Memoir on the Floridas, with a General Description from the Best Authorities,* by a Gentleman of the South (Baltimore, 1821), Introduction. *Moniteur,* Paris, Jan. 4, 1819; *Columbian Museum and Savannah Gazette,* Oct. 19, 1818; *Niles' Weekly Register,* Sept. 22, 1821; *Correspondence of Andrew Jackson,* ed. by J. S. Bassett, III, 430, Jackson to W. Williams, Sept. 25, 1819. Jackson denied participation in these schemes but some of his associates were involved.

25 *Niles' Weekly Register,* July 10, 1819.

26 See chap. iv, *supra*. On the reputed land hunger of the West, see *Annals of Congress,* XXX, 14 Cong., 2 Sess., HR, 735.

however, the Adams-Onís treaty had satisfied all sections and groups in the country. Even the desire for Texas was still inchoate, as the unanimity of the Senate in ratifying the treaty indicated.[27]

When Spain refused its consent, however, the unity of opinion in the United States disappeared. Georgians wanted Florida but cared nothing about the other interests involved in the treaty;[28] Eastern holders of claims saw that a violent occupation of Southern lands would be of no use to them;[29] Southwestern sentiment belittled Florida and became increasingly vociferous for the occupation of Texas.[30] To cap the climax, these smaller sectional interests were overlaid by the rising jealousy between free and slave states. Southerners, east and west joined Jefferson in condemnation of Northern selfishness when that section, alarmed by the Missouri controversy, lost interest in territory to be gained to the southward.[31]

Another factor complicating the situation was the news of a revolution in Spain. A rebellion of the troops in Andalusia led by Riego had languished after the first moments of enthusiasm in January, but while Vives was crossing the ocean the political storm in Spain rose to a climax. In February and March several important cities in the North, Coruña, Pamplona, Zaragoza and Barcelona with their garrisons, declared for the revolution

27 See p. 189.

28 See p. 229, note 22.

29 Adams, *Memoirs*, V, 19, 54; *Columbian Centinel*, Boston, Jan. 5, 1820.

30 Adams, *Memoirs*, V, 53; *Correspondence of Andrew Jackson*, ed. by J. S. Bassett, III, 24, Calhoun to Jackson. For western sentiment a few months later, see *Niles' Weekly Register*, Mar. 24, 1821; Austin Papers in *Annual Report*, AHA., 1919, vol. ii, Austin to Baron Bastrop, Jan. 26, 1821, *Niles' Weekly Register*, July 7, 1821.

31 F. W. Hodder, "Sidelights on the Missouri Compromise," *Annual Report*, AHA., 1909, p. 158-9. Hodder quotes a letter from a senator elect from Missouri which accuses the North of a conspiracy to check expansion for political reasons. *Writings of James Monroe*, ed. by Hamilton, vol. vi, Monroe to Jackson, May 23, 1820; *Writings of Thomas Jefferson*, ed. by Ford, X, 162. Jefferson to C. Pinckney, Sept. 30, 1820, illustrates this view.

and proclaimed the Constitution of 1812. Ferdinand VII, after a fruitless attempt to temporize, swore to uphold the constitution he so heartily detested. By the middle of March the new regime was in complete control of the country.[32] The change of government in Spain in the direction of liberalism created a current of favorable opinion in the United States and tended to reduce the pressure for aggressive action against that country.[33]

Vives, as yet unaware of these latter developments, arrived in New York on April 7. A week later he reached Washington and began his correspondence with Adams.[34] The opening of the negotiation was not auspicious. Adams parried his opponent's opening note by asking whether he had with him the ratification of the treaty. The Spaniard, taken aback by this directness, admitted that he had not brought the document, but offered assurances that it would not be withheld if the United States replied satisfactorily to his note.[35]

Monroe and his cabinet found it difficult to decide what course to follow. It was suspected that Vives had no authority except to delay matters,[36] and Crawford objected to any further correspondence with him, but the more moderate views of the President prevailed.[37] Adams, accordingly offered to answer the Spanish objections to the treaty if Vives would agree to authorize the delivery of Florida if he were satisfied by the American reply.[38] Vives refused these terms and the failure of his mission seemed inevitable when Hyde de Neuville came to the

32 Baumgarten, *Geschichte Spaniens*, II, Chap. I, Book IV, pp. 244-285, especially, 247, 275 f.

33 Dearborn to Monroe, June 5, 1820, MP. LC.; Adams, *Memoirs*, V, 156; Vives to Sec. of State, May 14, 1820, AHN., Est. Leg. 5646.

34 De la Serna to San Fernando, April 7, 1820, Vives to Adams, April 14, 1820, AHN., Est. Leg. 5646.

35 Adams to Vives, April 18, 1820, Vives to Adams, April 19, 1820, *ibid*.

36 Monroe to Dearborn, April 22, 1820, MP. NYP.

37 Adams, *Memoirs*, V, 73.

38 Adams to Vives, April 21, 1820, AHN., Est. Leg. 5646.

rescue and arranged an informal meeting between the rival negotiators which relieved tension and raised Adams' hopes.[39] Vives was eager to prevent the collapse of his mission and was conciliatory. He declared himself satisfied with the measures adopted by the United States against privateering and filibustering, but insisted on an assurance that the United States would not recognize the independence of Buenos Aires. Adams declared this to be out of the question, but Vives understood him to say that if Spain ratified the treaty it need have no fear that the United States would proceed to such recognition.[40]

It is extremely improbable that Adams said this. It is more likely that Vives gathered this impression from some less explicit statement that Spain need fear no unfriendly act if the treaty was ratified. Such a statement was probably made for similar ones had been made earlier and it was Adams' thesis that recognition of the new states, if it was delayed until there was no question as to the *de facto* authority of their governments, could not be considered an unfriendly act toward Spain.[41] As for the land grants, Vives, after unsuccessfully

39 Adams, *Memoirs*, V, 78 ff.

40 Minute of conversation between Vives and Adams, enclosed with Vives to San Fernando, No. 7, April, 1820, AHN., Est. Leg. 5646. Spain had received alarming reports during the past year of another filibustering attack on Texas. James Long, who headed this latest move, though supported by certain Mexicans, relied more than any previous expedition on American backing. This was easy to secure owing to the resentment of Louisiana and Texas frontiersmen at the surrender of Texas in the Spanish Treaty. Recruiting was carried on openly at Natchez and there was much large talk which alarmed the Spanish consul at New Orleans. The three thousand men whom he reported to have crossed the Sabine, however, were actually not more than three hundred and they were ignominiously driven out after a very brief incursion. Adams was able to reassure Vives on this score. See L. E. Fisher, *The Background of the Revolution for Mexican Independence,* p. 376, and the same author in MVHR., XVIII (1932), 472-6; Bancroft, *History of the North Mexican States and Texas,* II, 48-51.

41 See chap. ix, *infra; cf.* Hyde de Neuville to Dessolle, Dec. 25, 1819, AAE., C. P. États Unis, vol. 76; *idem* to Richelieu, Nov. 8, 1819, *ibid.;* also, *Writings of John Quincy Adams,* ed. by W. C. Ford, VI, 520 f.

suggesting a compromise, stated that they were not a serious obstacle, and a later remark that he was *personally* satisfied on every point except that dealing with recognition of the rebels was taken by Adams to imply complete surrender of the Spanish position on the land question.[42]

During the next few days much bickering took place as to just what each had said. Another meeting on May 1 and the amiability of Hyde de Neuville, who managed to soothe ruffled feelings, led to an agreement which prevented a break.[43] Adams sent Vives a note summing up these conferences as he understood them. Adams' interpretation satisfied Vives on neutrality, but he denied having officially accepted the American stand on recognition of the Spanish Americans, though he agreed to forward it to his government. He also insisted that his agreement with Adams on the land grants was personal and that he could not bind his government to sustain him on that point. He excused this somewhat slippery conduct by the revolution in Spain which left him uncertain of his superiors' views.[44]

The cabinet again divided on what was to be done, but Adams, who was especially eager to salvage the treaty in which he felt so much personal pride, finally won over the others and it was decided to continue the waiting policy. Adams wrote a final note summarizing the American position and stating that matters would be left to Congress. This note of May 8 was a detailed and strongly worded presentation of the view that Spain was under moral and legal obligation to ratify the treaty of the previous year. It seems to have been written primarily to show Congress and the public that no surrender of American rights had been made.[45] A message was sent to Congress on the following day recommending further delay because of the

---

42 Adams, *Memoirs*, V, 80-83. The variation between Adams, and Vives' minutes of the conference are almost ludicrous.

43 *Ibid.*, V, 78-9, 94-5.

44 Vives to Adams, May 5, 1820, AHN., Est. Leg. 5646.

45 Adams to Vives, May 8, 1820, AHN., Est. Leg. 5646.

recent revolution in Spain and the hope of a friendly settlement with the new constitutional government.[46] Congress was
on the verge of adjournment when the message was received;
many members had already left Washington and the interest
of the House in Spanish affairs had apparently been exhausted
during a recent debate on a motion of Clay to provide for a
minister to South America; [47] the Missouri question also overshadowed all else in political circles. Adjournment came, accordingly, without any action having been taken and peace was
assured, at least until the next session.

The President showed great uncertainty during these weeks.
After Adams had informed Vives that Congress had admitted
further delay,[48] Monroe reopened the question in a cabinet meeting.[49] His doubts were produced by a letter from Jefferson,
who, though he had approved the Spanish treaty in 1819, now
thought that better terms could be made and that both Florida
and Texas could be acquired.[50] After some discussion, however,
the previous decision was allowed to stand.

The cry for Texas, which had grown since the previous year,
and the attack on his policy by Clay in the House had shaken
Monroe's confidence and he was much troubled. He wrote to a
friend complaining of the seductive passion for increasing
territory which seemed to have no limits.[51] The storm over the
Missouri question, however, enabled the President to resist the
temptation offered by Texas. That controversy, Monroe
declared:

46 Richardson, *Messages and Papers,* II, 70-72, Monroe to Congress,
May 9, 1820.

47 See chap. ix, *infra.*

48 Adams to Vives, May 16, 1820, AHN., Est. Leg. 5646.

49 Adams, *Memoirs,* V, 125.

50 *Writings of Thomas Jefferson,* ed. by Ford, VII, 160.

51 *Writings of James Monroe,* ed. by Hamilton, vol. vi, Monroe to Gallatin,
May 26, 1820.

. . . has excited feelings and raised difficulties . . . which did not exist before. Some parts of our Union became less anxious even for the acquisition of Florida, while others not content with that were desirous of taking possession of Texas. . . . Having long known the repugnance with which the eastern portion of our Union have seen its aggrandizement to the West and South, I have been decidedly of the opinion that we ought to be content with Florida for the present.[52]

The Secretary of State was less influenced by the demand for Texas and still felt his treaty a good bargain. In deference to the lack of enthusiasm for it in the cabinet he instructed Forsyth not to exert pressure in Madrid for ratification, but at the same time he ordered him to make it clear that if no action were taken there the United States would demand indemnity in addition to resuming all its original claims.[53] The United States now having agreed to wait, it remained to be seen what action would be taken by the new " Liberal " regime in Spain.[54]

The army officers and politicians, who were now in the saddle in Spain, surpassed their predecessors in literary and oratorical ability and in disinterested idealism more than they did in common sense. The leaders, Arguelles, Martínez de la Rosa, the Conde de Toreno, had more parliamentary and academic than administrative experience. They sincerely desired peace but they lacked foresight. Their outlook on the affairs of America was not essentially at variance with that of the ousted reaction-

52 *Ibid.*, Monroe to Jackson, May 23, 1820; *cf. ibid.*, Monroe to Jefferson in reply to Jefferson's letter of May 14. See also J. Roberts to N. Biddle, Jan. 8, 1821, Biddle Papers, LC., vol. vii, for confirmation of Monroe's view of the influence of the Missouri question.

53 Adams to Forsyth, May 25, 1820, DS., Instructions to Ministers, vol. ix. The contradictory nature of the sentence in the text above seems to have been due to a conflict between Adams and his subconscious.

54 Forsyth had little confidence in action by the new government except under pressure. Soon after the establishment of the constitution he wrote hoping that Florida would be occupied, as he preferred to face Spain with a *fait accompli*. Forsyth to Adams, Mar. 30, 1820, DS., Despatches, Spain, vol. xviii.

aries. In the first months after the success of the revolution their attention was focussed on domestic questions: the organization of the Cortes, the relations of Church and State, the regulation of the press, and the ever present financial problem.[55] On these issues a number of disputes arose which delayed consideration of the treaty with the United States.

The change at the Spanish court, however, did somewhat brighten the prospects of the treaty. Irujo, Pizarro and others who had been persecuted or neglected were restored to favor.[56] Onís was again employed in the foreign service,[57] and the favorites of the king under the old regime were publicly attacked.[58]

The abolition of the censorship of the press led to a flood of printed matter in the form of periodicals and pamphlets. One of these, which must have had considerable influence on the public and on the members of the Cortes when the American treaty was under consideration, was a memoir written by Onís in justification of his conduct. It dwelt in bitter language on the strength and aggressive character of the United States and its hostility to Spain; deplored past Spanish diplomatic errors; but urged ratification of the treaty as the safest course.[59] This exposition acquainted the Spanish reading public for the first time with the major outlines of the long continued dispute with the United States.

55 Baumgarten, *Geschichte Spaniens*, II, 306-307, 319-321, 324-329 and pages 325-394, *passim*. See also Cristobal de Castro, *Antología de las Cortes de 1820* (Madrid, 1910).

56 For the whitewashing of Irujo see AHN., Est. Leg. 94, Expediente No. 16.

57 Personal dossier of Onís, AHN., Est. Leg. 3446. He was appointed to the Naples mission and a year later sent to London.

58 Forsyth to J. Q. Adams, Mar. 30, 1820, DS., Despatches, Spain, vol. xviii.

59 *Memoria sobre las negociaciones entre España y los Estados Unidos que dieron motivo al tratado de 1819* (Madrid, 1820). This work was reprinted in Mexico in 1826 without the appendices. It was also translated into English and published both in Baltimore and in Washington in 1821. Forsyth, indignant at some of the reflections on the American government in this book, prepared a rebuttal, had it translated, and circulated it in MS among the deputies to the Cortes. See DS., Despatches, Spain, vol. xviii.

The new government, though much concerned at the unhappy state of Spanish colonial and foreign affairs did little to improve them. It depended a great deal on the hope that " Liberalism " and " Constitutionalism " would *per se* check rebellion and conciliate the United States.[60] In April, 1820, a renovated Council of State, which considered the American treaty, contented itself with merely advising caution and conciliation. Not long after, a proclamation of pardon to all American citizens under arrest for political offenses was issued in hope of relieving tension.[61]

Evaristo Pérez de Castro, who was appointed secretary of state under the new regime, had a long record in the Spanish diplomatic service going back to 1795. His reputation had been made in the Cortes during the war with France.[62] As a liberal Pérez de Castro had been forced into retirement in 1814 but had since returned to government service and at the time of his appointment was serving as minister at Hamburg.[63] He was a safe man, an upholder of the right wing or "moderados" among the groups that had effected the revolution. Not a dominant personality, in his conduct of foreign affairs he seems to have been largely the exponent of more influential members of the ministry.

Soon after Pérez de Castro took office Forsyth informed him, in accordance with orders from Adams, that ratification of the treaty would still be accepted, but that enough time had elapsed to make long deliberation unnecessary.[64] Though the official attitude toward Forsyth was cordial and his notes were

60 See Juan Jabat to De la Serna, April 27, 1820, AME., Estados Unidos, Cor. Pol., Leg. 227.

61 Juan Jabat to Vives, April 13, 1820, AME., Estados Unidos, Cor. Pol., Leg. 227 ; Forsyth to Adams, May 10, 1820, DS., Despatches, Spain, vol. xviii mentions the alarm in Madrid at news of the Florida occupation bill in Congress.

62 F. Antón del Olmet, *op. cit.*, II, 120-130.

63 Baumgarten, *Geschichte Spaniens*, II, 306.

64 Forsyth to Pérez de Castro, July 22, 1820, AHN., Est. Leg. 5662.

answered with unprecedented alacrity,[65] no immediate action was taken. According to the provisions of the constitution any cession of territory had to be authorized by the Cortes. Though Adams and Forsyth argued that the change in the form of government in Spain could not affect international obligations,[66] no serious objection was made to the submission of the treaty to the legislative assembly, perhaps because Pérez de Castro promised to rush the matter through as quickly as possible.[67]

Suiting the action to the word, Pérez de Castro, who had already prepared a preliminary report on the treaty, brought the matter to the Council of State.[68] Though the personnel of that body had been renovated, its attitude was very similar to that of the previous Council. The treaty was a bitter pill which only extreme danger could make palatable. Some still opposed it unconditionally, but the majority adopted a colorless resolution favoring ratification subject to the approval of the Cortes and still clung to the hope that Vives might secure a territorial guaranty from the United States in exchange for the ratification.[69]

In August the question was taken up by the Cortes. Pérez de Castro read his report, a lucid exposition of events leading to the existing situation. He recommended favorable action on the treaty as the only solution practicable at this time.[70] The

65 Forsyth to Adams, June 29, 1820, DS., Despatches, Spain, vol. xviii; Laval to Pasquier, July 31, 1820, AAE., C. P. Espagne, vol. 706.

66 Adams to Vives, June 8, 1820, AHN., Est. Leg. 5646.

67 Pérez de Castro to Forsyth, July 25, 1820, AHN., Est. Leg. 5662.

68 Pérez de Castro to Sec. of the Council of State, July 22, 1820, AHN., Est. Leg. 96.

69 Minutes of the Council of State, Aug. 4, 1820, AHN., Est. Leg. 5661.

70 Pérez de Castro, Memorandum for the Cortes, August 26, 1820, AHN., Est. Leg. 5662. According to Forsyth this report was largely the work of Narciso de Heredia who as under secretary to Pizarro and Irujo had been well acquainted with the past negotiations. Forsyth to Adams, July 13, 1820, DS., Despatches, Spain, vol. xviii.

report of the Council of State was also submitted but Pérez de Castro's *exposé* showed that its scruples and reservations were useless. After two secret sessions devoted to the reading of these reports the matter was referred to the committee on " Política " [71] (Foreign Affairs) of which Martínez de la Rosa was the most influential member. This committee felt indignation at the continual aggressions of the United States during the past generation, but saw the force of Pérez de Castro's survey of the problem and the majority report followed the recommendations of the ministry. It pointed out that non-ratification meant war and that war would mean American occupation of Texas as well as Florida, and attacks on Mexico and the Spanish West Indies which would greatly hamper attempts to win back the rebel colonies. Ratification, on the other hand, would ensure stricter neutrality enforcement in the United States.[72]

On October 5 another secret session of the Cortes was held and the committee report came up for debate. But little opposition developed and most of the talk was confined to denunciations of the land grants made by the king as an abuse of power. Some Cuban delegates feared that the loss of Florida might endanger that island,[73] but after a debate of not more than two hours and a quarter a resolution authorizing the cession of Florida was passed by a large majority. At the same time the Alagon and other similar land grants were expressly cancelled.[74]

71 Laval to Pasquier, Aug. 28, 1820, AAE., C. P. Espagne, vol. 706.

72 Report of the Committee on " Política ", September 30, 1820, AHN., Est. Leg. 5662. One committeeman, Vargas Ponce, voted against the report. He feared that cession ef territory would hurt the prestige of the government and thought that war would unite and strengthen the nation. *Ibid.*

73 According to Forsyth the opposition of Cuban and Mexican delegates was based on unavowed motives. They desired a conflict with the U. S. which might hasten Cuban and Mexican independence, Forsyth to Adams, July 13, 1820, DS., Despatches, Spain, vol. xviii.

74 Memorandum of the secret session of the Cortes, Oct. 5, 1820, AHN., Est. Leg. 5662; Laval to Pasquier, Oct. 5, Oct. 9, 1820, AAE., C. P. Espagne,

Public interest in this aspect of Spanish foreign relations was not very great. Of the many periodicals published in Madrid only two discussed the Florida cession and those were obviously inspired. *El Censor* in its article followed Pérez de Castro's point of view closely.[75] *La Minerva Nacional* edited by an important figure in Spanish liberal journalism, José Joaquin de Mora, was even more friendly to the United States and stressed the point that Spain should concentrate its efforts on more vital regions than Florida.[76]

The Cortes, together with their authorization of the Florida cession, had recommended that the government do all it could to secure the welfare of Spanish settlers in that province.[77] This request and the recommendation of the Council of State that some benefit to the treasury be sought from the public lands in Florida, led Pérez de Castro to seek some compromise from the United States on the land grant issue. On October 6 he notified Forsyth that there was no longer any obstacle in the way of ratification, but he tried to involve the latter in a further discussion of the status of Florida lands. Admitting the nullity of the Vargas grant, he adduced a number of plausible reasons for dividing the value of the Alagon and Puñonrostro grants between Spain and the United States, or at least that part of their value over and above the five million dollars which

vol. 707. According to testimony later presented in support of a claim of Richard Meade against the U. S. Treasury, one motive which strengthened the deputies in favor of ratification of the treaty was that Meade's claim, a large one for over $400,000 against the Spanish government, was considered cancelled by the treaty. One deputy claimed that Forsyth had assured him that Meade's claim was so cancelled. Forsyth later denied making any statement. *Compilation of the Reports of Committee on Foreign Regulations, U.S. Senate, 1789-1901,* I, 17-23, 74 and 203-204; F. W. Hackett, *The Meade Claim,* p. 9.

75 *El Censor* (Madrid), No. 11, Oct. 14, 1820.

76 *La Minerva Nacional,* extract enclosed in DS., Despatches, Spain, vol. xviii.

77 Sec. of the Cortes to Pérez de Castro, Oct. 5, 1820, AHN., Est. Leg. 5662.

the United States had agreed to pay its citizens in settlement of claims against Spain.[78] Forsyth refused to take any step leading to a revision of the treaty in any way. Pérez de Castro for a few days urged his point warmly both verbally and in a series of notes, but fearing that delay might lead to disaster, he declared on October 11 that the Spanish ratification would be sent to Vives.[79]

Forsyth must have breathed a sigh of relief at this point which marked the successful end of his thorny mission. The persistence of Spanish diplomacy, however, was to be shown once more in a final effort to better the bargain. Two sets of ratifications were drawn up and sent to Vives. One, made out in accordance with the American demands; the other, so framed as to recognize Spain's right to the proceeds of a part of the Florida lands. In the accompanying despatch Pérez de Castro instructed Vives not to alarm Adams and to state that he had received the instrument of ratification, but suggested that if the cancellation of the Alagon and Puñonrostro grants by the Cortes were kept secret the United States might allow Spain part of their value in return for the ratification. Only if he failed in this attempt was Vives authorized to bring the negotiation definitely to a close.[80] This move was doomed to failure in any case, but especially since Adams was well informed of the action taken by the Cortes.[81]

Vives received with these instructions an order to withhold the delivery of Florida for the six months maximum time allowed by the treaty in order to permit orderly evacuation and the transfer of the Seminole Indians from Florida to Texas, where they could help to defend the province against American encroachment and escape the extermination which threatened

78 Pérez de Castro to Forsyth, Oct. 9, 1820, AHN., Est. Leg. 5662.

79 Pérez de Castro to Forsyth, Oct. 11, 1820, *ibid.*; Forsyth to Adams, Oct. 11, 1820, ASP. FR., IV, 695.

80 Pérez de Castro to Vives, Oct. 24, 1820, AHN., Est. Leg. 5662.

81 Forsyth to Adams, Oct. 12, 1820, DS., Despatches, Spain, vol. xviii.

them in Florida. Nothing came of this order. The difficulties in the way of its execution are obvious. It was characteristic of the ineffectual paternalism of Spanish rule that one of the last orders emanating from Spain with regard to this part of its North American dominions related to the protection of the Indians. It is equally characteristic that the order was not carried out.

Vives, the soldier, had no taste for debate and no hope of success along the lines indicated by these instructions. He made a half hearted move to comply with the letter of his orders and then conceded defeat.[82]

Owing to the lapse of the former ratification of the treaty by the Senate it was considered necessary to consult that body again.[83] Opposition was slight, but four votes were cast against the treaty whereas the vote in 1819 had been unanimous. Senator Benton of Missouri was the outstanding enemy of the treaty, representing the dissatisfaction of the West at the surrender of the American claim to Texas.[84] The country as a whole desired peace and on February 22, 1821, two years to a day after John Quincy Adams proudly noted in his diary the signature of the treaty, the long delayed settlement went into effect.[85]

Friendly relations between the United States and Spain did not result, as the Spanish government had hoped. The occupation and temporary organization of the new United States territory was marked by a series of petty squabbles between American and Spanish officials which led a contemporary to remark that Florida if productive of nothing else was a fruitful source of public documents. Andrew Jackson, who was appointed governor of the territory by Monroe, was soon at odds

82 D. H. Miller, *Treaties*, III, 51, Vives delivered the Spanish ratification on Feb. 12, 1821. See Adams to Vives, Feb. 26, 1821, ASP. FR., IV, 703.

83 Richardson, *Messages and Papers*, II, 83-84.

84 T. H. Benton, *Thirty Years' View*, I, 17.

85 Richardson, *op. cit.*, II, p. 84.

with Colonel Callava, the retiring Spanish governor over alleged obstruction to the delivery of the public records dealing with land titles as specified in the treaty. The dispute soon became a personal quarrel. Spanish officials were unfriendly and Jackson acted with his usual violence. Part of the difficulty arose from the inability of the principals to understand each other except through interpreters. Charges and counter charges were made ending in the expulsion of Callava and some of his subordinates. The archives which had caused the original difficulty disappeared and were to lead to correspondence between the two governments for generations. At St. Augustine similar quarrels arose over the details of the evacuation of the Spanish garrison.[86] It would be hard to find an example of so considerable a concession by one nation to another which did less to create an atmosphere of good will. Spain reaped the harvest of its long years of dilatory and obstructive diplomacy.

86 ASP. FR., IV, 751-765; Moore, *Digest*, I, 282-284.

CHAPTER IX

THE RECOGNITION OF SPANISH AMERICAN INDEPENDENCE

DURING the period of critical relations with Spain related in the previous chapters the United States steadily maintained its official policy of neutrality toward the Spanish American revolution. The suggestion of a joint recognition of Buenos Aires made to Great Britain and France at a critical stage in the negotiation of the Adams-Onís treaty was not a deviation from this policy. The United States did not then suggest action apart from the European concert of nations and remained inactive when its suggestion met a cool reception.[1] Occasional menacing statements, like Adams' remark to Poletica in May, 1819, that recognition of the rebels by the United States would probably follow Spain's refusal to ratify the treaty,[2] were not borne out by subsequent events and can only be considered attempts to apply pressure to Spain. Shortly after the signature of the Spanish treaty Monroe wrote to Rush in London expressing his satisfaction with the American policy toward the " Colonists ", for it had been possible " to render to these people all the service that we could have rendered, had their interest been exclusively our object," and this had been done " without injury to, or serious compromitment of the United States ". Monroe hoped that the rebels would not be " the dupes of those among us who profess to be exclusively their friends." [3] This indicates the President's intention to maintain the attitude adopted by Madison and continued by himself up to this time. In May, 1820 he was still of the opinion that the United States should continue to " throw its moral weight in the scale on the side of the rebels without making itself a party to their

1 See pp. 183-84, *supra*.
2 Adams, *Memoirs*, IV, 380, May 29, 1819.
3 Monroe to Rush, Mar. 7, 1819, MP. LC.

struggle.[4] During the autumn of 1820 Monroe remained calm when the delay of the Spanish Cortes in dealing with the pending treaty led Adams to suggest occupation of Florida and recognition of Colombia.[5] The President's message of November, 1820, had little to say about Spanish America, except to note the continued successes of the rebels and the conclusion of an armistice between Bolívar and Morillo which, it was hoped, might soon lead to a peace and a general recognition of the new status of Spanish America by all the powers.[6]

For the maintenance of this policy various reasons can be given aside from the precedent of almost a decade. These were: unwillingness to exasperate Spain while there was any prospect of a peaceful conclusion of differences with that country; growing irritation at the rebel system of privateering; discouraging reports from South America by the late commissioners, and rumors of monarchical schemes at Buenos Aires. Somewhat paradoxically, the decisive successes of the patriots in 1819 and the truce arranged between Bolívar and the royalist general Morillo in 1820 also weakened the pressure for recognition, for as it began to appear almost certain that independence would eventually be secured by the rebels through their own efforts, the attempts of their friends in the United States to bring about recognition as an act of assistance to them became weaker.

The neutrality legislation of 1817 and 1818 had not put an end to the embarrassment of the United States government from the privateers. There was still much opposition to the

4 Monroe to Jackson, May 23, 1820, MP. LC.

5 Adams, *Memoirs*, V, 179 f.

6 Richardson, *Messages and Papers*, II, 77, Monroe to Congress, Nov. 14, 1820.

It was Calhoun, apparently, who was responsible for the moderate tone of this part of the message (Adams, *Memoirs*, V, 200). Calhoun had been friendly to the rebels (see Gaillard Hunt, *John C. Calhoun*, p. 46), but the current slavery controversy had led him to center his interest on domestic politics almost exclusively.

enforcement of the law in certain ports, and the press still counted some defenders of these irregular warships, though there was an increasing tendency to distinguish between vessels which comported themselves more or less regularly and others which were but thinly disguised pirates.[7] The author of a pamphlet published in 1820 still defended the right of the rebels to commission such vessels and spoke of them as a help to unemployed American seamen.[8] In Baltimore threats were made against any interference in the traffic by federal officials,[9] and two papers published in that city indulged in a spirited controversy over the so-called pirates. *The Telegraph* objected strenuously to what it called the " attempts of some editors in the United States to implicate the reputation of the citizens of Baltimore, by the general imputation of encouraging pirates." [10] Sentiment was turning against the practice, however, and it was more often referred to as piracy than as privateering. Editorials protesting and calling for further government action became numerous in 1819.[11]

The chief weakness of the neutrality enforcement legislation was its failure to take preventive action. From 1817 to 1821 dozens of cases were brought before the federal courts and in a great majority of instances ample proof was given of the violation of the law, not only by foreigners but by citizens of the United States.[12] Though the procedure of the higher courts

7 *Niles' Weekly Register*, April 17, 1819.

8 *Strictures on 'A Voyage to South America'*, pp. 54-59.

9 Adams, *Memoirs*, IV, 186.

10 Quoted in the *Baltimore Federal Gazette*, Jan. 8, 1819.

11 *Columbian Museum and Savannah Gazette*, Sept. 11, 1819; *Niles' Weekly Register*, April 3 and 17, 1819; *Norfolk Beacon*, quoted in the *Columbian Museum and Savannah Gazette*, Jan. 18, 1819; *New York Evening Post*, Jan. 8, 11, 29, 1819; *Baltimore Federal Gazette*, Jan. 7, 1819.

12 *Prize Cases Decided in the U. S. Supreme Court*, ed. by J. B. Scott, II, 1096, 1154, 1168, 1200, 1209, 1235. An interesting point decided by the Supreme Court was the denial of belligerent rights to certain groups of alleged rebels, particularly Aury at Amelia Island and elsewhere; *ibid.*, pp. 1167, 1080-3.

was unbiased and effective as far as it could go, the fact that so many cases came before them is ample proof of the insufficiency of the sanctions provided by law to stop this activity.

The administration attempted to enforce the law more stringently. Adams, especially, took great interest in the matter.[13] He complained of Crawford's sluggishness and his wish to avoid the onus of opposing the privateers.[14] The acquittal of Daniels, a notorious privateer captain who was tried for piracy at Baltimore, in spite of the fact that Attorney General Wirt in person had gone to that city to press the prosecution was discouraging to the administration.[15] The clamor against piracy, however, led to the passage of an act authorizing the use of the Navy against vessels guilty of depredations on American commerce. The U. S. S. *Firebrand* was sent to cruise in the West Indies on watch for such vessels.[16] This vigorous action and the conviction of several men for piracy in the courts in 1819 and 1820 led to the gradual disappearance of this abuse.[17]

The reports of the commissioners to South America were also discouraging to those who favored immediate recognition of Buenos Aires. The three commissioners were unable to agree and submitted separate statements. With the exception of Bland, who crossed the *pampa* and the *cordillera* to Chile, the envoys visited only Buenos Aires and Montevideo, then held by Portugal. The information contained in these reports,

13 Adams to E. Glenn, District Att'y at Baltimore, April 12, 1819, DS., Domestic Letters, vol. vii.

14 Adams, *Memoirs*, IV, 88; *cf.* Crawford to S. Smith, April 3, 1819, Samuel Smith Papers, LC.

15 Adams, *Memoirs*, IV, 372-373; Adams to Glenn, May 1, 1819, DS., Domestic Letters, vol. vii; Adams to C. Todd, June 5, 1820, DS., Despatches to Consuls, vol. ii; *Annals of Congress*, 15 Cong., 2 Sess., HR. 2523, gives the text of the act.

16 *Niles' Weekly Register*, April 17, 1819.

17 Currier, *Los corsarios . . .* , p. 55; the *Columbian Centinel*, Boston, Mar. 8, 1820. Those convicted were pardoned except for ten who were hanged.

aside from historical, geographical and statistical material gleaned from books available in Buenos Aires, was indefinite and unsatisfactory. Though all the commissioners were partial to the revolutionists before their departure, the tone of their reports showed disillusionment. Rodney was the most optimistic, Graham was less so, and Bland was apparently fully conscious of the difficulties faced by the patriot governments: their lack of political experience, and the non-existence of democratic and representative institutions worthy of the name. The civil war between Buenos Aires and the forces led by Artigas, factional disputes and plots in the city itself, and the isolation of Paraguay from the rest of the old viceroyalty, to say nothing of the continued occupation of much of the interior by the royalists, were discouraging factors.[18]

The official reports made no recommendations, but Bland had written previously that recognition of Buenos Aires was inadvisable.[19] His report on Chile described that government as a military despotism " trembling at the very name of the people." [20] Poinsett, when he was consulted on South American affairs in 1818, was even more forceful than Bland in his advice against recognition. He wrote Adams that the people having no part in the government of those countries, recognition would only strengthen the faction momentarily in power, which he characterized as having nothing but low cunning, tricks, and artifices.[21] These reports which, except for that of Poinsett, were printed [22] and soon reached the reading public tended to

18 Manning, *Diplomatic Correspondence*, II, 382 ff., Bland's report on Argentina; II, 486 ff. reports of Graham and Rodney; III, 946 ff., Bland's report on Chile.

19 Bland to Monroe, April 14, 1818, MP. LC. He based his advice on the internal dissensions of the patriots.

20 Manning, *op. cit.*, II, 957.

21 Manning, *Diplomatic Correspondence*, I, 439, Poinsett to Adams, Nov. 4, 1818.

22 Extracts from these reports were also printed widely in the press. See *Kentucky Reporter* (Lexington), Jan. 13, and Jan. 20, 1819.

moderate the enthusiasm of many whose previous opinions had been based largely on information from sources more friendly to the revolutionists.

The publication of Brackenridge's account of the voyage of the commission in 1820 which was sympathetic to the Buenos Aires government [23] was offset by a counterblast published anonymously.[24] This work which attacked Brackenridge and the Pueyrredon government was probably written by Baptis Irvine, who like Poinsett was prejudiced against the enemies of Carrera.[25]

During 1820 news reached the United States of the negotiations reported to have taken place between Pueyrredon and agents of the French government for the establishment of a monarchy under the Prince of Lucca, a Bourbon cousin of Ferdinand VII.[26] These reports were not without their effect on Adams, who spoke bitterly of the " hankerings of Buenos Aires for a European prince ".[27] He was no less caustic with regard to Bolívar whom he declared to have a " gigantic project of Napoleonic ambition ".

The effect of these developments on the American public can be judged partly by a decline in the strength of editorial propaganda for immediate recognition of the rebels and also by the appearance in several serious reviews of very critical articles on the Spanish Americans. A Philadelphia publication, *The Portfolio,* reviewed favorably a book by one Hackett, a disgruntled volunteer who had retired from the Venezuelan service. According to the reviewer it was the laudable purpose of the book to " warn his fellow countrymen of the utter fallacy of those

23 H. M. Brackenridge, *Voyage to South America in the Years 1817 and 1818 in the Frigate Congress* (London, 1820).

24 *Strictures on a " Voyage to South America,"* (Baltimore, 1820).

25 On the authorship of this book see Adams, *Memoirs,* V, 57.

26 C. A. Villanueva, *Bolívar y el General San Martín,* pp. 127-137; B. Mitre, *Historia de Belgrano,* III, 127 ff.; Manning, *op. cit.,* I, 545 ff., Prevost to Adams, Mar. 20, 1820.

27 Adams to Monroe, Aug. 25, 1820, MP. LC.

golden dreams which are inspired by the wandering Dons and accredited agents who are scattered through this country and Europe." [28] An extreme example of this point of view is furnished by a reviewer of Dean Funes' work on the history of Buenos Aires. " Though at first it might appear," he wrote, " that few subjects would awaken wider sympathy than the South American Revolution, in spite of declamation and poetry, the commercial and political relations of the United States with these people are insignificant compared to those with Europe ". A policy of interference in South America would be against the traditions of the country. Again, he asked, " What sympathy or concern can Americans have for people of a different stock, law, institution, religion? Their violence, laziness, are but the natural consequence of the degeneracy of a mixed race, ruined by tyranny, and afflicted by the evil influence of tropical climatic conditions.[29] Such opinions were due not only to anti-revolutionary sentiment among conservatives in New England, but also to disagreeable experiences of merchants and sailors. in South America.[30] A Boston newspaper which had been rather acid in its comment on the revolutionists became even bolder in 1820 and attacked the *Philadelphia Aurora* as a disseminator of false information about South America.[31] According to the *National Gazette* of Philadelphia, Monroe and his colleagues deserved applause for resisting the " temptations and importunities " to which they were subjected through the attraction that the ideas of freedom and independence had for the public. Though it wished the patriots well, this paper saw no hope that the revolution would bring any " real freedom " to Spanish America.[32] For such opinions it could find support even

28 *The Portfolio*, series iv, vol. vii, 219 (1819).

29 *North American Review*, XII, 432 ff. (1821).

30 *Columbian Centinel*, Boston, June 26, 1822, offers an example of how such experiences reached the press.

31 *Ibid.*, April 29, 1820.

32 *National Gazette*, Philadelphia, quoted by the *Columbian Centinel*, May 4, 1820.

from a veteran republican like Jefferson, who declared that the insurgents were unfit for civil or religious liberty and favored an accommodation between the Colonies and Spain.[33]

Though these years saw a partial disillusionment of the American public's enthusiasm for the patriots, there was little doubt that between the Spaniards and the Spanish Americans the sympathy of the bulk of the population was on the side of the latter. The waiting policy of the administration, however, met more general approbation than it had two years earlier.[34]

In Congress sympathy for the patriot cause was far from dead. In the spring of 1820, immediately after the failure of Clay's resolutions on the Spanish treaty, the tireless orator renewed his efforts to bring about the recognition of Buenos Aires. He introduced a motion that it was expedient to provide outfit and salary for " such minister to South America as the President may deem it expedient to send." [35] Not quite so much interest was aroused on this occasion as had been the case two years earlier, but because of the qualifying words " as the President may deem it expedient to send " there was less determined opposition to the resolution than in 1818. It was possible to support the resolution without committing the administration to any action. Observers did not expect that it would pass the House, but to their surprise it did succeed by a narrow margin.[36] It was known that Clay intended to retire from Congress and the passage of this motion may have been a gesture in recognition of his work. No specific conclusions

33 *Writings of Jefferson*, ed. by Ford, X, 174.

34 For the opinion that sympathy for the patriots was diminishing see Adams, *Memoirs*, IV, 472; *Analectic Magazine*, XV, 190 (1820). Even in the *Kentucky Reporter*, at this time devoted to Clay, articles criticizing the patriots appeared (August 4, 1819). That sentiment still preferred the patriots to Spain is also true, see A. Hodgeson, *Letters from North America* ... (London, 1824), I, 85.

35 *Annals of Congress*, XXXVI, 16 Cong., 1 Sess., HR, 1781-1782.

36 Smith Thompson to Van Buren, May 9, 1820, LC. Van Buren Papers; Antrobus to Castlereagh, May 16, 1820, PRO., FO-5, vol. 149; Adams, *Memoirs*, V, 108.

can be drawn from a comparison of this vote with that of 1818, for the resolutions varied in wording. It is interesting, however, to note that the additional support came chiefly from New York and Pennsylvania, though all sections gave a slightly larger number of votes in favor of Clay's motion. The movement for rebel recognition, strangely enough, though it was headed by the future leader of the Whig party, had its support in those regions that were to rally most strongly to the Jacksonian banner: the Southwest and the Middle Atlantic states.[37] Clay felt that this was a great personal triumph, but coming as it did at the end of a session overshadowed by the much more vital Missouri issue, it failed to win great notice and had little or no effect on the policy of the administration.

After 1818, in contrast with the earlier period of the Spanish American revolt, the administration had to deal with few official representatives of the rebels. After the departure of Aguirre in 1818 and of Lino de Clemente a few months later the only one remaining in the country was Manuel Tórres who was appointed chargé d'affaires of Venezuela and left in charge by Clemente. Tórres, a Spaniard by birth and a nephew of a former viceroy of New Granada, had been forced to take refuge in the United States as early as 1796 on account of his liberal views, and he had lived since that time in Philadelphia where he was liked and respected. He was intimate with Duane, the editor of the *Aurora,* and long before his official duties began had collaborated with him as a propagandist for the patriots, translating Spanish news and pamphlets for the latter and occasionally putting Duane's effusions into Spanish for the use of the patriot gazettes.[38] In addition to many unsigned articles

37 *Annals of Congress,* XXXVI, 16 Cong., 1 Sess., 2229-2230. The vote was 80 to 75 in favor of the resolution. The sectional distribution was as follows: *Yeas,* New England 10, Middle Atlantic 35, South Atlantic 17, West 18, total 80. *Nays,* New England 20, Middle Atlantic 18, South Atlantic 32, West 5.

38 R. Rivas, *Relaciones internacionales entre Colombia y los Estados Unidos, 1810-1850* (Bogotá, 1915), p. 11; N. Garcia Samudio, *Capítulos de*

he wrote a pamphlet guide for American merchants intending to do business in Spanish America in which he painted the golden possibilities of the region for foreign traders in addition to furnishing useful statistical information on commercial law and practice, customs duties, and exchange.[39]

Tórres was the most successful of the rebel agents in the United States. Perhaps because of his long residence and familiarity with conditions in the country he was able to avoid difficulties with the government and to achieve a respected position. His plan was to work quietly for his objects: the recognition of his government and the acquisition of munitions of war. He negotiated with the Bank of the United States for a loan at ten per cent but was unable to put the deal through, though he was personally liked by the president of the bank and had recommendations from Clay and from Lowndes of South Carolina. The stumbling block seems to have been the failure of Colombia to maintain its credit by living up to certain earlier obligations.[40] Tórres also tried to secure a loan from a Dutch firm with which he established contact through Joseph Idler of Philadelphia.[41]

Tórres established informal communication with Adams in November, 1819, without difficulty, managing to avoid the pitfalls into which earlier envoys had fallen.[42] In February, 1820, he attempted to secure arms from the government and had several conferences with Adams on the subject. Monroe was embarrassed by the request, which he wished neither to grant nor to refuse. Various men of influence favored the sale, among them Colonel Richard M. Johnson of Kentucky, General

historia diplomática (Bogotá, 1925), p. 45; Pedro I. Cadena, Anales diplomáticos de Colombia (Bogotá, 1878), pp. 98-99.

39 Manual Tórres, An Exposition of the Commerce of Spanish America (Philadelphia, 1816).

40 García Samudio, op. cit., pp. 55-56.

41 Cadena, op. cit., p. 101.

42 Adams to Tórres, Nov. 29, 1819, DS., Notes to Foreign Legations, vol. ii; Tórres to Adams, Nov. 19, 1819, Notes, Colombia, vol. i, part 1.

Mason, and a Colonel Bomford. Though it was under consideration for some time, the plain failed, principally on account of Adams' disapproval.[43]

The administration, however, finding Tórres discreet, consulted him on political events in Spanish America and treated him with such good will as to raise his hopes of a prompt recognition of his government.[44] This regard may have been due partly to the envoy's strong pro-American sympathies of which he made no secret,[45] urging strongly on his government the wisdom of economic and political approximation to the United States.[46] Tórres was therefore much annoyed by the failure of Francisco Zea, an envoy from Colombia of higher rank than himself, to put in his expected appearance at Washington, for he believed that a more pretentious mission might achieve the great objective of recognition.[47]

Though Adams and Monroe were as yet not prepared to change their policy toward Spanish America, they had felt it important to make their position clear to the insurgent governments, to win their friendship if possible, and at the same time to protest against the abuses committed by the privateers. In 1819 Adams had lost confidence in his agents on the ground in South America. Worthington had exceeded his instructions in negotiating a commercial convention in Buenos Aires and both Worthington and Prevost had identified themselves with the patriot cause too openly to please the punctilious and cautious Secretary of State.[48] It was decided, therefore, to send a naval officer to both Venezuela and Buenos Aires, the two

43 Cadena, *op. cit.*, p. 110 ff.; García Samudio, *op. cit.*, pp. 58-59; Adams to Tórres, Mar. 30, 1820, DS., Notes to Foreign Legations, vol. ii.

44 Cadena, *op. cit.*, pp. 123-130.

45 Tórres to Adams, Aug. 11, 1820, DS., Notes, Colombia, vol. i, part I.

46 Cadena, *op. cit.*, p. 130, Tórres to Revenga, May 20, 1820.

47 *Ibid.*; also F. J. Urrutia, *op. cit.*, p. 194; for another angle see *Cartas del Libertador*, ed. by V. Lecuna, II, 232.

48 Adams, *Memoirs*, IV, 70, 158-9; H. M. Wriston, *Executive Agents in American Foreign Relations*, p. 421.

principal foci of the independence movement. Captain Oliver H. Perry was chosen for the mission and instructions for his guidance were issued in May, 1819. They gave an excellent survey of American policy as Adams wished the patriots to see it.

In the main, the argument was that the United States must remain neutral both for its own benefit and for the good of the rebels themselves. As a neutral the United States had been able to throw its influence against the attempted " mediation " or intervention by the European powers and to bring about a similar attitude on the part of Great Britain, which feared the loss of its trade with the patriots to the United States if it adhered to the plan. While Spain maintained its opposition to independence the most effective policy for the United States was to neutralize Europe, and at the same time to offer to act jointly with France and Great Britain whenever they were ready to recognize the independence of the new republics. To this rather exaggerated account of the international aspect of Spanish American affairs was appended a series of complaints against the ill-regulated privateers, and an explanation of the reasons for the refusal of the United States to receive Lino de Clemente, the Venezuelan agent, and De Forest, the consul sent by Buenos Aires.[49]

Perry's mission to South America came to an abrupt end due to his death while he had as yet completed only the first part of his assignment in Venezuela. One of his subordinates reported for him that Venezuela had repudiated the action of Clemente with regard to Amelia Island, and that it was grateful for the information given it with regard to the European situation. The officer reporting also added that the people of Venezuela seemed to think the United States unsympathetic, an attitude he attributed, as Irvine had before him, to British influence.[50]

49 Adams to Smith Thompson (Sec. of the Navy), May 20, 1819, DS., Domestic Letters, vol. vii.

50 Manning, *Diplomatic Correspondence*, II, 1178, C. O. Handy to Adams, Sept. 29, 1819.

A private citizen of the United States, Samuel D. Forsyth, did a good deal to improve relations between Venezuela and the United States during the following year. He had gone to Angostura as agent for some American claimants against the patriot government there, and through his adroitness and tact managed to secure a partial settlement, and so far won the confidence of the Venezuelans as to be charged with business for them in the United States.[51] In June, 1820 another agent was despatched, Charles Todd, of Lexington, Kentucky.[52] He was instructed to avoid any discussion of recognition and to restrict himself to prosecuting American claims and to securing a modification of the prize code in force.[53] The Venezuelan government was again disappointed to find that this envoy was not invested with formal diplomatic character, but they received him amiably enough at Margarita Island, which was as far as he went.[54] Todd, however, did try to justify the American attitude, pointing out that the United States had refused to give Spain any promise not to recognize the new governments, and that there was a regular though unofficial communication between Adams and Tórres at Washington.[55] The specific objects of his mission were not accomplished, though there was much show of friendliness on both sides. Todd's health led him to return to the United States after a stay of only a few months.[56]

51 S. D. Forsyth to Adams, Sept. 22, 1820, DS., Special Agents, vol. ix; Adams to Tórres, April 3, 1820, Notes to Foreign Legations, vol. ii.

52 Adams to Todd, Feb. 22, 1820, DS., Despatches to Consuls, vol. ii, Todd had a salary of $4,500 and passage on a warship.

53 Adams to Todd, June 5, 1820, ibid.

54 Memorias del General O'Leary, ed. by S. B. O'Leary, VIII, Roscio to Bolívar, Sept. 27, 1820. He was well received partly because he was a relative of Clay, whose fame was bright in Venezuela at that time.

55 Todd to Adams, Aug. 10, 1820; Todd to J. G. Roscio, Aug. 2, 1820, DS., Despatches from Colombia, vol. i.

56 Todd to F. Z. Yañez, Oct. 14, Nov. 1, Dec. 9, 1820, Todd to Lino de Clemente, Dec. 24, 1820, ibid.

The attitude of Venezuelans [57] towards the United States at this time seems to have been one of mingled friendly expectation and resentment which tended to neutralize each other. They spoke of the United States as their brother of the North, but at the same time bewailed the indifference of that brother to their cause.[58] They were angered by the claims for damages presented by Americans at a time when the treasury was empty and they were engaged in a life and death struggle. Bolívar spoke in 1820 of the " conduct of business arithmetic " followed by the United States,[59] but such barbed language was varied by enthusiasm when hope of assistance reappeared.[60] Venezuelan leaders watched the United States closely and considered its attitude a matter of importance to their cause, but many disappointments had taught them not to count too heavily on the favor of any foreign power. An official memorandum, composed by J. R. Revenga, at that time one of Bolivar's chief civil subordinates, sketches a policy of playing on the mutual jealousy of the United States and Great Britain. The latter he considered to be less favorably disposed than the former, but as its power was greater its good will should be cultivated as far as possible.[61]

As this document suggests, there was no strong bias in favor of any one foreign power in the new Colombian republic. England had furnished thousands of volunteers, but American merchants had often brought in supplies in times of great need and many Americans served in the naval squadron under the

57 Officially the term used should be Colombians for after the battle of Boyacá in 1819 Bolívar proclaimed the union of Venezuela and New Granada under that name. The people with whom the U. S. agent dealt were, however, Venezuelans.

58 *Cartas del Libertador*, ed. by V. Lecuna, II, 126.

59 *Ibid.*, II, 157.

60 *Ibid.*, II, 146-147.

61 *Memorias del General O'Leary*, VI, 454.

command of Admiral Brion.[62] The irritation occasionally shown against the United States was due to the fact that more was expected from it than from the European powers because of the sentimental tie that supposedly united peoples owing their existence to revolution.

Though no agents from southern South America were present in the United States after 1818, American agents continued their activity in that region. The death of Captain Perry left Worthington and Prevost still in charge of American interests. They spent most of their time on the Pacific coast, but Worthington came to Buenos Aires in 1819 and took over the consulate there from Halsey. His stay was short, for he was soon after recalled and left the office in charge of a local merchant.[63] Prevost, who followed Worthington to the River Plate country also spent little time there, but enough to embroil himself with the authorities.

As it has been noted, Pueyrredon's government now leaned toward Europe rather than the United States. The Supreme Director supported the cause of independence from Spain, but

62 On the subject of British volunteers, see A. Hasbrouck, *Foreign Legionaries in the Liberation of Spanish America* (New York, 1928). C. A. Wilgus surveys American participation in " Some Activities of United States Citizens in the South American Wars of Independence", *Louisiana Historical Quarterly*, XIV (1931), 182-203. See also Chandler, *Inter-American Acquaintances*, p. 89 ff. The following reports of arms shipments from the United States to Venezuela and New Granada indicate the importance of this traffic: In November, 1811 Caracas agents were reported to have shipped 24,000 rifles from the U. S. (Onís to Bardaxí, Nov. 20, 1811, AHN., Est. 5637) ; 1500 stand of arms reached Cartagena from the U. S. in the same year (*Richmond Enquirer*, Jan. 18, 1812) ; Onís reported another shipment to Cartagena from Baltimore in 1815 (Onís to Cevallos, April 16, 1815, AHN., Est. Leg. 5640) ; In January 1820 Brion stated the situation was saved by a brig from Boston (*Memorias de O'Leary*, XII, 10) ; In July 1820 the Venezuelan gov't. received 5,000 muskets and other arms from the U. S. (C. Todd to Adams, July 12, 1820, DS., Despatches from Colombia, vol. i), 3000 more arrived in October, 1820 (*Memorias de O'Leary*, viii, 22 ff.). The above is far from a comprehensive list.

63 Worthington to Adams, Mar. 6, 1819, DS., W. G. D. Worthington, Special Agent, Argentine Republic, vol. i, part i.

a monarchical rather than a republican form of government appealed to him, as to San Martín and others. They saw the difficulty of stable government in countries racially heterogeneous and lacking experience in self government, unless it were buttressed by the familiar external aspect of monarchy. The French government encouraged these hopes for the establishment of a South American monarchy, sending agents to Buenos Aires and receiving the Argentine envoy, Valentín Gómez.[64]

In 1820, the efforts of Pueyrredon and his associates to establish a monarchy became known to the public and were partly responsible for the collapse of his influence.[65] Prevost had not hesitated to show his approval of the change,[66] and he was suspected of having had a hand in the downfall of the " Unitario " party. The ascendency of the " Federal " party did not last long. After a year of anarchical civil commotion the " Unitarios " were again in power in Buenos Aires and their leaders—Rodríguez, the governor, and Bernardino de Rivadavia, his secretary and the leading light of the party—immediately expelled Prevost.[67]

Before Adams heard of this misadventure to his agent he had sent still another American to this part of South America. As Worthington had been recalled, and as it was considered desirable to have a resident agent both at Buenos Aires and on the west coast, John M. Forbes, a friend and classmate of Adams, was instructed to reside in whichever of the two areas

64 See p. 249, *supra*. On the monarchist plans in Buenos Aires, see B. Mitre, *Historia de Belgrano*, III, 128 ff., 314-322; Webster, *op. cit.*, p. 423 ff.; Manning, *op. cit.*, I, 545-557; for the attitude of France see C. A. Villanueva, *Bolívar y el General San Martín*, pp. 79, 87, 139. *Cf.* Hyde de Neuville to Richelieu, despatches of Jan. to June 1818, AAE., C. P. États Unis, vol. 75 which show his interest in these monarchical schemes. See also Laval to Richelieu, Oct. 5, 1818, AAE., C. P. Espagne, vol. 702; *id.* to *id.*, Aug. 21, 1818, *ibid.*

65 Mitre, *op. cit.*, III, 323-324.

66 Prevost to Adams, Mar. 15, 1820, DS., Special Agents, vol. vii.

67 Forbes to Adams, Dec. 4, 1820, DS., Consular Letters, Buenos Aires, vol. i, part 2; Prevost to Adams, Jan. 16, 1821, Special Agents, vol. vii.

Prevost should leave vacant.[68] Prevost was censured for his pro-patriot bearing and warned to maintain a more neutral attitude.[69] The expulsion of Prevost from Buenos Aires left him no choice of residence and he departed for Chile leaving Forbes, somewhat to his disappointment, in the former place.[70]

Forbes was able, eventually, to establish normal relations with Rivadavia. By a combination of conciliatory and forthright tactics which indicate his marked ability, he was able to secure the abolition of privateering under the Buenos Aires flag.[71] His despatches, however, indicate clearly that he was laboring under difficult conditions. The tone of the Buenos Aires press was very critical of the United States.[72] Anonymous articles, according to Forbes, cast insulting aspersions " not only on the character of our government but on the total want of religion and honor among the North Americans ".[73] Such squibs were probably due in large measure to personal grudges against individual Americans, and should be discounted to some extent. Forbes did his best to turn the current of opinion and was able in one case to win a newspaper editor, a Dr. Castro. This man avowed that though he had once distrusted the motives of the United States, he now believed that its course had been wise and magnanimous.[74] In spite of individual instances like the above, the United States was not so highly regarded in 1820 and 1821 at Buenos Aires as had previously been the case.[75]

68 *Dictionary of American Biography*, " John M. Forbes "; Adams to Forbes, June 17, 1820, DS., Despatches to Consuls, vol. ii.

69 Adams to Prevost, July 10, 1820. DS., Despatches to Consuls, vol. ii.

70 Forbes to Adams, Dec. 4, 1820, Consular Letters, Buenos Aires, vol. i, part 1.

71 Manning, *Diplomatic Correspondence*, I, 583-591.

72 *Strictures on 'A Voyage to South America' etc.*, p. 78.

73 Forbes to Adams, Dec. 4, 1820, Consular Letters, Buenos Aires, vol. i, part 1.

74 *Ibid.*

75 This generalization is born out by the preceding paragraphs in the text. See also Manning, *op. cit.*, II, 706-7 for a letter from Buenos Aires confirming this view.

Among the patriots of Chile British influence and British trade continued to flourish and the United States continued to be eclipsed. Perhaps more important than any other factor was the credit which British merchants were extending to Chileans, and which had become an indispensable factor in Chilean economy.[76] An attempt to float an American loan to the Chilean government failed, partly because of the dishonor of promissory notes issued by Aguirre during his mission to the United States.[77]

Here as elsewhere in Spanish America the earlier enthusiasm for the " brothers of the North " led to embarrassment. More was expected of the United States than of England.[78] Chileans accused the United States of not maintaining true neutrality and declared that the Neutrality Acts of 1817 and 1818 went beyond the letter of neutral obligation in order to humor Spain.[79] The close relations between the governments of Chile and Buenos Aires from 1816 to 1820 also prejudiced the United States, as the leaders in the latter region communicated their irritation to the Chilean authorities.[80]

Of course there were variations in opinion among Chileans. San Martín, O'Higgins, and their close associates were less friendly beneath the surface. The editor of the *Telegrafo* took his tone from them, but General Freire and some others showed a more amicable disposition.[81] Rumors of a recognition of Chile by the United States also excited flurries of good will.[82]

The employment of Lord Cochrane, a brilliant but temperamental British naval officer to head the Chilean naval service

---

76 J. Robinson to Adams, Jan. 19, 1819, DS., Special Agents, vol. v.

77 J. Robinson to Adams, Oct. 31, 1819, Aug. 2, 1821, DS., *ibid.*

78 J. Robinson to Adams, July 29, 1819, DS., *ibid.*

79 *Ibid.*

80 J. Robinson to Adams, Jan. 22, 1820, *ibid.*

81 *Ibid.*

82 *Ibid.*; see also J. Robinson to Adams, Oct. 9, 1820 and Nov. 21, 1820, *ibid.*

was a further blow to American prestige. He was accused by
Worthington of attempting to set the patriot authorities against
the United States.[83] Shortly after he took command a noisy
quarrel occurred between Lord Cochrane and Captain Biddle
of the U. S. S. *Ontario* over questions of precedence and eti-
quette. Biddle refused to salute the Chilean flag on one occasion,
and he was accused of smuggling Spanish property from Lima
to Rio de Janeiro. Whatever the truth of the matter was, the
incident caused irritation among the Chileans, and led to a
formal protest from the Chilean authorities.[84]

This was the first of a series of unpleasant controversies
growing out of the activities of Cochrane's fleet. During 1819
Chile declared a blockade of the Peruvian coast and seized a
number of American ships for infraction of it.[85] The United
States protested as it had to Spain on a similar occasion in
1816. The Chilean government did not persist in upholding
the legality of the blockade, but Cochrane did very much as he
pleased, and incidents continued to crop up.[86]

As at Buenos Aires, the encouragement of desertion among
the crews of American merchant ships was another source of
irritation. Chile, having but few sailors, depended on foreign
enlistments to man her naval vessels and privateers. Many
American merchantmen were held in Valparaiso short-handed
in consequence.[87]

The commercial relations of certain American merchants
with Lima during the latter part of the revolution, when communication between that port and Spain were interrupted, were

83 Manning, *op. cit.*, II, 1029.

84 *Documentos del archivo de San Martin*, VIII, 242, Álvarez Jonte to
San Martín, Jan. 10, 1819; Manning, *op. cit.*, II, 1024, Worthington to
Echevarría, Jan. 4, 1819; J. Robinson to Adams, Jan. 19, 1819, DS., Special
Agents, vol. v; Prevost to Adams, Mar. 20, 1819, and Echevarría to Prevost,
Mar. 16, 1819, DS., Special Agents, vol. vii.

85 J. Robinson to Adams, Jan. 17, 1820, DS., Special Agents, vol. v.

86 Manning, *op. cit.*, Prevost to Adams, May 16, 1819, II, 1037.

87 See affidavit of S. Townsend, April 27, 1818, DS., Special Agents, vol. v.

regarded with displeasure by the Chileans. Licenses had been given by the Viceroy to certain Americans to bring goods to Peru. In 1818 three thousand muskets were reported to have arrived there on an American vessel.[88] In the following year the royalists depended even more on the use of neutral flags, as Cochrane's cruisers had made their own unsafe. Two American ships, the *Alexander* and the *Flying Fish* brought in munitions of war.[89] Another vessel despatched from the United States under a license issued by Onís and loaded with munitions for Peru was captured by the Chileans.[90] Though it was perfectly legal for neutrals to engage in such business at their own risk, this traffic hurt American influence in Chile. The coincidence of these commercial relations with Lima and the signature of the Adams-Onís treaty led some Chileans to believe that the United States favored a Spanish victory.[91]

Cochrane was much annoyed by the insistence of British and American warships on running his blockade with freight and passengers on board. At this time it was customary for such vessels to carry small amounts of freight and a few passengers as a private venture of the captain. The business done in this way was necessarily small in volume but it led to much irritation. The patriots had themselves taken advantage of the practice before they gained control of the South Pacific,[92] but in a most human manner they objected to the use of the system by their adversaries. It was in the exportation of specie, which occupied little space in relation to its value and was a great risk to shippers, that the men-of-war were particularly active.

88 *Documentos del archivo de San Martin,* VI, 306, Álvarez Jonte to San Martín, Sept. 9, 1818.

89 *Archivo de San Martín,* V, 212, Pezuela to Casa Flores, June 15, 1819.

90 *Ibid.,* VIII, 251, Álvarez Jonte to O'Higgins, June 5, 1819.

91 J. Robinson to Adams, July 29, 1819, DS., Special Agents, vol. v. The capture of the *Macedonian* by Cochrane with an important cargo of specie caused indignation in Boston, *Columbian Centinel,* Jan. 26, 1820.

92 *Archivo de San Martín,* VI, 322, Tomás Guido to San Martín, Feb. 18, 1819.

The U. S. S. *Macedonia* carried a considerable sum in silver from Lima to Rio de Janeiro in 1820.[93]

Animosity between the naval forces of Chile and these neutral warships became so serious that the United States Navy Department sent instructions to its commanders in the Pacific Ocean that, though paper blockade could not be recognized as legal, the greatest care should be used to avoid antagonizing the Chilean authorities.[94]

These difficulties were not to be overcome by the efforts of Worthington and Prevost to make themselves agreeable to San Martín and O'Higgins. They were personally in the good graces of these leaders, and not without cause. Prevost, when in Lima assisting at the negotiation of a convention for the exchange of prisoners, brought back information and letters from patriots in Peru, acting virtually as a Chilean spy.[95] He also quarrelled with Biddle over what he called the latter's unneutral conduct toward Chile, but he seems to have erred more than that officer, though in the opposite direction.

These incidents on the sea account for the coolness between the United States and Chile which increased in 1820. The Chilean press was reported to contain many diatribes against the United States,[96] and they could be matched by similar outbursts in the American newspapers.[97] Overshadowing these rather petty incidents, however, was the growth of a national spirit in Chile, fostered by the great victories won by San Martín. This led to anti-foreign feeling of which Americans

93 *Documentos del archivo de San Martín,* V, 164, Goyeneche to Lastra, Feb. 22, 1821.

94 *Memorias de O'Leary,* XII, 414, Smith Thompson to A. C. P. Ridgeley, Mar. 22, 1821. This order was apparently called forth by the complaints of J. Robinson, an unofficial correspondent of Monroe and Adams from South America. See Rush to Monroe, Jan. 29, 1822, MP. LC.

95 Manning, *op. cit.,* I, 553, Guido to San Martín, Sept. 30, 1819.

96 *Strictures on 'A Voyage to South America'* ..., p. 97.

97 *Columbian Centinel,* Boston, Jan. 26, 1820.

were the victims because of their ubiquitous presence on the Chilean and Peruvian coasts.[98]

In Mexico, contact between the patriots and the United States almost lapsed entirely. Only in 1821 after the establishment of the Iturbide government were they renewed. The State Department received a favorable report on the new regime from an unofficial correspondent, one Smith Wilcocks, and in November, 1821, Herrera, the one-time envoy of the republicans who was now the foreign minister of Iturbide, wrote Adams suggesting the establishment of relations. This move was disregarded by the United States for some months, nor does it seem to be evidence of a friendly feeling in Mexico. The instructions furnished the first Mexican minister to the United States in 1822 show fear and suspicion of the United States both because of the hostility of the American people to the monarchical form of government and their aggressive policy on the border. This fear was shown even by those who were on the whole friendly to the United States.[99]

While Monroe's administration continued its cautious policy and while the new states in South America were losing hope of America assistance and turning either to other powers or to confidence in their own strength, Henry Clay, not satisfied with the success of his resolution of May, 1820, was carrying on his campaign for recognition with unabated energy. On February 6, 1821 he moved an amendment to the appropriation bill to include $18,000 for outfit and salary for an envoy to South America. In favor of the motion it was stated that it was the evident wish of the public that Congress should take action, while opponents declared that it would be of no assistance to the patriots and might embarrass the United States. After a

98 J. Robinson to Adams, June 29, 1821, DS., Special Agents, vol. v.

99 Smith Wilcocks to Adams, 1821, DS., Consular Letters, Mexico, vol. i; Fabela, *op. cit.*, p. 150 ff.; *Memoria politico instructiva enviada a los gefes de Anahuac* (Philadelphia, 1821), p. 13. This work is attributed both to Vicente Rocafuerte, a native of Quito, and to Fray Servando Teresa Mier, a Mexican friar, see Lockey, *op. cit.*, p. 202.

spirited debate, in the course of which Clay spoke twice, the motion was defeated.[100]

Clay then gave up the idea of an appropriation and offered instead a declaration of sympathy with the Spanish Americans and of a desire to cooperate with the President whenever he might choose to recognize any of the new governments.[101] During the debate on this motion Montgomery of Kentucky created a stir by doubting whether his constituents were interested in the matter.[102] His colleague, Stevens, strongly rebutted this view of Kentucky sentiment and insisted that *his* constituents favored a Congressional declaration. Cobb of Georgia felt that the liberal revolution in Spain demanded sympathy and that the issue between mother country and colonies was not as clear as it had been before that event.[103] The resolution was divided into two parts for voting. On Feb. 10 the first part, the declaration of sympathy, passed by an overwhelming vote of 134 to 12; the second part, endorsing recognition when the president should decide to act, passed by the smaller margin of 87 to 68.[104] Like the resolution of the preceding year this vote was merely an expression of feeling on the part of the House of Representatives and left matters where they had been.[105]

100 *Works of Henry Clay*, ed. by C. Colton, I, 262; Clay to Rodney, Feb. 16, 1821, Rodney Papers, LC.; the motion was first put in committee of the whole and defeated by a vote of 77 to 73. On being voted on again before the House, it was lost by a slightly larger margin. *Niles' Weekly Register,* Feb. 10, 17, 1821; *Annals of Congress,* XXXVII, 16 Cong., 2 Sess., HR, 1071 ff.

101 *Annals of Congress,* XXXVI, 16 Cong., 2 Sess., HR, 1081.

102 *Ibid.,* p. 1082.

103 *Ibid.,* p. 1084.

104 *Ibid.,* p. 1092. The sectional distribution of this vote was as follows: *Yeas,* New England 9, Middle Atlantic 33, South Atlantic 26, West 19. *Nays,* New England 28, Middle Atlantic 16, South Atlantic 18, West 6.

105 On this occasion ten Crawfordites who had previously voted against Clay's South American resolutions supported him.

These proceedings in Congress, however, encouraged Tórres, the Colombian agent, to approach Adams again to request the formal recognition of his government and muskets from the government arsenals.[106] Finding that this move was not made as a result of new instructions from Colombia, Adams evaded the question, declaring that the President wished to see the outcome of the current negotiations between Bolívar and Morillo.[107] The final ratification of the treaty with Spain, which came a few days after these occurrences, failed to bring any immediate change in the attitude of the administration. Monroe's second inaugural address and his annual message to Congress followed the pattern of the previous years in so far as they alluded to the struggle in Spanish America.[108]

With the departure of Clay from the halls of Congress there was a lull in the agitation for recognition. Clay himself no longer showed the same vehemence on the subject, and was friendlier to the administration. Early in March, 1821 he visited Adams and was treated to a lengthy exposition of the secretary's views on Spanish America. Adams insisted, though he admitted the natural sympathy of Americans with the rebels, that they were disorderly and that no one could tell what sort of political organization they might adopt. The United States had no interest whatever of a practical nature in taking sides in the conflict. Clay seems, however, to have parted from Adams on good terms, satisfied perhaps by his victory in the House.[109]

From the foregoing survey of the relations of the United States with the insurgent Spanish American governments from 1818 to the end of 1821, and of the course of the agitation for recognition of those states in the American Congress and elsewhere, it will be evident that there was no rapprochement be-

106 F. J. Urrutia, *op. cit.*, p. 212.
107 Adams, *Memoirs*, V, 283.
108 Richardson, *Messages and Papers*, II, 88-89, 105.
109 Adams, *Memoirs*, V, 324-325.

tween the two regions and that the campaign for recognition had passed its climax. Nevertheless, only a few months later the United States was to take the action so long discussed and so cautiously avoided by the American government. What explanation can be given for this action?

First of all, Spain received three staggering blows during the year 1821, which completely altered the political geography of Spanish America. An expeditionary force from Chile forced the evacuation of Lima, the citadel of royalism in South America. This was followed by the organization of a new state in Peru by San Martín, and by its formal declaration of independence from Spain. Further north, Bolívar added to his laurels by winning the smashing victory of Carabobo, which decided the fate of Venezuela as definitely as Boyacá, in 1819, had freed New Granada. These victories though highly important were not totally unexpected; they were steps in the triumphal procession of the patriot arms initiated by San Martín's Andean campaign in 1816, and by Bolívar's command of the Orinoco at about the same time. From Mexico came news that was more sensational. In 1820 New Spain appeared to have been totally pacified by the viceroy, Ruíz de Apodaca. The revolution had dwindled until it had almost lost organized existence, but the Spanish grip on the country was more apparent than real. When Iturbide raised the standard of revolt on a basis that appealed to the upper creole class as well as to the humbler folk who had followed earlier leaders the edifice of Spanish power collapsed with surprising rapidity. During the summer of 1821 a Spanish general sent to retrieve the disaster was forced to accept terms which practically ended Spanish sovereignty.

By the end of 1821, then, the final result of the wars of independence in Spanish America could no longer be held doubtful, though Spanish armies still held out in parts of Peru and Colombia. It became consistent now, in accordance with Adams' view that recognition was not a matter of right but of fact,[110] to recognize the new governments. By 1822, also, the situation in Europe made an isolated move by the United States safer than it had been. Adams, throughout his term of office, had held that America must remain aloof to prevent European meddling in Spanish America.[111] The Alliance of the great powers, however, now seemed less ominous than it had been during 1818 when the Congress of Aix-la-Chapelle discussed the Spanish-American question. Great Britain had remained aloof from the continental powers at Troppau; the wave of ' liberalism ' that had swept over Italy, Spain and Portugal had not yet spent all its force; not yet had intervention in Spain brought the further threat of an extension of intervention to America as in 1823.

Anglo-American commercial rivalry must be considered an equally important factor. For years the agents sent by Madison and later by Monroe to Spanish America had been reporting the growth of Britain's interests.[112] How long should the United States stand aside before making a friendly gesture which might help to counteract this trend?

No concerted effort by mercantile interests to force through the recognition of the rebels is apparent, but that does not justify the opinion that interest in trade did not play an important part in bringing it about. Politics and economics have their contacts even without the presence of organized pressure groups. In this case, in addition to the point of view of the American agents alluded to above, the repeated references to trade and commercial relations in the instructions issued by the State Department must be remembered.[113] The total existing

110 *Writings of John Quincy Adams*, ed. by Ford, VI, 472; Adams to Monroe, Aug. 24, 1818.

111 See pp. 137 f., 255, *supra*. *Cf.* also Adams to Monroe, *Writings*, V, 551.

112 See pp. 59 f., 65, 151 ff., *supra*, for expressions of this opinion.

113 See chaps. ii, iv, *supra*; for further examples of the commercial point of view of American agents see J. Robinson to Adams, July 29, 1819, DS., Special Agents, V; Memorandum on Venezuela by B. Irvine, DS., Special Agents, VIII; see also, Manning, *op. cit.*, I, 6, 11 and *passim*, also see chap. ii, *supra*, footnotes 34 and 35.

trade of the United States with the rebellious colonies was slight, as it has more than once been pointed out, but the influence of the future prospects of that trade was considerable at this difficult time in the history of American foreign commerce.[114]

Is it right to assume that President Monroe did not have business as well as political interests in mind when he wrote to Madison in May, 1822 that:

The time had certainly come when it became our duty to recognize them, provided it was intended to maintain friendly relations with them in future, and not to suffer them under a feeling of resentment towards us and the artful practice of European powers to become the dupes of their policies.[115]

All these factors were undoubtedly taken into consideration by Monroe and Adams in the early days of 1822.   In addition it may be surmised that they saw the value of rebel recognition in domestic politics. Clay had attempted to make political capital out of the South American question. Was it not to the interest of Monroe, and even more so of the aspirants to the presidency in his cabinet to take the wind out of his sails?

Perhaps an indication of the coming move might have been noticed by a far-sighted observer in the summer of 1821. Adams delivered a Fourth of July oration in Washington in that year, which among other things touched on the injustice of colonial rule which could not serve the true ends of government.[116] The address was an eloquent defense of the policy adhered to by the United States in Spanish-America up to that time, but according to Adams himself it " prepared the

114 This differs from the point of view of Professor Perkins, in *The Monroe Doctrine, 1823-1826*. The present writer does not question the facts given in this work, but he believes that commercial *hopes* have not been given sufficient weight.

115 *Writings of James Monroe*, VI, 285; *cf.* Robertson in HAHR, I (1918), 258.

116 *Niles' Weekly Register*, July 21, 1821.

way for an acknowledgement upon the principle of public law of that independence (i.e., of Spanish America) whenever it shall be sufficiently established by the fact ".[117]

Adams' insistence that recognition of a government depended on its established authority *de facto* could now bring forth its fruits. Though the Secretary of State's views were less spectacularly derived from the republican and democratic climate of opinion in the United States than those of Henry Clay, they were none the less rooted there, and in the long run they were to lead to a more valuable defense of the political foundations of the new world than those of his contemporary because they were formulated with legal precision and based on legal precedents. The doctrine which Adams upheld had been stated by Vattel and hinted at by other writers on international law,[118] but the 'legitimate' state system of Europe which was reaffirmed at Vienna in 1815 was fundamentally hostile to it. The existence of the United States was the only breach in this system. If the United States had recognized the Spanish American states according to Clay's plan, its action would have been similar to that of France and Holland during the war of the American Revolution and could have been considered a justification for war. By systematically formulating a neutral policy, and going beyond the usual practice of states in that era in the enforcement of it; by resisting all temptations to recognize the independence of the new states while their future was still in reasonable doubt, Adams was paving the way for the acceptance of his doctrine which once accepted by other states would make a great breach in the barriers of legitimacy.

Accordingly, when the House of Representatives at the motion of Nelson of Virginia called for information on the state of South America and for communications received by

117 *Writings of John Quincy Adams*, ed. by Ford, VII, 197, Adams to Everett, Jan. 31, 1822.

118 Julius Goebel, *The Recognition Policy of the United States* (New York, 1915), p. 41. The ideas expressed in this paragraph are based on this work.

the government from envoys from that region,[119] a good opportunity was afforded the administration to take a step forward. On January 31, 1822, Trimble of Kentucky moved that the President be requested to recognize the Republic of Colombia and to exchange ministers with it and with any others that should be actually independent.[120] A few weeks later the resolution came before the committee of the whole and the author spoke in favor of his measure,[121] but some inkling of a move by the executive must have reached Congressional circles for the debate went no further, nor was a vote taken.

On March 8, 1822, Congress received Monroe's message in reply to the previous call for information. It recommended recognition of the new states in the following language:

When we regard, then, the great length of time which this war has been prosecuted, the complete success which has attended it in favor of the provinces, the present condition of the parties and the utter inability of Spain to produce any change in it, we are compelled to conclude that its fate is settled, and that the provinces which have declared their independence and are in the enjoyment of it ought to be recognized.[122]

To sugar the pill for Spain the message was careful to make it clear that no question of right was being judged; that the recognition was not to be considered a hostile act toward Spain; and that the United States would continue to act with the most perfect neutrality.[123]

This recommendation by the executive was the decisive step, but Monroe sought Congressional backing and carefully

119 *Annals of Congress*, 17 Cong., 1 Sess., vol. i, p. 825.

120 *Ibid.*, p. 854; *Niles' Weekly Register*, Feb. 2, 1822.

121 *Annals of Congress*, 17 Cong., 1 Sess., vol. i, p. 1382 ff.; *Columbian Centinel*, Boston, Feb. 20, 1822.

122 Richardson, *Messages and Papers*, II, 116-118.

123 This point was further elaborated in instructions to Forsyth in Spain. Adams to Forsyth, March 9, 1822, DS., Instructions, vol. vii.

avoided action while Congress was considering his message. The House committee on foreign relations concurred with the President's message and its report dwelt at length on the essential neutrality of the proposed action. The documents furnished with the message in addition to reports on the progress of the Spanish American states tended to produce the impression that Spain itself was on the point of making peace with the rebels. It was suggested that a negotiation with that in view had been contemplated by the Cortes. The House of Representatives, however, does not seem to have cared very much what Spain had done or would do. Poinsett, now a member from South Carolina, showed in an able speech that Madrid would probably consider recognition of the colonies a hostile act, but he did not favor further delay. The keynote of his speech was not sympathy for struggling Spanish America, but belief that the contemplated move would raise American prestige and aid American commerce in that region to withstand the competition of European rivals.[124] The resolution reported from the committee included a generous appropriation of one hundred thousand dollars for the support of missions to the new republics. It passed the House on March 28 by a unanimous vote except for that of one Garnett who gained momentary notoriety by his single handed opposition.[125]

The Senate acted with more caution. Though rumors were current that Spain also had recognized the independence of the Colonists, that view was soon exploded when it became known that the Cortes had repudiated the treaty of Cordoba with the new Mexican authorities.[126] Rufus King, Nathaniel Macon and a few others were disturbed by this news, and an amendment to the resolution passed by the House of Representatives was introduced, providing that no money should be drawn until the President was fully satisfied that missions to South America

124 *Annals of Congress*, 17 Cong., 1 Sess., vol. ii, p. 1395.
125 *Ibid.*, p. 1404.
126 Adams, *Memoirs*, V, 489.

would not interrupt peaceful relations with other powers. The amendment secured only a few scattering votes [127] and the resolution passed soon after by a vote of 39 to 3.[128]

As soon as Congress had acted Adams wrote to Tórres, whose official reception as minister from Colombia was to be the outward symbol of the new attitude of the United States. The illness of the veteran patriot caused some delay in holding the reception which finally took place in June, 1822, to the enormous satisfaction of Tórres who was suffering from what was soon to prove a fatal illness.[129] Beyond this point it is unnecessary to pass, the establishment of regular diplomatic relations with Mexico, and with the United Provinces of Rio de la Plata followed soon after.[130]

The administration attempted to make it clear that the action now taken was the natural consequence of a policy laid down for over a decade, that it was not yielding to pressure, nor veering from the course travelled by the United States up to this time. That it was right in making this claim is partly shown by the reaction of the country to the recognition of the new republics. Although all previous attempts to induce the administration to make this step had been supported by only a part of the public and a minority in Congress, the approval of the action once taken was universal. It was but natural that those who had favored the move for years should be pleased, but in 1822 those who had counselled caution were even more approving. This can only be explained by the fact that motives and occasion alike were different in 1822 from what they had been in 1818.

The *North American Review,* still maintaining its aloof and disdainful attitude towards the Spanish Americans, approved

127 *Annals of Congress,* 17 Cong., 1 Sess., vol. i, p. 430.

128 *Ibid.,* p. 431.

129 Urrutia, *op. cit.,* p. 162 f., William Duane to Clay, July 15, 1822, Clay Papers, LC.

130 On this subject see the monograph of Prof. W. S. Robertson, "The First Legations of the United States in Latin-America" in MVHR., vol. ii.

the President's move on account of its importance for commerce.[131] The Boston *Columbian Centinel,* while it rejoiced in the news that the House had voted for recognition, stated that this was " no rash sentimentality " and showed no enthusiasm for the newly recognized states.[132] Only a few weeks earlier the same paper had strongly defended the policy of the administration up to that time.[133] The independence of Mexico, once the monarchical and imperial complexion it bore was realized, was far from popular in the United States,[134] yet the *fact* had much to do with the action taken by the government. One of Clay's supporters gave a clue to an important fact when he wrote to his pálladin: " recognition would at one time have been a noble deed " now it " flows from the calculations of a sordid interest alone ".[135] This sentiment, though exaggerated, was symptomatic of the difference in feeling between the earlier enthusiasts of the cause and the administration and its supporters. Neither was uninfluenced by economic motives, but there was less emotion and more calculation among the latter.[136]

What Clay's correspondent failed to realize was the importance of the question of international law. A government in

131 *North American Review,* XIV (1822), p. 420 ff.

132 *Columbian Centinel,* Boston, Mar. 27, April 3, 1822.

133 *Ibid.,* March 16, 1822.

134 I. Fabela, *Los precursores de la diplomacia Mejicana,* p. 154 citing the testimony of the first Mexican minister in the U. S., Bermudez Zozaya; Vicente Rocafuerte, *Memoria político-instructiva, etc.* (Philadelphia, 1821), p. 37.

135 H. Shaw to Clay, Clay Papers, LC., vol. iii.

136 That there was a realization on the part of commercial interests that the situation had changed since 1817-18 is evident. The success of the patriots made it appear that the trade in munitions and foodstuffs would not continue long (*Niles' Weekly Register,* Sept. 1, 1821). South American markets at this time were glutted, and a need was felt for action that might revive commerce (Chandler, " Commerce of the United States with South America on the Eve of the Monroe Doctrine ", *Quarterly Journal of Economics,* XXXVIII, 473. On the eve of the action taken by Monroe efforts were being made to initiate trade between New Orleans and Vera Cruz (T. Reilly to C. A. Rodney, Feb. 20, 1822, MP. LC.).

which lawyers played so great a part, and a Department of State headed by John Quincy Adams would naturally believe in the importance of that aspect. The policy followed by the United States was closely based on a theory of recognition, as it has been pointed out above. No one, Adams least of all, would have claimed that the United States had acted on motives of ideal love of justice, but Adams did believe that the enlightened self interest of the nation could and should be carried out through channels of action justifiable by legal principle.

CHAPTER X
LOOKING BACKWARD

During the years covered by this study the most significant change in the United States was its emergence from its earlier constant preoccupation with the affairs of Europe and its increasing attention to internal problems. This trend, already evident before the War of 1812, was stronger after the providentially favorable outcome of that struggle and the new era of peace in Europe. This national tendency was to reach its culmination in the field of foreign policy with the enunciation of the Monroe Doctrine in 1823, a doctrine almost every aspect of which is implicit in the attitude of American statesmen, diplomats, and publicists during the first three decades of United States history.

The period under review was one of transition, and the ideas and forces working in it were often discordant. Though the keynote of American policy was national aggrandizement, it was envisaged in different ways: some saw it best accomplished by territorial expansion, an aim now more frankly and definitely acknowledged than in earlier years; others thought of new markets and the expansion of foreign trade and of the merchant marine as the more vital interest of the nation. These objectives were not necessarily in conflict, but they did not coincide and were often supported by opposing groups. Of the two interests the urge for territory was predominant. It was in harmony with the new vision of a republic of continental proportions while the other, in spite of the vigor and ingenuity of its proponents, was framed by the older eighteenth century view of American economic life. In the incidents surveyed in this volume the workings of both forces have been noted.

But these major economic interests do not explain everything. The interaction of American aims with those of other countries, the play of personality upon personality, and even the fortuitous way in which seemingly unrelated phenomena come together to form a pattern must be taken into consideration. The data accumulated in these pages suggest an interpretation of the main lines of development.

From 1810 to 1815 the boundary controversy overshadowed other matters in the relations of the United States and Spain. While war raged in Europe and America and diplomatic relations between the two countries were interrupted, the administration of Madison continued the traditional American policy of taking advantage of European disturbances to promote national American interests. Florida was almost completely torn from the weakened grasp of Spain. The district of Baton Rouge was occupied in 1810 and that of Mobile three years later. Spanish authority in the rest of Florida was paralysed by the insurrection in East Florida, fostered by General Mathews, and by Jackson's operations in West Florida in 1814.

Towards the Spanish American revolutions which broke out in 1810 the United States looked with sympathetic interest. At the outset this sympathy was much confused and qualified by party spirit and by mistaken views of the relation between the rebels and the various warring nations of Europe, but by 1812 the attitude of government and people alike had become clearly benevolent. Agents were sent to and received from the new governments, though on an informal and non-diplomatic basis; the rebel aims of republican independence were encouraged; and their ships were accorded equal rights with those of Spain in American ports. The war of 1812, by cutting off contact with the region to the south and by focussing attention on territorial issues nearer home that were emphasized by the threat of British attack in Florida, reduced the interest of the United States in Spanish American independence.

The basic motive for these aggressions against Spain was the desire of Southern frontiersmen and planters for additional territory and for control of the fluvial lines of communication which afforded better access to lands already owned by the United States. Closely allied with this land hunger was the need for security on the border, which faced in Spanish Florida a constant menace of Indian or foreign attack and a haven for fugitives from the United States. This expansionist sentiment in the South and West also affected the relations of the United States with the Spanish American rebels. Those who favored strong measures against Spain for one reason sided with the enemies of Spain on another issue. In the revolutionary movements in territory adjoining the United States the connection was even closer. Through the agency of revolution, real or synthetic, and by encouraging filibustering, American expansion was carried forward.

Commercial and financial interests also stood to gain from territorial expansion, through the growth of population which meant larger markets and a greater volume of trade for urban centers. This identity of interest accounts for the similarity of outlook between New Orleans and the West as a whole. The Eastern cities, in those days of undeveloped communications, did not yet see clearly their interest in expansion in the distant South and West, and the influence of existing lines of business outweighed future problematical developments. Even so, the attitude of Eastern merchants and financiers was not uniform. Those involved in the trade with Spain and with Cuba would not favor a bellicose policy. The holders of claims against Spain also favored a policy which would bring about a peaceful settlement. On the other hand it must be recognized that certain ports had already begun trade relations with regions controlled by the patriots and that these trade interests would be helped by friendly political relations with the rebels and could expect little advancement unless the latter were successful in their struggle with the mother country. The volume of this trade was smaller than that with Cuba and Spain, however, and it may perhaps be presumed that it consequently exercised less political pressure.

In Spain the period 1810-1815 was one of war against a foreign invader and intense domestic political unrest followed by a restoration that failed to bring real peace or prosperity. During most of this time the American interests of Spain were necessarily neglected. Attempts of varying nature and importance were made to secure the intervention of European powers against the aggression of the United States in Florida, especially after the return of peace in Europe, but they were all unavailing. The ultimate aims of the constitutionalist government from 1810 to 1814 were national while those of Ferdinand VII after his restoration were dynastic and personal, but their concrete objectives and their methods in foreign affairs were similar. Both sought the preservation of the Spanish colonial empire intact. The liberals in 1812 and 1813 realized the importance of the dispute with the United States not only for the territory directly involved, but also for the future of the empire as a whole. The government of Ferdinand overestimated its own strength and underestimated that of the United States, consequently failing to recognize the critical nature of the pending negotiations.

The insurgents, at the outset of their struggle, very generally looked to the United States for aid and sometimes turned to its constitutional experience for guidance. This was especially true in Venezuela, New Granada and Chile; less so in Mexico and in Buenos Aires. Almost all these areas sent envoys to the United States to seek moral and material support. Aware of the conflict between the United States and Spain, the rebels hoped that the United States would espouse their cause. When the war of 1812 cut them off from contact with the United States, the patriots, except those of Mexico, established closer relations with Great Britain.

In 1815, with the re-establishment of peace in Europe and between Great Britain and the United States, the situation changed. Diplomatic relations were renewed between the United States and Spain, and Madison and Monroe tried to negotiate a settlement with that power. From this time the Spanish American rebels played a larger part in the conflict between the two powers. In order to avoid a break with Spain and to live up to the American policy of complete neutrality, the Neutrality Acts of 1817 and 1818 were passed, and the popular movement for official recognition of the rebels was gently but firmly checked by the administration. Negotiations with Spain did not progress until 1818 owing to the unyielding policy of both governments. The Florida campaign of Jackson in the latter year helped to break the deadlock. In the United States it led to a withdrawal of the long maintained claim to Texas. In Spain it jolted the court into a more compliant attitude on the boundary question, which was also furthered by a ministerial change which occurred at the same time. The treaty of 1819 was a compromise of the claims and boundary issues. The question of neutrality in the Spanish colonial war was not mentioned in it, though a principal motive for its conclusion had been the Spanish hope of restraining the United States from hostile action.

From 1815 to 1819 the land hunger of the South and West changed in character. It had been partially satisfied by the acquisition of most of West Florida in 1810 and 1813. The remaining Spanish territory east of the Mississippi was desired for other reasons. The irritation produced by a series of annoying incidents on Florida soil played a larger part. Florida was wanted more for reasons of military defense, communication, national pride, than because of any strong urge to settle Florida lands, though there was some speculation in those lands. This change was counterbalanced by a growing interest in Texas into which province increasing numbers of Americans were drifting.

The relation of commercial interests to Spanish affairs also shifted. In the West, stirred by Clay's campaign in favor of recognition, the sentiment was abroad that Spanish America would provide a market for the produce of the Mississippi valley. The more extensive direct interests of the East were affected by the phenomenal growth of the privateering business under the flags of the insurgent states. Trade with many parts of Spanish America was renewed after the interruption caused by the British war. Trade with Spain, however, languished. The balance between commerce with loyal and rebel parts of the Spanish empire was still in favor of the former because of Cuba, but the current was setting in the other direction. Certain ports, especially Baltimore and New Orleans became centers of pro-patriot and anti-Spanish feeling.

In Spain the shift from a policy of inaction that characterized the Cevallos ministry to one of conciliation under Pizarro and Irujo has been mentioned. It was in 1817 that the aid received in American ports by rebel privateers and the possible recognition of their governments by the United States began seriously to occupy the attention of the Spanish foreign office. It was this which made the treaty of 1819 a possibility.

In these years the influence of the United States in Spanish America was on the wane. Military men, less impressed than their predecessors by American political experience, were at the head of the patriot forces in Buenos Aires, Chile and Venezuela. They considered the neutrality legislation of the United States unfair and they were also antagonized by the misadventures of rebel agents in that country. The Florida-Texas controversy between the United States and Spain encouraged them to hope that there might be a break between the contestants, but that hope was again and again deferred. The governments of independent South America turned toward France and England and some of them considered the establishment of constitutional monarchies ruled by European princes. The attempts of American agents to counteract this tendency and to win the friendship of the insurgents for the United States were not markedly successful.

The years 1819 and 1820 during which ratification of the Adams-Onís treaty was deferred brought various changes of alignment in the United States. The administration, though it considered various alternatives, finally adhered to a waiting policy which was rewarded by the acceptance of the treaty by Spain in the autumn of 1820. Toward the new Spanish American states the executive maintained its previous stand, though there was talk of recognition at moments when relations with Spain were critical. The Missouri question in 1820 led to opposition in the North to territorial expansion in the South. Even in the areas heretofore united on that issue there came to be a division of opinion. Clay, Benton, and other exponents of western sentiment wished to scrap the 1819 treaty and to insist on the claim to Texas. Adams, Monroe, and—strangely enough —Jackson as well, favored adherence to the terms of the treaty. Public opinion east of the Appalachian chain supported them.

Commercial interests favored the treaty, which arranged for the settlement of private claims, and this conservative influence was strengthened by the disfavor with which the rebel privateers were regarded after 1818. A decline in the volume of trade with southern South America and the series of disputes which arose on the Pacific coast due to interference with American merchantmen by the Chilean fleet may also be regarded as factors which retarded recognition of the rebels. These years also saw the growth of disillusionment among certain groups in the United States as to the political capacity and republican principles of the Patriots.

In Spain the treaty, embodying Irujo's policy of conciliation, was not well regarded. Its ratification was at first defeated by a combination of interests: the Florida grantees, personal enemies of Irujo, and those who objected on traditional and sentimental grounds to any territorial cession. After the first two interests mentioned ceased to have much influence the Spanish court continued to feel that a treaty which did not explicitly bind the United States not to act counter to Spanish inerests in America was of no advantage to the monarchy. The liberal revolution of 1820 produced a reversal of this policy. Spain, weakened by domestic political feuds and regarded with suspicion by the continental powers, was forced to adopt a more compliant attitude toward the United States; a necessity which was made more acceptable because those who now directed affairs were able to blame their predecessors for allowing a situation to develop which made surrender unavoidable.

During 1821 the situation became simpler. The ratification of the Adams-Onís treaty eliminated boundary and other controversies between the United States and Spain, leaving only an aftermath of minor irritation over the evacuation of Florida. Popular pressure for recognition of the rebel states was not very strong at this time and there seemed to be greater willingness to allow the administration to choose its own way of handling the situation. Other factors, however, led the United States government to take the long delayed step and recognize the independence of the new states. One was the series of victories of the patriots in Colombia and Peru together with the collapse of Spanish rule in Mexico; another, the growing rivalry between the United States and Great Britain for a favored position in the trade with Spanish America. The relatively highly advanced state of British industry made the ambitions of Americans illusory, but the United States, not yet aware of the great alternative openings for capital employment at home, still felt that foreign commerce and the carrying trade was to be as important as it had been in earlier times, and was unwilling to concede British supremacy in Spanish American markets. These motives are more apparent in the words of politicians than in any sign of pressure from mercantile interests, but were not for that reason any less potent as political factors. At the end of 1821, too, the unity of the European powers in support of reaction was less ominous than it had seemed a year or two earlier. Lastly, it must be kept in mind that in accordance with the theory of recognition maintained by Adams, the time had now arrived when action toward recognition could be taken without disavowing the policy maintained up to this juncture.

A survey of American policy toward Spain in this period can not be complete without pointing to the influence of personalities. On the American side those who played influential roles were: Madison, Monroe, and John Quincy Adams. Calhoun, Crawford and Clay also exerted influence, nor should the redoubtable Jackson be forgotten. All these men, with the possible exception of Adams and Calhoun, were strongly prejudiced against Spain. In addition to sharing a widely diffused sentiment each had more personal reasons. Madison had had one of the bitterest quarrels of his career with Irujo during Jefferson's administration; Monroe had been deeply humiliated by his unsuccessful negotiations with Cevallos in 1805; Jackson was known as a hater of " the Dons " long before he began his attacks on Florida.

It does not appear that Adams, the most nationalistic of them all, was animated by special antipathy against Spain, but he was deeply suspicious of all foreigners, and it was only his long service in Europe and his recognition of the strength of the great powers that prevented his aggressive conduct of the negotiations from becoming rash. Adams at this stage of his career was less affected by sectional sentiments and interests than most of his contemporaries. He was ambitious, but he was able to combine his personal hopes and his loyalty to state and nation with a deep regard for law. He sometimes strained his logic to suit his ends but was not, apparently, aware of it. Altruism is seldom the motive power of national policy, but a regard for the forms of civilized intercourse between nations, and adherence to principles which outlive the expediency of the passing moment, can hardly be too highly praised. For his influence in this direction, as well as for his devotion to his country, great respect is due to the Secretary of State from Massachusetts.

Those who directed the affairs of Spain at this time were all subordinate to the king, Ferdinand VII. In spite of his unpleasant traits he must not be made the scape-goat for all the ills of Spain during his reign. In foreign affairs it was the lack of steady adherence to men or measures rather than his reactionary views which adversely affected his career. He was more of a Spaniard and less of a Bourbon than his predecessors. He knew well one aspect of the paradoxical Spanish spirit, but he was blind to the generous idealism symbolized by Don Quixote. It has already been related how the *camarilla,* and especially Tatistcheff, Ugarte, Alagon, Lozano de Tórres and others affected the foreign relations of Spain. Of the foreign ministers of Spain during the regency none left any mark on relations with the United States. After the restoration the same can be said of the Duke of San Carlos. Cevallos, who succeeded him, failed to keep abreast of his times, and though he posed as an expert on American affairs was singularly ignorant, not only in that sphere but of the European international situation. Pizarro, though he was a more intelligent man, failed to do much better. He lacked the confidence of the king, and he had too much liking for long drawn out and finely argued negotiations on non-essential details. Irujo, had a more incisive mind, but like Pizarro he lacked firm royal support, and he was handicapped by his intense Anglophobia. Of all Spain's diplomats during this period, however, Irujo and Onís stand out as the clearest minded and the best informed.

Finally a word may be said about the two most influential leaders in South America, Bolívar and San Martín. Both were men of genius. Temperamentally they were as divergent as the poles but circumstances led them at times along similar paths. They had a common devotion to the cause of independence; both came to the front after the close of the first period of revolution, when the influence of the United States was on the wane; both were convinced of the need for strong government in Spanish America to combat a tendency toward anarchy which was quick to show itself. Neither was strongly or more than temporarily prejudiced against the United States, but neither were they particularly friendly to that country. Not by diplomacy, but by their military successes, were they so largely responsible for bringing about the recognition of the South American republics by the United States.

The significance of this study which now draws to a close is multiple. It throws some additional light on a chapter in the territorial expansion of the United States, bringing out the complicated nature of the forces involved and the close connection between the border conflict and the Spanish American revolution. It also attempts to indicate the beginnings of the Hispanic American relations of the United States, and may help to correct too idealistic a view of the early contacts between the great republic of the North and its younger neighbors. Since the period covered in this study the relative economic position of the United States and Hispanic America has changed a great deal. These pages do not relate the contacts of a great industrial nation with others still struggling for political and economic integration. Yet motives and attitudes of mind have not changed as much as might be expected. The dual threads of sympathy and repulsion which exist today were not absent at the birth of the Spanish American republics at which the United States played the part of so interested an observer.

FINIS

BIBLIOGRAPHY

MANUSCRIPT SOURCES

Archives du Ministère des Affaires Étrangères, Paris.

Correspondance Politique, Espagne, Vols. 700 to 708.
Correspondance Politique, Espagne, Supplement No. 25.

Instructions to, and despatches from, the French ambassador in Madrid, 1817-1821.

Correspondance Politique, États Unis, Vols. 75 to 80.

Instructions to, and despatches from, the French minister in Washington from 1817-1821.

Archivo General de Simancas, Simancas, Spain.

Sección de Estado, Embajada de Inglaterra, Legajos 8289 (2675 moderno) and 8294 (2676 moderno).

Containing selections from the papers of the Spanish Embassy at London dealing with American affairs, 1815-1820.

Archivo Histórico Nacional, Madrid.

Sección de Estado, Negociación de Estados Unidos, Legajos 5636 to 5648 inclusive.

Containing the despatches of the Spanish ministers in the United States (original) and drafts of instructions to them from 1810 to 1822.

Legajos 5660, 5661 and 5662.

A varied assortment of documents dealing with the negotiation and ratification of the treaty of 1819.

Legajos 5554 to 5564 inclusive.

Expedientes or *dossiers* on special subjects relating to the United States.

Sección de Estado, Negociación de Francia, Legajo 6797.

Papers dealing with Louisiana, 1803 to 1818, an incomplete file of material on this subject selected from the correspondence of the Spanish Embassy at Paris.

Sección de Estado, Miscellaneous,

Legajo 3420.

Data on the personnel of the Spanish diplomatic service. *Dossiers* of Pizarro, Irujo and others.

Legajo 3412.

Documents dealing with the arrest and imprisonment of Irujo, 1819.

Legajo 3446.

Miscellaneous papers in the possession of Irujo.

Legajo 2770.

Miscellaneous letters of Onís.

Sección de Estado, Actas del Consejo de Estado,

Actas y Minutas de Consejo, 1818-1821, one bound volume, record in-incomplete.

Legajo 94, Expediente 16, Consulta del Consejo de Estado, sobre la conducta del Marqués de Casa Irujo, 1820.

Legajo 96, Expediente 7, Consulta del Consejo de Estado, sobre la cesión de las Floridas. 1820.

Archivo del Ministerio de Estado, Madrid.

Correspondencia del ministro de Su Majestad en los Estados Unidos, Correspondencia Política, 1815 to 1821, Legajos 222 to 227 inclusive and 237.

> *Note:* The originals of these papers were not seen by the writer. He consulted them from transcripts made for him by an employee of the ministry.
> These bundles contain the returned legation files from the Spanish legation in Washington for the years mentioned.

Public Record Office, London (Photocopies in the Division of Manuscripts, Library of Congress, Washington).

Foreign Office. 5, Volumes 114 to 150 inclusive.

> Correspondence between the British ministers and chargés d'affaires in Washington and the Foreign Office and drafts of instructions to them 1815 to 1822.

Department of State, Washington, D. C.

Despatches from Spain, Vols. XIII to XVIII (1814-1821).

> Original despatches from the American Ministers at Madrid and copies of correspondence at Madrid with the Spanish Foreign Office.

Instructions to Ministers, Vols. VIII and IX.

> Copies of the original instructions.

Special Agents, Vols. II to IX.

> Despatches from the following men: William Shaler, Jeremy Robinson, J. B. Prevost, Baptis Irvine, Samuel Forsyth, A. Scott, J. Lewis, J. R. Poinsett, A. Morris.

South American Mission, 1817-1818.

> Reports and correspondence of the mission composed of Rodney, Graham and Bland.

Argentine Republic, Notes, Vol. I, parts 1 and 2.

> Communications from the government of Buenos Aires.

Argentine Republic (Buenos Aires, Chile and Peru) W. G. D. Worthington, Special Agent, Vol. I, parts 1 and 2.

Despatches from Argentina, Vol. I.
> Correspondence of J. Forbes. 1820–

Consular Letters, Buenos Aires, Vol. I, parts 1 and 2.
> Despatches from Poinsett, Halsey, Miller and others in charge of the U. S. consulate at Buenos Aires, 1810-1822.

Colombia, Notes, Vol. I, parts 1 and 2.
> Communications from the various governments later united as Colombia from 1810 to 1818, and the communications of M. Tórres, chargé and later minister from Colombia from 1818-22.

Despatches from Colombia, Vol. I.
> Despatches of Charles Todd, 1820.

Consular Letters, La Guayra, Vol. I.
> Reports of Robert Lowry, 1810-12 and 1819-

Consular Letters, Mexico. Vol. 1, 1811-25.
> Reports of Smith Wilcocks and others and early communications from Mexican agents in the United States.

Mexico, Filibustering Expeditions against the Government of Spain, 1811-16.
> Letters of Álvarez de Toledo, Gutiérrez de Lara, William Shaler, J. H. Robinson and others.

Consular Letters, Galveston, Vol. I.
> Correspondence relating to Lafitte, Lallemand, and others, 1818–

Despatches to Consuls, Vols. I and II.
> Instructions are filed under the name of the officials.

Notes to Foreign Legations, Vol. II.
> Official communications of the Department of State to these legations, copies, filed under the name of the foreign envoys.

Domestic Letters, Vol. VII.
> Miscellaneous letters from the Department of State to persons in the United States.

Division of Manuscripts, Library of Congress, Washington, D. C.
> Biddle Papers.
> Clay Papers.
> Monroe Papers.
> Monroe Papers, Johnson Collection.

Rodney Papers.

Smith Papers.

Papers of William Taylor, Baltimore, Vol. 62 contains data on Buenos
Aires privateering.

Thornton Papers.

Van Buren Papers.

Crittenden Papers.

Note: In all the above collections, material dating from 1810 to 1822
has been consulted.

Division of Manuscripts, New York Public Library.

Barbour Papers, Correspondence of an influential Virginia family.

Monroe Papers.

Letters to Madison.

Library of the University of California.

P. C. Brooks, "The Adams-Onís Treaty as a Territorial Agreement." MS.
of doctoral dissertation. (See notes on pp. 176 and 186, *supra.*)

CONTEMPORARY NEWSPAPERS AND OTHER PERIODICALS

American Monthly Magazine, 1818.
Alexandria (La.) *Herald,* Aug. 11, 1812.
Analectic Magazine, 1818.
Aurora de Chile, La, 1812-13 (reprinted, Santiago, 1903).
Baltimore Federal Republican and Commercial Gazette, 1810.
Baltimore Federal Gazette, 1819.
Baltimore Telegraph, July, 1819.
Blackwood's Magazine, 1817.
Censor, El (Buenos Aires), June 6, 1818.
Censor, El (Madrid), 1820.
Columbian Centinel (Boston, Mass.), 1817, 1820-22.
Columbian Museum and Savannah Gazette, 1815-22.
Correo del Orinoco, El, Oct. 10, 1818.
Gaceta de Buenos Aires, 1810-20 (reprinted, Buenos Aires, 1910-14).
Gaceta de Texas, La (Nacogdoches), 1813.
Gaceta de Madrid, La, 1815-1821.
Gaceta Ministerial de Chile (Santiago), Nov. 7, 1818.
Kentucky Reporter (Lexington, Ky.), Jan. to Oct., 1819.
Louisiana Courier (New Orleans), Mar. 30, 1812, April 6, 1818.
Louisiana Gazette and Commercial Advertiser, April 28, 1818.
Mexicano, El (Natchitoches), Nos. 1 and 2, June, 1813.
Moniteur, Le (Paris), 1819.
Monhtly Anthology and Boston Review (Boston), 1808.
National Intelligencer (Washington), 1810-1822.

New York Evening Post, 1817-1820, 1822.
New York National Advocate, 1817.
New York Spectator, 1810-11.
Niles' Weekly Register (Baltimore), 1811 to 1822.
North American Review, Vols. I to XXV, 1815—
Philadelphia Aurora and General Advertiser, 1810-12, 1817-22.
Portfolio (Philadelphia), 1815-1820.
Richmond Enquirer, 1811-12, 1817-18.
Savannah Republican, July 27, 1819, May 26, 1819.

DIARIES, MEMOIRS, AND CORRESPONDENCE

Adams, John, *The Works of John Adams, Second President of the United States: with a Life of the Author, Notes and Illustrations, by his Grandson*, Charles Francis Adams (Boston, 1850-56, 10 v.).

Adams, John Quincy, *Writings of John Quincy Adams*, ed. by W. C. Ford (New York, 1913-17, 7 v.).

——, *Memoirs of John Quincy Adams, comprising Portions of his Diary from 1795 to 1848*, ed. by C. F. Adams (Philadelphia, 1874-77, 12 vols.).

——, "Letters of John Quincy Adams to Alexander Hill Everett, 1811-1837", *American Historical Review*, XI (1905-06).

Benton, Thomas H., *Thirty Years' View; or a History of the Working of the American Government for Thirty Years, from 1820 to 1850 . . .* (New York, 1854-56, 2 v.).

Bolívar, Simón, *Cartas del Libertador*, ed. by Vicente Lecuna (Caracas, 1929-30, 10 v.).

——, "Cartas de Bolívar á Baptis Irvine", *Boletín de la Academia de Historia Nacional* (Caracas), XVI.

Calhoun, John C., *Correspondence of John C. Calhoun*, ed. by J. F. Jameson (Washington, 1900). *Annual Report* (AHA., 1899, Vol. II).

Castlereagh, Lord (R. W. Stewart), *Correspondence, Despatches and Other Papers of Viscount Castlereagh*, ed. by C. W. Vane, Marquess of Londonderry (London, 1850-53, 12 v.).

Claiborne, W. C. C., *The Official Letter Books of W. C. C. Claiborne, 1801-1816*, ed. by Dunbar Rowland (Jackson, Miss., 6 v.).

Clay, Henry, *The Works of Henry Clay, comprising His Life, Correspondence and Speeches*, ed. by Calvin Colton (New York and London, 1904, 10 v.).

Cochrane, Lord, *Memorias de Lord Cochrane* (Madrid, 1918). (Biblioteca Ayacucho).

Coffin, Isaac F., *Diario de un joven norte-americano detenido en Chile durante el período revolucionario de 1817 a 1819*, traducido del inglés por J. T. Medina (Santiago, 1898).

Cutler, Manasseh, *Life, Journals, and Correspondence of the Rev. Manasseh Cutler*, by William P. Cutler and J. P. Cutler (Cincinnati, 1888).

Duane, William, "Letters of William Duane", *Proceedings*, MHS., Second Series, XX.

Gallatin, Albert, *The Writings of Albert Gallatin*, ed. by Henry Adams, Philadelphia, 1879, 3 v.).

García de León y Pizarro, José, *Memorias de la vida del exmo. señor D. José García de León y Pizarro, escritas por si mismo* (Madrid, 1894-97, 3 v.).

Gutiérrez de Lara, José Bernardo, "Diary of José Bernardo Gutiérrez de Lara", ed by E. West, *American Historical Review*, XXXIV (1928).

Hamilton, Alexander, *The Works of Alexander Hamilton*, ed. by H. C. Lodge (1885-86, 9 v.).

Heredia, Narciso de, *Escritos del Conde de Ofalia*, publicados por su nieto, el Marques de Heredia, senador por derecho propio (Bilbao, 1894).

Hyde de Neuville, J. G., *Mémoires et souvenirs* (Paris, 1890-92, 3 v.).

Jackson, Andrew, *Correspondence of Andrew Jackson*, ed. by J. S. Bassett (Washington, 1926-33, 6 v.).

Jefferson, Thomas, *The Writings of Thomas Jefferson*, ed. by P. L. Ford (New York, 1892-99, 10 v.).

——, *The Writings of Thomas Jefferson*, Monticello ed. (Washington, 1904).

Johnston, Samuel, *Diario de un tipógrafo yanqui en Chile y Peru durante la guerra de la independencia*, introducción de Armando Donoso (Madrid, 1919).

King, Rufus, *Life and Correspondence of Rufus King*, by C. R. King (New York, 1894-1900, 6 v.).

Madison, James, *The Writings of James Madison, comprising his Public Papers and his Private Correspondence, . . .* ed. by Gaillard Hunt (New York, 1900-10, 9 v.).

Monroe, James, *The Writings of James Monroe, including a Collection of his Public and Private Papers and Correspondence now for the First Time Printed*, ed. by S. M. Hamilton (New York, 1898-1903, 7 v.).

Moreno, Mariano, *Escritos de Mariano Moreno* (Buenos Aires, 1896).

O'Higgins, Bernardo, "Epistolario de O'Higgins", *Revista Chilena de Historia y Geografía* (1927), LII.

Porter, David, *Journal of a Cruise to the Pacific Ocean* (Philadelphia, 1815, 2 v.).

Pozzo di Borgo, Charles André Comte de, *Correspondance politique depuis la restauration des Bourbons jusqu'au congres d'Aix-la-Chapelle de Charles André Comte de Pozzo di Borgo et le Comte de Nesselrode* (Paris, 1890-1897, 2 v.).

Pueyrredon, Juan Manuel de, *Documentos del archivo de Pueyrredon* (Publicación del Museo Mitre) (Buenos Aires, 1912, 4 v.).

Rush, Richard, *Memoranda of a Residence at the Court of London, comprising Incidents Official and Personal from 1819 to 1825 . . .* (London, 1845).

San Martín, José de, *Documentos del archivo de San Martín* (Publicación del Museo Mitre) (Buenos Aires, 1910-12, 12 v.).

Taggart, Samuel, *Letters of Samuel Taggart*, in *Proceedings of the American Antiquarian Society*, New Series, XXXIII.

Van Halen, Juan, *Memoirs of Don Juan Van Halen* (London, 1830, 2 v.).

Wellesley, Sir Henry, *Diary and Correspondence of Henry Wellesley, First Lord Cowley, 1790-1846* (London, 1930), ed. by F. A. Wellesley.

Winder, W. H., "Letters of General W. H. Winder to President Monroe", ed. by M. Kenway, *Hispanic American Historical Review*, XII (1932), p. 458 ff.

Wirt, William, "Letter of William Wirt to J. Coulter" in *American Historical Review*, XXV.

DOCUMENTARY COLLECTIONS

Abridgement of the Debates of Congress from 1789 to 1856, ed. by T. H. Benton (New York, 1857-61, 16 v.). Vol. VI.

American State Papers, Class I, Foreign Relations, ed. by Gales and Seaton (Washington, 1832-59, 6 v.) ; *Class V, Commerce and Navigation* (Washington, 1832-34, 2 v.).

Annals of Congress, 1789-1824 (Washington, 1834-56, 42 v.).

Compilation of the Messages and Papers of the Presidents, 1789 to 1900 (American Bureau of Literature and Art, 1909, no place given, 11 v.), ed. by J. D. Richardson.

Compilation of the Reports of Committee on Foreign Relations, U. S. Senate, 1789 to 1901 (Washington, 1901, 8 v.).

"Correspondence of the Russian Ministers in Washington," ed by W. C. Ford in *American Historical Review*, XVIII (1913).

"Correspondence of George Rogers Clark and Citizen Genêt" in *Annual Report*, AHA., 1896, Vol. I.

Diplomatic Correspondence of the United States concerning the Independence of the Latin-American Nations, ed. by W. R. Manning (New York and London, 1925, 3 v.).

Documentos para la historia de la vida pública del Libertador de Colombia, Perú y Bolivia,..., ed. by J. F. Blanco and R. Azpurúa (Caracas, 1875-77, 14 v.).

Louisiana under the Rule of Spain, France, and the United States, 1785-1807, ed. by J. A. Robertson (Cleveland, 1911, 2 v.).

Memorias del general O'Leary, publicados por su hijo, Simón Bolívar O'Leary (Caracas, 1879-88, 32 v.).

Parliamentary Debates, published by Hansard, Vol. XL (London, 1819).

Privateering and Piracy in the Colonial Period, ed. by J. F. Jameson (New York, 1923).

Prize Cases Decided in the United States Supreme Court, 1789-1918, ed. by J. B. Scott (Oxford, 1923, 3 v.).

Tratados, convenios, y declaraciones de paz y comercio que han hecho con las potencias estranjeras los monarcas españoles de la casa de Borbón desde el año 1700 hasta el día, ed. by Alejandro Cantillo (Madrid, 1843).

Treaties and Other International Acts of the United States of America, ed. by D. H. Miller (Washington, 1931– 4 v.).

Miscellaneous Primary Sources

Al Avisador Patriota y Mercantil de Baltimore, un ciudadano de Buenos Aires (Buenos Aires, 1817), Nos. 1-3.

Bonnycastle, R. H., *Spanish America* (Philadelphia, 1819).

Brackenridge, Henry M., *South America; a Letter on the Present State of that Country, to James Monroe, President of the United States* (London, 1818) in *Pamphleteer*.

——, *Voyage to South America, Performed by Order of the American Government, in the Years 1817 and 1818* (London, 1820, 2 v.).

Cobbett, William, *Our Anti-neutral Conduct Reviewed; letter III to Major Cartwright from Cobbett's Political Register* (New York, 1818).

Hodgeson, A., *Letters from North America Written during a Tour of the United States and Canada* (London, 1824, 2 v.).

Martínez de la Rosa, Francisco, *Bosquejo histórico de la política de España desde los tiempos de los Reyes Católicos hasta nuestros días* (Madrid, 1857, 2 v.).

Onís, Luis de, *Memoria sobre las negociaciones entre España y los Estados Unidos que dieron motivo al tratado de 1819* (Madrid, 1820, 2 v.).

——, *Memoir upon the negotiations between Spain and the United States which led to the treaty of 1819*, by Don Luis de Onís, Madrid, 1820, translated from the Spanish by Tobias Watkins (Baltimore, 1821).

Original Memoir on the Floridas, with a General Description from the Best Authorities, by a Gentleman of the South (Baltimore, 1821).

[Palacio Fajardo, M.], *Outline of the Revolution in Spanish America, or an Account of the Origin, Progress and Actual State of the War Carried on between Spain and Spanish America* ... (New York, 1817) by a South American.

Pazos, Vicente, *Letters on the United Province of South America, Addressed to the Hon. Henry Clay* ... (New York, 1819), translated by P. H. Crosby.

Pitkin, *A Statistical View of the Commerce of the United States* ... (New York, 1817).

Rattenberry, J. F., *Remarks on the Cession of Florida to the United States of America, and on the Necessity of Acquiring the Island of Cuba by Great Britain* (London, 1820) in the *Pamphleteer*, XV.

Robinson, W. D., *Memoirs of the Mexican Revolution, including a Narrative of the Expedition of General Xavier Mina* (Philadelphia, 1820).

——, *A Cursory View of Spanish America* in the *Magazine of History*, XXXVI, reprinted from the edition of 1815.

[Rocafuerte, Vicente], *Memoria politico-instructiva enviada a los gefes de Anahaac* (Philadelphia, 1821).

Sherman, John W., *A General Account of Miranda's Expedition including the Trial and Execution of Ten of His Officers* (New York, 1808).

Spanish America and the United States, or Views on the Actual Commerce of the United States with the Spanish Colonies, by a Merchant of Philadelphia (Philadelphia, 1818).

Strictures on a Voyage to South America as Indited by the "Secretary of the (Late) Mission" to La Plata ... (Baltimore, 1820).

Taylor, Robert B., *Argument in Support of the Memorial of the Marine Insurance Companies of Baltimore, to the Congress of the United States, Praying Compensation for the Losses Sustained under the Treaty with Spain of the 22nd February, 1819* (Norfolk, 1826).

Tórres, Manuel, *An Exposition of the Commerce of Spanish-America* ... (Philadelphia, 1816).

Vignoles, C. B., *Observations upon the Floridas* (New York, 1823).

SECONDARY WORKS

Adams, Henry, *History of the United States during the Administrations of Jefferson and Madison* (New York, 1889-91, 9 v.).

Alamán, Lucas, *Historia de México hasta la época presente* (Mexico, 1850, 4 v.).

Altamira, Rafael, "Spain, 1815-1840" in *Cambridge Modern History*, Vol. X, *The Restoration*, chap. vii (Cambridge, 1907).

Álvarez, Alejandro, *Rasgos generales de la historia diplomática de Chile, 1810-1910, Primera época, la emancipación* (Santiago, 1911).

Ambler, C. H., *Thomas Ritchie, a Study of Virginia Politics* (Richmond, 1913).

Amunátegui, Miguel Luis, *Los precursores de la independencia de Chile* (Santiago, 1909-10, 2 v.).

——, *Camilo Enriquez* (Santiago, 1911, 2 v.).

Amunátegui, Miguel Luis and Vicuña McKenna, B., *La dictadura de O'Higgins* (Madrid, 1917) (Biblioteca Ayacucho).

Antokoletz, Daniel, *Histoire de la diplomatie argentine* (Paris and Buenos Aires, 1914).

Antón del Olmet, F. (Marqués de Dos Fuentes), *Proceso de los orígenes de la decadencia española, El cuerpo diplomático español durante la guerra de la independencia* (Madrid, no date, 6 v.).

Bancroft, H. H., *History of Mexico* (San Francisco, 1883-88, 6 v.).

——, *History of the North Mexican States and Texas* (San Francisco, 1884-89, 2 v.).

Barbagelata, Hugo, *Artigas y la revolución americana* (Paris, no date).

Barros Arana, Diego, *Historia jeneral de la independencia de Chile* (Santiago, 1854-58, 4 v.).

——, "Poinsett, primer consul estranjero en Chile", *Obras completas*, Vol. XI (Santiago, 1908-11, 11 v.).

——, "La acción del clero en la independencia Americana", *Obras completas*, Vol. X.

Bassett, J. S., *Life of Andrew Jackson* (New York, 1911, 2 v.).

Baumgarten, H., *Geschichte Spaniens vom Ausbruch der französichen Revolution bis auf unsere Tage* (Leipzig, 1865-71, 3 v.).

Becker, Jerónimo, *Historia de las relaciones exteriores de la España durante el siglo XIX* (Madrid, 1924, 3 v.).

Bemis, Samuel F., ed., *The American Secretaries of State and their Diplomacy* (New York, 1927-1929, 10 v.), Vols. III and IV.

——, *A Diplomatic History of the United States* (New York, 1936).

——, *Pinckney's Treaty; a Study of America's Advantage from Europe's Distress, 1783-1800* (Baltimore, 1926).

——, *The Foundations of American Diplomacy: I, The Revolution* (New York, 1935).

Bolton, H. E., ed., *Arredondo's Historical Proof of Spain's Title to Georgia* (Berkeley, 1925).

Cadena, Pedro I., *Anales diplomáticos de Colombia* (Bogotá, 1878).

Castro, Cristobal de, *Antología de las Cortes de 1820* (Madrid, 1910).

Chadwick, F. E., *The Relations of the United States and Spain*, Vol. I (New York, 1909).

Chandler, C. L., *Inter-American Acquaintances* (Sewanee, Tenn., 1917).

Clauder, A. C., *American Commerce as Affected by the Wars of the French Revolution and Napoleon, 1793-1812* (Philadelphia, 1932).

Coleman, Mrs. Chapman, *Life of J. J. Crittenden and Selections from his Correspondence and Speeches* (Philadelphia, 1871, 2 v.).

Collier, W. C. y Feliú Cruz, G., *La primera misión de los Estados Unidos en Chile* (Santiago, 1927).

Cox, Isaac J., *The West Florida Controversy; 1798-1813, a Study in American Diplomacy* (Baltimore, 1918).

Cresson, W. P., *The Holy Alliance* (New York, 1922).

Currier, T. S., *Los corsarios del Rio de la Plata* (Buenos Aires, 1929).

Davis, Mathew L., *Memoirs of Aaron Burr* (New York, 1869, 2 v.).

Fabela, I., *Precursores de la diplomacia Mejicana* (Mexico, 1926).

Fenwick, C. G., *The Neutrality Laws of the United States* (Washington, 1913).

Fisher, L. E., *The Background of the Revolution for Mexican Independence* (Boston, 1934-).

Fuller, H. B., *The Purchase of Florida, its History and Diplomacy* (Cleveland, 1906).

García Samudio, Nicolás, *Capítulos de historia diplomática* (Bogotá, 1925).

Goebel, Julius, *The Recognition Policy of the United States* (New York, 1915) (Columbia University Studies in History, Economics and Public Law, Vol. LXVI).

Gouchon, Emilio, *La masonería y la independencia americana* (Valparaíso, 1917).

Gray, L. C. and Thompson, E. K., *History of Agriculture in the Southern United States to 1860* (Washington, 1933, 2 v.).

Guido, José, T., *Biografía de Manuel Dorrego* (Buenos Aires, 1877).

Hackett, F. W., *The Meade Claim* (Washington, 1910).

Hasbrouck, A., *Foreign Legionaries in the Liberation of Spanish America* (New York, 1928).

Hyneman, C. S., *The First American Neutrality, a Study of American Understanding of Neutral Obligations during the Years 1792 to 1815* (Urbana, Ills., 1934).

Hunt, Gaillard, *John C. Calhoun* (Philadelphia, 1908).

Johnson, E. R. and others, *History of the Domestic and Foreign Commerce of the United States* (Washington, 1915, 2 v.).

Konkle, B. A., *Life of Joseph Hopkinson* (Philadelphia, 1931).

Larrazabal, Felipe, *Vida de Simón Bolívar* (Madrid, 1917, 2 v.) (Biblioteca Ayacucho).

Lea, H. C., *The Inquisition in the Spanish Dependencies* (New York, 1922).

Legal Opinions on the Title of Richard S. Hackley and Others to Lands in Florida (New York, 1841).

Lockey, J. B., *Pan-Americanism, Its Beginnings* (New York, 1920).

Lyon, E. W., *Louisiana in French diplomacy, 1759-1804* (Norman, Okla., 1934).

Mancini, Jules, *Bolívar y la emancipación de las colonias españolas desde los orígenes hasta 1815* (Paris, 1923).

McCaleb, W. F., *The Aaron Burr Conspiracy; a History Largely from Original and hitherto Unused Sources* (New York, 1903).

McMaster, J. B., *Life and Times of Stephen Girard* (Philadelphia, 1918, 2 v.).

——, *History of the People of the United States* ... (New York, 1884-1913, 8 v.).

Medina, J. T., *Historia del tribunal del santo oficio de la inquisición en Chile* (Santiago, 1890, 2 v.).

Meyer, Leland W., *Life of Colonel Richard M. Johnson of Kentucky* (New York, 1932).

Mitre, Bartolomé, *Historia de Belgrano y de la independencia argentina* (Buenos Aires, 1887, 3 v.).

Moore, John Bassett, *History and Digest of the International Arbitrations to which the United States has been a Party* (Washington, 1898, 6 v.).

——, *A Digest of International Law as embodied ... especially in Documents ... of the United States* (Washington, 1906, 7 v. and index).

Moses, B., *The Intellectual Background of the Revolution in South America* (New York, 1926).

Palomeque, A., *Oríjenes de la diplomacia argentina, misión Aguirre á norte América* (Buenos Aires, 1905, 2 v.).

Parks, E. T., *Colombia and the United States, 1765-1934* (Durham, N. C., 1935).

Paxson, Frederick L., *The Independence of the South American Republics, a Study in Recognition and Foreign Policy* (Philadelphia, 1916).

Pelliza, M. A., *Dorrego en la historia de los partidos Unitario y Federal* (Barcelona, 1878).

Perkins, Dexter, *The Monroe Doctrine, 1823-26* (Cambridge, Mass., 1927).

Petrie, F. L., *Simón Bolívar 'El Libertador', a Life of the Chief Leader in the Revolt against Spain in Venezuela, New Granada and Peru* (London, 1910).

Pilling, William, *The Emancipation of South America, being a Condensed Translation by William Pilling of the History of San Martín by General Don Bartolomé Mitre* (London, 1893).

Pratt, Julius W., *The Expansionists of 1812* (New York, 1925).

Ramírez de Villaurrutia, Wenceslao (Marques de Villa Urrutia), *Fernan-Nuñez, el embajador* (Madrid, 1931).

Reeves, J. S., *The Napoleonic Exiles in America, a Study in American Diplomatic History, 1815-1819* (Baltimore, 1905).

Rippy, J. F., *The Rivalry of the United States and Great Britain over Latin America, 1808-30* (Baltimore, 1929).

——, *Joel R. Poinsett, Versatile American* (Durham, N. C., 1935).

Riva Palacio V., *México a través de los siglos* . . . (Barcelona, 1888-9, 5 v.).

Rivas, Raimundo, *Relaciones internacionales entre Colombia y los Estados Unidos, 1810-1850* (Bogotá, 1915).

Robertson, W. S., *Life of Miranda* (Chapel Hill, 1929, 2 v.).

——, *Rise of the Spanish-American Republics as Told in the Lives of their Liberators* (New York, 1918).

——, *Hispanic-American Relations with the United States* (New York, 1923).

Rydjord, John, *Foreign Interest in the Independence of New Spain* (Durham, N. C., 1935).

Rutter, F. R., *The South-American Trade of Baltimore* (Baltimore, 1897).

Tatum, E. H., *The United States and Europe, 1815-1823* (Berkeley, Cal., 1936).

Torrente, M., *Historia de la Independencia de México* (Madrid, 1918).

Updyke, F. A., *The Diplomacy of the War of 1812* (Baltimore, 1915).

Urrutia, F. J., *Los Estados Unidos de América y las repúblicas hispano-americanas, de 1810 á 1830; páginas de historia diplomática* (Madrid, 1918).

Vicuña, McKenna, B., *El ostracismo de los Carreras* (Santiago, 1857).

Villanueva, Carlos A., *Napoleon y la independencia de America* (Paris, 1911).

——, *La monarquía en América, Bolívar y el general San Martín* (Paris, 1913).

Webster, Charles K., *The Foreign Policy of Castlereagh, 1815-1822* (London, 1925).

Whitaker, Arthur P., *The Spanish-American Frontier, 1783-95; the Westward Movement and the Spanish Retreat in the Mississippi Valley* (Boston and New York, 1927).

——, *The Mississippi Question, 1795-1803; a Study in Trade, Politics and Diplomacy* (New York and London, 1934).

Wriston, H. M., *Executive Agents in American Foreign Relations* (Baltimore and London, 1929).

Yela Utrillo, *España ante la independencia de los Estados Unidos* (Lerida, 1925, 2 v.).

Zubieta, Pedro A., *Apuntaciones sobre las primeras misiones diplomáticas de Colombia (primero y segundo períodos—1809 - 1810 - 1830)* (Bogotá, 1924).

ARTICLES IN PERIODICALS

Ames, Ellis, "Expedition against Cartagena", *Proceedings*, MHS., first series, Vol. XVIII.

Brooks, P. C., "The Pacific Coast's First International Boundary Delineation, 1816-1819", *Pacific Historical Review*, 1934.

Chandler, C. L., "United States Merchant Ships in the Rio de la Plata (1801-09) as Shown by Early Newspapers", *Hispanic American Historical Review*, 1919.

——, "United States Shipping in the La Plata Region, 1809-10", *Hispanic American Historical Review*, 1920.

——, "United States Commerce with Latin America at the Promulgation of the Monroe Doctrine", *Quarterly Journal of Economics*, 1923.

Cox, Isaac J., "The Panamerican Policy of Jefferson and Wilkinson", *Mississippi Valley Historical Review*, 1914.

——, "Monroe and the Early Mexican Revolutionary Agents", *Annual Report*, AHA., 1911, Vol. I.

——, "The Louisiana Texas Frontier during the Burr Conspiracy", *Mississippi Valley Historical Review*, 1923.

——, "Hispanic American Phases of the Burr Conspiracy", *Hispanic American Historical Review*, 1932.

——, "American Intervention in West Florida Revolution", *American Historical Review*, 1912.

——, "The Border Missions of General George Mathews", *Mississippi Valley Historical Review*, 1925.

Curry, J. L. M., "The Diplomatic Services of George W. Erving", *Proceedings*, MHS., second series, Vol. XX (1890).

Fisher, L. E., "American Influence upon the Movement for Mexican Independence", *Mississippi Valley Historical Review*, 1926.

Galpin, W. F., "American Grain Trade to the Spanish Peninsula", *American Historical Review*, XXVIII.

Garret, K., "The First Newspaper of Texas: Gaceta de Texas" in *Southwestern Historical Quarterly*, XL (1937).

Hodder, F. W., "Sidelights on the Missouri Compromise" in *Annual Report of the American Historical Association*, 1909.

Hoskins, H. L., "The Hispanic American policy of Henry Clay", *Hispanic American Historical Review*, 1927.

Nichols, R. F., "Trade Relations and the Establishment of United States Consulates in Spanish America", *Hispanic American Historical Review*, 1933.

Perkins, Dexter, "Russia and the Spanish Colonies", *American Historical Review*, 1923.

Ramírez de Villaurrutia W. (Marqués de Villa Urrutia), "España en el congreso de Viena", *Revista de Archivos, Bibliotecas y Museos*, Vols. XV, XVI, XVII (1906-08).

Robertson, W. S., "Beginnings of the Hispanic American Diplomacy of the United States" in *Essays in American History Dedicated to Frederick J. Turner* (New York, 1910).

——, "The United States and Spain in 1822", *American Historical Review*, 1915.

——, "First Legations of the United States in Latin America", *Mississippi Valley Historical Review*, 1915.

——, "The Recognition of the Hispanic American Nations by the United States", *Hispanic American Historical Review*, 1918.

Shepherd, William R., "Wilkinson and the Beginnings of the Spanish Conspiracy", *American Historical Review*, 1904.

——, Bolívar and the United States", *Hispanic American Historical Review*, 1918.

Stewart, W., "The South American Commission", *Hispanic American Historical Review*, 1929.

Whitaker, A. P., "The Retrocession of Louisiana in Spanish Policy", *American Historical Review*, 1934.

Wilgus, C. A., "Spanish American Patriot Activity along the Gulf Coast of the United States, 1811-1822", *Louisiana Historical Quarterly*, 1925.

——, "Some Activities of United States Citizens in the South American Wars of Independence, 1810-24", *Louisiana Historical Quarterly*, 1931.

Wyllys, R. K., "The East Florida Revolution, 1812-1814", *Hispanic American Historical Review*, 1929.

INDEX

Adams, John, 44-45, 173

Adams, John Quincy, at London, 70; cautioned by Castlereagh, 77; negotiations with Onís, 89, 164, 181, 185-88; and British mediation offer, 91; and projected European mediation in Sp. Am., 92, 145; and Bonapartist plot, 111, 113; on Clay's policy in Sp. Am., 133; policy in Sp. Am., 137-38, 244; secretary of state, 141; views in cabinet, 141; and Aguirre, 147; and McGregor, 149; disavows Worthington, 154; upholds Jackson, 165, 182; on Fla. land grants, 195; Spanish policy of, 211, 217-18; and Russia, 217; and Crawford, 217; negotiations with Vives, 231-34; on Spanish treaty, 235; favors Fla. occupation, 245; on neutrality enforcement, 247; on monarchies for Sp. Am., 249; contacts with Torres, 253-56; distrusts U. S. agents in Sp. Am., 254; views on recognition of Sp. Am., 267-69, 271; receives Tórres officially, 274.

Agrelo, José, 127, 153

Aguirre, Juan F., 59

Aguirre, Manuel H., 146-48, 152, 252, 261

Aix-la-Chapelle, Congress of, 171, 174, 269

Alabama, 113

Alagon, Duke of, 193-99, 201, 209, 240

Aldama, Ignacio, 67

Alexander I, 36, 75, 81, 144, 203-04, see Russia

Alexander, The, 263

Allende, Gen., 67

Allies, European and Spain, 33, 38, 169, 170; and Sp. Am., 48, 92-93, 138, 172; and U. S. policy, 141; mentioned, 269

Álvarez de Toledo, José, arrives U. S., contacts with administration, 53-54; filibusters in Texas, 71, 107-08; arrested in La., 108; deserts rebels, 109; and Onís, 115; and Thornton, 127, aids Onís, 130; and Mexican rebels, 156; at Madrid, 207-08

Álvarez, Ignacio, 152

Ambrister, Robert, 179

Amelia Island, 29; privateering in, 103; McGregor at, 112; occupation by U. S., 148, 135; Clay opposes occupation, 137; cabinet discussion on, 140; Monroe's message on, 141, 142; Venezuela repudiates action at, 255

America, *see* United States

American Monthly Magazine, The, 131, 157

Anaya, Juan Pablo, 107, 156

Andalusia, 221, 230

Andes Mountains, 121

Angostura, 121, 179, 256

Apure River, 121

Aranjuez, treaty of, 39

Arbuthnot, Alexander, 179

Argentina, *see* Buenos Aires

Arguelles, 235

Arkansas River, 175, 185-86

Arms and Munitions, trade in from U. S. to Spanish America, 50, 52-53, 64 fn., 99, 108, 115, 129, 153, 263; Monroe and sale of to rebels, 53; need of at Buenos Aires, 60; Mexicans seek at N. Orleans, 67; Spain protests at trade in, 99, 115

Armstrong, Gen., 24

Arroyo Hondo (River in Texas), 25

Artigas, José Gervasio, 59, 153, 248

Astor, J. J. 128

Astoria, 140

Aurora, The (Philadelphia) 47, 157, 250

Aurora de Chile, La. 60

Aury, Luis, 101, 110, 112, 142, 148, 156-57

Austria, 38, 171

Avila, Spain, 201

Bagot, Sir Charles, offers British mediation, 91; McGregor and, 111; on Bonapartist plots, 113; notes change in U. S. policy, 141; reports opinions on Jackson, 177; mentioned, 145, 211

Baltimore, Md., Sp. Am. agents at, 50, 100, 126; trade with Cartagena, 64; privateers of, 101, 104, 116; bank in, 102; Hq. of Gen.

Mina, 109; neutrality enforcement at, 116; opinion at, 49, 153, 158, 246; Carrera sails from, 129; trials for piracy at, 247

Bank of the United States, 253

Barataria, 102

Barcelona, 230

Barlow, Joel, 50

Barrancas, Fort (Pensacola), 219

Bathurst, Lord, 210

Baton Rouge, 26, 28, 29

Bayonne, 74

Belgrano, Manuel, 58

Bernabeu, 130

Benton, Thomas H., 189, 242

Biddle, Captain, U. S. N., 99, 262, 264

Biddle, Nicholas, 159

Bland, Theodoric(k), 126, 152, 154, 247-48

Blockade, conflicting views of Spain and U. S., 98; Venezuela, 150; Chilean, 262; U. S. views of Chilean, 264

Bogotá, Audiencia at, 63; mission to U. S. from 64, 64 fn.

Bolívar, Juan V., 50-51

Bolívar, Simón, visited U. S., 56; opposes federalism, 66; activities of, 96; meets Gen. Mina, Haiti, 109; British volunteers for, 119; in Orinoco area, 121; dispute with B. Irvine, 149-51; interest in Seminole War, 179; signs armistice, 245; Adams on, 249; attitude to U. S., 257; victories of, 268

Bomford, Col., 254

Bonaparte, see Joseph, Napoleon

Bonapartist exiles in the U. S., 88, 111-115, 128

Boquilla de Piedras, 103

Boston, Mass., 114, 158, 214, 218, 250, 275

Bourbon, House of, interests in Italy, 18; deposition of in Spain, 26; in Naples, 38; interests of in Franco-Spanish treaty (1814), 39; liberalism in Spain under, 57; monarchies for, in South America, 95-96, 249

Boyacá, Battle of, 268

Brackenridge, H. M., 122, 126, 142, 157, 249

Brent, T. L. L. 169

Brion, Admiral, 100, 150, 258

Buenos Aires, uprising at, 15; trade with the U. S., 43; news of revolt in, 46; influence of G. Britain and U. S. in 58; representative assembly at, 58; seeks U. S. aid, 59; dependent on British trade, 59; neutrality of in War of 1812, 60; seeks alliance with U. S., 60; privateers of, 100-103; American ships stranded at, 102; foreigners in navy of, 104; foreigners engaged in privateering at, 104; factions in, 125, 128; Carrera detained at, 129; Worthington in, 139; Halsey in, 153; Spain plans attack on, 177; monarchical schemes at, 245; war with Artigas, 248; U. S. press on, 249; desertion of American seamen at, 262; recognition of, 122, 140, 183, 274; agents of U. S. in, 49, 139, 154, 247-48, 258; agents of in U. S. 52, 148, 146, 255; attitude toward U. S., 58-60, 151-154, 260

Bulgary, Count, 214

Burke, William, 66

Burr, Aaron, 45, 46, 128

Cabinet, of the U. S., 141, 164-65, 211, 217, 231-34

Cadiz, 32, 105, 173, 198-99, 210, 212

Calcasieu River, 164

Calhoun, John C., 185, 211, 218

Callao, Peru, 43, 62

Callava, Col., 243

Camarilla, in Spain, 73, 81, 171, 203, 206, see also Ferdinand VII, Tatistcheff, Ugarte, Lozano de Tórres, Pizarro, Irujo, Cevallos, Spain, court of

Carabobo, battle of, 268

Caracas, revolt at, 15; U. S. views of, 47, 49; earthquake at, 50; Lowry agent of U. S. at, 65; see also Venezuela, Miranda, Bolívar

Caribbean Sea, 98, 101, 103, 210

Carlos, Don, 170, 192, 206

Carolina, 16, 229

Carrera, José Miguel de, 62, 63, 125-129, 154, 249

Carrera, Luis, 63

Carroll, Charles, 46

Cartagena, attacked by G. Britain, 16; agent to U. S. from, 53; civil war in, 64; trade with U. S., 64; captured by Morillo, 99; privateers of 100; arms for, from U. S., 115; Americans imprisoned at, 161; mission of Hughes to, 99

Casa Irujo, *see* Irujo

Castlereagh, Lord (R. W. Stewart), attitude to Sp. dispute with U. S., 38, 76-77, 94-95, 204, 208, 224; on mediation of Powers in Sp. Am., 144, 172; hostile to Pozzo di Borgo, 171; and Jackson in Fla., 179; on recognition of Sp. Am., 184; avoids rivalry with Russia at Madrid, 203; mentioned, 37, 85

Castro, Dr., 260

Censor, El (Madrid), 240

Censorship of press, relaxed in Sp. Am., 56; abolition of in Spain, 236, *see also* Newspapers

Cevallos, Pedro, signs convention with C. Pinckney, 20; negotiates with Monroe and Pinckney, 23; policy of 39-40, 73 f.; refuses to receive Erving, 69 fn.; correspondence with Monroe, 70; and Tatistcheff, 75; instructions to Onís, 75; moderates tone, 76; seeks aid from G. Britain and France, 76; scheme for delay, 78-79; removed from office, 80; mentioned, 92

Champ d'Asile, Le, French colony in Texas, 114

Charles III, of Spain, 17, 56

Charles IV, of Spain, 73

Charleston, S. C., 112, 114, 158

Chihuahua, Mexico, 32

Chile, mentioned 59; U. S. influence in, 60-63; Carrera in, 62; hopes of recognition by U. S., 62; U. S. S. *Essex* in, 63, 78; victories of rebels in, 96; navy of, 104; battle of Maipú, 121; factions in, 125; Worthington agent in, 139; Aguirre represents in U. S., 146; attitude to U. S., 154-55, 261-65; Bland in, 247; British in, 261; relations with B. A. gov't. 261; Biddle incident in, 262, blockades Peru, 262; maritime conflicts with U. S., 263-64; Prevost in, 264; press, in, 264, expeditionary force from, 268

Claiborne, W. C. C., 25-26, 28, 33, 46, 54

Claims, *see* names of countries involved

Clark, George Rogers, 44

Clemente, L., 127, 148-49, 252, 255

Clay, Henry, and neutrality bill, 117; campaign for recognition of Sp. Am., 133-37; 157, 234, 251-52, 265-

66; supports Amelia Island filibusters, 137; effect of his policy on Spain, 168; followers, 178; hostility to Spain, 123-4, 178, 226; neglects Sp. Am. question (1819), 183; attacks Jackson, 183; opposition to Adams-Onís treaty, 189, 225-26; and M. Tórres, 253; talks with Adams on recognition, 267; leaves Congress, 267; makes capital of Sp. Am. question, 270

Clergy, anti-Americanism of, in Chile, 62; in Venezuela, 66

Clinton, De Witt, 128

Cobb, Mr. (Rep. from Ga.), 266

Cobbett, William, 118, 150

Cochrane, Lord, 261-265 *passim*

Colombia, 124; Dr. Thornton and, 126; recognition of, 245, 253, 267, 272, 274; relations with U. S., 257 and fn.; Tórres seeks arms for, 267; Spanish troops in, 268; *see also* New Granada, Venezuela

Colorado River (Texas), 23, 82, 91, 94, 168, 175, 182

Columbia River, 140, 155, 135

Columbian Centinel, The (Boston), 158, 275

Commission to South America, 92-93, 139-40, 142, 154, 245, 247-49

Congress, of Aix-la-Chapelle, 171, 269; American Continental 64; of Mexico, 156; of Troppau, 269; of Tucumán, 151-52; of Venezuela, 64; of Vienna, 39

Congress, of the U. S., and Fla. occupation, 28, 30, 224-227, 233-34; and Sp. Am., 50, 117, 132-137, 251, 265-66, 271-74; and Adams-Onís treaty, 189, 233-34; votes relief for Caracas, 50; grants land to French exiles, 113; Neutrality Act, 117; and Seminole War, 178; Forsyth in, 197; Clay retires from, 267; mentioned, 212, 215, 216, *see* Votes in Congress

Congress, U. S. S. 142, 154

Consuls, of Buenos Aires, 148, 154; British, 102; French, 19; Spanish, in the U. S., 27, 102, 116, 130; of the U. S., 62, 193, 154

Convention of 1802, 20, 23, 89, 91, 168, 180

Cordoba (Mexico), treaty of, 273

Cortes, Juan, 107

Cortes, The, considers U. S. relations, 35; Alvarez De Toledo in,

53; of 1820, 236; and treaty with U. S., 238-240; annuls Fla. land grants, 240-41; policy in Sp. Am., 273

Coruña, La., 230

Council, of the Indies, 194

Council of State (Spanish), and negotiations with the U. S., 84-89, 94-95, 169-70, 176; and ratification of treaty, 192, 205-06, 237-240; Pizarro attacked in, 170; on Jackson in Fla., 176, mentioned 35

Courcier, Mr., 114

Courts (of Law) in the U. S., enforcement of neutrality by, 246-47; status of Sp. Am. in, 135

Crawford, W. H., 164, and Sp. negotiations, 181, 185, 197, 211, 231; and J. Q. Adams 217, 247

Creek Indians, 30-31

Cuba, annexation desired, 33; trade with U. S., 44; Monroe's interest in, 54; defense of, 207; occupation by G. Britain feared, 210; idem by U. S., 215; delegates in the Cortes, 239

Cundinamarca, 64

Dallas, Alexander, 54, 70

Daniels, Capt., 247

Darcy (Dacy) and Didier, 129, 147

Declaration of Independence, see countries involved

Declaration of Rights of Venezuela, 48, 64

De Forest, David C., 148, 255

Dessolle, Marquis, 217

Devereux, Joseph, 138, 152

Dorrego, Manuel, 127

Duane, William, 124, 252 see also Aurora

East Florida, 29, 30

Eguía, Gen., 173, 207

Enriquez, Camilo, 60-61

Erving, George W., minister to Spain, 69-72, 77-78; negotiations with Cevallos, 78-80; with Pizarro (1817), 85-86; idem (1818) 167-69; optimism of, 89, 93; instructions to, 91; on Neutrality Act, 118; and Irujo, 174; and Fla. land grants, 194; thinks Spain will accept treaty, 211

Essex, U. S. S., 62-63, 78

Etruria, 40

Europe, Wars in, 18, 46, see Allies, European

Family Compact, The, 39

Federalism, in New Granada, 64; in Venezuela, 64; opposed by Bolívar, 66

Federalists, diplomacy of, 18; opposition of, 19-20, 177; and Fla. occupation, 28, 30; favor Spanish liberals, 47; fear French influence in Fla., 47, deplore excesses of Sp. Am. rebels, 48; praise Venezuela, 49; oppose war policy, 177

Ferdinand VII, King of Spain, and Onís, 27; return to Spain, 33, 36; policy, 36-39; still recognized by New Granada, 64 fn.; and Cevallos, 73, 80; admires Tsar, 74; projected marriage, 75; diplomacy, 75; and Pizarro, 81, 84; and Council of State, 84; makes grants in Fla., 167; and Jackson episode, 169; and U. S. negotiation, 87, 95, 177; treatment of officials, 180; and Adams-Onís treaty, 200, 206, 208-09; and Tatistcheff, 203; and foreign affairs, 213; Clay on, 226; and Constitution of 1812, 231; mentioned, 178

Fernandina, Fla., 103, 148

Fernan-Nuñez, Duke of, 77, 85, 88, 223

Filibustering Expeditions, of Miranda, 46; of Álvarez de Toledo, 71; from the U. S., 101-02; of Gutiérrez and Magee, 106-07; of Javier Mina, 109-10; of McGregor in Fla., 111-112; Vives attitude to, 232; of General Long, 232 fn.

Firebrand, U. S. S., 161, 247

Florida, revolution in, 16, 29-30; negotiations for cession to U. S., 23-24, 82-86, 161-90; efforts of U. S. to seize, 29-32, 37, 91, 122, 211, 215, 218, 223-27, 245; opinions in U. S. on acquisition, 33, 177, 185, 226-27, 229, 234-35; G. Britain and, 16, 30, 36, 70, 72, 84, 162, 200, 210, 224; Indians in, 78, 163, 241; privateers and filibusters in, 101, 111 f.; Jackson in, 31, 163-67; Spain on cession of, 176, 192, 207-08, 240-43; see also Treaty (Adams-Onís), Louisiana, United States, Public Opinion,

Land Grants, Congress, of the U. S., etc.
Floridablanca, Count of, 173
Flying Fish, The, 262
Folch, Vicente, 25, 29
Forbes, John M., 259-60
Foronda, Valentin de, 26
Forsyth, John, and Neutrality Act, 117; opposes Clay, 136; character and career, 195-198; diplomacy at Madrid, 198-202, 205-09, 212-14, 237, 241; despatches from, 211; instructions to 212, 235
Forsyth, Samuel D., 256
Fowltown, 163
France, cession of La, to, 18; policy in Florida, 21-22, attitude in disputes of Spain and U. S., 22-23, 27, 38-39, 76, 85, 88, 90, 95; influence in Sp. Am. 44, 56-57, 64; policy in Sp. Am. 47, 95-96, 144, 172, 183-84, 215, 222, 225, 249, 259; and Sp. Am. privateers, 88, 93; and Bonapartists in U. S., 112 ff.; inroads on U. S. shipping, 19; evacuation of by Allies, 171; in Am. Revolution, 271
Francia, Dr., 59
Freire, General, 261
Franklin, Benjamin, 56, 59
Frontier, Spanish - American, *see* Texas, Louisiana, Florida, West Florida, Mississippi, etc.
Fulton, R. 126
Funes, Dean, 250

Gage Thomas, 42 and fn.
Gaines, Gen. 163
Gallatin, Albert, 211, 218, 223
Galveston (Texas), 103, 110, 135, 141
Garáy, Martin de, 81, 171-73
García de León y Pizarro, José de, *see* Pizarro
García de Sena, M., 55
Garnett, Mr. (Rep. from Pa.), 273
Garrido, Nicolás, 196
Genêt, Citizen, 44
Georgia, Anglo-Spanish conflict in, 16; settlement in, 30; citizens support McGregor, 112; opinion on Spanish affairs, 33, 162, 228-29; Indians in 163
Ghent, treaty of, 40, 140
Girard, Stephen, 52
Godoy, Manuel, 73, 173
Gómez, Valentin, 259

Gómez Labrador, Pedro, 39, 40
González Salmón, Manuel, 202, 207, 221
Graham J. 139, 142, 154, 248
Great Britain, relations with Spain (general), 26, 76, 81, 90, 207, 219; Spanish attempts to get aid from, 36, 38, 41, 76, 85, 223; policy toward disputes of Spain and U. S., 36, 38, 94, 192, 204, 210; mediation between Spain and U. S., 83, 87-90; rivalry with the U. S., 30, 60, 70, 153, 179, 209, 269; sea power of, 43, 63, 101; influence and interests in Sp. Am. 47, 56, 58, 66, 99, 111, 119, 151, 154-55; trade with Sp. Am. 59, 65, 95, 98, 103, 255; possible occupation of Fla., 33, 70, 162; attitude of U. S. to, 122, 124; relations with Russia, 75, 171, 203; mediation of Europe in Sp. Am. 144, 145, 171, 172; and recognition of Sp. Am., 183-84, 222; and Continental Powers, 143, 269; press and opinion in, 209, 210, 179, 182
Gual, Pedro, 111, 127, 149
Guaranty, territorial, offered by Pinckney (1803), 168; suggested by Pizarro (1818), 168; required by Council of State, 170; Spain abandons idea of, 177; suggested by Spain (1820), 222; 238
Gulf of Mexico, 22, 25, 100, 102, 103, 161, 164
Gutiérrez de Lara, José, Bernardo de, 54-55, 106, 107

Hackett, 249
Hackley, Richard S., 193
Haiti, 110
Hakluyt, R., 42
Halsey, Thomas L., U. S. consul at B. A., and privateering, 104; appointment, 138, activities, 151-52; exceeds powers, 152; and B. A. gov't, 153; and Artigas, 153; recalled, 153-54; mentioned, 258
Hamilton, Alexander, 44-45
Hardenberg, Prussian statesman, 144
Heredia, José de, 130
Heredia, Narciso de, 83 fn., 86
Herrera, José Manuel de, 156, 265
Hidalgo, Manuel, 67
Hispanic America, *see* Spanish America

Hispanophobia, 42, 42 fn., 44, 45, see also, Public Opinion
Holmes, Gov., 28
Holy Alliance, 75, 151
Hopkinson, J., 158 fn.
Hornet, U. S. S., 197, 198, 202, 211, 212
House of Representatives, see Congress of the U. S.
Hualde, Guillermo, 170, 192
Hughes, Christopher, 99
Humbert, Gen. 107, 156
Hyde de Neuville, J. G., instructions to, 88, 93; intermediary between Adams and Onís, 164-66, 170, 182, 185-6, 195, 216; between Adams and Vives, 223, 231-33; attitude towards Spain and U. S., 88-89, 181, 215-16; and Bonapartist plot, 113 ff.; and Sp. Am., 144; see also France, Adams-Onís treaty, etc.

Iberville River, 22
Idler, Joseph, 253
Imaz, José, 205
Independence of Spanish America, see Spanish America, also regions and countries
Indians, in Georgia, 30; and Mexican revolution, 67; in Fla. assisted against U. S., by Spain, 78; hostilities of Seminoles, 163ff.; Spain seeks to move from Fla., 241; see also names of individual tribes.
Infantado, Duke of, 170, 192
Inquisition, abolished in Venezuela, 48; relaxation of under Charles III, 56; C. Enriquez imprisoned by, 60; U. S. hostility toward, 161
Insurgents, see Spanish America and subheads, also names of countries, Buenos Aires, Chile, etc.
Irujo, Carlos Martínez de (Marquis of Casa Irujo), minister in U. S., 106, career to 1818, 173; foreign minister, 174; negotiations with the U. S., 175-78, 193; and ratification of treaty, 191, 198-201 and chap. vii *passim*; downfall, 201-03; hostility to G. Britain, 203; mentioned 206, 209, 211, 222, 236
Irvine, Baptis, 124, 126, 128, 149-51, 179, 249, 255
Iturbide, Augustin de 156, 265, 268

Jackson, Gen. Andrew, military operations in Fla., 31, 163-64; Gov. of Fla., 242-43; and Spain, 30-31, 75, 169, 174-76, 181, 218-19; and Indians, 30, 163-4; at N. Orleans, 41; and T. Ritchie, 125; and U. S. government, 33, 165, 182; and U. S. public, 177-78; executes British subjects, 179; and H. Clay, 183
Jefferson, Thomas, diplomacy of, 18-24; on Spanish treaty (1819), 234; and Sp. Am., 44, 251; influence in Sp. Am., 56, 61; and Miranda, 106; on Neutrality Act, 117; on Jackson in Fla., 177; on sections of U. S., 230
Johnson, Col. Richard M., 253
Joseph (Bonaparte), King of Spain, 24, 113, 128
Jovellanos, G. de, 57
Junta, established at Caracas, 15; in Spain, 26, 27; at Bogotá, 53 fn.; at Buenos Aires, 59-60; at Santiago, Chile, 60; at Socorro, N. Granada, 63; in Spain, 201; of Ministers in Spain, (1819), 206, 208

Kemper brothers, 25
Kentucky, 17, 266
King, Rufus, 44-45, 162-63; 177, 273
Kingston, Stephen, 227

Labrador, see Gómez Labrador, P.
Lafitte, 101, 114
La Guayra, 65
Lakanal, 113
La Lastra, 53, 64 fn.
L'Allemand, Gen. Charles, 113, 114
Land grants in Florida, 167; Erving and Pizarro on, 167; Adams and, 181, 186, 200; in negotiations for treaty, 194 fn., 192-97; Monroe and Forsyth on, 200; Irujo and, 201; grantees, 206; Spanish policy and, 222, 233, 239-42; U. S. position on, 212-13; Chap. vii *passim*
Lands, in W. Fla., 25, 28, 30; in E. Fla., 29; speculation in Texas, 107; granted to Bonapartists, 114; speculation in Fla., 229
Lansdowne, Marquis of, 210
La Plata, River, 127, see also Buenos Aires
La Rochefoucauld-Liancourt, 57
Larrain, faction in Chile, 62

Lautaro, Letters of, 125, 157

Laval, Duke of, French ambassador at Madrid, 167, 170, 176; intermediary between Irujo and Forsyth, 198-99; and Adams-Onís treaty's prospects, 202; and Forsyth and San Fernando, 212; mentioned 207

Leander, expedition of Miranda in, 106

Lewis, J., agent of the U. S., 138-139

Lima, Peru, 99, 262-64, 268

Liverpool, 224

Liverpool, Lord, 210

Livingston, Robert, 21

Loans, sought by Sp. Am., 253, 261

Long, James, 232 fn.

Los Adaes, 164

Louis XIV, King of France, 22

Louis XVIII, King of France, 95

Louisiana, boundaries of, 21-22, 77-89 *passim,* 174-76, 181-87; Spain and, 17, 19, 23, 38-39, 41, 75, 115; France and, 18, 21, 39-40, 77; U. S. and, 19, 21, 30, 44; Congress of Vienna and 39; G. Britain and, 41; A. Hamilton, 45; and Texas filibusters, 55, 107-08, 115; exchange for Fla.? 82, 84, 89; Bank of, 102

Lowndes, William, 227, 253

Lowry, Robert, 49, 65, 138

Lozano de Tórres, J. E., attacks Pizarro, 170; opposes Irujo, and Adams-Onís treaty, 191-92, 200; influence of, 202; and H. Wellesley, 205; rivalry with San Fernando, 207; intimate with Toledo, 208; mentioned, 209, 213

Lucca, Prince of, 249

Mably, 57

McCulloch, 126

McGregor, Gregor, 110-12, 142, 149

M'Kean, Gov of Pa., 173

Macedonian, U.S.S., 99, 264

Macon, N., 273

Madison, James, relations with Irujo, 26, 173; and W. Fla., 29-31; and mission of J. Robinson 32; sends A. Morris to Spain, 32; Spanish policy of, 1812-1815, 53; and Sp. Am. independence, 47-54, *passim;* sends Hughes to Cartagena, 99; B. A. Junta and, 60; influence of writings in Chile, 61; appoints Erving minister to Spain, 69; seeks accommodation with Spain, 70; neutrality policy of, 97, 108, 117; and Miranda, 106; and Carrera, 128-29; views on recognition of Sp. Am., 159; on Jackson in Fla., 177; his policy, 244

Magdalena River, 127

Magee, Augustus, 106-07

Maipú, battle of, 121

Málaga, Spain, 105

Margarita, island of, 103, 246

Martínez de Irujo, *see* Irujo

Martínez de la Rosa, Francisco, 235, 239

Massachusetts, 119, *see also* Boston

Mason, Gen., 254

Matagorda, Texas, 101

Mathews, Gen. George, 29, 30, 112

Maurepas, Lake, 22

Mediation of the European Powers, 143-45, 171, 255

Message to Congress, Jefferson, 1805, 23; secret message, 1805, 24; Irujo on, 1805, 26; Madison, 1811, 50; Madison 1816, neutrality legislation, 117; Monroe, 1817, Amelia Island, 135, 141; Monroe, 1818, 182-83; Monroe, 1819, 216-218; Monroe, Fla. occupation, 1820, March, 225; Monroe, 1820, Sp. negotiation, 233, 245; Monroe, 1821, 267; Monroe, Mar. 8, 1822, 272

Metternich, Prince, 40, 72, 144

Mexico plans to attack, 1793, 44; and Burr, 45; Claiborne, Wilkinson and liberation of, 46; U. S. agent sent to, 49 and fn., 274; influence of U. S. in, 57; of France, 57; character of revolution in, 67; Spain seeks to protect from the U. S., 93; privateers of, 100-01; J. H. Robinson in, 107-08; Mina attacks, 109-10; Toledo and, 109; N. Orleans merchants and attack on, 110; Bonapartists plots against, 113-14; interest of American West in liberation of, 104; course of revolution in, 155; contacts of rebels in with U. S., 67, 156; Spanish troops in, 219; fear of U. S. in, 265; fall of Spanish power in, 269; Iturbide in, 268; U. S. public and Iturbide, 275

Mina, Javier, 109-10, 127

Minerva Nacional, La (Madrid), 240

Miranda, Francisco de, 26; interest of Federalists in schemes of, 44; hostility of Burr to, 46; expedition to Venezuela, 46; in the U. S., 56; attitude to the U. S., 65-66; towards G. Britain, 66; Leander expedition, 106

Mississippi, Question, *see* Louisiana, Right of Deposit, Treaty of San Lorenzo, etc.

Mississippi, River, 17, 18, 22, 175

Mississippi, Territory, 25, 31

Mississippi Valley, 17, 18

Missouri, 189, controversy, 224, 230, 234-35, 252

Missouri, River 164, 175, 182, 185

Mitre, B., 57

Mobile 28, 30 33

Mobile Act, 20, 26

Mobile River, 25, 36

Molé, Comte de, 95

Monarchy in South America, 47, 95-96, 249, 258-9

Monroe Doctrine, 122

Monroe, James, European service, 19, 23; Spanish policy, 29, 70-71, 82, 165, 166-167, 178, 181, 211, 215, 217, 231, 234; policy in Sp. Am., 50-55 *passim*, 137-45, 244-45, 267, 270-72; and Sp. Am. agents in U. S., 54, 147-48, 253; and neutrality 109, 116; and T. Ritchie, 125; and Clay, 133, 226; tour of 139; and Jackson, 165, 178, 242; and Texas, 182; Fla. 29; cabinet, 217; Adams 186; Congress, 227, 273; Hyde de Neuville, 216; influences on, 215; on expansion, 235; *see also* Messages to Congress, United States, Spanish America, Spain

Monterosa, 59

Monteverde, 66

Montevideo, 43, 144, 168, 247

Montgomery (Rep. from Ky.), 266

Mora, José Joaquin de, 240

Morales, Juan V., 25

Morelos, José, M., 67, 156

Moreno, Manuel, 127

Moreno, Mariano, 58, 127

Morillo, Gen., 98, 115, 121, 161, 245

Morphy (Murphy?), Sp. consul at N. Orleans 130

Morris, Anthony, 32, 33, 69

Naples, King of, 38

Napoleon I, 23, 26, 36, 47, 74, 201

Napoleonic Association, 113

Nariño, Gen. Antonio, 64

Natchez, 18

Natchitoches, La., 54, 55, 108, 182

National Intelligencer, The (Washington, D. C.), 125, 141, 157, 188

Nelson, Hugh, 271

Neutral Zone, 23, 168

Neutrality, of Buenos Aires (War of 1812), 60; of Spain (War of 1812), 31, 35, 37, 93; of the U. S. (Sp. Am. Revolution), 93, 97-120 *passim*, 244-48; Monroe and, 137, 141; Bolívar and, 150; Spain and 175, 177, 181, 233; and Adams-Onís treaty, 209, *see also* Neutrality Acts

Neutrality Acts, of 1794, 97; of 1817, Spanish reaction, 93; passed, 117; opinion on, 117-119; enforcement, 119; amendments, 1818, 120; debate on, 1817, 134; Clay on, 134; Aguirre and, 146-148; Chilean sentiment on, 261; mentioned, 245

New England, opposition to Madison, 34; on neutrality bill (1817), 117; feeling against Spain in, 214; opinion on Sp. Am., 250

New Granada, independence movement in, 53; influence of U. S. in 63; disputes and civil war in, 64; U. S. and independence of, 64 fn.; coast blockaded by Spain, 98; barbarities in, 161; battle of Boyacá in, 268

New Mexico, 93, 186

New Orleans, right of deposit at, 17-19, 26; Federalists try to buy, 18; trade through, 20; French commission at, 22; Spanish officials in, 25; communications with Miss. territory, 25; Jackson at, 41; anti-Spanish feeling in, 45; trade with Cartagena, 64; Mexicans in, 67; privateering base, 101; Toledo in, 107; base for filibusters, 108; Mina in, 110; French retreat to from Texas, 114; Onís protests at privateering from, ·116; neutrality enforcement at, 116;

rebel agents at, 156-57; hostility to Spain, 162

New Spain, *see* Mexico

New York, Miranda in, 1806, 46, 106; trade with Venezuela, 52; and Mina, 109; and L'Allemand's schemes, 114; opinion in, 119, 124, 158, 252; Aguirre in, 147

Newspapers, in the U. S., 15, 47, 48, 59, 100, 118, 130, 153, 157 ff., 177, 189-90, 209; British, 76, 204; in Buenos Aires, 58, 59, 153, 260; in Chile, 60, 264; in Venezuela, 66; in Mexico, 68 *see also* names of cities.

Nichols, Major, in Fla., 31

Niles, Hezekiah, 49, 119, 125, 130

Norfolk, Va., 102, 109

North American Review, The, 274

Northeast (section of the U. S.), 178, 224, 227-31, 235

Onís y González, Luis de, minister of Spain in the U. S., 27; relations with U. S. prior to recognition, 27-28, 31-32, 36, 47, 71; activities, 27; and rebel agents, 51, 64 fn.; reports of to superiors, 72, 83, 133, 219; and treaty negotiations, 71, 82, 89-91, 164-67, 180-91; protests to U. S. gov't 71, 76, 106, 115, 135, 164; opinions of, 72, 80, 83, 90, 92; situation and state of mind 82, 131, 164, 167, 202; instructions to, 75, 80, 86, 89, 92-94; and rebel privateers, 83, 93, 102, 104, 106; and filibusters, 108-09, 115; and Bonapartists, 113; and Fla. grants, 195; bribe offered to, 227; Álvarez de Toledo, 207; Forsyth, 197; memoir published 236; trade to Peru licensed by, 263

O'Higgins, Bernardo, 62, 125, 128, 155, 261, 264

Olivenza, Portugal, 144

Omaña, agent from New Granada, 53 fn., 64 fn.

Ontario, U. S. S., 99, 262

Orb, privateer, 101

Orea, Telésforo de, 50-51, 52, 65

Oregon, 188, 190

Orinoco, Bolívar in valley of, 121; blockade of river, 150; mentioned, 268

Ortiz, Pascasio, 67

Pacific Ocean, U. S. boundary to, 16, 175, 181, 185; British navy in, 63; seapower in, 62, 98, 263; instructions to U. S. Navy officers in 264

Paez, Gen. 121

Paine, Thomas, 126

Palacio Fajardo, M., 53, 121, 131

Pamplona, 230

Pan-Americanism, of Enriquez, 61; of Clay 136

Paraguay, 59, 248

Pasquier, Baron, 223

Patriots, *see* Spanish American rebels

Pazos, Vicente, 111, 149, 123, 127, 148-9, 153

Pennsylvania 119, 252

Pensacola, authorities at, 28; Jackson at (1814), 31, (1818) 164; U. S. gov't and capture of, 33, 165, 182; interest of N. Orleans in attack on, 110; Sp. Am. interest in capture of, 179; mentioned, 219

Perdido River, 21, 30

Peredo, Francisco A., 67

Pérez de Castro, E., 237-242 *passim.*

Perry, Capt. Oliver H., 255, 258

Peru, Spanish navy in, 99; Worthington agent in, 139; maritime incidents at 261-265; Prevost in, 264; independence of, 268

Peter Porcupine, *see* Cobbett, William

Philadelphia, Álvarez de Toledo in, 54; Gutiérrez de Lara in, 54; inhabitants of mentioned, 63; commerce of, 64; Mina in, 109; and L'Allemand's schemes, 114; sentiment on neutrality enforcement, 119; newspapers in 215; opinions in, 218; Tórres in, 252, *see Aurora,* Duane, Biddle, Hopkinson etc.

Pickering T., 28

Picornell, 107

Pinckney, Charles, 20, 23, 94

Pinckney, Thomas 17 f.

Pinkney, William 126

Pittsburgh, Pa. 108

Pizarro, José García de León y, foreign minister, 80; position at Spanish court, 81, 84, 170-73, 236; policy towards the U. S., 82-85, 92, 169-70, 176, 222; negotiations with Erving, 85-86, 167-69, 222;

instructions to Onís, 86-87, 92-93, 164-65, 174-75; and rebel privateers, 93; recognition of rebels, 93-95; and France, 95; and G. Britain, 72, 85; land grants, 167; and European mediation, Sp. Am., 172

Poinsett, Joel R., agent to S. Am., 49; at Buenos Aires, 59; in Chile, 60-63; and Carrera in the U. S., 128, 138; offered post as commissioner to S. Am., 139; consulted on recognition of Sp. Am., 248; in Congress, 1822, 273

Poletica, Count Pierre, 179, 216-17, 223, 244

Pontchartrain, Lake, 22

Port-au-Prince, Haiti, 109, 110

Porter, Capt. David, 128

Portfolio The (Denny's), 157, 249

Portugal, 60, 144, 168-69, 202, 247, 269

Pozzo di Borgo, General, 75, 144, 171, 217, 223

Press see Newspapers, Censorship

Prevost, J. B., agent to S. Am., 139-140; in Chile, 154-55; pro Sp. Am. attitude, 254; and B. A. gov't, 259; censured by Adams, 260; in Chile and Peru, 260, 264; quarrel with Capt. Biddle, 264; mentioned 258

Privateers, of Artigas, 152; British, 17; Chilean, 62, 262; French, 19, 20; Spanish 98-99, 219; Spanish American (Buenos Aires Venezuela, etc.), 82, 92, 99-105, 146, 162, 201; aid to same in U. S., 71, 93, 104-05, 146, 160, 232; objections to in U. S., 254-55, 142; various opinions on, 245-46; abolished in Buenos Aires, 260

Propaganda, Bonapartist in U. S., 28; combatted by Onís, 28; of early Sp. Am. revolutionists, 56; French in Mexico, 57; of U. S. agents at B. A. 58; of C. Enriquez in Chile, 60; of Poinsett in Chile, 61; of Lowry in Venezuela, 65; of the Sociedad Patriótica in Caracas, 65; in favor of Sp. Am. rebels in the U. S., 123 ff.; Spanish in U. S., 130; of Buenos Aires exiles in the U. S., 153

Prussia, 80, 171

Public Opinion in the United States, on neutrality 103, 117, 119; on

Adams-Onís treaty, 188-90; on G. Britain, 210; on Sp. Am. privateers, 246-47; on Spain, 19, 123, 124, 161-62, 214, 231; on U. S. policy towards Spain, 33-34, 177-78, 182, 218, 227-31; on Sp. Am. revolution, 44, 46, 48, 59, 121, 129, 157, 183, 209, 249-51; on recognition of Sp. Am., 130-33, 245 ff.; 274-76; see also names of other countries and regions.

Pueyrredon, Juan M. de 123, 127; detains Carrera, 129; gov't of, 148; and the U. S., 152-53, 154; mentioned, 155; attitude of the U. S. to, 249; monarchical schemes of, 249, 258-59; downfall, 259

Puerto Rico, 95

Puñonrostro, Count of, 193, 195, 196, 201, 240

Purchas, Samuel, 42

Quincy, Josiah, 28

Randolph, John, 24, 117, 133, 135

Rayon, Ignacio, 67

Rebels, see Spanish American Rebels and names of countries

Red River, 175, 181, 182, 186

Regency, Spanish, refuses to see Morris, 32; fate of, 33; on American affairs, 35; Pizarro's service under, 81; Irujo's service under, 173; see Spain

Religion, toleration of in Venezuela, 66; influence on politics, Chile, 62; in Mexican revolt, 67; anti-Catholic feeling in U. S., 134; Church and State in Spain, 236

Republicans (Party in U. S.) 24; in North oppose Fla. occupation, 30; fear British activity in W. Fla., 47; take up cause of Sp. Am. rebels, 48; and negotiations with Spain, 163; newspapers, 178

Revenga, J. R., 127, 257

Revolution, American, 17, 21, 63, 65, 271

Revolution, Spanish American, see Spanish America and names of regions

Rhode Island 119

Richelieu, Duke of, and La. boundary question, 77, 88; and Spanish gov't, 88; and proposed cession of Santo Domingo, 95; and the U. S., 95

Richmond Enquirer, The, 125, 157
Riego, Rafael, 230
Right of Deposit, *see* New Orleans
Rio de Janeiro, 173, 262
Rio Grande (del Norte), 89, 166
Ritchie, Thomas, 125
Rivadavia, Bernardino, 259-60
River Plate, *see* La Plata
Robertson, William, 42
Robinson, Dr. John H., 32; and Toledo, 107; in Mexico, 108; arrest in La., 108
Robinson, William Davis, 123-24
Rocky Mountains, 186
Rodney, Caesar A., 139, 142, 154, 215, 248
Rodríguez, Gov., of B. A., 259
Romp, privateer, 101-02
Root, Mr. (Rep. from N. Y.), 117
Roscio, J. G., 127
Ruiz de Apodaca, 268
Rush, Richard, 111, 144, 146, 184, 244
Russia, mediation of sought by Spain, 35, 79; support sought by Spain, 38; influence at Madrid, 74-75; influence causes Cevallos' downfall, 80; and mediation between Spain and colonies, 144, 172; rivalry with G. Britain and Austria, 171; U. S. sounds on recognition of Sp. Am., 183; Tatistcheff's action in Spain and policy of, 203, 204; urges moderation on U. S., 215, 225; policy on Fla. treaty, 216-17

Saavedra, Diego de, 59
Sabine River, 23, 25, 78, 94, 166, 168, 175, 224
Sacedon, Spain, 207
St. Augustine, Fla., 29, 196, 219, 243
St. Bartholomew, 103
St. Louis, 189
St. Marks, Fla., 164, 166, 167
St. Mary's River, Fla., 103, 229
St. Petersburg, 36, 144
St. Thomas, 103
Salcedo, Gov., at Chihuahua, 32
Salem, Mass., 43
San Antonio, Texas, 106
San Carlos, Duke of, 39, 69, 73, 204, 208, 223, 224
San Fernando, Duke of, 207, 212-14
San Ildefonso, treaty of, 18, 21
San Lorenzo, treaty of, 18, 20, 116

San Martin, General José de, 121; reconquers Chile, 128, 155; political views, 259; and U. S., 261; and Prevost, 264; victories of, 264; and independence of Peru, 268
Santiago, Chile, 60
Santo Domingo, 95
Savannah, Ga., 104, 112, 120, 158
Scott, Alexander, 50 fn., 138
Scott, Gen. Winfield, 109
Sections, of the United States, *see* Northeast, South, West
Seminoles, 162, 163, 241; war with, 163-4, 178
Senate of the U. S., *see* Congress
Serna, De la, 211
Shaler, William, 49, 55, 138
Sharp, Mr. (Rep. from Ky.), 117, 134
Sheffy, Mr. (Rep. from Va.), 135
Shipping, American, decline of, 101; desertion from, 102, 262; hurt by rebel privateers, 103; in Chile, 155, insurance of, 228; seizures of by Chilean navy, 262
Skinner, J. S., 125, 126, 128, 129
Smith, Mr. (Rep. from Md.), 117
Smith, Dennis A. 109
Smith, Robert, 34
Smith-Wilcocks, 265
Sociedad Patriótica, in Venezuela, 65
Socorro (New Granada), 63
South of the United States, influence of the *Richmond Enquirer* in, 125; attitude to Clay, 137; desires quick settlement with Spain, 162; bellicose feeling in, 163; and Jackson, 178; and Fla. occupation bill, 224; interests of, 227-231, *passim;* 235
South America, trade of with U. S., 43; U. S. interest in, 1810, 47; U. S. commission to, 92-93, 139-40, 142, 154, 245, 247-49; Spanish expeditionary force for, 204, 221; *see also* Spanish America.
Stevens, Mr. (Rep. from Ky.), 266
Spain, general situation, 24, 35-38, 72, 76, 130, 171-72, 230-31, 235-36, 238, 269; commerce, 28, 35, 43, 100; naval affairs, 98-99, 161; military affairs, 96, 114, 121, 128, 155, 268; court of, 37, 73-74, 169, 171, 176-77, 191, 203; colonial system of 18, 43, 55-56, 121, 124, 135; officials of, 28, 29, 31, 40, 93,

123, 219, 242-43; relations with France, 18, 21, 38-39, 94; with G. Britain, 35, 37, 39-41, 84, 94, 207, 219, 223; with Portugal 144, 168; with Russia, 34-35, 74-75, 79-80, 216-17; policy in Sp. Am., 177, 237; and rebel privateers, 93, 103; mediation of European powers with Colonies, 143-45, 171, 255; rivalry with U. S., 16-20, 31, 35, 37, 84, 219, 242; negotiations with U. S., 18, 20, 23, 75, 78-79, 82, 86, 90, 170, 213, 231-34, 237-42; policy toward U. S., 75, 82, 84, 89-93, 98, 115, 122, 179-182, 221-22, 237-42; and La., 18, 23; and right of deposit, 19; Florida, 21; treaty with U. S., 188; U. S. claims on, 19-20; public opinion on U. S., 192, 240; Bonapartists in U. S., 112-13; attitude of U. S. to, 47, 134, 135, 223; *see also,* Regency, Cortes, Ferdinand VII, and names of ministers and diplomats.

Spanish America, agents from, 50-55, 64 fn., 126, 131-2, 145, 148, 156-51, 252, 254, *see also* names of agents; exiles from, 127-28, 148; difficulty of communications in, 55; propagandists of revolt in, 56; revolts in, 15, 28, 29, 46-47, 55, 67, 96, 98, 99, 114, 121, 128, 155, 268; Spain and independence of, 89, 92-93, 170, 175, 182, 201, 206, 222, 232-34; U. S. and independence of, 50, 53, 122, 133-37, 142, 157, 182-83, 209, 215, 222, 232-34, 244, 247-49, 255-56, 269-70, 265-66, 272-74; *see also,* Buenos Aires, Chile, Colombia, France, Great Britain, Mediation, Mexico, New Granada, Privateers, Propaganda, Russia, South America, Spain, Trade, United States

Talleyrand, Prince, 37
Tatistcheff, Dmitri Pavlovitch, Russian minister to Spain, 74; intrigues, 75; aims and policies, 75; relations with Cevallos, 75; and Pizarro, 81; champions liberalism in Spain, 81; withdraws support from Pizarro and Garáy, 171; intrigues and influence of, 174; fall from power, 203; mentioned, 209
Taylor, Thomas, 100
Tennessee, 31, 229
Teran, Gen., 156

Texas, U. S., claims to, 21-23, 91, 166, 181, 186; U. S. interests in, 122, 215, 226-42; Spain and, 25, 90, 94, 174, 192; France and, 22, 115; Mexican rebels and 67; revolution in, 16, 71, 101-02, 106-10, 114-15, 156-57, 232 fn.; *see also* Filibustering Expeditions.
Thompson, Martin, 145
Thornton, Dr. William, 126
Times, The (London), 210
Todd, Charles, 256
Toledo, *see* Álvarez de Toledo
Tombigbee Association, 113
Toreno, Conde de, 235
Tórres, Manuel, and Duane, 124; and Dr. Thornton, 127; chargé of Venezuela and Colombia, 252-54; writes pamphlet, 253; seeks loan, 253; friendly to U. S., 254; and Adams, 256, 267; official reception in U. S. and death, 274
Trade, of France, 95; of Great Britain, 59, 60, 98, 103, 222, 257, 261-63; of Spain with America, 43, 98; of Spanish America, 56, 144; of Buenos Aires, 59-60; of Cartagena, 64; of Chile, 62, 261-63; of Venezuela, 65, 257; of the U. S., 89, 98, 100, 103, 122, 136; with Spain, 35, 115, 158-59, 214, 228; with Sp. Am., 43, 49, 158-59, 228, 261-63, 269, 277
Treaty, Adams-Onís (1819), negotiation of 71-92, 164-187; character and significance, 188-91; struggle for ratification, 192-242; mentioned 21, 263, 267
Treaty, of Cordoba (Mexico), 273
Treaty, Franco-Spanish (1814), 39
Treaty, Louisiana Purchase, 21, 30
Treaty, Paris (1783), 21, 94, (1814), 38
Treaty, of San Ildefonso (1800), 18, 21
Treaty, of San Lorenzo (1795), 18, 20, 116
Trimble, Mr., (Rep. from Ky.) 272
Trinity River, 114, 166
Tsar, The, *see* Alexander I
Tucumán, Congress of, 151
Two Million Act, 24

Ugarte, 203
United Kingdom, *see* Great Britain
United Provinces (of S. Am.), *see* Buenos Aires

United States of America, relations with Spain, 15-41, 69-83, 161-243; neutrality in Sp. Am., 97-120; relations with Sp. Am., 42-68, 121-60, 244-76; *see also* Public Opinion, Spanish America, Spain, France, G. Britain, Florida, Louisiana, Texas, Filibustering Expeditions, Neutrality, Privateers, Trade, Adams, J. Q., Monroe, J., etc.
Uruguay, 59, 153
Utrecht, treaty of, 94

Valparaiso, Chile, 62, 155, 262
Vargas, Sr. de, 193, 195, 240
Vasquez-Figueroa 173
Vattel, 271
Venezuela, revolution in, 15, 26, 47, 48, 49, 52, 64-65, 66, 96, 106, 268; relations with the United States, 49-51, 52, 55, 63-64, 126, 148-49, 149-51, 252-54, 255-57; blockade by Spain, 98; navy of, 100; privateers of, 101; McGregor in, 110; and Dr. Thornton, 126; intercepted Spanish despatches in, 179; and Amelia affair, 255; and Great Britain, 268
Vera Cruz, 49 and 49 fn., *see also* Mexico
Verus, pseudonym of Onís, 130
Virginia, 218
Vives, Francisco Dionisio, minister to U. S., career, 221; instructions to 221-22; in Paris, 223, in London, 223-34; negotiations with Adams, 231-34; mentioned, 238; new instructions to, 241-42, final action by on treaty, 242
von Humboldt, Alexander, 42
Votes, in U. S. Congress, neutrality bill, 117; Clay's resolutions, Spanish America, (1818) 136, (1820 252, (1821) 266; recognition of Spanish America, (1822), 273-74

War, of Austrian Succession, 17; Peninsular, 24; of U. S. and Creeks, 30; of 1812, 30, 34, 37, 64, 98; threat of between U. S. and Spain, 23, 35, 84, 91, 214, 217-20; Anglo-French (1793) 97; nature of in Sp. Am., 161; civil, in New Granada, 64
Washington, George, sends T. Pinckney to Spain, 17; influence of in Sp. Am., 56, 58, 59, 61; neutrality policy of, 97
Weed, Thurlow, 128
Wellesley, Sir Henry, 35, 37, 88, 203, 205
Wellington, Duke of, 40, 172
West, The (Section of the U. S.), public opinion in, 44, 124, 134, 136, 163, 178, 215, 218, 242; influence of Richmond Enquirer in, 125; interests of analyzed, 227-31 *passim*
West Florida, insurrection in, 15, 28; U. S. claims to, 21, 23; acquired by Spain, 21; France and, 21; sale of lands in, 25; Gov. Folch of, 25; inhabitants, 25; independence declared, 28; lands in, 28, 30; U. S. Congress and, 30; controversy with Spain over, 32; Spain seeks restoration, 36, 75, 90; foreign interest in feared in U. S., 47; Onís protests occupation of, 71
West Indies, 103, 210, 247, *see* Cuba, Puerto Rico, Margarita, St. Thomas, St. Bartholomew's
Whig Party, 178, 252
Wilkinson, Gen. James, 17, 25, 30, 46
Winder, General W. H., 148
Wirt, William, 247
Worthington, W. G. D., agent of U. S., 139, 152; at Buenos Aires, 154; in Chile, 154-55, 262, 264; recall of, 254, 259; mentioned, 259

Yrujo, *see* Irujo

Zaragoza, 230
Zea, Francisco, 254